T0265770

A Town Without Time

A Town Without Time

GAY TALESE'S NEW YORK

Gay Talese

MARINER CLASSICS

New York   Boston

The Bridge was originally published by Harper & Row in 1964. "New York Is a City of Things Unnoticed" was originally published in *New York: A Serendipiter's Journey*, New York: Harper & Brothers, 1961. The following essays first appeared in *Esquire* magazine: "Frank Sinatra Has a Cold" (1966), "The Kidnapping of Joe Bonanno" (1971), "The Kingdoms, the Powers, and the Glories of the *New York Times*" (1966), "*Vogue*land" (1961), "Looking for Hemingway" (1963), and "Mr. Bad News" (1966). "The Homeless Woman with Two Homes" (1989) and "My New York City Apartment" (2011) first appeared in *New York Magazine*. "Gino's Long Run" (1995) and "High Notes" (2011) first appeared in *The New Yorker*. "Journey Into the Cat Jungle" (1957) was originally published in *The New York Times Sunday Magazine*. "The Kingdom and the Tower" (2007) was originally published in *The New York Observer*. "Dr. Bartha's Brownstone" was originally published in *Bartleby and Me*, Mariner Books, 2023.

The Mariner flag design is a registered trademark of HarperCollins Publishers LLC.

HarperCollins books may be purchased for educational, business, or sales promotional use. For information, please email the Special Markets Department at SPsales@harpercollins.com.

FIRST EDITION

Photographs by Gay Talese

Library of Congress Cataloging-in-Publication Data has been applied for.

ISBN 978-0-06-339218-2

24 25 26 27 28 LBC 5 4 3 2 1

To the women in my life—Nan,
and our daughters,
Pamela and Catherine

Contents

Introduction

I

N HIS NINETY-SECOND YEAR, Gay Talese occupies a peerless perch in American journalism.

He's one of the last of the journalistic literary lions left. There's no practitioner of narrative nonfiction who doesn't have to reckon with his work. His stories are studied with the same scholarship reserved for literature. And there's nary a journalism student who can escape being assigned "Frank Sinatra Has a Cold."

So you might be wondering: Why does this guy need another book of his collected works?

The reason is that this book corrects an injustice. You see, despite all the veneration accorded to Talese, there's still one aspect of his journalism that has eluded sufficient critical recognition, which is his role as one of the great chroniclers of New York, worthy of a place as a spiritual contemporary to Joseph Mitchell.

The air is always getting sucked out of the room by his position as a pioneer of New Journalism, as a debonair Manhattan literary celebrity, as the author of the controversial *Thy Neighbor's Wife*, and as the writer of that damned Frank Sinatra profile. But the city has long been a vital character in Talese's work, even when he was writing about it indirectly, and it gave him his first creative fuel as a cub reporter for the *New York Times* seventy years ago.

For my own part, as a young reporter for the *Times* who writes about the city as his beat, Talese's writings on the metropolis have served as a North Star, so the absence of a book formally honoring them has always been glaring to me. Thankfully, this collection helps make the case for why Talese is on the level of Mitchell.

I'd argue that the city is what first defined Talese's work, which is why we must go back to the beginning to understand this element of his journalistic identity.

After paying his dues in the early 1950s as copy boy for the *Times*, his first job as a reporter at the paper was on the sports desk. There he filed beautiful and unlikely stories about bare-knuckle fighters, horse jockeys, barbell lifters, and a dentist who made mouthpieces for boxers. Although sport was ostensibly his beat, the city was undeniably present in these pieces, and he exploited it as a character in his reportage to bring readers into the sweaty boxing rings of Gleason's and the dugouts of Yankee Stadium.

This collection's first section, "The Unnoticed," picks up right after that.

Talese is now twenty-nine and working for the metro desk of the *Times*, and he's just published his debut book, *New York: A Serendipiter's Journey*. The book was a love letter to the city, filled with his vignettes about street barkers, Bowery bums, barflys, waterfront eccentrics, a George Washington impersonator, and New York's then tallest man, Eddie Carmel, who stood eight feet two. But the book, which featured photographs by Marvin Lichtner, would become an obscurity in Talese's back catalog, and copies of it are rare collectors' items today. The first inclusion in this collection is that book's wondrous reported essay "New York Is a City of Things Unnoticed."

In its opening, Talese gives E. B. White a run for his money:

> New York is a city of things unnoticed. It is a city with cats sleeping under parked cars, two stone armadillos crawling up St. Patrick's Cathedral, and thousands of ants creeping on top of the Empire State Building. The ants probably were carried up there by wind or birds, but nobody is sure; nobody in New York knows any more about the ants than they do about the panhandler who takes taxis to the Bowery; or the dapper man who picks trash out of Sixth Avenue trash cans; or the medium in the West Seventies who claims, "I am clairvoyant, clairaudient, and clairsensuous."

The second work in this section is *The Bridge*, Talese's 1964 book about the construction of the Verrazzano-Narrows, which is filled with humanistic tales about the hard and anonymous men who built the bridge. But again, until the *The Bridge* was reissued several years ago, it was also relegated to relative obscurity in Talese's back catalog. Just to ensure it won't be forgotten again, this collection includes no mere excerpt, but its entirety.

In the next section, "The Restless Voyeurs," Talese is now at *Esquire*, and he's becoming a figure of what will be called the New Journalism. Whereas a few years earlier he was writing short but artful pieces in the *Times*, now he is writing stories that are 15,000 words long and is developing his repute as a hero of literary nonfiction. It is during this period that I'd argue Gay's humble craft as a city chronicler begins to be overshadowed by his burgeoning celebrity, an eclipse that will follow him through his pursuit of the ambitious books that will each take him nearly a decade to write.

But you can't take serendipity out of a serendipiter. The city as an observed character looms in the rearview mirror of many of Talese's *Esquire* pieces, which fill this section of the collection. The city will become a motif he keeps soulfully evoking—even throughout his books—as though he were a jazz musician slyly repeating a line in a bebop solo.

The *Esquire* pieces here include "*Vogue*land," a 1961 profile of *Vogue* magazine's fashion editors and staff, and "Looking For Hemingway," a 1963 profile of George Plimpton and the *Paris Review*. Both serve as examples of proto–media industry reporting, and Manhattan is rendered in them as the stylish ecosystem that nourishes these movers and shakers.

There's also Talese's 1966 *Esquire* story "The Kingdoms, the Powers, and the Glories of the *New York Times*," which will lead to his book-length study of the *Times*, *The Kingdom and the Power*. In this piece, Talese profiles fabled *Times*men like Clifton Daniel and Turner Catledge, but the story is also a forensic examination of the *Times* newsroom, which he portrays as a dramatic, fantastical, complex, and even dangerous place that could only exist in New York.

The collection's third section, "The Offbeat Wonders," collects some of Talese's more unexpected city tales.

In "Gino's Long Run," which ran in the *The New Yorker* as a Talk of the Town piece in 1995, he offers a study of vanishing New York through the lens of the Italian restaurant on the Upper East Side that he's patronized for years. The piece is an ode to Gino's stubborn resistance to change. Fifteen years later, Talese will write another Talk story about Gino's, this time about its closure.

In "The Homeless Woman with Two Homes," which ran in *New York Magazine* in 1989, he pens an uncharacteristic work of social commentary. And his 1971 *Esquire* crime classic, "The Kidnapping of Joe Bonanno," opens with his anthropological study of the doormen of Park Avenue, namely one who witnessed the midnight kidnapping of mafia boss Joseph Bonanno and decided that it was probably best to say that he saw and heard nothing.

But the lost gem is "Journey into the Cat Jungle," which ran in the *New York Times Sunday Magazine* in 1957 and is a whimsical investigation into the secret lives of street cats. As you read it you can imagine a noirish version of Talese visiting the city's dark alleys and waterfront piers to get the story. He is only twenty-five when he writes this passage:

> In every neighborhood the strays are dominated by a "boss"—the largest, strongest tomcat. The boss's position is secure so long as he can whip every other tom in the neighborhood. Some bosses stay in power for years—surviving the average stray by nine or ten lives. They usually have many scars, like Mickey, a grisly-looking cat that roams about the Corvan Garage in the mid-Fifties.
>
> "For years, every cat in this block would run when they saw Mickey coming," said a workman at the garage. "He's fought everything—dogs, cats, taxicabs—and he's been bumped once or twice by the Cadillacs the chauffeurs park along here. That cat is afraid of nothing."

The collection's fourth section, "The City's Crooners," includes Talese's *New Yorker* story about Tony Bennett and Lady Gaga recording a duet album at a midtown recording studio. Not much narratively happens in the piece, but it's a late-career tour de force of observational reportage. There's also the obligatory inclusion of "Frank Sinatra Has a Cold," but upon rereading it, you're only reminded of how good it is. In the context of this book, that smoky scene in Jilly's saloon, Sinatra's old watering hole on West Fifty-second Street, reeks of atmosphere.

(Talese has repeatedly said that he does not consider "Frank Sinatra Has a Cold" to be his greatest magazine story; if you wish to read what he does consider his greatest magazine story, flip to the previous section and read "Mr. Bad News," his 1966 *Esquire* profile of Alden Whitman, the chief obituary writer for the *Times*.)

The collection's final section, "The Land Grabbers," regards an unsentimental aspect of life in New York: real estate.

"My New York City Apartment," which ran in *New York Magazine* in 2011, is a personal essay about Talese's yearslong odyssey to buy out each floor of the Upper East Side townhouse he started living in as a renter in the late 1950s. The second story, "Dr. Bartha's Brownstone," is also an Upper East Side yarn, originating from his 2023 memoir, *Bartleby and Me*.

It is an obsessively reported tale about the case of Nicholas Bartha, the Romanian doctor who blew up his Sixty-second Street townhouse in 2006, killing himself in the process, so that he could spite his ex-wife by ensuring that she wouldn't benefit financially from its court-ordered sale. The obsessive tone stems from the fact that the explosion occurred a block from Talese's own townhouse. When the incident was forgotten to New Yorkers after it faded from headlines, the story gnawed at Talese for years, an itch he scratched by finally writing this piece. The story would also deal heavily with the building plot's history, which Talese traced back to the colonial era and its earliest owner, Hugh Gaine, an Irish-born printer and publisher who was a turncoat during the Revolutionary War.

Being that it's the most recent of his works in the collection, its inclusion neatly ties things together, but the piece holds more significance than that.

When Talese initially began reporting the story, he was in a contemplative stage of his life. He was entering his late eighties, and the city as he knew it was changing faster than ever. Gino's was now a Sprinkles cupcake shop and his favorite old restaurants and martini haunts were vanishing around him. Painfully, he also found himself saying goodbye to contemporaries like Tom Wolfe, Pete Hamill, and Jimmy Breslin. *Bartleby and Me* would also become his first book of original reportage since the 2016 release of *The Voyeur's Motel*.

So maybe for reasons of reportorial superstition, or maybe just because he felt like lying low, Talese told few people about what he was working on. "It's a story about a building," he'd vaguely say. "It's a story about New York."

But as he clandestinely toiled away, I'd occasionally hear from people on the Upper East Side about a fedora-wearing figure who had taken an all-consuming interest in a plot of land on Sixty-second Street, the plot that housed that building that blew up all those years ago.

A hot dog vendor told me once that he'd seen this nattily dressed man just standing there, studying the site as he scribbled notes. A hairdresser reported to me that the man politely asked to enter his salon's building so that he could examine the area from an elevated view. And there were sightings of Talese sitting alone in a booth at the Viand diner, deep in thought over a bowl of chicken soup, as he annotated his pages of research.

These sightings surprised me. I was taken aback to hear that a journalistic lion like Talese was still working like this, scrappy and with his hands still deep in the dirt. But I guess I shouldn't have been so surprised.

Once a serendipiter, always a serendipiter, I guess.

—ALEX VADUKUL

PART I

The
Unnoticed

Flag Pole Painters

Deep-Sea Diver in New York (Berney Sweeney) SH8 8508

M. Landsman = OR 9-3500

CARPENTS & JOINERS Union — LE 4-5186

3 DIVERS → 1- EMIL AHLSTROM = Derrick & Salvage dummon
                                  21834 Reverville Drive
          2- Magnus Sonnergren 273 Wordwell ave., SI
          3- Gus Marcussen, 1364 68th St - Bklyn
                         Sweeney

Frenchy Trahan
2002 Murray Place
merrick, L.I.

FR 8-2550

Marine Diver = HAS 36 divers
42nd St. Power House → 38th & East River
12 MIDNIGHT — at the gate House

Res

1 -

GROCER-1

"For many years there has been a kind of
Hatfield-McCoy gun feud on upper Lexington
Ave between a sharp-shooting grocer, Chas
DiMaggio, and a number of unsavory neighbors
who frequently seek to rob him...
      "Whatta neighborhood," his wife kept say.
      He, all the while, bragging...
            (good dialogue)

FROM THE AUTHOR'S NOTEPAD

New York Is a City of Things Unnoticed

FROM *New York: A Serendipiter's Journey*, 1961

N EW YORK IS A city of things unnoticed. It is a city with cats sleeping under parked cars, two stone armadillos crawling up St. Patrick's Cathedral, and thousands of ants creeping on top of the Empire State Building. The ants probably were carried up there by wind or birds, but nobody is sure; nobody in New York knows any more about the ants than they do about the panhandler who takes taxis to the Bowery; or the dapper man who picks trash out of Sixth Avenue trash cans; or the medium in the West Seventies who claims, "I am clairvoyant, clairaudient, and clairsensuous."

New York is a city for eccentrics and a center for odd bits of information. New Yorkers blink twenty-eight times a minute, but forty when tense. Most popcorn chewers at Yankee Stadium stop chewing momentarily just before the pitch. Gum chewers on Macy's escalators stop chewing momentarily just before they get off—to concentrate on the last step. Coins, paper clips, ballpoint pens, and little girls' pocketbooks are found by workmen when they clean the sea lions' pool at the Bronx Zoo.

Each day New Yorkers guzzle 460,000 gallons of beer, swallow 3,500,000 pounds of meat, and pull 21 miles of dental floss through their teeth. Every day in New York about 250 people die, 460 are born, and 150,000 walk through the city wearing eyes of glass or plastic.

A Park Avenue doorman has parts of three bullets in his head—there since World War I. Several young gypsy daughters, influenced by television and literacy, are running away from home because they do not want to grow up and become fortune-tellers. Each month 100 pounds of hair are delivered to Louis Feder at 545 Fifth Avenue, where blonde hairpieces are made from German women's hair; brunette hairpieces from French and Italian women's hair; but no hairpieces from American women's hair, which, says Mr. Feder, is weak from too-frequent rinses and permanents.

Some of New York's best-informed men are elevator operators, who rarely talk but always listen—like doormen. Sardi's doorman listens to the comments made by Broadway's first-nighters walking by after the last act. He listens closely. He listens carefully. Within ten minutes of the curtain's fall he can tell you which shows will flop and which will be hits.

On Broadway in the evening, a big, dark 1948 Rolls-Royce pulls in—and out hops a little lady armed with a Bible and a sign reading "The Damned Shall Perish." She proceeds to stand on the corner screaming at the multitudes of Broadway sinners sometimes until 3 a.m., when the chauffeur-driven Rolls picks her up and drives her back to Westchester.

By this time Fifth Avenue is deserted by all but a few strolling insomniacs, some cruising cabdrivers, and a group of sophisticated females who stand in store windows all night and day wearing cold, perfect smiles—smiles formed by lips of clay, eyes of glass, and cheeks that will glow until the paint wears off. Like sentries, they line Fifth Avenue—these window mannequins who gaze onto the quiet street with tilted heads and pointed toes and long, rubber fingers reaching for cigarettes that aren't there. At 4 a.m., some store windows become a strange fairyland of gangling goddesses, all of them frozen in the act of dashing to a party, diving into a swimming pool, or sashaying skyward in a billowy blue negligee.

While this wild illusion is partly due to the runaway imagination, it is also partly due to the incredible skill of mannequin makers, who have endowed mannequins with certain individual characteristics—the theory being that no two females, not even plastic or plaster females, are quite alike. As a result, the mannequins at Peck & Peck are made to look young and prim, while at Lord & Taylor they seem wiser and windblown. At Saks they are demure but mature, while at Bergdorf's they look agelessly elegant and quietly rich. The profiles of Fifth Avenue's mannequins have been fashioned after some of the world's most alluring women—women like Suzy Parker, who posed for the Best & Co. mannequins, and Brigitte Bardot, who inspired some mannequins at Saks. The preoccupation with making mannequins almost human, and equipping them with curves, is perhaps responsible for the rather strange fascination so many New Yorkers have for these synthetic virgins. This is why some window decorators frequently talk to mannequins and give them pet names, and why naked manne- quins in windows inevitably attract men, disgust women, and are banned in New York City. This is why some mannequins are attacked by perverts, and why the svelte mannequin in a White Plains shop was discovered in the basement not long ago with her clothes torn off, her makeup smeared, and her body possessing evidence of attempted rape. The police laid a trap one night and caught the attacker—a shy little man: the porter.

When street traffic dwindles and most people are sleeping, some New York neighborhoods begin to crawl with cats. They move quickly through the shadows of buildings; night watchmen, policemen, garbage collectors, and other nocturnal wanderers see them—but never for very long. A majority of them hang around the fish markets, in Greenwich Village, and in the East and West Side neighborhoods where garbage cans abound. No part of the city is without its strays, however, and all-night garage attendants in such busy neighborhoods as Fifty-fourth Street have counted as many as twenty of them around the Ziegfeld Theatre early in the morning. Troops of cats patrol the waterfront piers at night searching for rats. Subway track- walkers have discovered cats living in the darkness. They seem never to get hit by trains, though some are occasionally liquidated by the third rail. About twenty-five cats live seventy-five feet below the west end of Grand Central Terminal, are fed by the underground workers, and never wander up into the daylight.

The roving, independent, self-laundering cats of the streets live a life strangely different from New York's kept, apartment-house cats. Most are flea-bitten. Many die of food poisoning, exposure, and malnutrition; their average life span is two years, whereas the stay-at-home cats live ten to twelve years or more. Each year the ASPCA kills about 100,000 New York street cats for whom no homes can be found.

Social climbing among the stray cats of Gotham is not common. They rarely acquire a better mailing address out of choice. They usually die within the blocks of their birth, although one flea-bitten specimen picked up by the ASPCA was adopted by a wealthy woman; it now lives in a lux- urious East Side apartment and spends the summer at the lady's estate on Long Island. The American Feline Society once moved two strays into the headquarters of the United Nations after having heard that some rodents had infested UN filing cabinets. "The cats took care of 'em," says Robert Lothar Kendell, society president. "And they seemed happy at the UN. One of the cats used to sleep on a Chinese dictionary."

In every New York neighborhood the strays are dominated by a "boss"—the largest, strongest tomcat. But, except for the boss, there is not much organization in the street cat's society. Within the society, however, there are three "types" of cats—wild cats, Bohemians, and part-time grocery store (or restaurant) cats.

The wild cats rely on an occasional loose garbage lid or on rats for food and will have little or nothing to do with people—even those who would feed them. These most unkempt of strays have a recognizable haunted look, a wide-eyed, wild expression, and they usually are found around the waterfront.

The Bohemian, however, is more tractable. It does not run from people. Often, it is fed in the streets daily by sensitive cat lovers (mostly women) who call the strays "little people," "angels," or "darlings" and are indignant when the objects of their charity are referred to as "alley cats." So punctual are most Bohemians at feeding time that one cat lover has advanced the theory that cats can tell time. He cited a gray tabby that appears five days a week, precisely at 5:30 p.m., in an office building at Broadway and Seventeenth Street, where the elevator men feed it. But the cat never shows up on Saturdays or Sundays; it seems to know people don't work on those days.

The part-time grocery store (or restaurant) cat, often a reformed Bohemian, eats well and keeps rodents away, but it usually uses the store as a hotel and prefers to spend the nights prowling in the streets. Despite its liberal working schedule, it still assumes most of the privileges of a related breed—the full-time, or wholly nonstray, grocery store cat—including the right to sleep in the window. A reformed Bohemian at a Bleecker Street delicatessen hides behind the door and chases away all other Bohemians looking for handouts.

The number of full-time cats, incidentally, has diminished greatly since the decline of the small food store and the rise of supermarkets in New York. With better rat-proofing methods, improved packaging of foods, and more sanitary conditions, such chain stores as the A&P rarely keep a cat full-time.

On the waterfront, however, the great need for cats remains unchanged. Once a longshoreman who was allergic to cats poisoned them. Within a day rats were all over the place. Every time the men turned around, they would find rats on crates. And on Pier 95 the rats began stealing the longshoremen's lunch and even attacking the men. So the street cats were recruited from nearby neighbors, and now most of the rats are controlled.

"But cats don't get much sleep around here," said one longshoreman. "They can't. Rats would overrun them. We've had cases here where the rat has torn up the cat. But it doesn't happen often. Most waterfront cats are mean bastards."

At 5 a.m. Manhattan is a town of tired trumpet players and homeward-bound bartenders. Pigeons control Park Avenue and strut unchallenged in the middle of the street. This is Manhattan's mellowest hour. Most *night* people are out of sight—but the *day* people have not yet appeared. Truck drivers and cabs are alert, yet they do not disturb the mood. They do not disturb the abandoned Rockefeller Center, or the motionless night watchmen in the Fulton Fish Market, or the gas-station attendant sleeping next to Sloppy Louie's with the radio on.

At 5 a.m. the Broadway regulars have gone home or to all-night coffee shops where, under the glaring light, you see their whiskers and wear. And on Fifty-first Street a radio press car is parked at the curb with a photographer who has nothing to do. So he just sits there for a few nights, looks through the windshield, and soon becomes a keen observer of life after midnight.

"At 1 a.m.," he says, "Broadway is filled with wise guys and with kids coming out of the Astor Hotel in white dinner jackets—kids who drive to dances in their fathers' cars. You also see cleaning ladies going home, always wearing kerchiefs. By 2 a.m., some of the drinkers are getting out of hand, and this is the hour for bar fights. At 3 a.m. the last show is over in the nightclubs, and most of the tourists and out-of-town buyers are back in hotels. At 4 a.m., after the bars close, you see the drunks come out—and also the pimps and prostitutes who take advantage of drunks. At 5 a.m., though, it is mostly quiet. New York is an entirely different city at 5 a.m."

At 6 a.m. the early workers begin to push up from the subways. The traffic begins to move down Broadway like a river. And Mrs. Mary Woody jumps out of bed, dashes to her office, and phones dozens of sleepy New

Yorkers to say in a cheerful voice, rarely appreciated: "Good morning. Time to get up." For twenty years, as an operator of Western Union's Wake-Up Service, Mrs. Woody has gotten millions out of bed.

At 7 a.m. a floridly robust little man, looking very Parisian in a blue beret and turtleneck sweater, moves in a hurried step along Park Avenue visiting his wealthy lady friends—making certain that each is given a brisk, before-breakfast rubdown. The uniformed doormen greet him warmly and call him either "Biz" or "Mac" because he is Biz Mackey, a ladies' masseur extraordinaire.

Mr. Mackey is spry and straight-spined, and always carries a black leather grip containing liniments, creams, and the towels of his trade. Up the elevator he goes; then, half an hour later, he is down again, and off to another lady—an opera singer, a movie actress, a lady police lieutenant.

Biz Mackey, a former featherweight prizefighter, started rubbing women the right way in Paris, in the twenties. He had lost a fight during a European tour and decided he'd had enough. A friend suggested he go to a school for masseurs, and six months later he had his first customer—Claire Luce, the actress then starring in the Folies-Bergère. She liked him, and sent him more clients—Pearl White, Mary Pickford, and a beefy Wagnerian soprano. It took World War II to get Biz out of Paris.

When he returned to Manhattan, his European clientele continued to patronize him when they visited here, and though he is now pushing seventy, he is still going strong. Biz handles about seven women a day. His muscular fingers and thick arms have a miraculously soothing touch. He is discreet, and that is why New York ladies prefer him. He visits each of them in her apartment and has special keys to the bedrooms; he is often the first man they see in the morning, and they lie in bed waiting for him. He never reveals the names of his customers, but most of them are middle-aged and rich.

"Women don't want other women to know their business," Biz explains. "You know women," he adds, offhandedly, leaving no doubt that he does.

The doormen that Biz passes each morning are generally an obliging, endlessly articulate group of sidewalk diplomats who list among their friends some of Manhattan's most powerful men, most beautiful women, and snootiest poodles. More often than not the doormen are big, slightly

Gothic in design, and possessors of eyes sharp enough to spot big tippers a block away in the year's thickest fog.

Some East Side doormen are as proud as grandees, and their uniforms, heavily festooned, seem to have come from the same tailor who outfitted Marshal Tito. Most hotel doormen are superb at small talk, big talk, and back talk, at remembering names and appraising luggage leather. (They size up a guest's wealth by the luggage he has, not by the clothes he wears.)

In Manhattan today there are 650 apartment-house doormen, 325 hotel doormen (14 at the Waldorf-Astoria), and an unknown, but formidable, number of restaurant and theater doormen, nightclub doormen, barking doormen, and doorless doormen.

Doorless doormen, who are nonunion vagabonds, usually without uniforms (but with rented hats), pussyfoot about town opening car doors when traffic is thick—on nights of the opera, concerts, championship fights, and conventions. The Brass Rail doorman, Christos Efthimiou, says that doorless doormen know when he is off (Mondays and Tuesdays) and that on these days they freelance off his spot on Seventh Avenue at Forty-ninth Street.

Barking doormen, who sometimes wear rented uniforms (but own their hats), post themselves in front of jazz clubs with floor shows, such as along Fifty-second Street. In addition to opening doors and lassoing cabdrivers, the barking doormen might whisper to passing pedestrians, softly but distinctly, "Psssst! No cover charge—girls inside . . . the new Queen of Alaska!"

Though there is hardly a doorman in town who does not swear up and down that he is underpaid and underrated, many hotel doormen admit that on some good, rainy weeks they have made close to $200 in tips alone. (More people desire cabs when it is raining, and doormen who provide umbrellas and cabs rarely go untipped.)

When it rains in Manhattan, automobile traffic is slow, dates are broken, and, in hotel lobbies, people slump behind newspapers or walk aimlessly about with no place to sit, nobody to talk to, nothing to do. Taxis are harder to get; department stores do between 15 to 25 percent less business; and the monkeys in the Bronx Zoo, having no audience, slouch grumpily in their cages looking more bored than the lobby loungers.

While some New Yorkers become morose with rain, others prefer it, like to walk in it, and say that on rainy days the city's buildings seem some-how cleaner—washed in an opalescence, like a Monet painting. There are fewer suicides in New York when it rains; but when the sun is shining, and New Yorkers seem happy, the depressed person sinks deeper into depres-sion and Bellevue Hospital gets more attempted suicides.

Yet a rainy day in New York is a bright day for umbrella and raincoat salesmen, for hatcheck girls, bellhops, and for members of the British Consulate General's office, who say rain reminds them of home. Consol-idated Edison claims New Yorkers burn $120,000 worth more electricity than they do on bright days; thousands of trouser creases lose their sharp-ness in rain, and Norton Cleaners on Forty-fifth Street presses an average of 125 more pants on such days.

Rain ruins the mascara on the eyes of fashion models who cannot find cabs; and rain makes it a lonely day for Times Square's recruiting sergeants, demonstrators, bootblacks, and burglars—who all tend to lose their enthusiasm when wet.

Shortly after 7:30 each morning, while most New Yorkers still are in a bleary-eyed slumber, hundreds of people are lined along Forty-second Street waiting for the 8 a.m. opening of the ten movie houses that stand almost shoulder to shoulder between Times Square and Eighth Avenue.

Who are these people who go to the movies at 8 a.m.? They are the city's night watchmen, derelicts, or people who can't sleep, can't go home, or have no home. They are truck drivers, homosexuals, cops, hacks, clean-ing ladies, and restaurant men who have worked all night. They are also alcoholics who are waiting at 8 a.m. to pay forty cents to get a soft seat and sleep in the cool, dark, smoky theater.

And yet, aside from being smoky, each Times Square theater has a spe-cial quality, or lack of quality, about it. At the Victory Theatre one finds only horror films, while at the Times Square Theater they feature only cowboy films. There are first-run films for forty cents at the Lyric, while at the Selwyn there are always second-run films for thirty cents. At both the Liberty and the Empire are reissues, and at the Apollo they run only foreign films. Foreign films have been making money at the Apollo for twenty years, and William Brandt, one of the owners, never could under-stand why. "So one day I investigated the place," he said, "and saw people in the lobby talking with their hands. I realized they were mostly deaf and dumb. They patronize the Apollo because they read the subtitles that go with foreign films; the Apollo probably has the biggest deaf-and-dumb movie audience in the world."

New York is a town of 8,485 telephone operators, 1,364 Western Union messenger boys, and 112 newspaper copyboys. An average baseball crowd at Yankee Stadium uses over ten gallons of liquid soap per game—an unofficial high mark for cleanliness in the major leagues; the stadium also has the league's top number of ushers (360), sweepers (72), and men's rooms (34).

In New York there are 500 mediums, from semitrance to trance to deeptrance types. Most of them live in New York's West Seventies, Eighties, and Nineties, and on Sundays some of these blocks are communicating with the dead, vibrating to trumpets, and solving all problems.

In New York the Fifth Avenue Lingerie Shop is on Madison Avenue, the Madison Pet Shop is on Lexington Avenue, the Park Avenue Florist is on Madison Avenue, and the Lexington Hand Laundry is on Third Avenue. New York is the home of 120 pawnbrokers, and it is where Bishop Sheen's brother, Dr. Sheen, shares an office with one Dr. Bishop.

Within a serene brownstone on Lexington Avenue, on the corner of Eighty-second Street, a pharmacist named Frederick D. Lascoff for years has been selling leeches to battered prizefighters, catnip oil to lion hunters, and thousands of strange potions to people in exotic places around the world.

Within a somber West Side factory each month a long, green line of cardboard crawls like an endless reptile up and down a printing press until it is chopped into thousands of little, annoying pieces. Each piece is designed to fit into a policeman's pocket, decorate the windshield of an illegally parked car, and relieve a motorist of fifteen dollars. About 500,000 fifteen-dollar tickets are printed for New York's police each year on West Nineteenth Street by the May Tag and Label Corp., whose employees sometimes see their workmanship boomerang on their own windshields.

New York is a city of 200 chestnut vendors, 300,000 pigeons, and 600 statues and monuments. When the equestrian statue of a general has both front hoofs off the ground, it means the general died in battle; if one hoof is off the ground, he died of wounds received in battle; if all four hoofs are on the ground, the general probably died in bed.

In New York from dawn to dusk to dawn, day after day, you can hear the steady rumble of tires against the concrete span of the George Washington Bridge. The bridge is never completely still. It trembles with traffic. It moves in the wind. Its great veins of steel swell when hot and contract when cold; its span often is ten feet closer to the Hudson River in summer than in winter. It is an almost restless structure of graceful beauty which, like an irresistible seductress, withholds secrets from the romantics who gaze upon it, the escapists who jump off it, the chubby girl who lumbers across its 3,500-foot span trying to reduce, and the 100,000 motorists who each day cross it, smash into it, shortchange it, get jammed up on it.

Few of the New Yorkers and tourists who breeze across it are aware of the workmen riding elevators through the twin towers 612 feet above, and few people know that wandering drunks occasionally have climbed blithely to the top and fallen asleep up there. In the morning they are petrified and have to be carried down by emergency crews.

Few people know that the bridge was built in an area where Indians used to roam, battles were fought, and where, during early colonial times, pirates were hanged along the river as a warning to other adventurous sailors. The bridge now stands where Washington's troops fell back before the British invaders who later captured Fort Lee, New Jersey, and who found kettles still on the fire, the cannon abandoned, and clothing strewn along the path of Washington's retreating garrison.

The roadway at the George Washington Bridge is more than 100 feet above the little red lighthouse that became obsolete when the bridge went up in 1931; its Jersey approach is two miles from where Albert Anastasia lived behind a high wall guarded by Doberman pinschers; its Jersey tollage is twenty feet from where a truck driver without a license tried to drive four elephants across in his trailer—and would have if one elephant hadn't fallen out. The upper span is 220 feet from where a Port Authority guard once climbed up to tell an aspiring suicide, "Listen, you SOB, if you don't come down, I'm going to shoot you down"—and the man crawled quickly down.

Around the clock the bridge guards stay alert. They have to. At any moment there may be an accident, breakdown, or a suicide. Since 1931, 100 people have jumped from the bridge. More than twice that number have been stopped. Bridge jumpers intent on committing suicide go quickly and quietly. On the edge of the roadway they leave automobiles, jackets, eyeglasses, and sometimes a note reading, "I wish to take the blame for everything" or "I don't want to live anymore."

A lonely out-of-town buyer who'd had a few drinks checked into a Broadway hotel near Sixty-fourth Street one night, went to bed, and awoke in the middle of the night to a shocking view. He saw, floating past his window, the shimmering image of the Statue of Liberty.

Immediately he imagined himself shanghaied—sailing past Liberty Island toward certain disaster on the high seas. But then, after a closer look, he found that he was actually seeing New York's *second* Statue of Liberty—the obscure, almost unnoticed statue that stands on top of the Liberty-Pac warehouse at 43 West Sixty-fourth Street.

This reasonable facsimile, erected in 1902 at the request of William H. Flattau, a patriotic warehouse owner, stands 55 feet high above its pedestal as compared with Bartholdi's 151-footer on Liberty Island. This smaller Liberty also had a lighted torch, a spiral staircase, and a hole in the head through which Broadway could be seen. But in 1912 the staircase became weakened, the torch blew off in a storm, and schoolchildren were no longer permitted to run up and down inside. Mr. Flattau died in 1931, and with him went much of the information on the history of this statue.

From time to time, however, employees in the warehouse, as well as people in the neighborhood, are asked by tourists about the statue. "People usually come over and say, 'Hey, what's *that* doing up *there?*'" said a Kinney parking-lot attendant who works across from the statue. "The other day a Texan pulls in, looks up, and says, 'I thought that statue was supposed to be in the water somewhere.' But some people are really interested in the statue and take pictures of it. I consider it a privilege to work under it, and when tourists come I always remind them that this is the 'Second Largest Statue of Liberty in the World.'"

But most neighborhood folks pay no attention to the statue. The gypsy fortune-tellers who work to the left of it do not; the habitués of Mrs. Stern's tavern below it do not; the soup slurpers in Bickford's restaurant across the street do not. A New York cabby, David Zickerman (Cab No. 2865), has whizzed by the statue hundreds of times and never knew it existed. "Who the hell looks up in this town?" he asks.

For decades this statue has carried a burned-out torch over this neighborhood of punchball players, short-order cooks, and warehouse watchmen; over undertipped bellhops and cops and high-heeled transvestites who leave their fire-escaped walls after midnight and stroll through this town of perhaps too much liberty.

New York is a city of movement. Artists and beatniks live in Greenwich Village, where the Negroes first settled. Negroes live in Harlem, where the Jews and Germans once lived. The wealth has moved from the West to the East Side. Puerto Ricans cluster everywhere. Only the Chinese have stability in their enclave around the ancient angle of Doyer Street.

To some people, New York is best remembered by the smile of an airline stewardess at LaGuardia, or the patience of a shoe salesman on Fifth Avenue; to others the city represents the smell of garlic in the rear of a Mulberry Street church, or a hunk of "turf" for juvenile gangs to fight over, or a chunk of real estate to be bought and sold by Zeckendorf.

But beyond the New York City guidebooks and the chamber of commerce, New York is no summer festival. For most New Yorkers it is a town of hard work, too many cars, too many people. Many of the people are anonymous, like busmen, charwomen, and those creepy pornographers who mark up advertising posters and are never caught. Many New Yorkers seem to have only one name, like barbers, doormen, bootblacks. Some New Yorkers go through life with the wrong name—like Jimmy Buns, who lives across from Police Headquarters on Centre Street. When Jimmy Buns, whose real surname is Mancuso, was a little boy, the cops sitting across the street would yell to him, "Hey, kid, how 'bout going down the corner and getting us some coffee and buns?" Jimmy always obliged, and soon they called him "Jimmy Buns" or just "Hey Buns." Now Jimmy is a white-haired, elderly man with a daughter named Jeannie. But Jeannie never had a maiden name; everybody just calls her "Jeannie Buns."

New York is the city of Jim Torpey, who has been flashing headlines around Times Square's electric sign since 1928 without burning a bulb for himself; and of George Bannan, Madison Square Garden's official timekeeper, who has held up like an imperishable grandfather's clock through 7,000 prizefights and has rung the bell 2 million times. It is the city of Michael McPadden, who sits behind a microphone in a subway booth near the Times Square shuttle train yelling in a voice wavering between futility and frustration, "Watch your step getting off, please, watch your step." He delivers this advice 500 times a day and sometimes would like to ad-lib. Yet he rarely tries. He has long been convinced that his is a forgotten voice lost in the clamor of slamming doors and pushing bodies; and before he can think of anything witty to say, another train has arrived from Grand Central, and Mr. McPadden must say (one more time!), "Watch your step getting off, please, watch your step."

When it begins to get dark in New York, and all the shoppers have left Macy's, ten black Doberman pinschers begin to tip-tap up and down the aisles sniffing for prowlers who may be hiding behind counters or lurking in clothes racks. They wander through all twenty floors of the big store and are trained to climb ladders, jump through window frames, leap over hurdles, and bark at anything unusual—a leaky radiator, broken steamline, smoke, or a thief. Should a thief try to escape, the dogs can easily overtake him, run between his legs—and trip him. Their barks have alerted Macy's guards to many minor hazards but never to a thief—none has dared remain in the store after closing hours since the dogs arrived in 1952.

New York is a city in which large, cliff-dwelling hawks cling to skyscrapers and occasionally zoom to snatch a pigeon over Central Park, or Wall Street, or the Hudson River. Bird watchers have seen these peregrine falcons circling lazily over the city. They have seen them perched atop tall buildings, even around Times Square.

About twelve of these hawks patrol the city, some with a wingspan of thirty-five inches. They have buzzed women on the roof of the St. Regis Hotel, have attacked repairmen on smokestacks, and, in August 1947, two hawks jumped women residents in the recreation yard of the Home of the New York Guild for the Jewish Blind. Maintenance men at the Riverside Church have seen hawks dining on pigeons in the bell tower. The hawks remain there for only a little while. And then they fly out to the river, leaving pigeons' heads for the Riverside maintenance men to clean up. When the hawks return, they fly in quietly—*unnoticed*, like the cats, the ants, the doorman with three bullets in his head, the ladies' masseur, and most of the other offbeat wonders in this town without time.

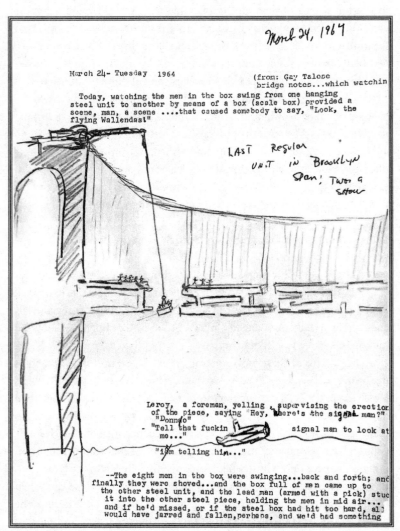

March 24, 1964

March 24- Tuesday 1964

(from: Gay Talese
bridge notes...which watchin

Today, watching the men in the box swing from one hanging
steel unit to another by means of a box (scale box) provided a
scene, man, a scene ....that caused somebody to say, "Look, the
flying Wallendas!"

LAST Regular
UNIT IN Brooklyn
Span; Two; a
show

Leroy, a foreman, yelling , supervising the erection
of the piece, saying "Hey, where's the signal man?"
"Donngo"
- "Tell that fuckin   signal man to look at
me..."

"i'm telling him..."

--The eight men in the box were swinging...back and forth; and
finally they were shoved...and the box full of men came up to
the other steel unit, and the lead man (armed with a pick) stuc
it into the other steel piece, holding the men in mid air...
and if he'd missed, or if the steel box had hit too hard, all
would have jarred and fallen,perhaps, and we'd had something

AUTHOR'S DRAWING FROM THE BRIDGE SITE

The Bridge

FROM *The Bridge*, Harper & Row, 1964

Preface

A GREAT BRIDGE IS A poetic construction of enduring beauty and utility, and in the early 1960s, as the rainbow-shaped roadway of the Verrazano-Narrows Bridge was being extended for two and a half miles across the New York Harbor, connecting the boroughs of Brooklyn and Staten Island, I often put on a hard hat and followed the workers across the catwalk and watched for hours as they crawled like spiders up and down the cable ropes and straddled beams while tightening bolts with their spud wrenches. Sometimes they would give a shove with their gloved hands against a stalled spinning wheel, or bang a shoulder against tons of framework dangling from a crane, or wiggle their toes within their boots as they bent their bodies closer to the task while seeking stable footing in the shifting winds a few hundred feet above the sea.

From the bridge's two towers, each seventy stories high, one can survey the panorama of the city—the Empire State Building, the Chrysler Building, the venerable Brooklyn Bridge, completed in 1883, the spires of Wall Street, and, rising out of the chaos of September 11, 2001, the needle-topped 104-story Tower 1 of the new World Trade Center.

When I first moved to New York in the mid-1950s, I often asked myself: Whose fingerprints are on the bolts and beams of these soaring edifices in this overreaching city? Who are these high-wire walkers in boots and hard hats who earn their living while risking their lives in places where falls are often fatal and where the bridges and skyscrapers are looked upon as sepulchers by the families and coworkers of the deceased? Although we often know the identities of the architects or chief engineers of renowned structures, the workers' names are rarely mentioned in the written accounts or archival materials associated with such landmarks.

I kept this in mind when I decided to write a book about the development of the Verrazano-Narrows Bridge, which began with a groundbreaking ceremony along the harbor on August 14, 1959.

The bridge opened for business about five years later, on November 21, 1964, with a traffic jam that was led by fifty-two black limousines bearing politicians and business executives, most of whom had earlier attended a ribbon cutting ceremony. Currently, more than 170,000 vehicles cross the span every weekday, generating a daily revenue of $950,000.

Now, as the Metropolitan Transportation Authority is about to mark the fiftieth anniversary of the bridge's opening, this new edition of my original 1964 book, *The Bridge*, commemorates that milestone. This edition, like the older one, is less a celebration of the bridge than of the high-stepping men who built it—the very men who, incidentally, were not invited to attend the opening-day ceremony fifty years ago.

I have kept in touch with many of these men during the last half-century, and this book represents an invitation to become acquainted with the uninvited.

I. The Boomers

They drive into town in big cars, and live in furnished rooms, and drink whiskey with beer chasers, and chase women they will soon forget. They linger only a little while, only until they have built the bridge; then they are off again to another town, another bridge, linking everything but their lives.

They possess none of the foundation of their bridges. They are part circus, part gypsy—graceful in the air, restless on the ground; it is as if the wide-open road below lacks for them the clear direction of an eight-inch beam stretching across the sky six hundred feet above the sea.

When there are no bridges to be built, they will build skyscrapers, or highways, or power dams, or anything that promises a challenge—and overtime. They will go anywhere, will drive a thousand miles all day and night to be part of a new building boom. They find boom towns irresistible. That is why they are called "the boomers."

In appearance, boomers usually are big men, or if not always big, always strong, and their skin is ruddy from all the sun and wind. Some who heat rivets have charred complexions; some who drive rivets are hard of hearing; some who catch rivets in small metal cones have blisters and body burns marking each miss; some who do welding see flashes at night while they sleep. Those who connect steel have deep scars along their shins from climbing columns. Many boomers have mangled hands and fingers sliced off by slipped steel. Most have taken falls and broken a limb or two. All have seen death.

They are cocky men, men of great pride, and at night they brag and build bridges in bars, and sometimes when they are turning to leave, the bartender will yell after them, "Hey, you guys, how's about clearing some steel out of here?"

Stray women are drawn to them, like them because they have money and no wives within miles—they liked them well enough to have floated a bordello boat beneath one bridge near St. Louis, and to have used up-turned hardhats for flowerpots in the red-light district of Paducah.

On weekends some boomers drive hundreds of miles to visit their families, are tender and tolerant, and will deny to the heavens any suggestion that they raise hell on the job—except they'll admit it in whispers, half proud, half ashamed, fearful the wives will hear and then any semblance of marital stability will be shattered.

Like most men, the boomer wants it both ways. Occasionally his family will follow him, living in small hotels or trailer courts, but it is no life for a wife and child.

The boomer's child might live in forty states and attend a dozen high schools before he graduates, if he graduates, and though the father swears he wants no boomer for a son, he usually gets one. He gets one, possibly, because he really wanted one, and maybe that is why boomers brag so much at home on weekends, creating a wondrous world with whiskey words, a world no son can resist because this world seems to have everything: adventure, big cars, big money, and gambling on rainy days when the bridge is slippery, and booming around the country with Indians who are sure-footed as spiders, with Newfoundlanders as shifty as the sea they come from, with roaming Rebel riveters escaping the poverty of their small Southern towns, all of them building something big and permanent, something that can be revisited years later and pointed to and said of: "See that bridge over there, son—well one day, when I was younger, I drove twelve hundred rivets into that goddamned thing."

They tell their sons the good parts, forgetting the bad, hardly ever describing how men sometimes freeze with fear on high steel and clutch to beams with closed eyes, or admitting that when they climb down they need three drinks to settle their nerves; no, they dwell on the glory, the overtime, not the weeks of unemployment; they recall how they helped build the Golden Gate and Empire State, and how their fathers before them worked on the Williamsburg Bridge in 1902, lifting steel beams with derricks pulled by horses.

They make their world sound as if it were an extension of the Wild West, which in a way it is, with boomers today still regarding themselves as pioneering men, the last of America's unhenpecked heroes, but there are probably only a thousand of them left who are footloose enough to go anywhere to build anything. And when they arrive at the newest boom town, they hold brief reunions in bars, and talk about old times, old faces: about Cicero Mike, who once drove a Capone whiskey truck during Prohibition and recently fell to his death off a bridge near Chicago; and Indian Al Deal, who kept three women happy out West and came to the bridge each morning in a fancy silk shirt; and about Riphorn Red, who used to paste twenty-dollar bills along the sides of his suitcase and who went berserk one night in a cemetery. And there was the Nutley Kid, who smoked long Italian cigars and chewed snuff and used toilet water and, at lunch, would drink milk and beer—without taking out the snuff. And there was Ice Water Charley, who on freezing wintry days up on the bridge would send apprentice boys all the way down to fetch hot water, but by the time they'd climbed back up, the water was cold, and he would spit it out, screaming angrily, "*Ice water, ice water!*" and send them all the way down for more. And there was that one-legged lecher, Whitey Howard, who, on a rail bridge one day, did not hear the train coming, and so he had to jump the tracks at the last second, holding on to the edge, during which time his wooden left leg fell off, and Whitey spent the rest of his life bragging about how he lost his left leg twice.

Sometimes they go on and on this way, drinking and reminiscing about the undramatic little things involving people known only to boomers, people seen only at a distance by the rest of the world, and then they'll start a card game, the first of hundreds to be played in this boom town while the bridge is being built—a bridge many boomers will never cross. For before the bridge is finished, maybe six months before it is opened to traffic, some boomers get itchy and want to move elsewhere. The challenge is dying. So is the overtime. And they begin to wonder: "Where next?" This is what they were asking one another in the early spring of 1957, but some boomers already had the answer: New York.

New York was planning a number of bridges. Several projects were scheduled upstate, and New York City alone, between 1958 and 1964, planned to spend nearly $600,000,000 for, among other things, the double-decking of the George Washington Bridge, the construction of the Throgs Neck Bridge across Long Island Sound—and, finally, in what might be the most challenging task of a boomer's lifetime, the construction of the world's largest suspension span, the Verrazano-Narrows Bridge.

The Verrazano-Narrows, linking Brooklyn and Staten Island (over the futile objections of thousands of citizens in both boroughs), would possess a 4,260-foot center span that would surpass San Francisco's Golden Gate by sixty feet, and would be 460 feet longer than the Mackinac Bridge in upper Michigan, just below Canada.

It was the Mackinac Bridge, slicing down between Lake Huron and Lake Michigan and connecting the cities of St. Ignace and Mackinaw City, that had attracted the boomers between the years 1954 and 1957. And though they would now abandon it for New York, not being able to resist the big movement eastward, there were a few boomers who actually were sorry to be leaving Michigan, for in their history of hell-raising there never had been a more bombastic little boom town than the once tranquil St. Ignace.

Before the boomers had infiltrated it, St. Ignace was a rather sober city of about 2,500 residents, who went hunting in winter, fishing in summer, ran small shops that catered to tourists, helped run the ferryboats across five miles of water to Mackinaw City, and gave the local police very little trouble. The land had been inhabited first by peaceful Indians, then by French bushrangers, then by missionaries and fur traders, and in 1954 it was still clean and uncorrupt, still with one hotel, called the Nicolet— named after a white man, Jean Nicolet, who in 1634 is said to have paddled in a canoe through the Straits of Mackinac and discovered Lake Michigan.

So it was the Nicolet Hotel, and principally its bar, that became the boomers' headquarters, and soon the place was a smoky scene of nightly parties and brawls, and there were girls down from Canada and up from Detroit, and there were crap games along the floor—and if St. Ignace had not been such a friendly city, all the boomers might have gone to jail and the bridge might never have been finished.

But the people of St. Ignace were pleased with the big new bridge going up. They could see how hard the men worked on it and they did not want to spoil their little fun at night. The merchants, of course, were favorably disposed because, suddenly, in this small Michigan town by the sea, the sidewalks were enhanced by six hundred or seven hundred men, each earning between $300 and $500 a week—and some spending it as fast as they were making it.

The local police did not want to seem inhospitable, either, and so they did not raid the poker or crap games. The only raid in memory was led by some Michigan state troopers; and when they broke in, they discovered gambling among the boomers another state trooper. The only person arrested was the boomer who had been winning the most. And since his earnings were confiscated, he was unable to pay the $100 fine and therefore had to go to jail. Later that night, however, he got a poker game going in his cell, won $100, and bought his way out of jail. He was on the bridge promptly for work the next morning.

It is perhaps a slight exaggeration to suggest that, excepting state troopers, everybody else in St. Ignace either fawned upon or quietly tolerated boomers. For there were some families who forbade their daughters to date boomers, with some success, and there were young local men in town who despised boomers, although this attitude may be attributed as much to their envy of boomers' big cars and money as to the fact that comparatively few boomers were teetotalers or celibates. On the other hand, it would be equally misleading to assume that there were not some boomers who were quiet, modest men—maybe as many as six or seven—one of them being, for instance, a big quiet Kentuckian named Ace Cowan (whose wife was with him in Michigan), and another being Johnny Atkins, who once at the Nicolet drank a dozen double martinis without causing a fuss or seeming drunk, and then floated quietly, happily out into the night.

And there was also Jack Kelly, the tall 235-pound son of a Philadelphia sailmaker, who, despite years of work on noisy bridges and despite getting hit on the head by so much falling hardware that he had fifty-two stitches in his scalp, remained ever mild. And finally there was another admired man on the Mackinac—the superintendent, Art "Drag-Up" Drilling, a veteran boomer from Arkansas who went west to work on the Golden Gate and Oakland Bay bridges in the thirties, and who was called "Drag-Up" because he always said, though never in threat, that he'd sooner drag-up and leave town than work under a superintendent who knew less about bridges than he.

So he went from town to town, bridge to bridge, never really satisfied until he became the top bridgeman—as he did on the Mackinac, and as he hoped to do in 1962 on the Verrazano-Narrows Bridge.

In the course of his travels, however, Drag-Up Drilling sired a son named John. And while John Drilling inherited much of his father's soft Southern charm and easy manner, these qualities actually belied the devil beneath. For John Drilling, who was only nineteen years old when he first joined the gang on the Mackinac, worked as hard as any to leave the boomer's mark on St. Ignace.

John Drilling had been born in Oakland in 1937 while his father was finishing on the Bay Bridge there. And in the next nineteen years he followed his father, living in forty-one states, attending two dozen schools, charming the girls—marrying one, and living with her for four months. There was nothing raw nor rude in his manner. He was always extremely genteel and clean-cut in appearance, but, like many boomers' offspring, he was afflicted with what old bridgemen call "rambling fever."

This made him challenging to some women, and frustrating to others, yet intriguing to most. On his first week in St. Ignace, while stopped at a gas station, he noticed a carload of girls nearby and, exuding all the shy and bumbling uncertainty of a new boy in town, addressed himself politely to the prettiest girl in the car—a Swedish beauty, a very healthy girl whose boyfriend had just been drafted—and thus began an unforgettable romance that would last until the next one.

Having saved a few thousand dollars from working on the Mackinac, he became, very briefly, a student at the University of Arkansas and also bought a $2,700 Impala. One night in Ola, Arkansas, he cracked up the car and might have gotten into legal difficulty had not his date that evening been the judge's daughter.

John Drilling seemed to live a charmed life. Of all the bridge builders who worked on the Mackinac, and who would later come east to work on the Verrazano-Narrows Bridge, young John Drilling seemed the luckiest—with the possible exception of his close friend, Robert Anderson.

Anderson was luckier mainly because he had lived longer, done more, survived more; and he never lost his sunny disposition or incurable optimism. He was thirty-four years old when he came to the Mackinac. He had been married to one girl for a dozen years, to another for two weeks. He had been in auto accidents, been hit by falling tools, taken falls—once toppling forty-two feet—but his only visible injury was two missing inside fingers on his left hand, and he never lost its full use.

One day on the north tower of the Mackinac, the section of catwalk upon which Anderson was standing snapped loose, and suddenly it came sliding down like a rollercoaster, with Anderson clinging to it as it bumped and raced down the cables, down 1,800 feet all the way to near the bottom where the cables slope gently and straighten out before the anchorage. Anderson quietly got off and began the long climb up again. Fortunately for him, the Mackinac was designed by David B. Steinman, who preferred long, tapering backspans; had the bridge been designed by O. H. Ammann, who favored shorter, chunkier backspans, such as the type he was then creating for the Verrazano-Narrows Bridge, Bob Anderson would have had a steeper, more abrupt ride down, and might have gone smashing into the anchorage and been killed. But Anderson was lucky that way.

Off the bridge, Anderson had a boomer's luck with women. All the moving around he had done during his youth as a boomer's son, all the shifting from town to town and the enforced flexibility required of such living, gave him a casual air of detachment, an ability to be at home anywhere. Once, in Mexico, he made his home in a whorehouse. The prostitutes down there liked him very much, fought over him, admired his gentle manners and the fact that he treated them all like ladies. Finally the madam invited him in as a full-time house guest and each night Anderson would dine with them, and in the morning he stood in line with them awaiting his turn in the shower.

Though he stands six feet and is broad-shouldered and erect, Bob Anderson is not a particularly handsome fellow; but he has bright alert eyes, and a round, friendly, usually smiling face, and he is very disarming, a sort of Tom Jones of the bridge business—smooth and swift, somewhat gallant, addicted to good times and hot-blooded women, and yet never slick or tricky.

He is also fairly lucky at gambling, having learned a bit back in Oklahoma from his uncle Manuel, a guitar-playing rogue who once won a whole carnival playing poker. Anderson avoids crap games, although one evening at the Nicolet, when a crap game got started on the floor of the men's room and he'd been invited to join, he did.

"Oh, I was drunk that night," he said, in his slow Southwestern drawl, to a friend some days later. "I was so drunk I could hardly see. But I jes' kept rolling them dice, and all I was seeing was sevens and elevens, sevens and elevens, *Jee-sus Kee-rist*, all night long it went like that, and I kept winning and drinking and winning some more. Finally lots of other folks came jamming in, hearing all the noise and all, and in this men's toilet room there's some women and tourists who also came in—jes' watching me roll those sevens and elevens.

"Next morning I woke up with a helluva hangover, but on my bureau I seen this pile of money. And when I felt inside my pockets they were stuffed with bills, crumpled up like dried leaves. And when I counted it all, it came to more than one thousand dollars. And that day on the bridge, there was guys coming up to me and saying, 'Here, Bob, here's the fifty I borrowed last night,' or, 'Here's the hundred,' and I didn't even remember they borrowed it. Jee-sus Kee-rist, what a night!"

When Bob Anderson finally left the Mackinac job and St. Ignace, he had managed to save five thousand dollars, and, not knowing what else to do with it, he bought a round-trip airplane ticket and went flying off to Tangier, Paris, and Switzerland—"Whoring and drinking," as he put it—and then, flat broke, except for his return ticket, he went back to St. Ignace and married a lean, lovely brunette he'd been unable to forget.

And not long after that, he packed his things and his new wife, and along with dozens of other boomers—with John Drilling and Drag-Up, with Ace Cowan and Jack Kelly and other veterans of the Mackinac and the Nicolet—he began the long road trip eastward to try his luck in New York.

II. Panic in Brooklyn

"You *sonamabitch*!" the old Italian shoemaker cried, standing in the doorway of the Brooklyn real estate office, glaring at the men who sat behind desks in the rear of the room. "You *sonamabitch*," he repeated when nobody looked up.

"*Hey*," snapped one of the men, jumping up from his desk, "who are *you* talking to?"

"You," said the shoemaker, his small disheveled figure leaning against the door unsteadily, as if he'd been drinking, his tiny dark eyes angry and bloodshot. "You take-a my store . . . you no give-a me notting, you . . ."

"Now listen here," said the real estate man, quickly walking to where the shoemaker stood and looking down at him hard, "we will have none of *that* talk around here. In fact I am going to call the cops . . ."

He grabbed the phone nearest him and began to dial. The shoemaker watched for a moment, not seeming to care. Then he shrugged to himself and slowly turned and, without another word, walked out the door and shuffled down the street.

The real estate man, putting down the telephone, watched the shoemaker go. He did not chase him. He wanted nothing further to do with him—neither with him nor with any of those boisterous people who had been making so much noise lately, cursing or signing petitions or issuing threats, as if it had been the *real estate men's* idea to build the Verrazano-Narrows Bridge and the big highway leading up to it, the highway that would cut into the Bay Ridge section of Brooklyn where seven thousand people now lived, where eight hundred buildings now stood—including a shoestore—and would level everything in its path into a long, smooth piece of concrete.

No, it was not their idea, it was the idea of Robert Moses and his Triborough Bridge and Tunnel Authority to build the bridge and its adjoining highways—but the real estate men, hired by the Authority, were getting most of the direct blame because it was they, not Moses, who had to face the people and say, "Abandon your homes—we must build a bridge."

Some people, particularly old people, panicked. Many of them pleaded with the Authority's representatives and prayed to God not to destroy these homes where their children had been born, where their husbands had died. Others panicked with anger, saying this was *their* home, *their* castle, and Mr. Moses would have to drag them from it bodily.

Some took the news quietly, waiting without words to be listed among the missing—waiting for the moving van as if it meant death itself. With the money the Authority paid them for their old home, they went to Florida, or to Arizona, or to another home in Brooklyn, any home, not seeming to care very much because now they were old people and new homes were all the same.

The old shoemaker, nearly seventy, returned to Southern Italy, back to his native Cosenza, where he had some farmland he hoped to sell. He had left Cosenza for America when he was twenty-two years old. And now, in 1959, seeing Cosenza again was seeing how little it had changed. There were still goats and donkeys climbing up the narrow roads, and some peasant women carrying clay pots on their heads, and a few men wearing black bands on their sleeves or ribbons in their lapels to show that they were in mourning; and still the same white stone houses speckled against the lush green of the mountainside—houses of many generations.

When he arrived, he was greeted by relatives he had long forgotten, and they welcomed him like a returning hero. But later they began to tell him about their ailments, their poverty, all their problems, and he knew what was coming next. So he quickly began to tell them about *his* problems, sparing few details, recalling how he had fallen behind in the rent of his shoestore in Brooklyn, how the Authority had thrown him out without a dime, and how he now found himself back in Italy where he had started—all because this damned bridge was going to be built, this bridge the Americans were planning to name after an Italian explorer the shoemaker's relatives had never heard of, this Giovanni da Verrazano, who, sailing for the French in 1524, discovered New York Bay. The shoemaker went on and on, gesturing with his hands and making his point, making certain they knew he was no soft touch—and, a day or two later, he went about the business of trying to sell the farmland. . . .

On the Staten Island side, opposition to the bridge was nothing like it was in Brooklyn, where more than twice as many people and buildings were affected by the bridge; in fact, in Staten Island there had long been powerful factions that dreamed of the day when a bridge might be built to link their borough more firmly with the rest of New York City. Staten Island had always been the most isolated, the most ignored of New York's five boroughs; it was separated from Manhattan by five miles of water and a half-hour's ride on the ferry.

While New Yorkers and tourists had always enjoyed riding the Staten Island Ferry—"A luxury cruise at a penny a mile"—nobody was ever much interested in getting to the other side. What was there to see? Sixty percent of the island's fifty-four square miles were underdeveloped as of 1958. Most of its 225,000 citizens lived in one-family houses. It was the dullest of New York's boroughs, and when a New York policeman was in the doghouse with headquarters, he was often transferred to Staten Island.

The island first acquired its rural quality when the British controlled it three hundred years ago, encouraging farming rather than manufacturing, and that was the way many Staten Islanders wanted it to remain—quiet and remote. But on the last day of 1958, after years of debate and doubt, plans for the building of the Verrazano-Narrows Bridge finally became definite and the way of those who cherished the traditional life was in decline. But many more Staten Island residents were overjoyed with the news; they had wanted a change, had grown bored with the provincialism, and now hoped the bridge would trigger a boom—and suddenly they had their wish.

The bridge announcement was followed by a land rush. Real estate values shot up. A small lot that cost $1,200 in 1958 was worth $6,000 in 1959, and larger pieces of property worth $100,000 in the morning often sold for $200,000 that afternoon. Tax-delinquent properties were quickly claimed by the city. Huge foreign syndicates from Brazil, Italy, and Switzerland moved in for a quick kill. New construction was planned for almost every part of Staten Island, and despite complaints and suits against contractors for cheaply built homes (one foreman was so ashamed of the shoddy work he was ordered to do that he waited until night to leave the construction site) nothing discouraged the boom or deglamorized the bridge in Staten Island.

The bridge had become, in early 1959, months before any workmen started to put it up, the symbol of hope.

"We are now on our way to surmounting the barrier of isolation," announced the borough president, Albert V. Maniscalco—while other leaders were conceding that the bridge, no matter what it might bring, could not really hurt Staten Island. What was there to hurt? "Nothing has ever been successful in Staten Island in its entire history," said one resident, Robert Regan, husband of opera singer Eileen Farrell. He pointed out that there had been attempts in the past to establish a Staten Island opera company, a semi-professional football team, a dog track, a boxing arena, a symphony orchestra, a midget auto track, a basketball team—and all failed. "The only thing that might save this island," he said, "is a lot of new people."

Over in Brooklyn, however, it was different. They did not need or want new people. They had a flourishing, middle-class, almost all-white community in the Bay Ridge section, and they were satisfied with what they had. Bay Ridge, which is in western Brooklyn along the ridge of Upper New York Bay and Lower New York Bay, commands a superb view of the Narrows, a mile-wide tidal strait that connects the two bays, and through which pass all the big ships entering or leaving New York. Among its first settlers were thousands of Scandinavians, most of them Danes, who liked Bay Ridge because of its nearness to the water and the balmy breeze. And in the late nineteenth century, Bay Ridge became one of the most exclusive sections of Brooklyn.

It was not that now, in 1959, except possibly along its shorefront section, which was lined with trees and manicured lawns and with strong sturdy homes, one of them occupied by the body builder Charles Atlas. The rest of Bay Ridge was almost like any other Brooklyn residential neighborhood, except that there were few if any Negroes living among the whites. The whites were mostly Catholic. The big churches, some with parishes in excess of 12,000, were supported by the lace-curtain Irish and aspiring Italians, and the politics, usually Republican, were run by them, too. There were still large numbers of Swedes and Danes, and also many Syrian shopkeepers, and there were old Italian immigrants (friends of the shoemaker) who were hanging on, but it was the younger, second- and third-generation Italians, together with the Irish, who determined the tone of Bay Ridge. They lived, those not yet rich enough for the shorefront homes, in smaller brown brick houses jammed together along tree-lined streets, and they competed each day for a parking place at the curb. They shopped along busy sidewalks clustered with tiny neighborhood stores with apartments above, and there were plenty of small taverns on corners, and there was the Hamilton House for a good dinner at night—provided they wore a jacket and tie—and there was a dimly lit sidestreet supper-club on the front barstool of which sat a curvesome, wrinkled platinum blonde with a cigarette, but no match.

So Bay Ridge, in 1959, had things in balance; it was no longer chic, but it was tidy, and most people wanted no change, no new people, no more traffic. And they certainly wanted no bridge. When the news came that they would get one, the local politicians were stunned. Some women began to cry. A number of people refused to believe it. They had heard this talk before, they said, pointing out that as far back as 1888 there had been plans for a railroad tunnel that would link Brooklyn and Staten Island. And in 1923 New York's Mayor Hylan even broke ground for a combined rail-and-automobile tunnel to Staten Island, and all that happened was that the city lost a half-million dollars and now has a little hole somewhere going nowhere.

And there had been talk about this big bridge across the Narrows for *twenty years*, they said, and each time it turned out to be just talk. In 1950 there was talk that a bridge between Brooklyn and Staten Island was a good thing, but what if the Russians blew it up during a war: Would not the United States Navy ships docked in New York Harbor be trapped behind the collapsed bridge at the harbor's entrance? And a year later, there was more talk of a tunnel to Staten Island, and then more debate on the bridge, and it went on this way, on and on. So, they said, in 1959, maybe this is still all talk, no action, so let's not worry.

What these people failed to realize was that about 1957 the talk changed a little; it became more intense, and Robert Moses was getting more determined, and New York City's Fire Commissioner was so sure in 1957 that the bridge to Staten Island would become a reality that he quickly got in his bid with the City Planning Commission for a big new Staten Island firehouse, asking that he be given $379,500 to build it and $250,000 to equip it. They did not realize that the powerful Brooklyn politician Joseph T. Sharkey saw the bridge as inevitable in 1958, and he had made one last desperate attack, too late, on Robert Moses on the City Council floor, shouting that Moses was getting too much power and was listening only to the engineers, not to the will of the people. And they did not realize, too, that while they were thinking it was still *all talk*, a group of engineers around a drawing board were quietly inking out a large chunk of Brooklyn that would be destroyed for the big approachway to the bridge—and one of the engineers, to his horror, realized that his plan included the demolition of the home of his own mother-in-law. When he told her the news, she screamed and cried and demanded he change the plan. He told her he was helpless to do so; the bridge was inevitable. She died without forgiving him.

The bridge was inevitable—and it was inevitable they would hate it. They saw the coming bridge not as a sign of progress, but as a symbol of destruction, as an enormous sea monster that soon would rise out of the water and destroy eight hundred buildings and force seven thousand Bay Ridge people to move—all sorts of people: housewives, bartenders, a tugboat skipper, doctors, lawyers, a pimp, teetotalers, drunks, secretaries, a retired light-heavyweight fighter, a former Ziegfeld Follies girl, a family of seventeen children (two dogs and a cat), a dentist who had just spent $13,000 installing new chairs, a vegetarian, a bank clerk, an assistant school principal, and two lovers, a divorced man of forty-one and an unhappily married woman who lived across the street. Each afternoon in his apartment they would meet, these lovers, and make love and wonder what next, wonder if she could ever tell her husband and leave her children. And now, suddenly, this bridge was coming between the lovers, would destroy their neighborhood and their quiet afternoons together, and they had no idea, in 1959, what they would do.

What the others did, the angry ones, was join the "Save Bay Ridge" committee which tried to fight Moses until the bulldozers were bashing down their doors. They signed petitions, and made speeches, and screamed, "This bridge—*who needs it*?" News photographers took their photographs and reporters interviewed them, quoting their impassioned pleas, and Robert Moses became furious.

He wrote letters to a newspaper publisher saying that the reporter had distorted the truth, had lied, had emphasized only the bad part, not the good part, of destroying people's homes. Most people in Brooklyn did not, in 1959, understand the good part, and so they held on to their homes with determination. But sooner or later, within the next year or so, they let go. One by one they went, and soon the house lights went out for the last time, and then moving vans rolled in, and then the bulldozers came crashing up and the walls crumbled down, and the roofs caved in and everything was hidden in an avalanche of dust—a sordid scene to be witnessed by the hold-out next door, and soon he, too, would move out, and then another, and another. And that is how it went on each block, in each neighborhood, until, finally, even the most determined hold-out gave in because, when a block is almost completely destroyed, and one is all alone amid the chaos, strange and unfamiliar fears sprout up: the fear of being alone in a neighborhood that is dying; the fear of a band of young vagrants who occasionally would roam through the rubble smashing windows or stealing doors, or picket fences, light fixtures, or shrubbery, or picking at broken pictures or leftover love letters; fear of the derelicts who would sleep in the shells of empty apartments or hanging halls; fear of the rats that people said would soon be crawling up from the shattered sinks or sewers because, it was explained, rats also were being dispossessed in Bay Ridge, Brooklyn.

One of the last hold-outs was a hazel-eyed, very pretty brunette divorced woman of forty-two named Florence Campbell. She left after the lovers, after the dentist, and after the former Ziegfeld Follies girl, Bessie Gros Dempsey, who had to pack up her 350 plumed hats and old scrapbooks; she left after the crazy little man who had been discovered alone in an empty apartment house because, somehow, he never heard the bulldozers beneath him and had no idea that a bridge was being built.

She left after the retired prizefighter, Freddy Fredericksen, who had only lost twice before, and after Mr. and Mrs. John G. Herbert, the parents of seventeen children—although Florence Campbell's leaving was nowhere as complex as the Herberts'. It had taken them twelve trips to move all their furniture, all the bicycles, sleds, dishes, dogs to their new house a little more than a mile away—twelve trips and sixteen hours; and when they had finally gotten everything there, Mr. Herbert, a Navy Yard worker, discovered that the cat was missing. So early the next morning he sent two sons back to the old house, and they discovered the cat beneath the porch. They also discovered an old axe there. And for the next hour they used the axe to destroy everything they could of the old house; they smashed windows, walls, the floors, they smashed their old bedroom, the kitchen shelves, and the banister of the porch, where they used to gather on summer nights, and they smashed without knowing exactly why, only knowing, as they took turns swinging, that they felt a little wild and gleeful and sad and mad as they smashed—and then, too tired to continue, they retrieved the cat from under the smashed porch and they left their old home for the last time.

In the case of Florence Campbell, it took more than even a murder to make her abandon her home. She had been living, since her divorce, with her young son in a sixty-four-dollar-a-month spacious apartment. It was difficult for her to find anything like it at a rental she could afford. The relocation agent, who had lost patience with her for turning down apartments he considered suitable but she considered too expensive, now forgot about her, and she was on her own to search alone at night after she had returned from her bookkeeping job with the Whitehall Club in Manhattan.

Then one morning she started smelling a strange odor in the apartment. She thought perhaps that her son had gone fishing the day before, after school, and had dumped his catch in the dumbwaiter. He denied it, and the next night, when the odor became worse, she telephoned the police. They soon discovered that the elderly man living on the first floor, the only other tenant in the house, had three days before murdered his wife with shotgun bullets and now, dazed and silent, he was sitting next to the corpse, empty whiskey bottles at his feet.

"Lady, do me a favor," the police sergeant said to Florence Campbell. "Get out of this block, will ya?"

She said she would, but she still could not find an apartment during her searchings. She had no relatives she could move in with, no friends within the neighborhood, because they had all moved. When she came home at midnight from apartment hunting, she would find the hall dark—somebody was always stealing the light bulb—or she might stumble over a drunken derelict sleeping on the sidewalk in front of the downstairs door.

A few nights after the sergeant's warning she was awakened from sleep by the sounds of shuffling feet outside her door and the pounding of fists against the wall. Her son, in the adjoining bedroom, jumped up, grabbed a shotgun he kept in his closet, and ran out into the hall. But it was completely dark, the light bulb had been stolen again. He tripped and Florence Campbell screamed.

A strange man raced up the steps to the roof. She called the police. They came quickly but could find no one on the roof. The police sergeant again told her to leave, and she nodded, weeping, that she would. The next day she was too nervous to go to work, and so she went to a nearby bar to get a drink and told the bartender what had happened, and, very excited, he told her he knew of an apartment that was available a block away for sixty-eight dollars a month. She ran to the address, got the apartment—and the landlord could not understand why, after she got it, she began to cry.

III. Survival of the Fittest

The bridge began as bridges always begin—silently. It began with underwater investigations and soil studies and survey sheets; and when the noise finally started, on January 16, 1959, nobody in Brooklyn or Staten Island heard it.

It started with the sound of a steam pile driver ramming a pipe thirty-six inches in diameter into the silt of a small island off the Brooklyn shore. The island held an old battered bastion called Fort Lafayette, which had been a prison during the Civil War, but now it was about to be demolished, and the island would only serve as a base for one of the bridge's two gigantic towers.

Nobody heard the first sounds of the bridge because they were soft and because the island was six hundred feet off the Brooklyn shore; but even if it had been closer, the sounds would not have risen above the rancor and clamor of the people, for when the drilling began, the people still were protesting, still were hopeful that the bridge would never be built. They were aware that the city had not yet formally condemned their property— but that came three months later. On April 30, 1959, in Brooklyn Supreme Court, Justice J. Vincent Keogh—who would later go to jail on charges of sharing in a bribe to fix another case—signed the acquisition papers, and four hundred Bay Ridge residents suddenly stopped protesting and submitted in silence.

The next new noise was the spirited, high-stepping sound of a marching band and the blaring platitudes of politicians echoing over a sun-baked parade ground on August 14, 1959—it was ground-breaking day for the bridge, with the ceremony held, wisely, on the Staten Island side. Over in Brooklyn, when a reporter asked State Senator William T. Conklin for a reaction, the Bay Ridge representative snapped, "It is not a ground-breaking—to many it will be heart-breaking." And then, slowly and more emotionally, he continued: "Any public official attending should always be identified in the future with the cruelty that has been inflicted on the community in the name of progress."

Governor Nelson Rockefeller of New York had been invited to attend the ceremony in Staten Island, but he sent a telegram expressing regret that a prior engagement made it impossible for him to be there. He designated Assembly Speaker Joseph Carlino to read his message. But Mr. Carlino did not show up. Robert Moses had to read it.

As Mr. Moses expressed all the grand hope of the future, a small airplane chartered by the Staten Island Chamber of Commerce circled overhead with an advertising banner that urged "Name it the Staten Island Bridge." Many people opposed the name Verrazano—which had been loudly recommended by the Italian Historical Society of America and its founder, John N. La Corte—because they could not spell it. Others, many of them Irish, did not want a bridge named after an Italian, and they took to calling it the "Guinea Gangplank." Still others advocated simpler names— "The Gateway Bridge," "Freedom Bridge," "Neptune Bridge," "New World Bridge," "The Narrows Bridge." One of the last things ever written by Ludwig Bemelmans was a letter to the *New York Times* expressing the hope that the name "Verrazano" be dropped in favor of a more "romantic" and "tremendous" name, and he suggested calling it the "Commissioner Moses Bridge." But the Italian Historical Society, boasting a large membership of emotional voters, was not about to knuckle under, and finally after months of debate and threats, a compromise was reached in the name "Verrazano-Narrows Bridge."

The person making the least amount of noise about the bridge all this time was the man who was creating it—Othmar H. Ammann, a lean, elderly, proper man in a high starched collar, who now, in his eightieth year, was recognized as probably the greatest bridge engineer in the world. His monumental achievement so far, the one that soared above dozens of others, was the George Washington Bridge, the sight of which had quietly thrilled him since its completion in 1931. Since then, when he and his wife drove down along the Hudson River from upstate New York and suddenly saw the bridge looming in the distance, stretching like a silver rainbow over the river between New York and New Jersey, they often gently bowed and saluted it.

"That bridge is his firstborn, and it was a difficult birth," his wife once explained. "He'll always love it best." And Othmar Ammann, though reluctant to reveal any sentimentality, nevertheless once described its effect upon him. "It is as if you have a beautiful daughter," he said, "and you are the father."

But now the Verrazano-Narrows Bridge presented Ammann with an even larger task. And to master its gigantic design he would even have to take into account the curvature of the earth. The two 693-foot towers, though exactly perpendicular to the earth's surface, would have to be one and five-eights inches farther apart at their summits than at their bases.

Though the Verrazano-Narrows Bridge would require 188,000 tons of steel—three times the amount used in the Empire State Building—Ammann knew that it would be an ever restless structure, would always sway slightly in the wind. Its steel cables would swell when hot and contract when cold, and its roadway would be twelve feet closer to the water in summer than in winter. Sometimes, on long hot summer days, the sun would beat down on one side of the structure with such intensity that it might warp the steel slightly, making the bridge a fraction lower on its hot side than on its shady side. So, Ammann knew, any precision measuring to be done during the bridge's construction would have to be done at night.

From the start of a career that began in 1902, when he graduated from the Swiss Federal Polytechnic Institute with a degree in civil engineering, Ammann had made few mistakes. He had been a careful student, a perfectionist. He had witnessed the rise and fall of other men's creations, had seen how one flaw in mathematics could ruin an engineer's reputation for life—and he was determined it would not happen to him.

Othmar Hermann Ammann had been born on March 26, 1879, in Schaffhausen, Switzerland, into a family that had been established in Schaffhausen since the twelfth century. His father had been a prominent manufacturer and his forebears had been physicians, clergymen, lawyers, government leaders, but none had been engineers, and few had shared his enthusiasm for bridges.

There had always been a wooden bridge stretching from the village of Schaffhausen across the Rhine, the most famous of them being built at a length of 364 feet in the 1700s by a Swiss named Hans Ulrich Grubenmann. It had been destroyed by the French in 1799, but had been replaced by others, and as a boy Othmar Ammann saw bridges as a symbol of challenge and a monument to beauty.

In 1904, after working for a time in Germany as a design engineer, Ammann came to the United States—which, after slumbering for many decades in a kind of dark age of bridge design, was now finally experiencing a renaissance. American bridges were getting bigger and safer; American engineers were now bolder than any in the world.

There were still disasters, but it was nothing like it had been in the middle 1800s, when as many as forty bridges might collapse in a single year, a figure that meant that for every four bridges put up one would fall down. Usually it was a case of engineers not knowing precisely the stress and strain a bridge could withstand, and also there were cases of contractors being too cost-conscious and willing to use inferior building materials. Many bridges in those days, even some railroad bridges, were made of timber. Others were made of a new material, wrought iron, and nobody knew exactly how it would hold up until two disasters—one in Ohio, the other in Scotland—proved its weakness.

The first occurred on a snowy December night in 1877 when a train from New York going west over the Ashtabula Bridge in Ohio suddenly crumbled the bridge's iron beams and then, one by one, the rail cars fell into the icy waters, killing ninety-two people. Two years later, the Firth of Tay Bridge in Scotland collapsed under the strain of a locomotive pulling six coaches and a brakeman's van. It had been a windy Sunday night, and seventy-five people were killed, and religious extremists blamed the railroad for running trains on Sunday. But engineers realized that it was the wrought iron that was wrong, and these two bridge failures hastened the acceptance of steel—which has a working strength 25 percent greater than wrought iron—and thus began the great era that would influence young Othmar Ammann.

This era drew its confidence from two spectacular events—the completion in 1874 of the world's first steel bridge, a triple arch over the Mississippi River at St. Louis designed and built by James Buchanan Eads; and the completion in 1883 of the Brooklyn Bridge, the first steel cable suspension span, designed by John Roebling and, upon his tragic death, completed by his son, Washington Roebling. Both structures would shape the future course in American bridge-building, and would establish a foundation of knowledge, a link of trial and error, that would guide every engineer through the twentieth century. The Roeblings and James Buchanan Eads were America's first heroes in high steel.

James B. Eads was a flamboyant and cocky Indiana boy whose first engineering work was raising sunken steamers from the bottom of the Mississippi. He also was among the first to explore the river's bed in a diver's suit, and he realized, when it came time for him to start constructing the foundations for his St. Louis bridge, that he could not rely on the Mississippi River soil for firmness, because it had a peculiar and powerful shifting movement.

So he introduced to America the European pneumatic caisson—an airtight enclosure that would allow men to work underwater without being hindered by the shifting tides. Eventually, as the caisson sank deeper and deeper and the men dug up more and more of the river bed below, the bridge's foundation could penetrate the soft sand and silt and could settle solidly on the hard rock beneath the Mississippi. Part of this delicate operation was helped by Eads's invention—a sand pump that could lift and eject gravel, silt, and sand from the caisson's chamber.

Before Eads's bridge would be finished, however, 352 workmen would suffer from a strange new ailment—caisson's disease or "the bends"—and twelve men would die from it, and two would remain crippled for life. But from the experience and observations made by James Eads's physician, Dr. Jaminet, who spent time in the caisson with the men and became temporarily paralyzed himself, sufficient knowledge was obtained to greatly reduce the occurrence of the ailment on future jobs.

When the St. Louis steel bridge was finished, James Eads, to show its strength, ran fourteen locomotives across each of the bridge's three arches. Later a fifteen-mile parade marched across it, President Grant applauded from the reviewing stand, General Sherman drove in the last spike on the Illinois side, and Andrew Carnegie, who had been selling bonds for the project, made his first fortune. The bridge was suddenly instrumental in the development of St. Louis as the most important city on the Mississippi River, and it helped develop the transcontinental railroad systems. It was credited with "the winning of the West" and was pictured on a United States stamp in 1898; and in 1920 James Buchanan Eads became the first engineer elected to the American Hall of Fame.

He died an unhappy man. A project he envisioned across the Isthmus of Tehuantepec did not work out.

John Augustus Roebling was a studious German youth born in 1806, in a small town called Muhlhausen, to a tobacco merchant who smoked more than he sold and to a mother who prayed he would someday amount to more than his father. Largely through her ambition and thrift he received a fine education in architecture and engineering in Berlin, and later he worked for the Prussian government building roads and bridges.

But there was little opportunity for originality, and so at the age of twenty-five he came to America and soon, in Pennsylvania, he was working as a surveyor for the railroads and canals. And one day, while observing how the hemp rope that hauled canal boats often broke, John Roebling began to experiment with a more durable fiber, and soon he was twisting iron wire into the hemp—an idea that would eventually lead him and his family into a prosperous industry that today, in Trenton, New Jersey, is the basis for the Roebling Company—world's largest manufacturers of wire rope and cable.

But in those days it led John Roebling toward his more immediate goal, the construction of suspension bridges. He had seen smaller suspensions, hung with iron chains, during his student days in Germany, and he wondered if the suspension bridge might not be more graceful, longer, and stronger with iron wire rope, maybe even strong enough to support rail cars.

He had his chance to find out when, in 1851, he received a commission to build a suspension bridge over Niagara Falls. This opportunity arose only because the original engineer had abandoned the project after a financial dispute with the bridge company—this engineer being a brilliant but wholly unpredictable and daring man named Charles Ellet. Ellet, when confronted with the problem of getting the first rope across Niagara, found the solution by offering five dollars to any boy who could fly a kite across it. Ellet later had a basket carrier made and he pulled himself over the rushing waters of Niagara to the other side; and next he did the same thing accompanied by his horse, as crowds standing on the cliffs screamed and some women fainted.

Things quieted down when Ellet left Niagara, but John Roebling, in his methodical way, got the job done. "Engineering," as Joseph Gies, an editor and bridge historian, wrote, "is the art of the efficient, and the success of an engineering project often may be measured by the absence of any dramatic history." In 1855, Roebling's 821-foot single span was finished, and on March 6 of that year a 368-ton train crossed it—the first train in history to cross a span sustained by wire cables.

The success quickly led Roebling to other bridge commissions, and in 1867 he started his greatest task, the Brooklyn Bridge.

It would take thirteen years to complete the Brooklyn Bridge, and both John Roebling and his son would be its victims. One summer morning in 1869, while standing on a pier off Manhattan, surveying the location of one of the towers, and paying no attention to the docking ferryboat that was about to bump into the pier, John Roebling suddenly had his foot caught and crushed between the pier floor and piles; tetanus set in, and two weeks later, at the age of sixty-three, he died.

At the death of his father, Washington Roebling, then thirty-two years old and the chief engineering assistant for the bridge, took over the job. Roebling had previously supervised the construction of other bridges that his father had designed, and had served as an engineering officer for the Union Army during the Civil War. During the war he had also been one of General Grant's airborne spies, ascending in a balloon to watch the movement of Lee's army during its invasion of Pennsylvania.

When he took over the building of the Brooklyn Bridge, Washington Roebling decided that since the bridge's tower foundations would have to be sunk forty-four feet into the East River on the Brooklyn side and seventy-six feet on the New York side, he would use pneumatic caissons—as James Eads had done a few years before with his bridge over the Mississippi. Roebling drove himself relentlessly, working in the caissons day and night, and he finally collapsed. When he was carried up, he was paralyzed for life. He was then thirty-five years old.

But Washington Roebling, assisted by his wife Emily, continued to direct the building of the bridge from his sickbed; he would watch the construction through field glasses while sitting at the window of his home on the Brooklyn shore; and then his wife—to whom he had taught the engineer's language, and who understood the problems involved—would carry his instructions to the superintendents on the bridge itself.

Washington Roebling was the first bridge engineer to use steel wire for his cables—it was lighter and stronger than the iron wire cables used by his father on the Niagara bridge—and he had every one of the 5,180 wires galvanized as a safeguard against rust. The first wire was drawn across the East River in 1877, and for the next twenty-six months, from one end of the bridge to the other, the small traveling wheels—looking like bicycle wheels with the tires missing—spun back and forth on pulleys, crossing the East River 10,360 times, each time bringing with them a double strand of wire which, when wrapped, would form the four cables that would hold up the center span of 1,595 feet and its two side spans of 930 feet each. This technique of spinning wire, and the use of a cowbell attached to each wheel to warn the men of its approaches, is still used today; it was used, in a more modern form, even by O. H. Ammann in the cable-spinning phase of his Verrazano-Narrows Bridge in the 1960s.

The Brooklyn Bridge was opened on May 24, 1883. Washington Roebling and his wife watched the celebrations from their windows through field glasses. It was a great day in New York—business was suspended, homes were draped with bunting, church bells rang out, steamships whistled. There was the thunder of guns from the forts in the harbor and from the Navy ships docked near the bridge, and finally, in open carriages, the dignitaries arrived. President Chester A. Arthur, New York's Governor Grover Cleveland, and the mayors of every city within several miles of New York arrived at the bridge. Later that night there was a procession in Brooklyn that led to Roebling's home, and he was congratulated in person by President Arthur.

To this day the Brooklyn Bridge has remained the most famous in America, and, until the Williamsburg Bridge was completed over the East River between Brooklyn and Manhattan in 1903, it was the world's longest suspension. In the great bridge boom of the twentieth century, nineteen other suspension spans would surpass it—but none would cast a longer shadow. It has been praised by poets, admired by aesthetes, and sought by the suicidal. Its tower over the tenement roofs of the Lower East Side so electrified a young neighborhood boy named David Steinman that he became determined to emulate the Roeblings, and later he would become one of the world's great bridge designers; he alone, until his death in 1960, would challenge Ammann's dominance.

David Steinman at the age of fourteen had secured a pass from New York's Commissioner of Bridges to climb around the catwalks of the Williamsburg Bridge, then under construction, and he talked to bridge builders, took notes, and dreamed of the bridges he would someday build. In 1906, after graduating from City College in New York with the highest honors, he continued his engineering studies at Columbia, where, in

1911, he received his doctor's degree for his thesis on long-span bridges and foundations. Later he became consulting engineer on the design and construction of the Florianopolis Bridge in Brazil, the Mount Hope Bridge in Rhode Island, the Grand Mere in Quebec, the Henry Hudson arch bridge in New York. It was Dr. David Steinman who was called upon to renovate the Brooklyn Bridge in 1948, and it was he who was selected over Ammann to build the Mackinac Bridge—although it was Ammann who emerged with the Verrazano-Narrows commission, the bridge that Steinman had dreamed of building.

The two men were never close as friends, possibly because they were too close in other ways. Both had been assistants in their earlier days to the late Gustav Lindenthal, designer of the Hell Gate and the Queensboro bridges in New York, and the two men were inevitably compared. They shared ambition and vanity, and yet possessed dissimilar personalities. Steinman was a colorfully blunt product of New York, a man who relished publicity and controversy, and who wrote poetry and had published books. Ammann was a stiff, formal Swiss gentleman, well born and distant. But that they were to be lifelong competitors was inevitable, for the bridge business thrives on competition; it exists on every level. There is competition between steel corporations as they bid for each job, and there is competition between even the lowliest apprentices in the work gangs. All the gangs—the riveters, the steel connectors, the cable spinners battle throughout the construction of every bridge to see who can do the most work, and later in bars there is competition to see who can drink the most, brag the most. But here, on the lower level, among the bridge workers, the rivalry is clear and open; on the higher level, among the engineers, it is more secret and subtle.

Some engineers quietly go through life envying one another, some quietly prey on others' failures. Every time there is a bridge disaster, engineers who are unaffiliated with its construction flock to the site of the bridge and try to determine the reason for the failure. Then, quietly, they return to their own plans, armed with the knowledge of the disaster, and patch up their own bridges, hoping to prevent the same thing. This is as it should be. But it does not belie the truth of the competition. When a bridge fails, the engineer who designed it is as good as dead. In the bridge business, on every level, there is an endless battle to stay alive—and no one has stayed alive longer than O. H. Ammann.

Ammann was among the engineers who, in 1907, investigated the collapse of a cantilever bridge over the St. Lawrence River near Quebec. Eighty-six workmen, many of them Indians, who were just learning the high-construction business then, fell with the bridge, and seventy-five drowned. The engineer whose career ended with his failure was Theodore Cooper, one of America's most noted engineers—the same man who had been so lucky years before when, after falling one hundred feet into the Mississippi River while working on James Eads's bridge, not only survived but went back to work the same day.

But now, in 1907, it was the opinion of most engineers that Theodore Cooper did not know enough about the stresses involved in the cantilever bridge. None of them did. There is no way to know enough about bridge failure until enough bridges have failed. "This bridge failed because it was not strong enough," one engineer, C. C. Schneider, quipped to the others. Then they all returned to their own bridges, or to their plans for bridges, to see if they too had made miscalculations.

One bridge that perhaps was saved in this manner was Gustav Lindenthal's Queensboro Bridge, which was then approaching completion over the East River in Manhattan. After a re-examination, it was concluded that the Queensboro was inadequate to safely carry its intended load. So the four rapid transit tracks that had been planned for the upper deck were reduced by two. The loss of the two tracks was compensated by the construction of a subway tunnel a block away from the bridge—the BMT tunnel at Sixtieth Street under the East River, built at an additional cost of $4,000,000.

In November of 1940, when the Tacoma Narrows Bridge fell into the waters of Puget Sound in the state of Washington, O. H. Ammann was again one of the engineers called in to help determine the cause. The engineer who caught the blame in this case was L. S. Moisseiff, a man with a fine reputation throughout the United States.

Moisseiff had been involved in the design of the Manhattan Bridge in New York, and had been the consulting engineer of the Ambassador Bridge in Detroit and the Golden Gate in California, among many others, and nobody had questioned him when he planned a lean, two-lane bridge that would stretch 2,800 feet over the waters of Puget Sound. True, it was a startlingly slim, fragile-looking bridge, but during this time there had been an aesthetic trend toward slimmer, sleeker, lovelier suspension bridges. This was the same trend that led David Steinman to paint his Mount Hope Bridge over Narragansett Bay a soft green color, and to have its cables strung with lights and approaches lined with evergreens and roses, costing an additional $70,000 for landscaping.

There was also a prewar trend toward economizing on the overall cost of bridge construction, however, and one way to save money without spoiling the aesthetics—and supposedly without diminishing safety—was to shape the span and roadway floor with solid plate girders, not trusses that wind could easily pass through. And it was partially because of these solid girders that, on days when the wind beat hard against its solid mass of roadway, the Tacoma Narrows Bridge kicked up and down. But it never kicked too much, and the motorists, far from becoming alarmed, actually loved it, enjoyed riding over it. They knew that all bridges swayed a little in the wind—this bridge was just livelier, that was all, and they began calling it, affectionately, "Galloping Gertie."

Four months after it had opened—on November 7—with the wind between thirty-five and forty-two miles an hour, the bridge suddenly began to kick more than usual. Sometimes it would heave up and down as much as three feet. Bridge authorities decided to close the bridge to traffic; it was a wise decision, for later it began to twist wildly, rising on one side of its span, falling on the other, rising and falling sometimes as much as twenty-eight feet, tilting at a forty-five-degree angle in the wind. Finally, at 11 a.m., the main span ripped away from its suspenders and went crashing into Puget Sound.

The factors that led to the failure, the examining engineers deduced, were generally that the tall skinny bridge was too flexible and lacked the necessary stiffening girders; and also they spoke about a new factor that they had previously known very little about: "aerodynamic instability."

And soon, on other bridges, on bridges all over America and elsewhere, adjustments were made to compensate for the instability. The Golden Gate underwent alterations that cost more than $3,000,000. The very flexible Bronx-Whitestone Bridge in New York, which Leon Moisseiff had designed—with O. H. Ammann directing the planning and construction—had holes punched into its plate girders and had trusses added. Several other bridges that formerly had been slim and frail now became sturdier with trusses, and twenty years later, when Ammann was creating the Verrazano-Narrows Bridge, the Tacoma lesson lived on.

Though the lower second deck on the Verrazano-Narrows was not yet needed, because the anticipated traffic could easily be accommodated by the six-lane upper deck, Ammann made plans for the second deck to go on right away—something he hadn't done in 1930 with his George Washington Bridge. The six-lane lower deck of the Verrazano will probably be without an automobile passenger for the next ten years, but the big bridge will be more rigid from its opening day.

After the Tacoma incident, Moisseiff's talents were no longer in demand. He never tried to pass off any of the blame on other engineers or the financiers; he accepted his decline quietly, though finding little solace in the fact that with his demise as an influential designer of bridges the world of engineering knowledge was expanded and bigger bridges were planned, bringing renown to others.

And so some engineers, like Leon Moisseiff and Theodore Cooper, go down with their bridges. Others, like Ammann and Steinman, remain high and mighty. But O. H. Ammann is not fooled by his fate.

One day, after he had completed his design on the Verrazano-Narrows Bridge, he mused aloud in his New York apartment, on the thirty-second floor of the Hotel Carlyle, that one reason he has experienced no tragedy with his bridges is that he has been blessed with good fortune.

"I have been lucky," he said, quietly.

"Lucky!" snapped his wife, who attributes his success solely to his superior mind.

"Lucky," he repeated, silencing her with his soft, hard tone of authority.

IV. Punks and Pushers

Building a bridge is like combat; the language is of the barracks, and the men are organized along the lines of the noncommissioned officers' caste. At the very bottom, comparable to the Army recruit, are the apprentices—called "punks." They climb catwalks with buckets of bolts, learn through observation and turns on the tools, occasionally are sent down for coffee and water, seldom hear thanks. Within two or three years, most punks have become full-fledged bridgemen, qualified to heat, catch, or drive rivets; to raise, weld, or connect steel—but it is the last job, connecting the steel, that most captures their fancy. The steel connectors stand highest on the bridge, their sweat taking minutes to hit the ground, and when the derricks hoist up new steel, the connectors reach out and grab it with their hands, swing it into position, bang it with bolts and mallets, link it temporarily to the steel already in place, and leave the rest to the riveting gangs.

Connecting steel is the closest thing to aerial art, except the men must build a new sky stage for each show, and that is what makes it so dangerous—that and the fact that young connectors sometimes like to grandstand a bit, like to show the old men how it is done, and so they sometimes swing on the cables too much, or stand on unconnected steel, or run across narrow beams on windy days instead of straddling as they should—and sometimes they get so daring they die.

Once the steel is in place, riveting gangs move in to make it permanent. The fast, four-man riveting gangs are wondrous to watch. They toss rivets around as gracefully as infielders, driving in more than a thousand a day, each man knowing the others' moves, some having traveled together for years as a team. One man is called the "heater," and he sweats on the bridge all day over a kind of barbecue pit of flaming coal, cooking rivets until they are red—but not so red that they will buckle or blister. The heater must be a good cook, a chef, must think he is cooking sausages not rivets, because the other three men in the riveting gang are very particular people.

Once the rivet is red, but not too red, the heater tong-tosses it fifty, or sixty, or seventy feet, a perfect strike to the "catcher," who snares it out of the air with his metal mitt. Then the catcher relays the rivet to the third man, who stands nearby and is called the "bucker-up"—and who, with a long cylindrical tool named after the anatomical pride of a stud horse, bucks the rivet into the prescribed hole and holds it there while the fourth man, the riveter, moves in from the other side and begins to rattle his gun against the rivet's front end until the soft tip of the rivet has been flattened and made round and full against the hole. When the rivet cools, it is as permanent as the bridge itself.

Each gang—whether it be a riveting gang, connecting gang, or raising gang—is under the direct supervision of a foreman called a "pusher." (One night in a Brooklyn bar, an Indian pusher named Mike Tarbell was arrested by two plainclothes men who had overheard his occupation, and Tarbell was to spend three days in court and lose $175 in wages before convincing the judge that he was not a pusher of dope, only of bridgemen.)

The pusher, like an Army corporal who is bucking for sergeant, drives his gang to be the best, the fastest, because he knows that along the bridge other pushers are doing the same thing. They all know that the bridge company officials keep daily records of the productivity of each gang. The officials know which gang lifted the most steel, drove the most rivets, spun the most cable—and if the pusher is ambitious, wants to be promoted someday to a better job on the bridge, pushing is the only way.

But if he pushes too hard, resulting in accidents or death, then he is in trouble with the bridge company. While the bridge company encourages competition between gangs, because it wants to see the bridge finished fast, wants to see traffic jams up there and hear the clink of coins at toll gates, it does not want any accidents or deaths to upset the schedule or get into the newspapers or degrade the company's safety record with the insurance men. So the pusher is caught in the middle. If he is not lucky, if there is death in his gang, he may be blamed and be dropped back into the gang himself, and another workman will be promoted to pusher. But if he is lucky, and his gang works fast and well, then he someday might become an assistant superintendent on the bridge—a "walkin' boss."

The walkin' boss, of which there usually are four on a big bridge where four hundred or five hundred men are employed, commands a section of the span. One walkin' boss may be in charge of the section between an anchorage and a tower, another from that tower to the center of the span, a third from the center of the span to the other tower, the fourth from that tower to the other anchorage—and all they do all day is walk up and down, up and down, strutting like gamecocks, a look of suspicion in their eyes as they glance sideways to see that the pushers are pushing, the punks are punking, and the young steel connectors are not behaving like acrobats on the cables.

The thing that concerns walkin' bosses most is that they impress *the* boss, who is the superintendent, and is comparable to a top sergeant. The superintendent is usually the toughest, loudest, foulest-mouthed, best bridgeman on the whole job, and he lets everybody know it. He usually spends most of his day at a headquarters shack built along the shore near the anchorage of the bridge, there to communicate with the engineers, designers, and other white-collar officers from the bridge company. The walkin' bosses up on the bridge represent him and keep him informed, but about two or three times a day the superintendent will leave his shack and visit the bridge, and when he struts across the span the whole thing seems to stiffen. The men are all heads down at work, the punks seem petrified.

The superintendent selected to supervise the construction of the span and the building of the cables for the Verrazano-Narrows Bridge was a six-foot, fifty-nine-year-old, hot-tempered man named John Murphy, who, behind his back, was known as "Hard Nose" or "Short Fuse."

He was a broad-shouldered and chesty man with a thin strong nose and jaw, with pale blue eyes and thinning white hair—but the most distinguishing thing about him was his red face, a face so red that if he ever blushed, which he rarely did, nobody would know it. The red hard face—the result of forty years' booming in the high wind and hot sun of a hundred bridges and skyscrapers around America—gave Murphy the appearance of always being boiling mad at something, which he usually was.

He had been born, like so many boomers, in a small town without horizons—in this case, Rexton, a hamlet of three hundred in New Brunswick, Canada. The flu epidemic that had swept through Rexton in the spring of 1919, when Murphy was sixteen years old, killed his mother and father, an uncle and two cousins, and left him largely responsible for the support of his five younger brothers and sisters. So he went to work driving timber in Maine, and, when that got slow, he moved down to Pennsylvania and learned the bridge business, distinguishing himself as a steel connector because he was young and fearless. He was considered one of the best connectors on the George Washington Bridge, which he worked on in 1930 and 1931, and since then he had gone from one job to another, booming all the way up to Alaska to put a bridge across the Tanana River, and then back east again on other bridges and buildings.

In 1959 he was the superintendent in charge of putting up the Pan Am, the fifty-nine-story skyscraper in mid-Manhattan, and after that he was appointed to head the Verrazano job by the American Bridge Company, a division of United States Steel that had the contract to put up the bridge's span and steel cables.

When Hard Nose Murphy arrived at the bridge site in the early spring of 1962, the long, undramatic, sloppy, yet so vital part of bridge construction—the foundations—was finished, and the two 693-foot towers were rising.

The foundation construction for the two towers, done by J. Rich Steers,

Inc., and the Frederick Snare Corporation, if not an aesthetic operation that would appeal to the adventurers in high steel, nevertheless was a most difficult and challenging task, because the two caissons sunk in the Narrows had been among the largest ever built. They were 229 feet long and 129 feet wide, and each had sixty-six circular dredging holes—each hole being seventeen feet in diameter—and, from a distance, the concrete caissons looked like gigantic chunks of Swiss cheese.

Building the caisson that would support the pedestal which would in turn bear the foundation for the Staten Island tower had required 47,000 cubic yards of concrete, and before it settled on firm sand 105 feet below the surface, 81,500 cubic yards of muck and sand had to be lifted up through the dredging holes by clamshell buckets suspended from cranes. The caisson for the Brooklyn tower had to be sunk to about 170 feet below sea level, had required 83,000 cubic yards of concrete, and 143,600 cubic yards of muck and sand had to be dredged up.

The foundations, the ones that anchor the bridge to Staten Island and Brooklyn, were concrete blocks the height of a ten-story building, each triangular-shaped, and holding, within their hollows, all the ends of the cable strands that stretch across the bridge. These two anchorages, built by The Arthur A. Johnson Corporation and Peter Kiewit Sons' Company, hold back the 240,000,000-pound pull of the bridge's four cables.

It had taken a little more than two years to complete the four foundations, and it had been a day-and-night grind, unappreciated by sidewalk superintendents and, in fact, protested by two hundred Staten Islanders on March 29, 1961; they claimed, in a petition presented to Richmond County District Attorney John M. Braisted, Jr., that the foundation construction between 6 p.m. and 6 a.m. was ruining the sleep of a thousand persons within a one-mile radius. In Brooklyn, the Bay Ridge neighborhood also was cluttered with cranes and earth-moving equipment as work on the approachway to the bridge continued, and the people still were hating Moses, and some had cried foul after he had awarded a $20,000,000 contract, without competitive bidding, to a construction company that employs his son-in-law. All concerned in the transaction immediately denied there was anything irregular about it.

But when Hard Nose Murphy arrived, things were getting better; the bridge was finally crawling up out of the water, and the people had something to *see*—some visible justification for all the noise at night—and in the afternoons some old Brooklyn men with nothing to do would line the shore watching the robin-red towers climb higher and higher.

The towers had been made in sections in steel plants and had been floated by barge to the bridge site. The Harris Structural Steel Company had made the Brooklyn tower, while Bethlehem made the Staten Island tower—both to O. H. Ammann's specifications. After the tower sections had arrived at the bridge site, they were lifted up by floating derricks anchored alongside the tower piers. After the first three tiers of each tower leg had been locked into place, soaring at this point to about 120 feet, the floating derricks were replaced by "creepers"—derricks, each with a lifting capacity of more than one hundred tons, that crept up the towers on tracks bolted to the sides of the tower legs. As the towers got higher, the creepers were raised until, finally, the towers had reached their pinnacle of 693 feet.

While the construction of towers possesses the element of danger, it is not really much different from building a tall building or an enormous lighthouse; after the third or fourth story is built, it is all the same the rest of the way up. The real art and drama in bridge building begins after the towers are up; then the men have to reach out from these towers and begin to stretch the cables and link the span over the sea.

This would be Murphy's problem, and as he sat in one of the Harris Company's boats on this morning in May 1962, idly watching from the water as the Staten Island tower loomed up to its tenth tier, he was saying to one of the engineers in the boat, "You know, every time I see a bridge in this stage, I can't help but think of all the problems we got coming next— all the mistakes, all the cursing, all the goddamned sweat and the death we gotta go through to finish this thing . . ."

The engineer nodded, and then they both watched quietly again as the derricks, swelling at the veins, continued to hoist large chunks of steel through the sky.

V. Keeping the Wheel from Benny

After the towers had been finished in the winter of 1962, the cable spinning would begin—and with it the mistakes, the cursing, the sweat, the death that Murphy had anticipated.

The spinning began in March of 1963. Six hundred men were up on the job, but Benny Olson, who had been the best cableman in America for thirty years, was not among them. He had been grounded. And though he had fumed, fretted, and cursed for three days after he'd gotten the news, it did not help. He was sixty-six years old—too old to be climbing catwalks six hundred feet in the sky, and too slow to be dodging those spinning wheels and snapping wires.

So he was sent four miles up the river to the bridge company's steel-yard near Bayonne, New Jersey, where he was made supervisor of a big tool shed and was given some punks to order around. But each day Olson would gaze down the river and see the towers in the distance, and he could sense the sounds, the sights, the familiar sensation that pervades a bridge just before the men begin to string steel thread across the sea. And Benny Olson knew, as did most others, that he had taught the cable experts most of what they knew and had inspired new techniques in the task, and every-body knew, too, that Benny Olson, at sixty-six, was now a legend securely spun into the lore and links of dozens of big bridges between Staten Island and San Francisco.

He was a skinny little man. He weighed about 135 pounds, stood five feet six inches; he was nearly bald on the top of his head, though some strands grew long and loose down the back of his neck, and he had tiny blue eyes, rimmed with steel glasses, and a long nose. Everybody referred to him as "Benny the Mouse." In his long career he had been a pusher, a walkin' boss, and a superintendent. He compensated for his tiny stature by cutting big men down to size, insulting them endlessly and ruthlessly as he demanded perfection and speed on each cable-spinning job. At the slightest provocation he would fire anyone. He would fire his own brother. In fact, he had. On a bridge in Poughkeepsie in 1928, his brother, Ted, did not jump fast enough to one of Benny Olson's commands, and that was all for Ted.

"Now look, you idiots," Olson then told the other men on the bridge, "things around here will be done my way, hear? Or else I'll kick the rest of you the hell off, too, hear?"

Very few men would ever talk back to Benny Olson in those days be-cause, first, they respected him as a bridgeman, as a quick-handed artist who was faster than anybody at pulling wires from a moving wheel and at inspiring a spinning gang to emulate him, and also because Olson, when enraged, was wholly unpredictable and possibly dangerous.

In Philadelphia one day, shortly after he had purchased a new car and was sitting in it at an intersection waiting for the red light to change, a jalopy filled with Negro teenagers came screeching up from behind and banged into the rear bumper of Olson's new car. Quickly, but without saying a word, Olson got out of his car and reached in the back seat for the axe he knew was there. Then he walked back to the boys' car and, still without saying a word, he lifted the axe into the air with both hands and then sent it crashing down upon the fender of the jalopy, chopping off a headlight. Two more fast swings and he had sliced off the other headlight and put a big incision in the middle of the hood. Finally he chopped off a chunk of the aerial with a wide sweep of his axe, and then he turned and walked back to his car and drove slowly away. The boys just sat in their jalopy. They were paralyzed with fear, stunned with disbelief.

Olson was in Philadelphia then because the Walt Whitman Bridge was going up, and the punks hired to work on that bridge were incessantly tormented by Olson, especially the larger ones, and particularly one six-foot-two-inch, 235-pound Italian apprentice named Dominick. Every time Benny Olson saw him, he would call him "a dumb bastard" or, at best, a "big, stupid ox."

Just the mere sight of Olson walking down the catwalk would terrorize Dominick, for he was a very high-strung and emotional type, and Olson could get him so nervous and shaky that he could barely light a cigarette. One day, after Olson had hurled five minutes' worth of abuse at Dominick, the big Italian, turning red, lunged toward Olson and grabbed him by the scrawny neck. Then Dominick lifted Olson into the air, carried him toward the edge of the catwalk, and held him out over the river.

"You *leetle preek*," Dominick screamed, "now I throw you off."

Four other bridgemen rushed up from behind, held Dominick's arms, pulled him back, and tried to calm him. Olson, after he'd been let loose, said nothing. He just rubbed his neck and smoothed out his shirt. A moment later he turned and walked idly up the catwalk, but after he had gotten about fifty feet away, Benny Olson suddenly turned and, with a wild flare of fury, yelled to Dominick, "You know, you really *are* a big, dumb stupid bastard." Then he turned again and continued calmly up the catwalk.

Finally, a few punks on the Walt Whitman Bridge decided to get revenge on Benny Olson. One way to irritate him, they decided, was to stop the spinning wheels, which they could do merely by clicking one of the several turn-off switches installed along the catwalk—placed there in case an accident to one of the men or some flaw in the wiring demanded an instant halt.

So this they did—and, at first, Olson was perplexed. He would be standing on one end of the bridge with everything going smoothly, then, suddenly, a wheel would stop at the other end.

"Hey, what the hell's the matter with that wheel?" he'd yell, but nobody knew. So he would run toward it, running the full length of the catwalk, puffing and panting all the way. Just before he would reach the wheel, however, it would begin to move again—a punk at the other end of the bridge would have flipped the switch back on. This conspiracy went on for hours sometimes, and the game became known as "Keeping the Wheel from Benny." And at 3 a.m. a few punks in a saloon would telephone Benny Olson at his hotel and shout, "Who's got the wheel, Benny?"—and then hang up.

Benny Olson responded without humor, and all day on the bridge he would chase the wheel like a crazy chimpanzee—until, suddenly, he came up with an idea that would stop the game. With help from an engineer, he created an electrical switchboard with red lights on top, each light connected with one of the turn-off switches strung along the bridge. So now if any punk turned off a switch he would give away his location. Olson also appointed a loyal bridge worker to do nothing but watch the switchboard, and this bridgeman was officially called the "tattletale." If the wheel should stop, all Benny Olson had to do was pick up the telephone and say, "Who's got the wheel, Tattletale?" The tattletale would give the precise switch that had been flipped off, and Olson, knowing who was working nearest that spot, could easily fix the blame. But this invention did more than just put an end to the game; it also created a new job in bridge building—the tattletale—and on every big bridge that has been built since the Walt Whitman Bridge, there has been a bridge worker assigned to do nothing but watch the switchboard and keep track of the location of the wheels during the cable-spinning phase of construction. There was a tattletale on the Verrazano-Narrows Bridge, too, but he did little work, for, without Benny Olson to irritate, the demonic spirit had died—there was just no point anymore to "Keeping the Wheel from Benny." And besides, the men involved in spinning the cables on the Verrazano were very serious, very competitive men with no time for games. All they wanted, in the spring of 1963, was to get the catwalks strung up between the towers and the anchorages, and then to get the spinning wheels rolling back and forth across the bridge as quickly and as often as possible. The number of trips that the wheels would make between the anchorages during the daily workshift of each gang would be recorded in Hard Nose Murphy's office—and it would be a matter of pride for each gang to try to set a daily mark that other gangs could not equal.

Before the spinning could begin, however, the men would have to build a platform on which to stand. This platform would be the two catwalks, each made of wire mesh, each twenty feet wide, each resembling a long thin road of spider web or a mile-long hammock. The catwalks would each be held up by twelve horizontal pieces of wire rope, each rope a little more than two inches thick, each more than a mile long. The difficult trick, of course, would be in getting the first of these ropes over the towers of the bridge—a feat that on smaller bridges was accomplished by shooting the rope across with a bow and arrow or, in the case of Charles Ellet's pedestrian bridge, by paying a boy five dollars to fly a rope across Niagara on the end of a kite.

But with the Verrazano, the first rope would be dragged across the water by barge, then, as the Coast Guard temporarily stopped all ship movements, the two ends of the rope would be hoisted out of the water by the derricks on top of the two towers, more than four thousand feet apart. The other ropes would be hoisted up the same way. Then all would be fastened between the towers, and from the towers back to the anchorages on the extremities of the bridge, following the same "sag" lines that the cables would later follow. When this was done, the catwalk sections would be hauled up. Each catwalk section, as it was lifted, would be folded up like an accordion, but once it had arrived high up on the tower, the bridgemen standing on platforms clamped to the sides of the tower would hook the catwalk sections onto the horizontal ropes, and then shove or kick the catwalk sections forward down the sloping ropes. The catwalks would glide on under the impetus of their own weight and unfurl—as a rolled-up rug might unfurl if pushed down the steep aisle of a movie theater.

Once all the catwalk sections glided, bumper to bumper, in place, they would be linked end to end, and would be further stiffened by crossbeams.

A handrail wire "banister" would also be strung across the catwalks, as would several wooden cross planks to give the men better footing in places where the catwalk was quite steep.

After the two catwalks were in place, another set of wires would be strung above each catwalk, about fifteen feet above, and these upper wires would be the "traveling ropes" that would pull the wheels back and forth, powered by diesel engines mounted atop the anchorages.

Four spinning wheels, each forty-eight inches in diameter and weighing a few hundred pounds apiece, would run simultaneously along the bridge—two wheels atop each of the two catwalks. Each wheel, being double-grooved, would carry two wires at once, and each wheel would take perhaps twelve minutes to cross the entire bridge, averaging eight miles per hour, although it could be speeded up to thirteen miles an hour downhill. As the wheels passed overhead, the men would grab the wires and clamp them down into the specified hooks and pulleys along the catwalk; when a wheel arrived at the anchorage, the men there would remove the wire, hook it in place, reload the wheel, and send it back as quickly as possible in the opposite direction.

After the wheel had carried 428 wires across the bridge, the wires would be bound in a strand, and when the wheel had carried across 26,018 wires—or sixty-one strands—they would be squeezed together by hydraulic jacks into a cylindrical shape. This would be a cable. Each cable—there would be four cables on the Verrazano—would be a yard thick, 7,205 feet long, and would contain 36,000 miles of pencil-thin wire. The four cables, collectively, would weigh 38,290 tons. From each cable would later be hung, vertically, 262 suspender ropes—some ropes as long as 447 feet—and they would hold the deck more than two hundred feet above the water, holding it high enough so that no matter how hot and limp the cables got in summer the deck would always be high enough for the *Queen Mary* to easily pass beneath.

From the very first day that the wheels began to roll—March 7, 1963—there was fierce competition between the two gangs working alongside one another on the two catwalks. This rivalry existed both between the gangs on the early-morning shift as well as the gangs on the late-afternoon shift. The goal of each gang, of course, was to get its two wheels back and forth across the bridge more times than the other gang's wheels. The result was that the cable-spinning operation turned into a kind of horse race or, better yet, a dog race. The catwalks became a noisy arena lined with screaming, fist-waving men, all of them looking up and shouting at their wheels—wheels that became mechanical rabbits.

"Com'on, you mother, move your ass," they yelled as their wheel skimmed overhead, grinding away and carrying the wire to the other end. "Move it, com'on, move it!" And from the other catwalk, there came the same desperate urgings, the same wild-eyed competition and anger when their wheel—their star, their hope—would drag behind the other gang's wheel.

The men from one end of the catwalk to the other were all in rhythm with their wheels, all quick at pulling down the wire, all glancing sideways to study the relative position of the other gang's wheels, all hoping that the diesel engines propelling their wheels would not conk out, all very angry if their men standing on the anchorages were too slow at reloading their wheel once it had completed the journey across. It was in such competition as this that Benny Olson had excelled in his younger days. He used to stand on the catwalk in front of an anchorage inspiring his gang, screaming insults at those too slow at pulling down the wire, or too sluggish at reloading the wheel, or too casual about the competition. Olson was like a deck master hovering over a shipload of slave oarsmen.

On Wednesday, June 19, to the astonishment of the engineers who kept the "score" in Hard Nose Murphy's office, one gang had moved its wheels back and forth across the bridge fifty times. Then, on June 26, a second gang also registered fifty trips. Two days later, in the heat of battle, one of the wheels suddenly broke loose from its moorings and came bouncing down onto the catwalk, skipping toward a bridgeman named John Newberry. He froze with fright. If it hit him, it might knock him off the bridge; if he jumped out of its path too far, he might lose his balance and fall off himself. So he held his position, waiting to see how it jumped. Fortunately, the wheel skimmed by him, he turned slightly like a matador making a pass, and then it stopped dead a few yards down the catwalk. He breathed relief, but his gang was angry because now their daily total was ruined. The other gang would win.

On July 16, one gang got the wheels back and forth fifty-one times, and on July 22, another gang duplicated it. A few days later, the gang under Bob Anderson, the boomer who had been so irresistible to women back on the Mackinac Bridge, was moving along with such flawless precision that with an hour to go of working time it had already registered forty-seven trips. If all went well in the remaining hour, six more trips could be added—meaning a record total of fifty-three.

"Okay, let's move it," Anderson yelled down the line to his gang, all of them focusing on what they hoped would be the winning wheel.

They watched it move smoothly along the tramway overhead, then it rolled higher to the tower, then down, down faster to the anchorage, then up again, quickly reloaded, up the tramway—"Keep moving, you mother!"—closer and closer to the tower now . . . then it stopped.

"*Bitch!*" screamed one of the punks.

"What the hell's wrong?" shouted Anderson.

"The engine's conked out," someone finally yelled. "Those goddamn idiots!" said the punk.

"Let's go beat their asses," yelled another punk, quite serious and ready to run down the catwalk.

"Calm down," Anderson said, with resignation, looking up at the stilled wheel, shaking his head.

"Let me go down and see what can be done."

He went down to the anchorage, only to learn that the engine failure could not be fixed in time to continue the race within the hour. So Anderson walked back up, sadly giving the news to his men, and when they walked down the catwalk that night, their hardhats under their arms, their brows sweaty, they looked like a losing football team leaving the field after the game. In the remaining two months, no gang could top the mark of fifty-one, but in September, when the gangs started to place the two-thousand-pound castings over the cables (the castings are metal saddles which would help support the 262 suspender ropes that would stream down vertically from each cable to hold up the deck), a new kind of competition began: a game to see who could bolt into position the most castings, and this got to be dangerous. Not only were bolts dropping off the bridge in this frenzied race—bolts that could pepper the decks of passing vessels and possibly kill anybody they hit—but the castings themselves were unwieldy, and if one of them fell . . .

"Chrissake, Joe, let's get the bolts out and put that mother on," one pusher yelled to Joe Jacklets, who was being cautious with the casting.

The pusher, noticing that another gang working down the catwalk had already removed the bolts and were clamping the casting into place, was getting nervous—his gang was behind.

"Take it easy," Joe Jacklets said, "this thing might not hold."

"It'll hold."

So Joe Jacklets removed the last bolt of the two-section casting and, as soon as he did, one half of the casting—weighing one thousand pounds—toppled off the cable and fell from the bridge.

"Jes-sus!"

"Ohhhhhhh."

"*Kee-rist.*"

"Nooooooooooo!"

"Jes-SUS."

The gang, their hardhats sticking out over the catwalk, watched the one-thousand-pound casting falling like a bomb toward the sea. They noticed, too, a tiny hydrofoil churning through the water below, almost directly below the spot where it seemed the casting might hit. They watched quietly now, mouths open, holding their breaths. Then, after a loud plopping sound, they saw a gigantic splash mushroom up from the water, an enormous fountain soaring forty feet high.

Then, swishing from under the fountain, fully intact, came the hydrofoil, its skipper turning his head away from the splashing spray and shooting his craft in the opposite direction.

"Oh, that lucky little bastard," one of the men said, peering down from the catwalk, shaking his head.

Nobody said anything else for a moment. They just watched the water below. It was as if they hated to turn around and face the catwalk—and later confront Hard Nose Murphy's fiery face and blazing eyes. They watched the water for perhaps two minutes, watched the bubbles subside and the ripples move out. And then, moving majestically into the ripples, moving slowly and peacefully past, was the enormous gray deck of the United States aircraft carrier *Wasp.*

"Holy God!" Joe Jacklets finally said, shaking his head once more.

"You silly bastard," muttered the pusher. Jacklets glared at him.

"What do you mean? I told you it might not hold."

"Like hell you did, you . . ."

Jacklets stared back at the pusher, disbelieving; but then he knew it was no use arguing—he would collect his pay as soon as he could and go back to the union hall and wait for a new job . . .

But before he could escape the scene, the whole line of bridgemen came down the catwalk, some cursing, a few smiling because it was too ridiculous.

"What are you stupid bastards laughing at?" said the walkin' boss.

"Aw, com'on, Leroy," said one of the men, "can't you take a little joke?"

"Yeah, Leroy, don't take it so hard. It's not as if we lost the casting. If we know where a thing is, we ain't lost it."

"Sure, that's right," another said. "We know where it is—it's in the river."

The walkin' boss was just too sick to answer. It was he who would later have to face Murphy.

Across on the other catwalk, the rival gang waved and a few of the younger men smiled, and one yelled out, "Hey, we set ten castings today. How many did you guys set?"

"Nine and a half," somebody else answered.

This got a laugh, but as the workday ended and the men climbed down from the bridge and prepared to invade Johnny's Bar, Joe Jacklets was seen walking with his head down.

If a casting had to fall, it could not have fallen on a better day—September 20, a Friday—because, with work stopped for the weekend anyway, the divers might be able to locate the casting and have it pulled up out of the water before the workers returned to the bridge on Monday. There was no duplicate of the casting, and the plant where it was made was on strike, and so there was no choice but to fish for it—which the divers did, with no success, all day Saturday and Sunday. They saw lots of other bridge parts down there, but no casting. They saw riveting guns, wrenches and bolts, and there was a big bucket that might have been the one that had fallen with four bolt machines, each worth eight hundred dollars.

Even if it was, the machines as well as the other items were now unserviceable, having been ruined either by the water or the jolt they received when hitting the sea from such high altitudes. Anyway, after a brief inspection of all the tools down there, the divers could easily believe the old saying, "A bridgeman will drop everything off a bridge but money."

Yet this is not precisely true; they drop money off, too. A few five-dollar and ten-dollar bills, even twenty-dollar bills, had been blown off the bridge on some windy Fridays—Friday is payday. And during the cable-spinning months, inasmuch as the men were working long hours, they received their pay on the bridge from four clerks who walked along the catwalks carrying more than $200,000 in bundles of cash in zippered camera cases. The cash was sealed in envelopes with each bridgeman's name printed on the outside, and the bridgeman would have to sign a receipt as he received his envelope from the clerk. Some bridgemen, however, after signing the receipt slip, would rip open the envelope and count the money—and that is when they would lose a few bills in the wind. More cautious men would rip off a corner of the envelope, clutching it tight, and count the tips of the bills. Others would just stuff the envelope into their pockets without counting. Still others seemed so preoccupied with their work, so caught up in the competitive swing of spinning, that when the pay clerk arrived with the receipt slip, a pencil, and the envelope, the bridgeman would hastily scribble his name on the slip, then turn away without taking the envelope. Once, as a joke, a clerk named Johnny Cothran walked away with a man's envelope containing more than four hundred dollars, wondering how far he could get with it. He got about twenty feet when he heard the man yelling, "*Hey!*"

Cothran turned, expecting to face an angry bridgeman. But instead the bridgeman said, "You forgot your pencil." Cothran took the pencil, then handed the bridgeman his envelope. "Thanks," he said, stuffing it absently into his pocket and then quickly getting back to the cable-spinning race.

On Monday, September 23, shortly before noon, the casting was discovered more than one hundred feet below the surface of the Narrows, and soon the cranes were swooping over it and pulling it up out of the water. The whole bridge seemed, briefly, to breathe more easily, and Murphy (who had been swearing for three straight days) suddenly calmed down. But two days later, Murphy was again shaking his head in disgust and frustration. At 3:15 p.m. on Wednesday, September 25, somebody on the catwalk had dropped a six-inch steel bolt and, after it had fallen more than one hundred feet, it had hit a bridgeman named Berger Hanson in the face and gone four inches through his skin right under his left eye.

Berger had been standing below the bridge at the time and had been looking up. If he hadn't been looking up the fallen bolt might have hit his hardhat and merely jarred him, instead of doing the damage it did—lifting his eyeball upward, crushing his jawbone, getting stuck in his throat.

Rushed to Victory Memorial Hospital in Brooklyn, Berger was met by the surgeon, Dr. S. Thomas Coppola, who treated all injuries to the bridge-men. Quickly, Dr. Coppola removed the bolt, stopped the bleeding with stitches, then realigned by hand the facial bones and restitched the jaw.

"How do you feel?" Dr. Coppola asked. "Okay," said Berger.

Dr. Coppola was flabbergasted. "Don't you have any pain?"

"No."

"Can I give you anything—an aspirin or two?"

"No, I'm okay."

After plastic surgery to correct the deformation of his face, and after a few months' recuperation, Berger was back on the bridge.

Dr. Coppola was amazed not only by Berger but by the stoicism he encountered in so many other patients among bridgemen.

"These are the most interesting men I've ever met," Dr. Coppola was telling another doctor shortly afterward. "They're strong, they can stand all kinds of pain, they're full of pride, and they live it up. This guy Berger has had five lives already, and he's only thirty-nine. . . . Oh, I'll tell you, it's a young man's world."

True, the bridge is a young man's world, and old men like Benny Olson leave it with some bitterness and longing, and hate to be deposited in the steelyard on the other side of the river—a yard where old men keep out of trouble and younger men, like Larry Tatum, supervise them.

Larry Tatum, a tall, broad-shouldered, daring man of thirty-seven, had been spotted years ago by Murphy as a "stepper," which, in bridge parlance, means a comer, a future leader of bridgemen.

Tatum had started as a welder when he was only seventeen years old, and had become a riveter, a fine connector, a pusher. He had fallen occasionally, but always came back, and had never lost his nerve or enthusiasm. He had four younger brothers in the business, too—three working under Murphy on the bridge, one having died under Murphy after falling off the Pan Am building. Larry Tatum's father, Lemuel Tatum, had been a boomer since the twenties, but now, pushing seventy, he also was in the steelyard, working under his son, the stepper, watching the boy gain experience as a walkin' boss so that, quite soon, he would be ready for a promotion to the number-one job, superintendent.

It was just a little awkward for Larry Tatum, though it was not obvious, to be ordering around so many old boomers—men with reputations, like

Benny the Mouse, and Lemuel Tatum, and a few dozen others who were in the yard doing maintenance on tools or preparing to load the steel links of the span on barges soon to be floated down to the bridge site. But, excepting for some of Olson's unpredictable explosions, the old men generally were quiet and cooperative—and none more so than the former heavyweight boxing champion, James J. Braddock.

Once they had called Braddock the "Cinderella Man" because, after working as a longshoreman, he won the heavyweight title and earned almost $1,000,000 until his retirement in 1938, after Joe Louis beat him.

Now Braddock was nearly sixty, and was back on the waterfront. His main job was to maintain a welding machine. His clothes were greasy, his fingernails black, and his arms so dirty that it was hard to see the tattoos he had gotten one night in the Bowery, in 1921, when he was a frolicsome boy of sixteen.

Now Braddock was earning $170 a week as an oiler, and some men who did not know Braddock might say, as men so often like to say of former champions, "Well, easy come, easy go. Now he's broke, just like Joe Louis."

But his was not another maudlin epic story about a broken prizefighter. Braddock, as he walked slowly around the steelyard, friendly to everyone, his big body erect and his chest out, still was a man of dignity and pride—he was still doing an honest day's work, and this made him feel good.

"What the hell, I'm a working man," he said. "I worked as a longshoreman before I was a fighter, and now I need the money, so I'm working again. I always liked hard work. There's nothing wrong with it."

He lost $15,000 on a restaurant, Braddock's Corner, once on West Forty-ninth Street in Manhattan, and the money he had put into a marine supply house, which he operated for ten years, proved not to be a profitable venture. But he still owns the $14,000 home he bought in North Bergen, New Jersey, shortly after the Joe Louis fight, he said, and he still loves his wife of thirty-three years' marriage, and still has his health and a desire to work hard, and has two sons who work hard, too.

One son, Jay, who is thirty-two, weighs 330 pounds and stands six feet five inches. He works in a Jersey City powerhouse; the other, thirty-one-year-old Howard, is a 240-pounder who is six feet seven inches and is in road construction.

"So don't feel sorry for me," James J. Braddock, the former Cinderella

Man, said, inhaling on a cigarette and leaning forward on a big machine. "Don't feel sorry for me one bit." But he did admit that bridge building, like boxing, was a young man's game.

And of all the eager young men working on the Verrazano-Narrows Bridge under Hard Nose Murphy in the fall of 1963, few seemed better suited to the work or happier on a bridge job than the two men working together atop the cable 385 feet over the water behind the Brooklyn tower.

One was very small, the other very large. The small man, standing five feet seven inches and weighing only 138 pounds—but very sinewy and tough—was named Edward Iannielli. He was called "The Rabbit" by the other men because he jumped the beams and ran across wires, and everybody said of the twenty-seven-year-old Iannielli that he would never live to be thirty.

The big boy was named Gerard McKee. He was a handsome, wholesome boy, about two hundred pounds and six feet three and one-half inches. He had been a Coney Island lifeguard, had charm with women and a gentle disposition, and all the men on the bridge immediately took to him, although he was not as friendly and forward as Iannielli.

On Wednesday morning, October 9, the two climbed the cables as usual, and soon, amid the rattling of the riveters and clang of mallets, they were hard at work, heads down, tightening cable bolts, barely visible from the ground below.

Before the morning was over, however, the attention of the whole bridge would focus on them.

VI. Death on a Bridge

It was a gray and windy morning. At 6:45 a.m. Gerard McKee and Edward Iannielli left their homes in two different parts of Brooklyn and headed for the bridge.

Iannielli, driving his car from his home in Flatbush, got there first. He was already on the catwalk, propped up on a cable with one leg dangling 385 feet above the water, when Gerard McKee walked over to him and waved greetings.

The two young men had much in common. Both were the sons of bridgemen, both were Roman Catholics, both were natives of New York City, and both were out to prove something—that they were as good as any boomer on the bridge.

They quietly resented the prevailing theory that boomers make the best bridgemen. After all, they reasoned, boomers were created more out of necessity than desire; the Indian from the reservation, the Southerner from the farm, the Newfoundlander from the sea, the Midwesterner from the sticks—those who composed most of the boomer population—actually were escaping the poverty and boredom of their birthplaces when they went chasing from boom town to boom town. Iannielli and McKee, on the other hand, did not have to chase all over America for the big job; they could wait for the job to come to them, and did, because the New York area had been enjoying an almost constant building boom for the last ten years.

And yet both were impressed with the sure swagger of the boomer, impressed with the fact that boomers were hired on jobs from New York to California, from Michigan to Louisiana, purely on their national reputations, not on the strength of strong local unions.

This realization seemed to impress Iannielli a bit more than McKee. Perhaps it was partly due to Iannielli's being so small in this big man's business.

He, like Benny Olson, desperately wanted to prove himself, but he would make his mark not by cutting big men to size, or by boasting or boozing, but rather by displaying cold nerve on high steel—taking chances that only a suicidal circus performer would take—and by also displaying excessive pride on the ground.

Iannielli loved to say, "I'm an *iron*worker." (Bridges are now made of steel, but iron was the first metal of big bridges, and the first bridgemen were called "ironworkers." There is great tradition in the title, and so Iannielli—and all bridgemen with pride in the past—refer to themselves as *iron*workers, never *steel*workers.)

When Edward Iannielli first became an apprentice ironworker, he used to rub orange dust, the residue of lead paint, into his boots before taking the subway home; he was naive enough in those days to think that passengers on the subway would associate orange dust with the solution that is coated over steel during construction to make it rustproof.

"When I was a little kid growing up," he had once recalled, "my old man, Edward Iannielli, Sr., would bring other ironworkers home after work, and all they'd talk about was ironwork, ironwork. That's all we ever heard as kids, my brother and me. Sometimes my old man would take us out to the job, and all the other ironworkers were nice to us because we were Eddie's sons, and the foreman might come over and ask, 'You Eddie's sons?' and we'd say, 'Yeah,' and he'd say, 'Here, take a quarter.' And that is how I first started to love this business.

"Later, when I was about thirteen or fourteen, I remember going out to a job with the old man and seeing this big ladder. And I yelled to my father, 'Can I climb up?' and he said, 'Okay, but don't fall.' So I began to climb up this thing, higher and higher, a little scared at first, and then finally I'm on the top, standing on this steel beam way up there, and I'm all alone and looking all around up there, looking out and seeing very far, and it was exciting, and as I stood up there, all of a sudden, I am thinking to myself, '*This* is what I want to do!'"

After his father had introduced him to the business agent of Local 361, the ironworkers' union in Brooklyn, Edward Iannielli, Jr. started work as an apprentice.

"I'll never forget the first day I walked into that union hall," he had recalled. "I had on a brand-new pair of shoes, and I saw all those big men lined up, and some of them looked like bums, some looked like gangsters, some just sat around tables playing cards and cursing.

"I was scared, and so I found a little corner and just sat there, and in my pocket I had these rosaries that I held. Then a guy walked out and yelled, 'Is young Iannielli here?' and I said, 'Here,' and he said, 'Got a job for you.' He told me to go down and report to a guy named Harry at this new twelve-story criminal court building in downtown Brooklyn, and so I rushed down there and said to Harry, 'I'm sent out from the hall,' and he said, 'Oh, so you're the new apprentice boy,' and I said, 'Yeah,' and he said, 'You got your parents' permission?' and I said, 'Yeah,' and he said, 'In writing?' and I said, 'No,' and so he said, 'Go home and get it.'

"So I get back on the subway and go all the way back, and I remember running down the street, very excited because I had a job, to get my mother to sign this piece of paper. Then I ran all the way back, after getting out of the subway, up to Harry and gave him the piece of paper, and then he said, 'Okay, now I gotta see your birth certificate.' So I had to run all the way back, get another subway, and then come back, and now my feet in my new shoes are hurting.

"Anyway, when I gave Harry the birth certificate, he said, 'Okay, go up that ladder and see the pusher,' and when I got to the top, a big guy asked, 'Who you?' I tell 'im I'm the new apprentice boy, and he says, 'Okay, get them two buckets over there and fill 'em up with water and give 'em to the riveting gang.'

"These buckets were two big metal milk cans, and I had to carry them down the ladder, one at a time, and bring them up, and this is what I did for a long time—kept the riveting gangs supplied with drinking water, with coffee and with rivets—no ifs and buts, either.

"And one time, when I was on a skyscraper in Manhattan, I remember I had to climb down a ladder six floors to get twenty coffees, a dozen sodas, some cake and everything, and on my way back, holding everything in a cardboard box, I remember slipping on a beam and losing my balance. I fell two flights. But luckily I fell in a pile of canvas, and the only thing that happened was I got splashed in all that steaming hot coffee. Some iron-worker saw me laying there and he yelled, 'What happened?' and I said, 'I fell off and dropped the coffee,' and he said, '*You dropped the coffee*! Well, you better get the hell down there fast, boy, and get some more coffee.'

"So I go running down again, and out of my own money—must have cost me four dollars or more—I bought all the coffee and soda and cake, and then I climbed back up the ladder, and when I saw the pusher, before he could complain about anything, I told him I'm sorry I'm late."

After Edward Iannielli had become a full-fledged ironworker, he fell a few more times, mostly because he would run, not walk across girders, and once—while working on the First National City Bank in Manhattan—he fell backward about three stories and it looked as if he was going down all the way. But he was quick, light, and lucky—he was "The Rabbit," and he landed on a beam and held on.

"I don't know what it is about me," he once tried to explain, "but I think it all has something to do with being young, and not wanting to be like those older men up there, the ones that keep telling me, 'Don't be reckless, you'll get killed, be careful.' Sometimes, on windy days, those old-timers get across a girder by crawling on their hands and knees, but I always liked to run across and show those other men how to do it. That's when they all used to say, 'Kid, you'll never see thirty.'

"Windy days, of course, are the hardest. Like you're walking across an eight-inch beam, balancing yourself in the wind, and then, all of a sudden, the wind stops—and you *temporarily lose your balance*. You quickly straighten out—but it's some feeling when *that* happens."

Edward Iannielli first came to the Verrazano-Narrows job in 1961, and while working on the Gowanus Expressway that cut through Bay Ridge, Brooklyn, to the bridge, he got his left hand caught in a crane one day.

One finger was completely crushed, but the other, cleanly severed, remained in his glove. Dr. Coppola was able to sew it back on. The finger would always be stiff and never as strong as before, of course; yet the surgeon was able to offer Edward Iannielli two choices as to how the finger might be rejoined to his hand. It could either be set straight, which would make it less conspicuous and more attractive, or it could be shaped into a grip-form, a hook. While this was a bit ugly, it would mean that the finger could more easily be used by Iannielli when working with steel. There was no choice, as far as Iannielli was concerned; the finger was bent permanently into a grip.

When, in the fall of 1963, Gerard McKee met Edward Iannielli and saw the misshapen left hand, he did not ask any questions or pay any attention. Gerard McKee was a member of an old family of construction workers, and to him malformation was not uncommon, it was almost a way of life. His father, James McKee, a big, broad-shouldered man with dark hair and soft blue eyes—a man whom Gerard strongly resembled—had been hit by a collapsing crane a few years before, had had his leg permanently twisted, had a steel plate inserted in his head, and was disabled for life.

James McKee had been introduced to ironwork by an uncle, the late Jimmy Sullivan, who had once been Hard Nose Murphy's boss in a gang. The McKee name was well known down at Local 40, the union hall in Manhattan, and it had been quite logical for James McKee, prior to his accident, to take his three big sons down to the hall and register them in the ironworkers' apprentice program.

Of the three boys, Gerard McKee was the youngest, tallest, and heaviest—but not by much. His brother John, a year older than Gerard, was 195 pounds and six feet two inches. And his brother Jimmy, two years older than Gerard, was 198 pounds and six feet three inches.

When the boys were introduced to union officials of Local 40, there were smiles of approval all around, and there was no doubt that the young McKees, all of them erect and broad-shouldered and seemingly eager, would someday develop into superb ironworkers. They looked like fine college football prospects—the type that a scout would eagerly offer scholarships to without asking too many embarrassing questions about grades. Actually, the McKee boys had never even played high school football. Somehow in their neighborhood along the waterfront of South Brooklyn, an old Irish neighborhood called Red Hook, the sport of football had never been very popular among young boys.

The big sport in Red Hook was swimming, and the way a young boy could win respect, could best prove his valor, was to jump off one of the big piers or warehouses along the waterfront, splash into Buttermilk Channel, and then swim more than a mile against the tide over to the Statue of Liberty.

Usually, upon arrival, the boys would be arrested by the guards. If they weren't caught, they would then swim all the way back across Buttermilk Channel to the Red Hook side.

None of the neighborhood boys was a better swimmer than Gerard McKee, and none had gotten back and forth through Buttermilk Channel with more ease and speed than he. All the young boys of the street respected him, all the young girls who sat on the stoops of the small frame houses admired him—but none more than a pretty little Italian redhead named Margaret Nucito, who lived across the street from the McKees.

She had first seen Gerard in the second grade of the parochial school. He had been the class clown—the one the nuns scolded the most, liked the most.

At fourteen years of age, when the neighborhood boys and girls began to think less about swimming and more about one another, Margaret and Gerard started to date regularly. And when they were eighteen they began to think about marriage.

In the Red Hook section of Brooklyn, the Catholic girls thought early about marriage. First they thought about boys, then the prom, then marriage. Though they thought Hook was a poor neighborhood of shanties and small two-story frame houses, it was one where engagement rings were nearly always large and usually expensive. It was marriage before sex in this neighborhood, as the Church preaches, and plenty of children; and, like most Irish Catholic neighborhoods, the mothers usually had more to say than the fathers. The mother was the major moral strength in the Irish church, where the Blessed Virgin was an omnipresent figure; it was the mother who, after marriage, stayed home and reared the children, and controlled the family purse strings, and chided the husband for drinking, and pushed the sons when they were lazy, and protected the purity of her daughters.

And so it was not unusual for Margaret, after they tentatively planned marriage and after Gerard had begun work on the bridge, to be in charge of the savings account formed by weekly deductions from his ironworker's earnings. He would only fritter the money away if he were in control of it, she had told him, and he did not disagree. By the summer of 1965 their account had reached $800. He wanted to put this money toward the purchase of the beautiful pear-shaped diamond engagement ring they had seen one day while walking past Kastle's jewelry window on Fulton Street. It was a one-and-one-half-carat ring priced at $1,000. Margaret had insisted that the ring was too expensive, but Gerard had said, since she had liked it so much, that she would have it. They planned to announce their engagement in December.

On Wednesday morning, October 9, Gerard McKee hated to get out of bed. It was a gloomy day and he was tired, and downstairs his brothers were yelling up to him, "Hey, if you don't get down here in two minutes, we're leaving without you."

He stumbled down the steps. Everyone had finished breakfast and his mother had already packed three ham-and-cheese sandwiches for his lunch. His father, limping around the room, was quietly cross at his tardiness.

He had not been out late the night before. He had gone over to Margaret's briefly, then had had a few beers at Gabe's, a neighborhood saloon with a big bridge painted across the back-bar. He had been in bed by about midnight, but this morning he ached, and he suspected he might be getting a cold.

They all left the house at 6:45 a.m. and caught a bus near the corner; then at Forty-ninth Street they got a cab and rode it to 101st Street in Bay Ridge, and then they walked, with hundreds of other ironworkers, down the dirt road toward the Brooklyn anchorage of the Verrazano-Narrows Bridge.

"Wait, let me grab a container of coffee," Gerard said, stopping at a refreshment shack along the path.

"Hurry up."

"Okay," he said. He gulped down the coffee in three swallows as they walked, and then they all lined up to take the elevator up to the catwalk. That morning Jimmy and John McKee were working on the section of the catwalk opposite Gerard, and so they parted on top, and Gerard said, "See you tonight." Then he headed off to join Iannielli.

Edward Iannielli seemed his spry self. He was sitting up there on the cable, whistling and very chipper.

"Good morning," he said, and McKee waved and forced a smile. Then he climbed up on the cable, and soon they began to tighten the seven bolts on the top of the casting.

After they had finished, Iannielli slid down from the cable and McKee handed the ratchet wrench down to him. Iannielli then fitted the wrench to the first of the seven lower bolts.

It was now about 9:30 a.m. It was cloudy and windy, though not as windy as it had been in the first week of October. Iannielli pushed his hardhat down on his head. He gazed down the catwalk and could see hundreds of men, their khaki shirts and jackets billowing in the breeze, all working on the cable—bolting it, banging it with tools, pushing into it. Iannielli took the big wrench he held, fixed it to a bolt, and pressed hard. And then, suddenly, from the bottom of the cable he heard a voice yelling, "*Eddie, Eddie . . . help me, Eddie, help me . . . please, Eddie . . .*"

Iannielli saw, hanging by his fingers from the south edge of the catwalk, clutching tightly to the thin lower wires of the hand rail, the struggling figure of Gerard McKee.

"God," Iannielli screamed, "dear God," he repeated, lunging forward, lying across the catwalk and trying to grab onto McKee's arms and pull him up. But it was very difficult.

Iannielli was only 138 pounds, and McKee was more than 200. And Iannielli, with one finger missing on his left hand from the crane accident, and with the resewn second finger not very strong, could not seem to pull McKee's heavy body upward even one inch. Then McKee's jacket and shirt came loose, and he seemed to be just hanging there, dead weight, and Iannielli kept pleading, "Oh, God, God, please bring him up . . . bring him up . . ."

Other men, hearing the screams, came running and they all stretched down, grabbing wildly for some part of McKee's clothing, and Gerard kept saying, "Hurry, hurry please, I can't hold on any longer." And then, a few moments later, he said, "I'm going to go . . . I'm going to go . . ." and he let go of the wire and dropped from the bridge.

The men watched him fall, feet first for about one hundred feet. Then his body tilted forward, and Iannielli could see McKee's shirt blowing off and could see McKee's bare back, white against the dark sea, and then he saw him splash hard, more than 350 feet below, and Iannielli closed his eyes and began to weep, and then he began to slip over, too, but an Indian, Lloyd LeClaire, jumped on top of him, held him tight to the catwalk.

Not far from where Gerard McKee hit the water, two doctors sat fishing in a boat, and also nearby was a safety launch. And for the next thirty seconds, hysterical and howling men's voices, dozens of them, came echoing down from the bridge, "Hey, grab that kid, grab that kid . . . hurry, grab that kid . . ."

Even if Gerard McKee had landed within a yard of the safety boat, it would have been no use; anyone falling from that altitude is sure to die, for, even if his lungs hold out, the water is like concrete, and bodies break into many pieces when they fall that far.

The remains of Gerard McKee were taken out of the water and put into the safety launch and taken to Victory Memorial Hospital. Some of the men up on the bridge began to cry, and, slowly, all of them, more than six hundred of them, removed their hardhats and began to come down. Work was immediately suspended for the day. One young apprentice ironworker, who had never seen a death like this before, froze to the catwalk and refused to leave; he later had to be carried down by three others.

Jimmy and John McKee went home to break the news and be with their parents and Margaret, but Edward Iannielli, in a kind of daze, got into his automobile and began to drive away from the bridge, without any destination. When he saw a saloon he stopped. He sat at the bar between a few men, shaking, his lips quivering. He ordered one whiskey, then another, then three beers. In a few minutes he felt loose, and he left the bar and got into his car and began to drive up the Belt Parkway. He drove about fifty miles, then, turning around, he drove fifty miles back, seeing the bridge in the distance, now empty and quiet. He turned off the Belt Parkway and drove toward his home. His wife greeted him, very excitedly, at the door, saying that the bridge company had called, the safety officer had called, and what had happened?

Iannielli heard very little of what she was saying. That night in bed all he could hear, over and over, was "Eddie, Eddie, help me . . . help me." And again and again he saw the figure falling toward the sea, the shirt blowing up and the white back exposed. He got out of bed and walked through the house for the rest of the night.

The next day, Thursday, October 10, the investigation was begun to determine the cause of McKee's death. Work was again suspended on the bridge. But since nobody had seen how McKee had gotten off the cable, nobody knew whether he had jumped onto the catwalk and bounced off it or whether he had tripped—and they still do not know. All they knew then was that the morale of the men was shot, and Ray Corbett, business agent for Local 40, began a campaign to get the bridge company to string nets under the men on the bridge.

This had not been the first death around the bridge. On August 24, 1962, one man fell off a ladder inside a tower and died, and on July 13, 1963, another man slipped off the approach road and died. But the death of Gerard McKee was somehow different—different, perhaps, because the men had watched it, had been helpless to stop it; different, perhaps, because it had involved a very popular young man, the son of an ironworker who had himself been crippled for life.

Whatever the reason, the day of Gerard McKee's death was the blackest day on the bridge so far. And it would have made little difference for any company official to point out that the Verrazano-Narrows' safety record—just three deaths during thousands of working hours involving hundreds of men—was highly commendable.

McKee's funeral, held at the Visitation Roman Catholic Church in Red Hook, was possibly the largest funeral ever held in the neighborhood. All the ironworkers seemed to be there, and so were the engineers and union officials. But of all the mourners, the individual who seemed to take it the worst was Gerard's father, James McKee.

"After what I've been through," he said, shaking his head, tears in his eyes, "I should know enough to keep my kids off the bridge."

VII. Stage in the Sky

Gerard McKee's two brothers quit the bridge immediately, as their father had requested, but both were back within the month. The other ironworkers were a bit nervous when the McKees climbed up that first day back, but the brothers assured everyone that it was far more comfortable working up on the bridge, busy among the men, than remaining in the quietude of a mournful home.

Though nobody could ever have imagined it then, the death of Gerard McKee was just the beginning of a long, harsh winter—possibly the worst in Hard Nose Murphy's career. There would be a tugboat strike and a five-day ironworkers' strike to force management to put nets under the bridge; there would be freezing weather, powerful winds that would swing the bridge, careless mistakes that would result in a near disaster while the men were lifting a four-hundred-ton piece of steel; and, hovering over everything else, there would be the assassination on November 22 of President Kennedy, an event that demoralized men nowhere in the world more than it did on the bridge, where the majority of workers were of Irish ancestry. All of this would occur while Hard Nose Murphy and the American Bridge engineers were facing their greatest challenge—the span across the sea.

If construction was to remain on schedule, permitting the bridge to open in late November of 1964, then the steel skeleton of the span would have to be linked 6,690 feet across the sky by spring—a feat that now, in the winter of 1963, seemed quite impossible.

The task would involve the hoisting off barges of sixty separate chunks of steel, each the size of a ten-room ranch house (but each weighing four hundred tons), more than 220 feet in the air. Each of these steel pieces, in addition to several smaller ones, would then be linked to the suspender ropes dangling from the cables and would finally be locked together horizontally across the water between Brooklyn and Staten Island.

If one of these pieces dropped, it would set the bridge's schedule back at least six months, for each piece was without a duplicate. The sixty larger pieces, all of them rectangular in shape, would be about twenty-eight feet high, 115 feet wide, almost as long, and would be floated to the bridge, one at a time, from the American Bridge Company's steelyard four miles up the river in New Jersey, where Benny Olson, James Braddock, and the other old champs were working. The loaded barges, pulled by tugboats, would take an hour to make the trip. Once the steel pieces were lifted off the barges by two tremendous hoisting machines on the lower traverse strut of each tower, the whole bridge would sag under the pressure of weight; for instance, the first piece, when lifted up, would pull the main cables down twenty inches. The second and third pieces would lower the cables an additional four feet six inches. The fifth and sixth pieces would pull the cables down another four feet three inches. When all the pieces were hanging, the cables would be as much as twenty-eight feet lower than before. (All this was as O. H. Ammann had designed it—in fact, his design allowed for as much as a thirty-five-foot cable defection—but he did not take into account human and mechanical frailty, this being Murphy's problem.)

Murphy's problems did not begin with the lifting of the first few steel pieces. This was conducted in the presence of a boatload of television and news cameras, and all the workers were very much on the ball. His troubles began when the initial excitement was tempered by the rote of repetition and the coming of colder weather. One freezing day a small barge holding suspender ropes was tied too tightly to the pier and sank that night when the tide came in, and the guard not only slept through this but also permitted vagrants to ransack the tool shed.

Murphy, in his shack the next morning, pounding his fist against the desk, was on the phone screaming to one of the dock supervisors. "Jes-sus Kee-rist, I'm sick of this crap! That stupidbastardguard just stood in that warm shanty, sleeping instead of watching. Now that guard isn't supposed to be sleeping where it's warm, goddammit, he's supposed to be watching, and I'm not taking any more of this crap, so you get that goddam guard up here and I'll tell that stupidbastard a thing or two . . ."

In the outer office of the shack, Murphy's male secretary, a slim, dapper, well-groomed young man named Chris Reisman, was on the switchboard answering calls with a very polite, "Good morning, American Bridge . . ." and covering his ears to Murphy's profanity in the next room.

Male secretaries are the only sort that would survive in this atmosphere; a female secretary would probably not be safe around some of the insatiable studs who work on bridges, nor would any woman condone the language very long. But Chris Reisman, whose uncle was a riveter and whose stepfather died on a bridge six years before, worked out well as a secretary, although it took a while for the bridgemen to accustom themselves to Chris Reisman's polite telephone voice saying, "Good morning, American Bridge" (instead of "Yeah, whatyawant?"), and to his style of wearing slim, cuffless trousers, a British kneelength raincoat, and, sometimes in wet weather, high soft leather boots.

The day after Reisman had been hired by the American Bridge Company and sent to Murphy's shack on the Staten Island shore, Murphy's welcoming words were, "Well, I see we got another ass to sit around here." But soon even Murphy was impressed with twenty-three-year-old Reisman's efficiency as a secretary and his cool manner over the telephone in dealing with people Murphy was trying to avoid.

"Good morning, American Bridge . . ."

"Yeah, say, is Murphy in?"

"May I ask who's calling?"

"What?"

"May I ask who's calling?"

"Yeah, dis is an old friend, Willy . . . just tell 'im Willy . . ."

"May I have your last name?"

"Wha?"

"Your *last* name?"

"Just tell Murphy, well, maybe you can help me. Ya see, I worked on the Pan Am job with Murphy, and . . ."

"Just a minute, please," Chris cut in, then switched to Murphy on the intercom and said, "I have a Willy on the phone that worked for you . . ."

"*I don't want to talk to that bastard,*" Murphy snapped back.

Then, back on the phone, Reisman said, "I am sorry, sir, but Mr. Murphy is not in."

"Wha?"

"I said I do not expect Mr. Murphy to be in today."

"Well, okay, I'll try tomorrow."

"Fine," said Chris Reisman, clicking him off, then picking up another call with, "Good morning, American Bridge . . ."

On Thursday, November 21, there was a hoisting engine failure, and a four-hundred-ton steel unit, which was halfway up, could not go any farther, so it dangled there all night. The next day, after the engine trouble was corrected, there was union rumbling over the failure of the bridge company to put nets under the bridge. This fight was led by Local 40's business agent, Ray Corbett, himself a onetime ironworker—he helped put up the television tower atop the Empire State—and on Monday, December 2, the men walked off the bridge because of the dispute.

The argument against nets was not so much money or the time it would take to string them up, although both of these were factors, but mainly the belief that nets were not really a safeguard against death. Nets could never be large enough to cover the whole underbelly of the bridge, the argument went, because the steel had to be lifted up into the bridge through the path of any nets. It was also felt that nets, even small ones strung here and there, and moved as the men moved, might induce a sense of false security and invite more injury than might otherwise occur.

The strike lasted from December 2 to December 6, ending with the ironworkers' unions victorious—they got their nets, small as they seemed, and Ray Corbett's strong stand was largely vindicated within the next year, when three men fell off the bridge and were saved from the water by dropping into nets.

By January, with barges arriving every day with one and sometimes two four-hundred-ton steel pieces to be lifted, about half of the sixty box-shaped units were hanging from the cables, and things seemed, at least for the time being, to be under control. Each day, if the sun was out, the old bridge buffs with binoculars would shiver on the Brooklyn shoreline, watching and exchanging sage comments and occasionally chatting with the ironworkers who passed back and forth through the gate with its sign:

BEER OR ANY ALCOHOLIC BEVERAGES NOT PERMITTED ON THIS JOB. APPRENTICES WHO BRING ALCOHOLIC BEVERAGES ON JOB FOR THE MEN WILL BE TERMINATED.

"You *never* drink on the bridge, right?" a man near the gate asked an Indian ironworker named Bronco Bill Martin.

"Who?"

"You."

"No, I only drink beer."

"Well, doesn't beer ruin your sense of balance?"

"I donno," Bronco Bill said. "I just go to job, drink beer, climb bridge, and I feel better on bridge than I do on ground. I can drink a dozen can of beer and still walk a straight line on that bridge."

"A *dozen*?"

"Yeah," he said, "easy."

A few yards away, a group of white-haired men, some of them retired engineers or construction workers, all of them now "seaside superintendents," were peering up at the bridge, listening to the grinds of the hoisting machines and the echoes of "Red" Kelly shouting instructions up through his bullhorn from a barge below the rising four-hundred-ton steel unit. It was a fascinating water show, very visual and dramatic, even for these elderly men who only saw the finale.

The show had its beginning more than an hour earlier up the river on the Jersey side. There, along the waterfront of the American Bridge Company's yard, a four-hundred-ton chunk of steel (steel that had been made in smaller sections at U.S. Steel plants in other states, and then shipped by rail to the New Jersey yard for assembly) was resting on a gigantic twin barge and was now just being pulled away by one tug, pushed by another.

The ironworkers, about seventy of them, waved from the yard to the tugs—another four hundred tons was off. The tug pilot, a thin, blond Norwegian-American named Villy Knutsen, carefully churned through New York Harbor—crisscrossing with oil tankers, ferryboats, luxury cruisers, aircraft carriers, fishing boats, driftwood, floating beer cans— squinting his pale blue eyes in the sun and splashing spray. On this day he was talking to a deckhand, Robert Guerra, telling him how he had hated the bridge when it first began. The Knutsens had been one of the families in Bay Ridge whose homes had been threatened by the approaches to the bridge. Villy Knutsen and his wife had joined the protests and signed many petitions before finally moving to Port Jefferson, Long Island.

"But I really hated that bridge then, I'll tell ya," he repeated.

"Well, don't hate it anymore," Guerra said, "it's making you a day's pay."

"Yeah," agreed Knutsen, cutting his tugboat wheel around quickly to skirt past an oncoming tanker, then swinging his head around to observe the barges still slapping the sea under the big red steel; all was well.

Forty minutes later, Knutsen was bringing his tug with its big steel caboose toward the bridge. The old men on the shore lifted their binoculars, and the ironworkers on the bridge got ready, and under one of the towers a fat pusher, with a telephone pressed to his left ear, was looking up at the crane on the tower and frowning and saying, "Hello, Eddie? Eddie? Hello, Eddie?" Eddie, the signal man on top, did not answer.

"Hello, Eddie?" Still no answer.

"Gimme that phone," said another pusher, grabbing it. "Hello, Eddie? Hello, Eddie?"

"Hello," came a thin voice through the static. "Hello, Eddie?"

"No, Burt."

"Burt, this is Joe down the bottom. Eddie in the cab?"

Silence.

"Hello, *Burt*? Hello, *Burt*?"

"Christsakes!" the pusher with the phone shouted, holding it away from his ear and frowning at it again. Then he put it to his mouth again. "Hello, Burt? Burt, hello, Burt . . . ?"

"Yeah."

"Whatthehell's wrong, Burt?"

"You got a goddam broken splice in your hand down there."

"Well, keep talking, Burt."

"Okay, Joe."

"Keep talking, Burt . . . keep . . ." The phone went dead again.

"Christsakes," Joe shouted. "Hello, Burt? Hello? Hellohellohello? Nuthin' . . . Hello? . . . Nuthin'. Hello, Burt?"

"Hello," came the voice from the top.

"Burt?"

"No, this is Eddie."

"Keep talkin', Eddie . . ."

Finally the telephone system between the pusher on the ground and the man on top who controlled the movements of the crane was re-established. Soon Villy Knutsen's tug had bumped the barge into position, and the next step was to link the hauling ropes to the steel piece and prepare to hoist it from the barge up 225 feet to the span.

This whole operation would be under the direct supervision of one man, who now stepped out of a workboat onto the barge—onto the stage. He was a big, barrel-chested man of 235 pounds who stood six feet two inches, and he was very conspicuous, even from the shore, because he wore a red checkered jacket and a big brown hardhat tilted forward over his red hair and big ruddy nose, and because he carried in his right hand a yellow bullhorn through which his commands could be heard by all the men on top of the bridge. He was Jack "Red" Kelly, the number-two bridgeman, second only to Hard Nose Murphy himself.

Suddenly all the men's attention, and also the binoculars along the shore, were focused on Kelly as he carefully watched a dozen ironworkers link the heavy hoisting ropes to the four upper extremities of the steel piece as it gently rocked with the anchored barge. When the ropes had been securely bound, the men jumped off the barge onto another barge, and so did Kelly, and then he called out, "Okay, ease now . . . up . . . *UP* . . ."

Slowly the hauling machines on the tower, their steel thread strung up through the cables and then down all the way to the four edges of the steel unit on the sea, began to grind and grip and finally lift the four hundred tons off the barge.

Within a few minutes, the piece was twenty feet above the barge, and Kelly was yelling, "Slack down . . ." Then, "Go ahead on seven," "Level it up," "Go ahead on seven"; and up on the bridge the signal man, phones clamped to his ears, was relaying the instructions to the men inside the hauling vehicles.

Within twenty-five minutes, the unit had climbed 225 feet in the air, and the connectors on top were reaching out for it, grabbing it with their gloves, then linking it temporarily to one of the units already locked in place.

"Artfully done," said one of the old men with binoculars.

"Yes, good show," said another.

Most of the sixty pieces went up like this one—with remarkable efficiency and speed, despite the wind and bitter cold, but just after New Year's Day, a unit scheduled to be lifted onto the Brooklyn backspan, close to the shoreline, caused trouble, and the "seaside superintendents" had a good view of Murphy's temper.

As the steel piece was lifted a few feet off the barge, a set of hold-back lines that stretched horizontally from the Brooklyn tower to the rising steel unit broke loose with a screech. (The hold-back lines were necessary in this case because the steel unit had to rise at an oblique angle, the barge being unable to anchor close enough to the Brooklyn shoreline to permit the unit a straight ride upward.)

Suddenly, the four-hundred-ton steel frame twisted, then went hurtling toward the Brooklyn shore, still hanging on ropes, but out of control. It swished within a few inches of a guard-rail fence beneath the anchorage, then careened back and dangled uneasily above the heads of a few dozen workmen. Some fell to the ground; others ran.

"*Jes-sus*," cried one of the spectators on shore. "Did you see that?"

"Oh, my!"

"Oh, if old man Ammann were here now, he'd have a fit!"

Down below, from the pier and along the pedestals of the tower, as well as up on the span itself, there were hysterical cries and cursing and fist waving. A hurried telephone call to Hard Nose Murphy brought him blazing across the Narrows in a boat, and his swearing echoed for a half-hour along the waterfront of Bay Ridge.

"Which gang put the clamps on that thing?" Murphy demanded.

"Drilling's gang," somebody said.

"And where the hell's Drilling?"

"Ain't here today."

Murphy was probably never angrier than he was on this particular Friday, January 3. John Drilling, who had led such a charmed life back on the Mackinac Bridge in Michigan, and who had recently been promoted to pusher though he was barely twenty-seven years old, had called in sick that day. He was at his apartment in Brooklyn with his blond wife, a lovely girl whom he'd met while she was working as a waitress at a Brooklyn restaurant. His father, Drag-Up Drilling, had died of a heart attack before the cable spinning had begun, and some people speculated that if he had lived he might have been the American Bridge superintendent in place of Hard Nose Murphy. The loss of his father and the responsibility of a new wife and child had seemed to change John Drilling from the hell-raiser he had been in Michigan to a mature young man. But now, suddenly, he was in real trouble. Though he was not present at the time of the accident that could have caused a number of deaths, he was nevertheless responsible; he should have checked the clamps when they were put on by his gang the day before.

When John Drilling returned to the bridge, not yet aware of the incident, he was met by his friend and fellow boomer, Ace Cowan, a big Kentuckian who was the walkin' boss along the Brooklyn backspan.

"What you got lined out for today, Ace?" Drilling said cheerfully upon arrival in the morning.

"Er, well," Cowan said, looking at his feet, "they . . . the office made me put you back in the gang."

"The gang! What, for taking a lousy day off?"

"No, it was those clamps that slipped . . ."

Drilling's face fell.

"Anybody hurt?"

"No," Cowan said, "but everybody is just pissed . . . I mean Ammann and Whitney, and Murphy, and Kelly, and everybody."

"Whose gang am I in?"

"Whitey Miller's."

Whitey Miller, in the opinion of nearly every bridgeman who had ever worked within a mile of him, was the toughest, meanest, pushiest pusher on the Verrazano-Narrows Bridge. Drilling swallowed hard.

VIII. The Indians

That night in Johnny's Bar near the bridge, the men spoke about little else.

"Hear about Drilling?"

"Yeah, poor guy."

"They put him in Whitey Miller's gang."

"It's a shame."

"That Whitey Miller's a great ironworker, though," one cut in. "You gotta admit that."

"Yeah, I admit it, but he don't give a crap if you get killed."

"I wouldn't say that."

"Well, I would. I mean, he won't even go to your goddam funeral, that Whitey Miller."

But in another bar in Brooklyn that night, a bar also filled with ironworkers, there was no gloom—no worries about Whitey Miller, no anguish over Drilling. This bar, The Wigwam, at 75 Nevins Street in the North Gowanus section, was a few miles away from Johnny's. The Wigwam was where the Indians always drank. They seemed the most casual, the most detached of ironworkers; they worked as hard as anybody on the bridge, but once the workday was done they left the bridge behind, forgot all about it, lost it in the cloud of smoke, the bubbles of beer, the jukebox jive of The Wigwam.

This was their home away from home. It was a mail drop, a club. On weekends the Indians drove four hundred miles up to Canada to visit their wives and children on the Caughnawaga reservation, eight miles from Montreal on the south shore of the St. Lawrence River; on week nights they all gathered in The Wigwam drinking Canadian beer (sometimes as many as twenty bottles apiece) and getting drunk together, and lonely.

On the walls of the bar were painted murals of Indian chiefs, and there also was a big photograph of the Indian athlete Jim Thorpe. Above the entrance to the bar hung a sign reading: THE GREATEST IRONWORKERS IN THE WORLD PASS THRU THESE DOORS.

The bar was run by Irene and Manuel Vilis—Irene being a friendly, well-built Indian girl born into an ironworkers' family on the Caughnawaga reservation; Manuel, her husband, was a Spanish card shark with a thin upturned mustache; he resembled Salvadore Dalí. He was born in Galicia, and after several years in the merchant marine, he jumped ship and settled in New York, working as a busboy and bottle washer in some highly unrecommended restaurants.

During World War II he joined the United States Army, landed at Normandy, and made a lot of money playing cards. He saved a few thousand dollars this way, and, upon his discharge, and after a few years as a bartender in Brooklyn, he bought his own saloon, married Irene, and called his place The Wigwam.

More than seven hundred Indians lived within ten blocks of The Wigwam, nearly every one of them ironworkers. Their fathers and grandfathers also were ironworkers. It all started on the Caughnawaga reservation in 1886, when the Dominion Bridge Company began constructing a cantilever bridge across the St. Lawrence River. The bridge was to be built for the Canadian Pacific Railroad, and part of the construction was to be on Indian property. In order to get permission to trespass, the railroad company made a deal with the chiefs to employ Indian labor wherever possible. Prior to this, the Caughnawagas—a tribe of mixed-blood Mohawks who had always rejected Jesuit efforts to turn them into farmers—earned their living as canoemen for French fur traders, as raft riders for timbermen, as traveling circus performers, anything that would keep them outdoors and on the move, and that would offer a little excitement.

When the bridge company arrived, it employed Indian men to help the ironworkers on the ground, to carry buckets of bolts here and there, but not to risk their lives on the bridge. Yet when the ironworkers were not watching, the Indians would go walking casually across the narrow beams as if they had been doing it all their lives; at high altitudes the Indians seemed, according to one official, to be "as agile as goats." They also were eager to learn the bridge business—it offered good pay, lots of travel— and within a year or two, several of them became riveters and connectors. Within the next twenty years dozens of Caughnawagas were working on bridges all over Canada.

In 1907, on August 29, during the erection of the Quebec Bridge over the St. Lawrence River, the span collapsed. Eighty-six workmen, many Caughnawagas, fell, and seventy-five ironworkers died. (Among the engineers who investigated the collapse, and concluded that the designers were insufficiently informed about the stress capability of such large bridges, was O. H. Ammann, then twenty-seven years old.)

The Quebec Bridge disaster, it was assumed, would certainly keep the Indians out of the business in the future. But it did just the opposite. The disaster gave status to the bridgeman's job—accentuated the derring-do that Indians previously had not thought much about—and consequently more Indians became attracted to bridges than ever before.

During the bridge and skyscraper boom in the New York metropolitan area in the twenties and thirties, Indians came down to New York in great numbers, and they worked, among other places, on the Empire State Building, the R.C.A. Building, the George Washington Bridge, Pulaski Skyway, the Waldorf-Astoria, Triborough Bridge, Bayonne Bridge, and Henry Hudson Bridge. There was so much work in the New York City area that Indians began renting apartments or furnished rooms in the North Gowanus section of Brooklyn, a centralized spot from which to spring in any direction.

And now, in The Wigwam bar on this Friday night, pay night, these grandsons of Indians who died in 1907 on the Quebec Bridge, these sons of Indians who worked on the George Washington Bridge and Empire State, these men who were now working on the biggest bridge of all, were not thinking much about bridges or disasters: they were thinking mostly about home, and were drinking Canadian beer, and listening to the music.

"Oh, these Indians are crazy people," Manuel Vilis was saying, as he sat in a corner and shook his head at the crowded bar. "All they do when they're away from the reservation is build bridges and drink."

"Indians don't drink any more than other ironworkers, Manny," said Irene sharply, defending the Indians, as always, against her husband's criticism.

"The hell they don't," he said. "And in about a half-hour from now, half these guys in here will be loaded, and then they'll get in their cars and drive all the way up to Canada."

They did this every Friday night, he said, and when they arrived on the reservation, at 2 a.m., they all would honk their horns, waking everybody up, and soon the lights would be on in all the houses and everybody would be drinking and celebrating all night—the hunters were home, and they had brought back the meat.

Then on Sunday night, Manuel Vilis said, they all would start back to New York, speeding all the way, and many more Indians would die from automobile accidents along the road than would ever trip off a bridge. As he spoke, the Indians continued to drink, and there were ten-dollar and twenty-dollar bills all over the bar. Then, at 6:30 p.m., one Indian yelled to another, "Com'on, Danny, drink up, let's move." So Danny Montour, who was about to drive himself and two other Indians up to the reservation that night, tossed down his drink, waved goodbye to Irene and Manuel, and prepared for the four-hundred-mile journey.

Montour was a very handsome young man of twenty-six. He had blue eyes, sharp, very un-Indian facial features, almost blond hair. He was married to an extraordinary Indian beauty and had a two-year-old son, and each weekend Danny Montour drove up to the reservation to visit them. He had named his young son after his father, Mark, an ironworker who had crippled himself severely in an automobile accident and had died not long afterward. Danny's paternal grandfather had fallen with the Quebec Bridge in 1907, dying as a result of injuries. His maternal grandfather, also an ironworker, was drunk on the day of the Quebec disaster and, therefore, in no condition to climb the bridge. He later died in an automobile accident.

Despite all this, Danny Montour, as a boy growing up, never doubted that he would become an ironworker. What else would bring such money and position on the reservation? To not become an ironworker was to become a farmer—and to be awakened at 2 a.m. by the automobile horns of returning ironworkers.

So, of the two thousand men on the reservation, few became farmers or clerks or gas pumpers, and fewer became doctors or lawyers, but 1,700 became ironworkers. They could not escape it. It got them when they were babies awakened in their cribs by the horns. The lights would go on, and their mothers would pick them up and bring them downstairs to their fathers, all smiling and full of money and smelling of whiskey or beer, and so happy to be home. They were incapable of enforcing discipline, only capable of handing dollar bills around for the children to play with, and all Indian children grew up with money in their hands. They liked the feel of it, later wanted more of it, *fast*—for fast cars, fast living, fast trips back and forth between long weekends and endless bridges.

"It's a good life," Danny Montour was trying to explain, driving his car up the Henry Hudson Parkway in New York, past the George Washington Bridge. "You can see the job, can see it shape up from a hole in the ground to a tall building or a big bridge."

He paused for a moment, then, looking through the side window at the New York skyline, he said, "You know, I have a name for this town. I don't know if anybody said it before, but I call this town the City of Man-made Mountains. And we're all part of it, and it gives you a good feeling—you're a kind of mountain builder . . ."

"That's right, Danny-boy, old kid," said Del Stacey, the Indian ironworker who was a little drunk, and sat in the front seat next to Montour with a half-case of beer and bag of ice under his feet. Stacey was a short, plump, copper-skinned young man wearing a straw hat with a red feather in it; when he wanted to open a bottle of beer, he removed the cap with his teeth.

"Sometimes, though," Montour continued, "I'd like to stay home more, and see more of my wife and kid . . ."

"But we can't, Danny-boy," Stacey cut in, cheerfully. "We gotta build them mountains, Danny-boy, and let them women stay home alone, so they'll miss us and won't get a big head, right?" Stacey finished his bottle of beer, then opened a second one with his teeth. The third Indian, in the back seat, was quietly sleeping, having passed out.

Once Montour had gotten the car on the New York Thruway, he began to speed, and occasionally the speedometer would tip between ninety and one hundred miles per hour. He had had three or four drinks at The Wigwam, and now, in his right hand, he was sipping a gin that Stacey had handed him; but he seemed sober and alert, and the expressway was empty, and every few moments his eyes would peer into the rear-view mirror to make certain no police car was following.

Only once during the long trip did Montour stop; in Malden, New York, he stopped at a Hot Shoppe for ten minutes to get a cup of coffee—and there he saw Mike Tarbell and several other Indians also bound for Canada. By 11 p.m. he was speeding past Warrensburg, New York, and an hour or so later he had pulled off the expressway and was on Route 9, a two-lane backroad, and Stacey was yelling, "Only forty miles more to go, Danny-boy."

Now, with no radar and no cars coming or going, Danny Montour's big Buick was blazing along at 120 miles per hour, swishing past the tips of trees, skimming over the black road—and it seemed, at any second, that a big truck would surely appear in the windshield, as trucks always appear, suddenly, in motion-picture films to demolish a few actors near the end of the script.

But, on this particular night, there were no trucks for Danny Montour.

At 1:35 a.m., he took a sharp turn onto a long dirt road, then sped past a large black bridge that was silhouetted in the moonlight over the St. Lawrence Seaway—it was the Canadian railroad bridge that had been built in 1886, the one that got Indians started as ironworkers. With a screech of his brakes, Montour stopped in front of a white house.

"We're home, you lucky Indians," he yelled. The Indian in the back seat who had been sleeping all this time woke up, blinked. Then the lights went on in the white house; it was Montour's house, and everybody went in for a quick drink, and soon Danny's wife, Lorraine, was downstairs, and so was the two-year-old boy, Mark. Outside, other horns were honking, other lights burned; and they remained alive, some of them, until 4 a.m. Then, one by one, they went out, and the last of the Indians fell asleep—not rising again until Saturday afternoon, when they would be awakened, probably, by the almost endless line of bill collectors knocking on doors:

milkmen, laundrymen, newsboys, plumbers, venders of vacuum cleaners, encyclopedia salesmen, junk dealers, insurance salesmen. They all waited until Saturday afternoon, when the ironworker was home, relaxed and happy, to separate him from his cash.

The reservation itself is quiet and peaceful. It consists of a two-lane tar road that curves for eight miles near the south shore of the St. Lawrence River. Lined along both sides of the road and behind it are hundreds of small white frame houses, most of them with porches in front—porches often occupied by old Indian men. They slump in rocking chairs, puffing pipes, and quietly watch the cars pass or the big ships float slowly through the St. Lawrence Seaway—ships with sailors on deck who wave at any Indian women they see walking along the road.

Many of the younger Indian women are very pretty. They buy their clothes in Montreal shops, have their hair done on Friday afternoons. There is little about their style of clothing or about their homes that is peculiarly Indian—no papooses, no totems, no Indian gadgets on walls. Some Indian homes do not have running water, and have outhouses in the back, but all seem to have television sets. The only sounds heard on Saturday afternoon are the clanging bells of the Roman Catholic church along the road—most Indians are Catholics—and occasionally the honking of an Indian motorcade celebrating a wedding or christening.

The only road signs bearing Indian symbols are CHARLIE MOHAWK'S SNACK BAR and, on the other side of the road up a bit, the CHIEF POKING FIRE INDIAN MUSEUM. The snack bar's sign is hung principally to amuse the tourists who pass in a yellow bus each day; inside, however, the place looks like any soda fountain, with the booths cluttered with teenaged boys sporting ducktail haircuts and smoking cigarettes, and teenaged girls in skin-tight dungarees and ponytails, all of them twisting or kicking to the rock 'n' roll music blaring from the jukebox.

At Chief Poking Fire's museum, things are different; here it's strictly for the tourists, with the Chief and his family assembling in full regalia a few times each day to dance whoop and holler for the tourists and wave tomahawks so that the tourists, clicking their 16-mm cameras, will have something to show for their visit to an Indian reservation.

The Indian mayor of Caughnawaga is John Lazare, who believes he might be a Jewish Indian. He succeeded his brother, Matthew, as mayor, and Matthew succeeded their father. The Lazares run a gas station on the same side of the road as Chief Poking Fire's museum, and they also sell liquid gas to Indians for home use.

The political viewpoint that has kept the Lazares popular with other Indians all these years is Mayor Lazare's speeches that usually include the sentence, "The Indian should be allowed to do whatever he wants," and also the Lazares' long-time denunciation of the license plate on automobiles. Indians hate to drive with license plates on their cars and would like to remove them, presumably so they'll get fewer speeding tickets (although many Indians ignore all tickets on the grounds that they are not valid documents, having never been agreed to by treaty).

On Saturday afternoons, when the Indian men get out of bed (if they get out of bed), they usually play lacrosse, if it is not too cold. In summer months they might spend their afternoons skimming along the St. Lawrence Seaway in a motorboat they themselves built, or fishing or watching television. On Sunday morning they have their traditional breakfast of steak and cornbread, and usually loll around the house all morning and visit friends in the afternoon.

Then, anywhere from 8 p.m. to 11 p.m., the big cars filled with ironworkers will begin to rumble down the reservation's roads, and then toward the routes to the expressway back to New York. It is a sad time for Indian women, these Sunday evenings, and the ride back to New York seems twice as long to the men as did the Friday-night ride coming up. The alcohol that many of them sip all the way back to New York is the only thing that helps make the trip endurable—and the thing that may help kill them.

And so on this Sunday evening, Danny Montour kissed his wife goodbye, and hugged his son, and then went to pick up the others for the long ride back.

"Now be careful," Lorraine said from the porch.

"Don't worry," he said.

And all day Monday she, and other Indian women, half-waited for the phone calls, hoping they would never come. And when they did not come on this particular Monday, the women were happy, and by midweek the happiness would grow into a blithe anticipation of what was ahead—the late-Friday sounds of the horns, the croaking call of Cadillacs and Buicks and Oldsmobiles, the sounds that would bring their husbands home . . . and will take their sons away.

IX. Back to Bay Ridge

In the spring of 1964, to the astonishment of nobody in this neighborhood that had long suspected it, there was discovered behind the black curtains and awning and white brick wall at 125 Eighty-sixth Street, in the plush Colonial Road section of Bay Ridge, a whorehouse.

Some people, of course, blamed the boomers, recalling the sight of those slinky blondes who lingered along the shore behind the bridge. But the *Brooklyn Spectator*, which broke the story on March 20, after the police finally had sufficient evidence to make arrests, reported that there were some prominent Bay Ridge citizens among the clientele, although it gave no names. The story caused a sensation—"The first story of its kind to appear in this paper in its thirty-two-year history," announced the *Spectator*—and not only was every copy suddenly sold out, but the newspaper office was left with none for its files, and it hastily had to announce that it would re-purchase, at the regular price of ten cents, any copies of the March 20 issue in good condition.

After arresting a thirty-six-year-old blond madam who swore she was a "real estate broker," and two other blond women who gave their occupations as "baby nurse" and "hostess," the police revealed that even the kitchen of the house had been converted into a boudoir, that the wallpaper was "vivid," and that there were mirrors on the ceilings.

Many respectable, old-time Bay Ridge residents were shocked by the disclosure, and there was the familiar lament for yesteryear. And a few people, apprehensively gazing up at the almost-finished bridge, predicted that soon the bridge might bring many more changes for the worse—more traffic through residential streets, more and cheaper apartment houses (that might be crowded with Negroes), and more commercialism in neighborhoods traditionally occupied by two-family houses.

It had been five years since the bridge first invaded Bay Ridge, and, though the protestors were now quiet and the eight hundred buildings that stood in the path of the bridge's approachways had now all disappeared, many people had long memories, and they still hated the bridge.

Monsignor Edward J. Sweeney, whose parish at St. Ephrem's had lost two thousand of its twelve thousand parishioners, thus diminishing the Sunday collection considerably, still became enraged at the mere mention of the bridge. The dentist, Henry Amen, who had put on forty pounds in the last five years, and was now prosperous in a new office one mile north of his old office, was nevertheless still seething, saying, "I strongly resent the idea of being forced to move."

In some cases the anger in Bay Ridge was as alive in 1964 as it was back in 1959 when "Save Bay Ridge" banners flew; when people screamed "That bridge—who needs it?"; when an undertaker, Joseph V. Sessa, claimed he would lose 2,500 people "from which to draw"; and when the anti-bridge faction included the disparate likes of housewives, bartenders, a tugboat skipper, doctors, lawyers, a family of seventeen children (two dogs and a cat), a retired prizefighter, a former Ziegfeld Follies girl, two illicit lovers, and hundreds of others who reacted generally as people might react anywhere if, suddenly, the order was delivered: "Abandon your homes—we must build a bridge."

In all, it had taken eighteen months to move out the seven thousand people, and now, in 1964, though a majority of them had been relocated in Bay Ridge, they had lost touch with most of their old neighbors, and had nothing in common now but the memories.

"Oh, those were depressing days," recalled Bessie Gros Dempsey, the former Follies girl who now lives four blocks from the spot where her old home had stood. "When those demolition men moved into the neighborhood, you'd have flower pots full of dust on your window sills at night, and all day long you'd see them smashing down those lovely homes across the street.

"That crane was like the jaw of a monster, and when it cracked into those buildings, into the roof and ceiling and shingles, everything would turn into powder, and then the dogs would start barking because of all the strange sounds a building makes when it is falling.

"I remember back of where I used to live was this big brownstone—an artist lived there, and the place was built like an Irish castle. When the crane hit into it, it was a horrible sound I'll never forget. And I remember watching them tear down that colonial house that was directly across the street from me. It had columns in front, and a screened-in porch, and it was lived in by a nice elderly couple that had twin daughters, and also an uncle, Jack, a crippled fellow who used to trim those hedges. Such pride was in that home, and what a pity to see that crane smash it all down."

The couple with the twin daughters now lives in upstate New York, Mrs.

Dempsey said, adding that she does not know what became of the crippled uncle named Jack. The artist who lived in the brownstone behind her old home is now dead, she said, along with five other people she used to know in her neighborhood in the pre-bridge days.

Mrs. Dempsey and many others in Bay Ridge in 1964 were citing the bridge as an accomplice in the death of many residents of the old neighborhood; they said that the tension and frustration in losing one's home and the uncertainty of the future had all contributed to the death of many since 1959. One woman pointed out that her husband, never ill before, suddenly had a heart attack and died after a "Save Bay Ridge" rally, and another woman blamed the bridge for her faltering eyesight, saying she never had to wear glasses until the announcement that her home would be destroyed by "that bridge."

Most of the older people who had owned their homes, particularly those on pensions or small fixed incomes, said that the relocation caused them financial hardships because they could not match the price of a new home of comparable size in a comparable neighborhood.

There were, to be sure, a minority who said they were happy that the bridge had forced them to move, or who felt that they had been unjustifiably pessimistic about the changes the Verrazano-Narrows Bridge would bring. Mrs. Carroll L. Christiansen, who had moved from Bay Ridge to Tenafly, New Jersey, into a suburban home with a quarter-acre of land around it, said, "It's a lot better here than in Brooklyn." She added, "In Brooklyn the people didn't mix socially—and never had too much to do with one another. But here it is entirely different. I've learned to play golf since coming here. And my husband and I play cards with other couples in the evenings, and we go to dances at the country club. My daughter, who is seventeen now, felt uprooted for about a year or so, but since then she's also made lots of new friends and the whole life is much easier here."

The undertaker, Joseph Sessa, who had feared he would lose thousands of people, was surviving nicely in Bay Ridge five years later; and the two lovers—the divorced man and the unhappily married woman who used to live across the street from him—have gone their separate ways (she to Long Island, he to Manhattan) and neither blames the bridge for coming between them. "It was just a passing fancy," she says of her old affair, now being moderately contented with her new home, her husband, and children. The lover, a forty-six-year-old insurance company executive, has met a woman at the office, unmarried and in her middle thirties, and each evening they meet in a dimly lit cocktail lounge on Park Avenue South.

Florence Campbell, the divorcée who with her young son had held out in her old apartment until 1960, despite the murder on the floor below, now believes the bridge has changed her life for the better. In her new block, she was introduced by a friend to a merchant mariner, and a year later they were married and now live in a comfortable home on Shore Road.

The old shoemaker who had screamed "sonamabitch" at the bridge authorities for tearing down his little store five years ago, and who returned disillusioned to Cosenza in Southern Italy, has since come back to Brooklyn and is working in another shoe store. He became restless in Italy, and found life among his relatives unbearable.

Mr. and Mrs. John G. Herbert, parents of seventeen children, all of whom once lived in a noisy and tattered frame house on the corner of Sixty-seventh and Seventh Avenue in Bay Ridge before the bridge intruded, now live on Fifty-second Street in a three-story, nine-room house that they own, and, in a sense, they are better off than when they were only renting at the old place.

This newer house is two rooms larger than the other one, but it is not any more spacious, and it is also jammed in the middle of a block of teeming row houses. The Herbert children miss the rambling grass yard and trees that used to surround the old property.

Mr. Herbert, a short, muscular Navy Yard worker with blue eyes and a white crew cut, sometimes escapes the clatter and confusion of his home by drinking heavily, and when guests arrive he often greets them by pounding them on the back, pouring them a drink, and shouting, "Com'on, relax—take off your coat, sit down, have a drink, relax," and Mrs. Herbert, shaking her head sadly, half moans to the guests, "Oh, you're lucky you don't live here," and then Mr. Herbert, downing another drink, pounds the guests again and repeats, "Com'on, relax, have another drink, relax!"

Two of the Herbert boys—Eugene, who is twenty, and Roy, who is nineteen—are very sensitive to such scenes, and both recall how happy, how hopeful they'd been five years before when they had first heard that their old house would be torn down. Finally, they thought, they'd be out of the city altogether, and moving into the country as their father had so often said they would.

When this did not happen, the family being unable to afford any home except the one they now have, the boys felt a bit cheated; even five years afterward, they missed their old home, yearned for another like it. One day in the early spring of 1964, Eugene and Roy took a nostalgic journey back to their old neighborhood, a mile and a half away, and revisited the land upon which their old home had stood.

Now all was flattened and smoothed by concrete—it was buried by the highway leading to the bridge, the path toward the tollgates. The highway was three months away from completion, and so it was without automobiles. It was quiet and eerie. Eugene walked around in the middle of the empty highway and then stopped and said, "It was about here, Roy—this is where the house was."

"Yeah, I guess you're right," Roy said, "because over there's the telephone pole we used to climb . . ."

"And over here was where the porch was . . ."

"Yeah, and remember how we used to sit out there at night in the summertime with the radio plugged in, and remember when I'd be on that swinging sofa at night with Vera?"

"Boy, I remember that Vera. What a build!"

"And remember when on Friday nights we all used to sit on the steps waiting for Dad to come home from the Navy Yard with a half-gallon of ice cream?"

"I remember, and he never failed us, did he?"

"Nope, and I remember what we used to sing, all of us kids, as we waited for him . . . You remember?"

"Yeah," said Roy. Then both of them, in chorus, repeated their familiar childhood song:

You scream, I scream,
We all scream
For ice cream.
You scream, I scream,
We all scream
For ice . . .

They looked at one another, a little embarrassed, then remained quiet for a moment. Then they walked away from where the house had stood, crossed the empty highway, and, turning around slowly, they rediscovered, one by one, other familiar sights. There was the sidewalk upon which they used to rollerskate, the cement cracks as they had remembered them. There were some of the homes that had not been destroyed by the new highway. There was Leif Ericson Park, where, as boys, they played, and where they once had dug a deep hole in the grass within which to bury things—Scout knives, rings, toys, new baseballs—anything that they had wanted to keep away from their brothers and sisters, because at home nothing was private, nobody respected another's ownership.

They searched along the grass for the hole that they had covered with a metal plate, but could not find it. Then they crossed the street to one of the few houses left on the block, and an elderly woman was shaking a mop outside of a window, and Eugene called up to her, "Hello, Mrs. Johnson, we're the Herbert boys. Remember, we used to live across the street?"

"Why, yes," she said, smiling. "Hardly would have recognized you. How are you?"

"Fine. We're over on Fifty-second Street now."

"Oh," she said, softly. "And how's your mother?"

"Fine, Mrs. Johnson."

"Well, give her my regards," the woman said, smiling, then she pulled the mop in and closed the window.

The boys walked on through the vacated neighborhood, past the yellow bulldozers and cement mixers that were quiet on this Saturday afternoon; past the long dirt road that would soon be paved; past the places that had once been alive with part of them.

"Roy, remember that barking dog that used to scare hell out of us?"

"Yeah."

"And remember that candy store that used to be here?"

"Yeah, Harry's. We used to steal him blind."

"And remember . . ."

"Hey," Roy said, "I wonder if Vera is still around?"

"Let's get to a phone booth and look her up."

They walked three blocks to the nearest sidewalk booth, and Roy looked up the name and then called out, "Hey, here it is—SHore 5-8486."

He put in a dime, dialed the number, and waited, thinking how he would begin. But in another second he realized there was no need to think any longer, because there was only a click, and then the coldly proper voice of a telephone operator began "I am sorry. The number you have reached is not in service at this time . . . This is a recording . . ."

Roy picked out the dime, put it in his pocket. Then he and his brother walked quietly to the corner, and began to wait for the bus—but it never came. And so, without saying anything more, they began to walk back to their other home, the noisy one, on Fifty-second Street. It was not a long walk back—just a mile and a half—and yet in 1959, when they were young teenagers, and when it had taken the family sixteen hours to move all the furniture, the trip to the new house in a new neighborhood had seemed such a voyage, such an adventure.

Now they could see, as they walked, that it had been merely a short trip that had changed nothing, for better or for worse—it was as if they had never moved at all.

X. Ramblin' Fever

A disease common among ironworkers—an itchy sensation called "ramblin' fever"—seemed to vibrate through the long steel cables of the bridge in the spring of 1964, causing a restlessness, an impatience, a tingling tension within the men, and many began to wonder: "Where next?"

Suddenly, the bridge seemed finished. It was not finished, of course—eight months of work remained—but all the heavy steel units were now linked across the sky, the most dangerous part was done, the challenge was dying, the pessimism and cold wind of winter had, with spring, been swept away by a strange sense of surety that nothing could go wrong: a punk named Roberts slipped off the bridge, fell toward the sea—and was caught in a net; a heavy drill was dropped and sailed down directly toward the scalp of an Indian named Joe Tworivers—but it nipped only his toes, and he grunted and kept walking.

The sight of the sixty four-hundred-ton units all hanging horizontally from the cables, forming a lovely rainbow of red steel across the sea from Staten Island to Brooklyn, was inspiring to spectators along the shore, but to the ironworkers on the bridge it was a sign that boredom was ahead. For the next phase of construction, referred to in the trade as "second-pass steel," would consist primarily of recrossing the entire span while lifting and inserting small pieces of steel into the structure—struts, grills, frills—and then tightening and retightening the bolts. When the whole span had been filled in with the finishing steel, and when all the bolts had been retightened, the concrete mixers would move in to pave the roadway, and next would come the electricians to string up the lights, and next the painters to cover the red steel with coats of silver.

And finally, when all was done, and months after the last ironworker had left the scene for a challenge elsewhere, the bridge would be opened, bands would march across, ribbons would be cut, pretty girls would smile from floats, politicians would make speeches, everyone would applaud— and the engineers would take all the bows.

And the ironworker would not give a damn. He will do his boasting in bars. And anyway, he will know what he has done, and he would some- how not feel comfortable standing still on a bridge, wearing a coat and tie, showing sentimentality.

In fact, for a long time afterward he will probably not even think much about the bridge. But then, maybe four or five years later, a sort of ram- blin' fever in reverse will grip him. It might occur while he is driving to another job or driving off to a vacation; but suddenly it will dawn on him that a hundred or so miles away stands one of his old boom towns and bridges. He will stray from his course, and soon he will be back for a brief visit: maybe it is St. Ignace, and he is gazing up at the Mackinac Bridge; or perhaps it's San Francisco, and he is admiring the Golden Gate; or perhaps (some years from now) he will be back in Brooklyn staring across the sea at the Verrazano-Narrows Bridge.

Today he will doubt the possibility, most of the boomers will, but by 1968 or '69 he probably will have done it: he may be in his big car coming down from Long Island or up from Manhattan, and he will be moving swiftly with all the other cars on the Belt Parkway, but then, as they ap- proach Bay Ridge, he will slow up a bit and hold his breath as he sees, stretching across his windshield, the Verrazano—its span now busy and alive with auto traffic, bumper-to-bumper, and nobody standing on the cables now but a few birds.

Then he will cut his car toward the right lane, pulling slowly off the Belt Parkway into the shoulder, kicking up dust, and motorists in the cars be- hind will yell out the window, "Hey, you idiot, watch where you're driving," and a woman may nudge her husband and say, "Look out, dear, the man in that car looks drunk."

In a way, she will be right. The boomer, for a few moments, will be under a hazy, heady influence as he takes it all in—the sights and sounds of the bridge he remembers—hearing again the rattling and clanging and Hard Nose Murphy's angry voice; and remembering, too, the cable-spinning and the lifting and Kelly saying, "Up on seven, easy now, easy"; and seeing again the spot where Gerard McKee fell, and where the clamps slipped, and where the one-thousand-pound casting was dropped; and he will know that on the bottom of the sea lies a treasury of rusty rivets and tools.

The boomer will watch silently for a few moments, sitting in his car, and then he will press the gas pedal and get back on the road, joining the other cars, soon getting lost in the line, and nobody will ever know that the man in this big car one day had knocked one thousand rivets into that bridge, or had helped lift four hundred tons of steel, or that his name is Tatum, or Olson, or Iannielli, or Jacklets, or maybe Hard Nose Murphy himself.

Anyway, this is how, in the spring of 1964, Bob Anderson felt—he was a victim of ramblin' fever. He was itchy to leave the Verrazano job in Brooklyn and get to Portugal, where he was going to work on a big new suspension span across the Tagus River.

"Oh, we're gonna have a ball in Portugal," Anderson was telling the other ironworkers on his last working day on the Verrazano-Narrows Bridge. "The country is absolutely beautiful, we'll have weekends in Paris . . . you guys gotta come over and join me."

"We will, Bob, in about a month," one said.

"Yeah, Bob, I'll sure be there," said another. "This job is finished as far as I'm concerned, and I got to get the hell out. . . ."

On Friday, June 19, Bob Anderson shook hands with dozens of men on the Verrazano and gave them his address in Portugal, and that night many of them joined him for a farewell drink at the Tamaqua Bar in Brooklyn. There were about fifty ironworkers there by 10 p.m. They gathered around four big tables in the back of the room, drank whiskey with beer chasers, and wished Anderson well. Ace Cowan was there, and so was John Drilling (he had just been promoted back to pusher after three hard months in Whitey Miller's gang), and so were several other boomers who had worked with Anderson on the Mackinac Bridge in Michigan between 1955 and 1957.

Everyone was very cheerful that night. They toasted Anderson, slapping him on the back endlessly, and they cheered when he promised them a big welcoming binge in Portugal. There was reminiscing and joke-telling, and they all remembered with joy the incidents that had most infuriated Hard Nose Murphy, and they recalled, too, some of the merry moments they had shared nearly a decade ago while working on the Mackinac. The party went on beyond midnight, and then, after a final farewell to Anderson, one by one they staggered out.

Prior to leaving for Lisbon, Bob Anderson, with his wife, Rita, and their two children, packed the car and embarked on a brief trip up to St. Ignace, Michigan. It was in St. Ignace, during the Mackinac Bridge job, that Bob Anderson had met Rita. She still had parents and many friends there, and that was the reason for the trip—that and the fact that Bob Anderson wanted to see again the big bridge upon which he had worked between 1955 and 1957.

A few days later he was standing alone on the shore of St. Ignace, gazing up at the Mackinac Bridge from which he had once come bumping down along a cable, clinging to a disconnected piece of catwalk for 1,800 feet, and he remembered how he'd gotten up after, and how everybody then had said he was the luckiest boomer on the bridge.

He remembered a great many other things, too, as he walked quietly at the river's edge. Then, ten minutes later, he slowly walked back toward his car and drove to his mother-in-law's to join his wife, and later they went for a drink at the Nicolet Hotel bar, which had been boomers' headquarters nine years ago and where he had won that thousand dollars shooting craps in the men's room.

But now, at forty-two years of age, all this was behind him. He was very much in love with Rita, his third wife, and he had finally settled down with her and their two young children. They both looked forward to the job in Portugal—and the possibility of tragedy there never could have occurred to them.

In Portugal while looking for a house, the Andersons stayed at the Tivoli Hotel in Lisbon. Bob Anderson's first visit to the Tagus River Bridge was on June 17. At that time the men were working on the towers, and the big derricks were hoisting up fifty-ton steel sections that would fit into the towers. Anderson apparently was standing on the pier when, as one fifty-ton unit was four feet off the ground, the boom buckled and suddenly the snapped hoisting cable whipped against him with such force that it sent him crashing against the pier, breaking his left shoulder and cracking open his skull, damaging his brain. Nobody saw the accident, and the bridge company could only guess what had happened. Bob Anderson remained unconscious all day and night and two months later he was still in a coma, unable to recognize Rita or to speak. His booming days were over, the doctors said.

When word got back to the Verrazano in Brooklyn, it affected every man on the bridge. Some were too shocked to speak, others swore angrily and bitterly. John Drilling and other boomers rushed off the bridge and called Rita in Portugal, volunteering to fly over. But she assured them there was nothing they could do. Her mother had arrived from St. Ignace and was helping care for the children.

For the boomers, it was a tragic ending to all the exciting time in New York on the world's longest suspension span. They were proud of Bob Anderson. He had been a daring man on the bridge, and a charming man off it. His name would not be mentioned at the Verrazano-Narrows dedication, they knew, because Anderson—and others like him—were known only within the small world of the boomers. But in that world they were giants, they were heroes never lacking in courage or pride—men who remained always true to the boomer's code: going wherever the big job was

. . . and lingering only a little while . . .
then off again to another town, another bridge . . .
linking everything but their lives.

Afterword

Fifty years after its clamorous and life-altering completion, the Verrazano-Narrows Bridge is no longer an object of fascination or anxiety to the residents of Staten Island. Here a new generation of residents has casually grown up with the bridge, and they accept it as the highlight of their horizon, their route to economic development, their link to the mammoth mosaic that is Brooklyn and to the waterfront towers of Manhattan, which Truman Capote once described as a "diamond iceberg."

Although Staten Island's population of 470,000 (in a city of more than 8 million) is now nearly double that of the pre-bridge figure, and although the island's once sprawling farmlands have disappeared along with the country roads through which motorists once moved bumpily past herds of grazing cattle, a provincial atmosphere still prevails here.

Along tree-shaded residential streets, one sees row upon row of single-family white frame houses with shuttered windows and roadside mailboxes and tidy lawns with poles bearing American flags, which were on display long before the nationwide proliferation of patriotism prompted by the terrorist attacks of 2001.

Some of these houses and apartments are now occupied by retired ironworkers, including eighty-three-year-old Dick Brady, who began in the 1950s on several skyscrapers between midtown Park Avenue and downtown near Wall Street, and then in the early 1960s became one of the "pushers" on the Verrazano. In 1980, after returning to the bridge to assist with maintenance work, he was head-butted by a beam and gradually developed balance problems that terminated his career on high steel. While he misses the camaraderie and pride that had always accompanied his chosen profession, he is pleased that his fifty-two-year-old son, Paul, continues to make a living as an ironworker.

Among other retirees on Staten Island are seventy-two-year-old James McKee and seventy-year-old John McKee, two Brooklyn-born older brothers of the late Gerard McKee, who fell to his death off the Verrazano in 1963, at the age of nineteen. The McKee brothers' father was an ironworker who became permanently disabled after a collapsed crane sent him crashing to the ground two stories below. But both James and John McKee avoided career-ending incidents and labored as ironworkers well into their middle years.

Recently, one of James McKee's longtime friends, a "walking boss" at the new World Trade Center, invited him to Manhattan to watch the men as they began constructing the 408-foot antenna spire and broadcast facility that tops the 104-story Tower 1.

"Com' on, Jimmy," said his friend, "you can ride up with us in the elevator. It'll be like old times."

"No thanks," replied James McKee. "I've had my day. But I'm really tempted." If James McKee had joined the group he might have been introduced to a muscular and handsome twenty-nine-year-old ironworker named Joe Spratt, who had recently joined the crew. Joe Spratt's late grandfather and father, both ironworkers, had been close friends for years with the McKee family.

The grandfather, Eugene Spratt, had been a strapping dark-haired aspiring prizefighter who was born in Brooklyn in 1917. After getting married, he supported himself and his wife (and later their five children) as a welder in the Brooklyn Navy Yard. There he became a member of Local 40, the ironworkers' union based in Manhattan, and soon he was part of a high-altitude team performing a variety of tasks at such sites as the Manhattan Bridge in the 1950s, the Verrazano-Narrows Bridge in the 1960s, and the original Twin Towers in the 1970s, being joined there by dozens of other Verrazano veterans, including the McKee brothers and Edward Iannielli, who had briefly clung to, and then lost hold of, the two-hundred-pound body of Gerard McKee on the Verrazano span in 1963.

Hardly any of the Verrazano alumni took much pride in constructing the first Twin Towers, being appalled by the lightness of the floor beams they were directed to connect, the lack of interior support columns, the seeming fragility of the entire construction, and the hasty pace they were instructed to follow in adding to the skyline two tubular towers that suggested from afar a pair of elongated bird cages.

"Flimsy" was how Iannielli had characterized the construction to me during one of our later meetings; and "flimsy" was also the word used by Ronald O. Hamburger, a member of a team of structural engineers assessing the performance of the World Trade Center during the terrorist attacks, the ensuing fires, and ultimately the demolition. "The floor trusses were relatively flimsy . . . the trusses just fell apart." It was pointed out by other engineers that the buildings were about 90 percent "air," designed to achieve the utmost in rentable floor space and flexibility, unencumbered by columns, explaining why the rubble in the wake of the collapse was only a few stories high.

But when I recently spoke about the new World Trade Center to young Joe Spratt—his grandfather had died in 2000, and his father was killed in a boating accident during the summer of 1998, when Joe was thirteen—there was only approval and praise for what has replaced the fallen buildings.

"I cannot comment on the 'old' Twin Towers," he told me after work one evening in early 2014, "but I do know the new Tower 1 is built extremely strong. There is a cement core that runs through the center of the entire building. All the steel and iron is large and with short spans. The entire outside columns and beams are completely welded together. So it is basically one solid structure. Everyone on the job, including the old timers, are extremely proud at how this building was built and designed, making it one of the strongest in the world. Some of these older men had helped to clean up the mess after the 9/11 disaster, and so this new building holds special meaning for them."

Joe Spratt is a blue-eyed, auburn-haired bachelor who stands five-ten and weighs 200 pounds. He lives in a rented apartment in Long Beach, New York, just south of Long Island, and he has a girlfriend who teaches kindergarten on the island. He said he dropped out of college after only a year because he could no longer resist the allure of becoming an ironworker. Yes, it was part of his family tradition, he conceded, but he also felt singularly qualified for this difficult and risky occupation because of his physical stamina and competitive nature. He had been the captain of his high school's football and wrestling teams, and he believed that "this translates very well to ironwork—being determined, being in shape, and, this is particularly true of football, knowing how to function as a team."

After Joe Spratt had worked for six months at low-level tasks at the World Trade Center, he was assigned to become a fill-in with a raising gang on the roof of Tower 1, where it was constructing the communications ring and the antenna.

"We took about half of the antenna pieces off a barge in the Hudson River," Spratt recalled. "Everything had to come in at night because transportation had been shut down in the streets. I was really lucky and proud to be part of that process, and finally to be working with ironworkers at the very top of the antenna. The total height of the building is 1,776 feet. Pretty amazing. I doubt I'll ever be up that high again in my career."

Spratt said that having little or no fear of heights (he claims to have none) is what is unique about being an ironworker. When high in the air, he says he feels special. When on the ground, he is part of the masses. He rides an early-morning train from Long Island into Manhattan, sitting among multitudes of passengers who, in most cases, will be spending the day indoors doing nothing more strenuous than pressing their fingers upon keyboards. But in the train he does not feel detached from these people. Like them, he sits reading a newspaper, or navigating his smartphone, or relaxing with his head tilted back against the seat with his eyes closed.

Except for being more casually dressed than a majority of the passengers—he wears blue jeans, a windbreaker, and a pair of rubber-soled leather boots without heels (which ironworkers favor as a precaution against tripping while walking on beams)—he sees himself as a common daily commuter. He moves with the crowd along the platform, shoulder to shoulder, after the train has pulled into Pennsylvania Station. Then he follows many of these passengers into a subway car headed downtown. Ten minutes later he has ascended into the open air, crosses Vesey Street, and heads toward 1 World Trade Center.

There he submits his vinyl identity card to a security guard for scanning. Seeing other ironworkers gathered behind a gate, he approaches and greets them, and then accompanies them into an outdoor elevator that slowly rises along one side of the building to a level beyond ninety stories. Now he no longer feels that he is a common commuter but rather a citizen of the stratosphere. Within himself he senses a surge of increased energy and enthusiasm for this job, and there are also his fraternal feelings toward his companions as they step out of the elevator and take turns climbing a ladder that takes them to the roof.

The floor of the roof is covered with corrugated iron decking, and, as he moves ahead into the wind and sunlight—ironworkers do not work on rainy days, nor are they paid when not working—his face is sometimes lost in the shadows cast by the vertical columns and swooping cranes that surround him. Noise is everywhere, coming from the machines and the shouting voices of the various foremen. Joe Spratt takes his place within the five-man raising gang.

His role is to assist the two men who stand above him on a beam, holding wrenches and pry bars; these men are called "connectors." Spratt is filling in as a "hooker-on," and his job is to rig up a section of steel that is being hoisted in the direction of the connectors by the crane's cables. Spratt is assisted in this task by a "tag line man," and standing nearby is the "signal man," who communicates through a phone to the man sitting in the crane. The crane operator is sometimes working in the blind and is dependent on the signal man for directions. The signal man is also the foreman's extra eyes while the latter is busy organizing the efforts of the "bolt up gang," who, after the steel is hung in place by the connectors, will penetrate it with bolts and use various guns to tighten the bolts to specification.

From his vantage point, except on foggy days, Spratt can see in the distance the accomplishments of ironworkers who had performed at close to these heights in previous years. As he turns toward the harbor, glancing at the cables and seventy-story towers of the Verrazano-Narrows Bridge, he thinks of his grandfather Eugene. As he faces uptown, toward the sixty-eight-story Penn Plaza building, which overlooks Madison Square Garden, he recalls the work done there years ago by his father, Joseph, and also his late uncle, Bobby, his father's older brother. His co-workers at the World Trade Center have other men in mind when they look upon skyscrapers and other towering structures. For everyone in this occupation, the skyline of New York is a family tree.

All of the Spratt men were members of Local 40, and it was young Joe's uncle, Bobby, who first escorted him as a recruit to the Raymond R. Corbett Building, the ten-story granite union headquarters at 451 Park Avenue South, between Thirtieth and Thirty-first Streets.

As an ironworker, Ray Corbett, who died in 1992 at seventy-seven, climbed to the top of the Empire State Building to help erect the television tower. In the lobby of the union's headquarters there is a large mural portraying men in hardhats strolling across beams extended high over midtown Manhattan. A smaller mural in the entryway shows Ray Corbett dangling in the air next to a fellow ironworker—his father, Pat. In the executive offices are hung several framed photos of other ironworkers, young and old. In his later years, Ray Corbett served as the union's business manager, and, in early December of 1963, he led a strike against the bridge's management at the Verrazano because it refused to install safety nets beneath the span. The four-day strike ended after management relented, and this decision subsequently saved the lives of fallen workers.

One nineteen-year-old apprentice on the Verrazano, Robert Walsh, who was twice saved after falling into nets, would gradually take over Corbett's title as Local 40's business manager. Walsh is now sixty-nine. He is a tall, broad-shouldered, sandy-haired figure who is not only the son of an ironworker but the father and grandfather of present-day ironworkers.

Walsh's main responsibility these days is finding jobs for his union's 1,300 members.

"With us it's either feast or famine," said Walsh's associate, Danny Doyle, an ex-ironworker and now the business agent.

An old ironworker named Lemuel Tatum once told me, "So many of us were looking for work during the Depression that, if a man fell off a building, somebody else was rushing to apply for the job before the other man hit the ground."

But jobs are currently plentiful in New York, Robert Walsh told me early in 2014. He said that among the big projects ahead will be the renovation of the upper deck of the Verrazano. The steel will be shipped in from China, but Americans will do the work.

Earning excellent hourly wages, workers may anticipate what Danny Doyle calls a "feast," perhaps considerable sums, if the workers are not cursed by abnormal amounts of bad weather, and if they are blessed with an abundance of overtime. But as Doyle's boss, Robert Walsh, emphasizes: What mainly motivates ironworkers is not money. "With us it is mostly about pride," Walsh said. "It is about being part of a proud tradition of men who love what they do, and love doing it well."

This is essentially what I have heard expressed by dozens of ironworkers that I have met during the past half-century—such individuals as young Joe Spratt ("We love building something from nothing."); Danny Montour, the boomer from an Indian reservation in Canada who saw New York as the "City of Man-Made Mountains"; and John Drilling, an Oakland-born boomer who told me in 1962, while working on the Verrazano-Narrows, "We may be the only hard workers left in this country. If I was wealthy, I wouldn't do this for a living. I would do it for a hobby."

Retired in Florida, but still thinking of themselves as ironworkers, are the three surviving sons of the late Lemuel Tatum: eighty-nine-year-old Larry Tatum; eighty-five-year-old Leonard Tatum; and seventy-two-year-old Ronald Tatum, who sadly retired a decade ago after fifty years on the job. (Their brother, Bruce, fell to his death in 1963 prior to the completion of the PanAm, on Park and Forty-fifth Street, a building that in 1992 was renamed MetLife.)

Another reluctant retiree, who now resides in Mystic, Connecticut, is Bruce Edgecomb—who nearly lost his job as an apprentice on the Verrazano in 1964 after someone in management accused him of celebrating July 4th by shooting fireworks into the cables. Bruce was successfully defended by his father, Barney Edgecomb, a veteran ironworker who knew the right people, although Bruce was sent down to work for a while in the steelyard, where he was supervised by his father's longtime friend, Lemuel Tatum. Bruce also got to know Lemuel's young son, Ronald, and they both hung out with a stalwart and friendly then-fifty-eight-year-old worker who maintained a welding machine and operated a crane. He was the ex-heavyweight champion of the world, James J. Braddock.

"Oh, if I had a chance, I'd be back on the job tomorrow," said Bruce Edgecomb, now sixty-nine, during a recent phone interview. Making light of his work-related leg injuries, back injuries, and the fact that he needs hip replacements, he mentioned only, "What fun we all had."

More than a half-century ago in Brooklyn, in a neighborhood along the western shoreline called Bay Ridge, the proposed construction of the Verrazano-Narrows Bridge was a loathsome idea to at least seven thousand residents. They were the occupants of eight hundred homes and small businesses that were slated to be destroyed in order to make room for an expressway leading toward the toll gates. In a series of street protests people displayed signs reading, WHO NEEDS THE BRIDGE? but they were unable to prevent its arrival nor the destruction of their dwellings, and their forced relocation.

Now, in 2014, memories of the late-1950s protests are retained by only a dwindling few. But one young resident of the area, born in 1962 and named David Capobianco, grew up appreciating the Brooklyn tower of the bridge as "the monument of our neighborhood"—and its looming presence, dominating the skyline wherever he turned, inspired him to one day achieve great things as an engineer.

Currently fifty-one, David Capobianco is overseeing the construction of the new four-tower Tappan Zee Bridge. Its 3.2-mile span, extending over the Hudson River and linking the towns of Tarrytown in Westchester County and South Nyack in Rockland County, will be finished in a few years and become the longest bridge in the state. It will also be the first bridge to make an appearance in New York since the completion of the Verrazano-Narrows a half-century ago.

PART II

The Restless Voyeurs

1-

Journalists are restless voyeurs who see ~~for~~ *they will not*
the warts on the world, the imperfections in *pub —*
people and places. Gloom is their game, the *— and there is*
spectacle their passion--normality their nemesis. *no title the*
most news is
The sane scene that is much of life, the great *staged of press—*
portions of the planet unmarked by madness are *reported or*
largely ignored as ~~nhn~~ front pages announce riots *there.*
and raids, crumbling countries and sinking ships, *They are important*
~~bankers banished to~~ Rio and burning Buddhist nuns. *what are others —*
~~Through it all the journalist remains restless, and~~ *news is*
~~involved and uninvolved uninvolved.~~ *not news*

are not a
At 4 P.M. each day, precisely, not a minute
late, Clifton Daniel presides iover a conferenc
of editors in his conference room at The New Yor
Times. The circlular table in his seats , and *on the*
the chairs are Bank of England. Daniel is an *wall —*
Anglophile, having spent the happiest years as *M.E's bros*
a cofrespondent there; but now, at 54, he is
no longer reports on world affairs, but presides *Van Anda*
over the newspaper and sits in this big office.. *Jones*
It is a lovely office. The hair, the rug, which *Catledge*
he selected himself, is blue--. The offices
irreverent people in office insist that he got it to fix

When furnished or
doesnt remember
thinks : it is

not ...

The Kingdoms, the
Powers, and the Glories
of the *New York Times*

FROM *Esquire*, 1966

MOST JOURNALISTS ARE RESTLESS voyeurs who see the warts on the world, the imperfections in people and places. The sane scene that is much of life, the great portion of the planet unmarked by madness, does not lure them like riots and raids, crumbling countries and sinking ships, bankers banished to Rio and burning Buddhist nuns—gloom is their game, the spectacle their passion, normality their nemesis.

Journalists travel in packs with transferable tension and they can only guess to what extent their presence in large numbers ignites an incident, turns people on. For press conferences and cameras and microphones have become such an integral part of the happenings of the sixties that nobody today knows whether people make news or news makes people—Premier Ky in Vietnam, feeling no doubt more potent after his sixth magazine-cover story, challenges Red China; after police in New York raided the headquarters of young hoodlums, it was discovered that some gang leaders keep scrapbooks; in Baltimore, a day after the *Huntley-Brinkley Report* mentioned that the city had survived the summer without a race riot, there was a race riot.

When the press is absent, politicians have been known to cancel their speeches, civil-rights marchers to postpone their parades, alarmists to withhold their dire predictions. The troops at the Berlin Wall, largely ignored since Vietnam stole the headlines, coexist casually watching the girls go by. News, if unreported, has no impact; it might as well have not happened at all. Thus the journalist is the important ally of the ambitious, a lamplighter for stars. He is invited to parties, is courted and complimented, has easy access to unlisted telephone numbers and to many levels of life. He may send to America a provocative story of poverty in Africa, of tribal threats and turmoil—and then he may go for a swim in the Ambassador's pool.

A journalist will sometimes mistakenly assume that it is his charm, not his usefulness, that gains such privilege; but most journalists are realistic men not fooled by the game. They use as well as they are used. Still they are restless. Their work, instantly published, is almost instantly forgotten, and they must endlessly search for something new, must stay alive with bylines and not be scooped, must nurture the insatiable appetites of newspapers and networks, the commercial cravings for new faces, fashions, fads, feuds; they must not worry when news seems to be happening because they are there, nor must they ponder the possibility that everything they have witnessed and written in their lifetime may someday occupy only a few lines in the plastic textbooks of the twenty-first century.

And so each day, unhaunted by history, plugged into the *instant*, journalists of every creed, quality, and quirk report the news of the world as they see it, hear it, believe it, understand it. Then much of it is relayed through America, millions of words a minute, some thousands of which penetrate a large fourteen-floor fact factory on Forty-third Street off Broadway, the New York Times Building, where each weekday afternoon at four o'clock—before it is fit to print, before it can influence the State Department and perplex the president and irritate David Merrick and get the ball rolling on Wall Street and heads rolling in the Congo—it is presented by *Times* editors seated around a conference table to one man, the managing editor, Clifton Daniel.

He is a most interesting-looking man but difficult to describe because the words that quickly catch him best, initially, seem entirely inappropriate for any man who is a man. But the impression persists. Clifton Daniel is almost lovely. It is his face, which is long and pale and soft and dominated by large dark eyes and very long lashes, and his exquisitely groomed, wavy gray hair that makes him seem almost lovely. His suits are very Savile Row, his hands and nails immaculate, his voice a soft, smooth blend of North Carolina, where he was born in a tiny tobacco town, and England, where he came of age as a journalist and squire of fashionable women and was sometimes referred to as the Sheik of Fleet Street.

London in those days, during and just after World War II, was a great city for young American journalists. There was the dramatic story of the blackout and the bombing raids, of the Allied counterattack and triumph. The Americans and British in London shared a warmth and common purpose; British society was democratic at every level, and the image of American correspondents, influenced to a degree by the presence of such eminent ones as Edward R. Murrow, was highly glamorous. If an American, particularly a well-tailored bachelor, also possessed, as did Clifton Daniel, a certain formality and reserve and understated charm—Tory manners that in Daniel's case were partly cultivated out of a small-town Southern boy's shyness—then London could be an even more responsive city; and for Daniel it was.

He was sought out by London hostesses, was often seen escorting distinguished women to the theater and ballet, and he generally avoided the men's clubs for the drawing-room scene where, sometimes in the company of Bea Lillie and Noel Coward, Margot Fonteyn and Clarissa Spencer-Churchill, who later married Anthony Eden, he could listen to the latest gossip about politics and people as he had many years before when he worked behind the fountain of his father's drugstore in Zebulon.

Zebulon is a quiet little town built up along the sides of a road to Raleigh in the bright leaf–tobacco region of North Carolina, a town with three traffic lights, five policemen, three Protestant churches, and about eighteen hundred people who live mostly in white frame houses and know just about everything there is to know about one another. They are friendly people who do their shopping along the one main street, and many of them stop in at Daniel's drugstore on the corner to catch up on the latest, have a Coke, and say hello to Elbert Clifton Daniel, Sr., a pharmacist in his eighties whose facial features, particularly his eyes, strongly resemble his son's, although his gray wavy hair is shorter and his clothes far less conservative.

Mr. Daniel will sometimes appear at his drugstore wearing a pair of formal gray-striped morning trousers and over them a brown double-breasted jacket, and under it a blue striped shirt and pale polka-dot bow tie, and also a brown hat, black shoes, a brown cane; all of which, on him, looks fine. He is thought of as the town's most distinguished living landmark, being the first man in Zebulon to have a telephone, and nearly everyone is very fond of him, although there are a few, very few, who find him a bit patronizing at times. Twice he served as mayor, first getting the city to put in running water, then to replace the kerosene streetlamps with electric lights. He had a brief fling at owning the Vakoo movie theater, and he once merchandised his own brand of liver pills and a diarrhea cure. In the back of his drugstore he usually keeps a bottle of bourbon for the nourishment of his friends and himself.

The marriage of his son to Margaret Truman in 1956 permitted him to become acquainted with Harry Truman, and the two men have gotten along splendidly ever since, Mr. Truman once telling Mr. Daniel: "Hell, you did just as well as I did—you just stayed down in your little town helping the poor people, and I went up and mixed with those rich bastards."

Had it not been for an attack of appendicitis in 1902, when Mr. Daniel was about eighteen years old, he might have never escaped the rugged farm life of his father, his grandfather, and nearly all the other Daniel kin; but the illness enabled him to meet a young doctor from Raleigh who later encouraged him to go into the drug business. And in 1905, after borrowing some money from his grandfather, Zachariah G. Daniel, an illiterate but industrious tobacco farmer who had migrated from England, and after acquiring a drug "permit" from the doctor friend, Clifton Daniel, Sr. bought an interest in his first drugstore.

He practiced pharmacy on his permit until 1911 when he supplemented his training with schooling at Greensboro. In the same year, in his drugstore one day, he saw seated at the counter with other girls, sipping a soda, Miss Elvah Jones. She was the daughter of a tobacco warehouseman, had attended college at Raleigh, having once been the May Queen, and she was very pretty. He quickly courted her and in December of that year, at her grandmother's house in the next county, they were married, and during the following September was born their only child, the future managing editor of the *New York Times*, Elbert Clifton Daniel, Jr.

The boy got all the attention and affection that an only child normally gets, and he did most of the right things. He had his first tooth at nine months, was walking within a year, but carefully, revealing a caution that would always be with him, and he displayed a premature aversion to dirt.

There was nothing of the farmer in him. He was like his mother in his quiet manner, neat about his clothing, clean and precise. His father later worried a bit when he preferred to stay indoors much of the time, sprawled on the rug reading books, but the boy was very bright in school and obedient at home, and after school he helped out in the drugstore and also sold *Grit* magazine around town, saving his pennies, and there was really nothing the father could justifiably complain about the boy.

The drugstore in those days, much more than now, was a center of social life. The deputy sheriff and the police chief hung out there, as did the farmers talking about the price of tobacco and cotton, and the visiting politicians would drop in to shake hands. There was a piano in the front of the place and, when he was not grinding ice for drinks or delivering things on his bicycle, Tad Chavis, the Negro man, was usually playing ragtime on it, although he was sometimes competing with a loud and scratchy rendition of "In a Little Spanish Town" blaring from the Edison phonograph that stood not far from the piano. There was no radio in the drugstore then, and so young Clifton Daniel, Jr. would occasionally slip across the street to the rear of a feedstore to hear the radio news and baseball scores, and it was there, too, that he remembers hearing about Lindbergh's flight. He never stayed away too long, however, for the drugstore was busy, and one of his jobs was to help with the curb service, thereby getting to know many of the pretty girls who sat out at the tables, and then he would be back inside taking telephone calls for the doctors, or listening to the deputy sheriff's account of some local brawl, and one night Daniel saw walking into the drugstore a man whose throat was cut from ear to ear. Daniel called a doctor. He also called the *Zebulon Record.*

He had been sending news items into the paper all summer, earning five dollars a week; the drugstore, the great clearinghouse for local gossip and news, was a perfect post for a young reporter. When he returned to high school in the fall he continued to write news stories for the *Zebulon Record*, covering student activities and sports. He was never an athlete himself. Young Clifton Daniel had absolutely no ambitions to fulfill on the ball field, and he was becoming a little deaf in his left ear, and he also was on the frail side, although for a while he did some calisthenics in his bathroom at home. One morning, however, he leaned over too far and slipped and broke a front tooth against the bathtub. This ended his physical-culture program for a while, and he sought to satisfy his ego by describing the actions of others, by getting his stories published, seeing his name in the paper. Sometimes, when writing a story that was a collection of local news items, he would separate each item with a small design bearing his initials—ECD—and a few people in town thought this was a bit much.

There was something a little cute and fancy about young Daniel, they said, those few who perhaps were put off by his formality in this so informal town. They saw him developing, too early, a sense of self and a manner that seemed mildly patronizing. But the girls whom he dated liked him very much, liked not only his fine clothes and politeness but also his respect for older people, especially his parents, and they liked the fact that he was the brightest boy in the class and voted the "best looking" in the Wakelon High School yearbook of 1929.

But the girls sensed that they did not have a chance with him, not from anything he said or did but from what he did not say or do. He did not get involved. He had plans, places to visit, things to do. And his first step away from Zebulon was Chapel Hill, home of the University of North Carolina, although now the Depression had begun and nobody had much money. The *Zebulon Record* was offering a year's subscription for a fat hen or a bushel of potatoes. The bank cashier with whom E. C. Daniel, Sr. had always dealt advised against sending the boy to college, urging instead that he be trained to someday take over the drug business. But Mr. Daniel, ignoring the advice, began trading drug supplies for corn and chickens, and Mrs. Daniel dressed the chickens and made chicken-salad sandwiches which were sold in the drugstore for ten cents apiece, money to put toward her son's room and board at college. He himself had saved sixty-five dollars from his summer earnings, and so in the fall of 1929 Elbert Clifton Daniel, Jr. began his career as a college freshman.

In 1929 the *New York Times* was in the process of becoming, if it had not already become, the most important newspaper in the world. Its great publisher, Adolph Ochs, who in 1896 had purchased the *Times* and begun to revitalize it, was now ill, but his credo—"To give the news impartially, without fear or favor, regardless of any party, sect or interest involved"— was firmly rooted in his staff, and the news department was still under the direction of Ochs's brilliant managing editor, Carr Vattel Van Anda.

Van Anda was an austere and impersonal man, possessing a look that one of his reporters, Alva Johnston, described as a "death ray," and when a group of *Times*men petitioned Van Anda to put bylines on their stories he snapped, "The *Times* is not running a reporters' directory!" Bylines were the exception on the *Times* then, going mainly to the few star journalists like Edwin L. James, a flamboyant Virginian who would himself become the *Times*' managing editor in the thirties (and be succeeded in turn by two other Southerners: Turner Catledge in 1951, Clifton Daniel in 1964).

But if Carr Van Anda was not a popular folk hero with his staff, as Edwin L. James would become, he was nonetheless respected as few editors would be; for he was not only a superb newsman but also a scholar, a mathematical genius and a student of science and logic. It was he who pushed the *Times* toward its expanded coverage of the great feats in polar exploration and aviation, forming the foundation for the paper's portrait of the space age. He was the first editor to publicize Einstein— and once, in checking over a story about one of Einstein's lectures, discovered that the scientist had made an error in an equation. Van Anda, who read hieroglyphics, printed many stories of significant excavations, and one night, after examining under a magnifying glass the inscription of a four-thousand-year-old Egyptian tomb, he discovered a forgery, and this fact, later confirmed by Egyptologists, led to the conclusion that a young Pharoah, Tut-ankh-Amen, had been assassinated by a military chief named Horemheb. It was Van Anda who disputed the new *Titanic's* claim to being unsinkable and when the ship's radio went silent, after an emergency call for help, he deduced what had happened and drove his staff to get the story of the disaster that would be a world scoop. During World War I, Carr Van Anda, equipping himself with every available military map, charted the course of battle and he anticipated many future campaigns, getting his reporters there in advance, and the *Times*' coverage during that time was unparalleled.

By 1929, too, while Clifton Daniel attended classes on the North Carolina campus, rarely reading the *Times* and having no particular ambition to work for it, there were rising on the paper many young and talented and ambitious men with their own singular styles and ideas—some of which would find favor for years, and some of which, when Daniel would emerge thirty years later, would be in conflict with the *Times*, would in fact be the foundation for a quiet revolution within the paper, a revolution distinguished for its tactics and intrigue, and one of the few that the *Times* has failed to cover fully.

It is still going on today, though the dust now seems to be settling in the *Times*' third-floor newsroom, and two figures stand very tall and clear, both of them small-town Southern boys. Both are very different. Both are very smooth.

One is Turner Catledge, a smiling, charming six-footer, born sixty-five years ago in Ackerman, Mississippi. His younger ally, Daniel, is now fifty-four. Catledge spent his best years getting the power; Daniel may spend his using it.

Catledge is a whiskey-drinking, joke-telling, onetime political reporter in Washington who could have become a very successful politician. He rarely makes enemies, never makes deals he cannot get out of, never hits things head-on. He moves at oblique angles and shifts, but always with gentility and always guided by what he truly believes to be in the best interest of the *Times*. During Catledge's years as managing editor, from 1951 to 1964—he has since moved up to the newly created position of executive editor, where he is directly answerable only to the forty-year-old publisher, Arthur Ochs Sulzberger—the *New York Times* enjoyed its greatest glory and power; but at that time Catledge was engaged in an almost constant power struggle within the paper, a battle with many distinguished editors and reporters who, during those almost slipshod years after Van Anda left and Edwin James was managing editor, were able to take some power themselves.

It was not that Edwin L. (Jimmy) James, the dashing correspondent of World War I, the boulevardier and horseplayer, the favorite son of Adolph Ochs and Carr Van Anda, was a weak or naive man; it was rather that he was of journalism's old school, a freewheeling reporter who, as an administrator, became easily bored with much of the necessary trivia of the job. While James was managing editor, from 1932 until his death in 1951, the newspaper was becoming bigger, less manageable, expanding its coverage all over the nation and the world; and it was understandable, given James's nature, that other men of talent and ambition, men with their *own* ideas of what was best for the *Times*, would move in and stake claims. Thus the *Times*, in a sense, became splintered into little dukedoms, each duke having his loyal followers and his special territory to protect.

This was contrary to Catledge's concept; he was a believer in the political organization, a self-perpetuating and coordinated institution with unchallenged hard power at the top. The challenge facing Turner Catledge when he became managing editor then was what to do about the dukes.

Had he been on another publication the solution would have been simpler, but on the *Times* it is not easy to remove people, particularly people with some power, or people who might have secret alliances with the publisher or members of his family. *Times*men in key positions like to stay there, they fight to stay there, for employment on the *Times* is very prestigious—doors open elsewhere, favors are for the asking, important people are available, the world seems easier. Also, from the early days of Adolph Ochs, there had been a traditional delicacy toward faithful employees, and people with prestige on the staff were rarely humiliated. Many of the dukes, too, were valuable men who had made, and were still making, important contributions to the paper which, in addition, was a very successful enterprise, and many people saw no reason for change.

If Turner Catledge wished to carve his concept upon the paper, if he wished to stage a revolution and demote the dukes and attempt to bring the power back under the managing editor's office, he had better do it subtly. And he had better be lucky.

In 1929, however, Catledge was just starting out as a *Times* reporter, and Daniel was a college freshman, and many of those who would be affected by the future revolution—Arthur Krock and Lester Markel, James Reston and Drew Middleton, Theodore Bernstein and Harrison Salisbury and Thomas J. Hamilton and A. M. Rosenthal, and dozens more—were either not yet on the scene, or not yet making their move, or many years away from the challenge.

Most of what Clifton Daniel wanted out of college life, he got; and that which he did not get, he did not miss. He joined Phi Delta Theta fraternity, did well in class, wrote for *The Daily Tarheel*. He would have liked to become editor of the *Tarheel*, but not long after joining it he was fired for being, or for seeming to be, a bit cocky with a senior editor. And by the time he was reinstated to the *Tarheel* staff he was out of line for the editor's job.

He did become editor of the campus literary magazine, the *Carolina*, and was elected vice-president of the student body. He could have run for the presidency later but he declined because he had the notion— "somewhat presumptuous," he later conceded—that he was a newspaperman, and he believed that newsmen, in the interest of objectivity, should stay out of party politics and never become irretrievably committed to any one cause or person, a policy shared by nearly all journalists, although at a price. For this detachment from the world they observe robs them of a deeper experience that springs from involvement, and they sometimes become merely voyeurs who see much, feel little. They take death and disaster as casually as a dock strike, and they take for granted their right to publicize the weakness in others, to second-guess the Senate, to criticize other men's plays, but they nearly have to lay it on the line themselves. Of course if journalists become committed to a cause or a great figure they might become apologists or propagandists, flunkies for the famous. Clifton Daniel would know some journalists to whom this would happen, but it would never happen to him. He was always too sure of what he was, what he wanted, and was possibly assisted by a natural aloofness, perhaps even a lack of passion. If he ever made a compromise in his professional or private life, few people would know it, there would be no scandal, he would cover his tracks well.

After graduating from the University of North Carolina in 1933, and after a year on a small newspaper downstate, Clifton Daniel joined the Raleigh *News & Observer*. There between 1934 and 1937 he covered politics and crime, all sorts of assignments, and he met many interesting people, among them Katharine Cornell, the first famous actress he ever interviewed, and Thomas Wolfe, whose novel, *Look Homeward, Angel*, had been published only a few years before. Daniel also met Turner Catledge one day in Raleigh, but it was only a quick, casual meeting—remembered by Daniel, forgotten by Catledge—and the two would not meet again for a couple of years.

Catledge was then the bright young man on the *New York Times*. He was a member of the Washington bureau headed by Arthur Krock, the latter being a powerful duke with more autonomy on the *Times* staff than anyone except Lester Markel, the Sunday editor whose style would one day be likened to that of Louis XIV, The Sun King. Arthur Krock became the chief of the *Times*' Washington bureau in 1932, a propitious move at the time because Krock's predecessor, Richard V. Oulahan, had run a rather disorganized bureau in which reporters did as they pleased, and if three of them wished to cover the same assignment on a particular day, they did, and sometimes all three versions would be sent to New York and be printed.

Krock quickly converted the bureau into a coordinated team, *his* team, and the most ambitious member of the team was Turner Catledge. Catledge sometimes wrote four or six major stories a day, became an expert on tax law, developed new sources throughout Washington; and all this tremendous energy and ambition could have worked against him if he did not also possess a quality that would redeem him.

He had a wonderful way with men. Particularly older men. Particularly older men with power. This is a quality that perhaps cannot be learned but is inherent in certain rare young men who, partly because they are very bright and do not flaunt it, and partly because they are respectful and not privileged, confident but not *too* confident, attract the attention of older men, self-made men, and receive from these men much advice and help. The older men probably see something of themselves in these bright young men, something of what they were, or *think* they were at a similar age. And so they help the younger men up the ladder, feeling no threat because these younger men are also endowed with a fine sense of timing.

Turner Catledge had all this as no other young *Times*men would have it until the arrival in 1939 of James Reston, and it is not surprising that these two would become, in their mannered ways, rivals throughout the forties and fifties, and especially during the *Times'* showdown of the sixties.

One of the first important men to help Catledge was Herbert Hoover who, as Secretary of Commerce in 1927, was on a survey of the Mississippi River flood area; Catledge was there for the Memphis *Commercial Appeal.* Catledge had left his home state of Mississippi for Memphis in 1923, riding the rails with $2.07 in his pocket, and now four years later he had come into prominence as a newsman principally for his vivid reporting on the Mississippi flood. Hoover, an orphan who always admired initiative in young men, was so charmed by Catledge that he wrote a letter in his behalf to Adolph Ochs, publisher of the *New York Times.* It was not until 1929, however, after Hoover had been elected President, that the *Times* hired Catledge.

Arthur Krock also was much impressed with Catledge and by 1936, when Krock was fifty and Catledge thirty-five, Krock hinted that he did not intend to spend his whole life in Washington and that Catledge had the makings of an ideal successor as bureau chief. Catledge was very pleased but he still continued to call him "Mr. Krock," and was not encouraged to do otherwise, and this formality later stiffened a bit when Krock heard that President Roosevelt was also becoming enchanted with Turner Catledge. Krock disliked Roosevelt, and vice versa, due in part to Krock's turning against the New Deal after 1936, and due also to an episode prior to Roosevelt's inauguration in March of 1933. Roosevelt suspected Krock of attempting to act as an intermediary between someone else and Roosevelt on some action Roosevelt was being pressed to take on becoming President. Roosevelt felt that the other person did not have to go through Krock but could have come directly to the President-elect, and Roosevelt blamed Krock for offering to act as a go-between in an effort to establish himself in an important role.

So after the Democratic National Convention of 1936, possibly as a way of embarrassing Arthur Krock, President Roosevelt told Catledge to feel free to check out stories or acquire information directly from the President; in short, Roosevelt was offering a line of communication that Catledge should use on his own without going through Krock.

Catledge immediately felt uncomfortable and he went to Krock and told him about it, and he also told a very close friend on the United Press, Lyle Wilson. Catledge wanted first to let Krock know that he was not available for such double-dealing and he wanted some intimate friend to know the story, too, and he was lucky that he did. For Krock got the episode mixed up, or at least Catledge felt that he did, and Krock let the word get around that Catledge had been intrigued by Roosevelt's proposition. Catledge, backed by Lyle Wilson, was able to counter Krock's suspicion and to reiterate that, far from being intrigued, he was actually offended by Roosevelt's move, even frightened.

Roosevelt's antipathy toward Krock was actually aimed at others on the *Times* as well, including Arthur Hays Sulzberger who, following the death in 1935 of his father-in-law, Adolph Ochs, assumed the position as publisher. Roosevelt thought he had an opportunity to benefit by a less independent *Times* at the time of the settlement of Mr. Ochs's estate tax. Roosevelt expected that the Ochs family would be forced to go into the money market or sell some of its stock in the *Times* in order to raise the necessary funds.

But when the family got the money by the sale of some of its preferred stock, not its common stock, Roosevelt became very distressed, and he admitted as much to some of his confidants in the Senate. Some editors on the newspaper felt then, and feel now, that Roosevelt's resentment of the *Times* was based on nothing more complicated than the fact that he could not control it. Few active presidents actually believe in a free press—Truman did not, nor did Eisenhower nor Kennedy nor Johnson; nor do most newspaper publishers, including those at the *Times*, whenever their own personal stakes are involved, a fact discovered by any writer who has ever attempted to do a publisher's biography.

Turner Catledge, at any rate, never became the Washington bureau chief of the *New York Times*. Krock, who in 1936 was saying that he did not intend to spend his whole life in Washington, was still there thirty years later. In 1938, in fact, a year in which he had condemned the Roosevelt administration for "official favors surreptitiously extended to syndicated columnists who are sympathetic," Krock strangely got an exclusive interview with Roosevelt, for which he received the Pulitzer Prize. Catledge at the same time felt his career had stalled—he was hitting his head "against the bottom of Arthur Krock's chair," he once described it to a friend—and in the winter of 1941, at the age of forty, Catledge quit the *New York Times*. He left for Chicago to become chief correspondent and later editor-in-chief of the *Chicago Sun*. But even before he left, Krock telephoned Sulzberger in New York and told the publisher to keep the door open—Catledge would probably be back.

By 1941, Clifton Daniel had left Raleigh and was working for the Associated Press. He had come up to New York in the spring of 1937 but had been turned down by nearly all the dailies in New York except the *World-Telegram*, and he turned it down when the offer was only thirty-five dollars a week, ten dollars less than he had been making in Raleigh. His interview at the *Times* was short and he was not very disappointed about being rejected, later explaining: "I was conscious of the *New York Times*, although I did not read it religiously, and I recognized the dignity and importance of working for the *New York Times*, but I did not regard it as a place where I would particularly want to work."

The newsmen whose work he knew best in those days were either working on the afternoon papers or the *Herald-Tribune*—such writers as H. Allen Smith and Joseph Mitchell, the latter a 1929 graduate of the University of North Carolina who would become the great reporter on the *New Yorker* magazine. The *Times* had, as always, many fine reporters and almost no fine writers, one notable exception being Meyer Berger. But some on the *Times* were even not impressed with Berger, one being a night

City editor who, shaking his head, once said to Berger, "Mike, you'll never make a newspaperman."

So when the Associated Press offered Clifton Daniel fifty dollars a week he quickly accepted, and for the next three years, from 1937 through 1940, he worked for the AP bureaus in New York and Washington; in November of 1940, at the age of twenty-eight, his dark wavy hair already turning gray, he sailed to Switzerland for the AP on a ship whose passengers included Lady Jersey, a stunning blue-eyed blonde who had been married to the Earl of Jersey, and before that to a Chicago lawyer and to Cary Grant. She would later, after the war, marry a Polish RAF pilot, but in London during the war—a year or so after meeting Daniel on the ship—she and Daniel would become sufficiently well acquainted to cause their friends to speculate the two would some day marry. But Daniel then, and for many years afterward, was not deeply serious about anything except his work, and he knew, too, that if he wished to distinguish himself on the Associated Press it would require a total commitment on his part because the AP had working for it many talented and ambitious young men. There was Drew Middleton and Gladwin Hill and William White, to name a few who would be hired away by the *New York Times*, and there was also James Reston, who by 1939 had already left the AP's London bureau for the *Times*, and had begun to rocket up through the *Times*' hierarchy more quickly, more smoothly than had any young man before him or since.

In addition to his energy and his very lucid style of writing, Reston had the rare quality that Catledge had, a wonderful way with older men. One of the first men to take an interest in him was the former Governor of Ohio, James M. Cox, who owned a string of newspapers and who, in 1920, had run as the Democratic candidate for President. Reston as a young teenager had caddied for Cox at the Dayton Country Club. Reston's family, very poor and pious (his mother wanted him to become a preacher, which as a columnist he later became), had immigrated from Scotland when he was eleven years old. Undistinguished as a student, he neglected books for the golf course, and soon he was shooting in the seventies and winning tournaments and he could have become a professional. But his mother was opposed—"Make something of yourself"—and James Cox advanced him money to help him through the University of Illinois; upon graduating in 1932, Reston went to work on one of Cox's newspapers.

He was hired away in 1933 by Larry MacPhail for a job as traveling secretary for the Cincinnati Reds baseball team, and in 1934 he was writing sports for the Associated Press. By 1937 he was in London with the AP bureau covering sports in summer and the Foreign Office in winter. He was then twenty-eight, was married to a very bright and lively girl who had already had their first son, and soon Reston had caught the eye of Ferdinand Kuhn, the *New York Times*' bureau chief in London. By 1939 Reston was with the *Times*.

His colleagues in the London bureau remember Scotty Reston as a man who seemed to be fast at everything except at a typewriter. There, surrounded by his notes and several open books out of which he picked tidbits of sagacity, he slowly composed his thoughts and arranged his words as few newsmen ever take the time to do. Outside the office he was neither the life of the party nor a playboy: it was work and then home to his wife, Sally, of whom he was both proud and impressed. She was a Fulton from Sycamore, Illinois, a member of Phi Beta Kappa, the daughter of a lawyer, of whom Reston said, smiling, "I married above me."

In 1941, with Sally expecting their second child, and with the big political story shifting to Washington as the United States prepared to move into the war, Reston arranged a transfer to Mr. Krock's bureau. A year later Reston's book, *Prelude to Victory*, was published to rave reviews, and the next thing that his colleagues in London heard was that Scotty Reston had become assistant to the *Times*' publisher, Arthur Hays Sulzberger, and would accompany Mr. Sulzberger on a trip to the Soviet Union. That it was a very valuable trip, one that broadened the understanding of both men, there is no doubt; that the trip was a social success that brought the *Times*' publisher and his young star closer as men—this is debatable. For the interoffice word after the trip was that Reston, with his early-to-bed habits and his rigidly moral character, palled on Sulzberger, an extremely sophisticated man who drank well and had an eye for an ankle, and who, away from his work, knew the art of relaxation. Sulzberger never ceased being an admirer of Reston the journalist; but Reston the epicurean, the man to take long trips with: this was something else. For this there was only one man. Catledge.

Turner Catledge had returned to the *Times* in the spring of 1943. He had been unhappy in Chicago, despite the $26,500 salary, and returned to the *Times* for $12,000. In the fall of 1944, while scouting the political campaign in Fargo, North Dakota, Catledge received a telegram from Arthur

Hays Sulzberger asking him if he would be interested in taking a trip with the publisher to inspect the Pacific front. Catledge wired back his acceptance, and in November they began their 27,000-mile flight with a stop at San Francisco. They checked into the Mark Hopkins Hotel, went almost immediately to the Top of the Mark for a few drinks before dinner. They were seated at a comfortable divan, and through the big windows that surrounded them they could see the panorama of the north side of the city, the neck of San Francisco Bay with the ships coming and going, and to the left, the Golden Gate Bridge.

They ordered a Scotch, then a second round. On the third round Sulzberger proposed that they be "doubles." Then they ordered two more "doubles" and continued to talk about everything—the *Times*, the San Francisco landscape, the *Times*, women, the *Times*. They ordered still another round of "doubles." When the waiter brought them, Sulzberger asked, "Are you sure these are doubles?" The waiter said, "Am I sure? You've drunk practically a bottle already."

They had a few more rounds and then they stood up to go to dinner. But before they left, Arthur Hays Sulzberger looked at Catledge, then extended his hand, saying, "Well, you pass."

In January 1945, Turner Catledge was named assistant managing editor, second in command to Edwin L. James. The other editors were neither surprised nor disappointed; none had regarded themselves as likely successors to James, except possibly Bruce Rae, a fine reporter who had become an assistant managing editor. But Rae made the mistake one day of sitting in James's chair when the managing editor was out ill. When James heard about it, he was furious.

Where one sits in the *Times*' newsroom is not a casual matter. Young reporters of no special status are generally assigned to sit near the back of the room, close to the Sports department; and as the years go by and people die and the young reporter becomes more seasoned and not so young, he is moved up closer to the front. But he must never move on his own initiative. There was one bright reporter who, after being told that he would help cover the labor beat, cleaned out his desk near the back of the room and moved up five rows into an empty desk vacated by one of the labor reporters who had quit. The recognition of the new occupant a few days later by an assistant City editor resulted in a reappraisal of the younger reporter's assets, and within a day he was back at his old desk; within a year or so he was out of the newspaper business.

Clifton Daniel, in February of 1944, resigned from the Associated Press in London and was hired by the *New York Times* on the recommendation of the *Times'* London bureau chief, Raymond Daniell, who is no relation. Raymond Daniell had been a first-rate *Times* reporter since 1928, reporting on the Scottsboro case and Huey Long's rise to power, the sharecropper disputes in Arkansas and coal-miner troubles in Kentucky. He had been in Mexico City in 1939 but, as the European war spread, he was quickly reassigned to London where, in 1940, his quarters at Lincoln's Inn were shattered by bombs and he and his colleagues moved the *Times* bureau into the Savoy Hotel, where they also lived. Since London time is five hours ahead of New York, the staff usually wrote until dawn while bombs shook the city; they slept through the afternoons, raids or no raids, and then after their customary round of martinis they were back at work on what were called "inraids" and "outraids"—the "inraids" being the German attacks on Great Britain, the "outraids" being the retaliation by the RAF.

When Raymond Daniell first became aware of the AP reporter with the similar name, he did not particularly like him, especially his looks. A little too smooth and suave. And this first impression was fortified by other reporters' observations about Clifton Daniel: he seemed haughty, he never removed his jacket in the office, he was the only newspaperman they had ever known who had lapels on his vests—and they made many other points about his clothes and his hair, as reporters would continue to do for years, even speculating in 1956 that Clifton Daniel owned more suits than Harry Truman ever sold.

But Raymond Daniell dug more deeply into the character of the man. And he learned that Clifton Daniel was not only a very fast and facile writer, but had often been put in charge of running the AP's London bureau during its most hectic hours and had always functioned calmly and efficiently; furthermore Daniel was known for his loyalty to the AP bureau chief and was not the sort who would ever overstep his boundaries or attempt to take over.

So Ray Daniell offered him a job and Daniel accepted. But first, taking some time off, he visited New York where a rather unusual thing happened that nearly cost him his job on the *New York Times*. Daniel had been invited to deliver a short speech about wartime London to a luncheon gathering of The Dutch Treat Club and, noticing the servicemen in the audience, he proceeded with anecdotes that he thought the G.I.'s might enjoy. He gave one vivid description of an American colonel falling into a fountain during the blackout, and he also told the servicemen that if they got to London they need not worry about women; there were plenty of girls on the streets, Daniel said, and they were easy to pick up.

Seated in the audience, becoming very indignant and barely suppressing his rage, was General Julius Ochs Adler, a high executive on the *Times* and a member of the ruling family. This profane and irreverent newspaperman was not *Times* material, General Adler declared later at the *Times* office. And it took a great deal of persuasion on the part of more tolerant *Times*men to get General Adler to withdraw his objection and give Daniel a chance. Daniel did well for the *Times* in London. Night after night he sat among his colleagues in the Savoy or in the field, writing stories that would carry his byline the next day on Page One.

On a single day in November, riding in a jeep behind the advancing First Army, Clifton Daniel visited three countries and filed news stories from each—Eupen, Belgium; Aachen, Germany; and Vaals, the Netherlands. Then, in March of 1945, he was in Paris watching as "the big, dirty, green trucks speed along the Rue La Fayette, their heavy tires singing on the cobblestones and their canvas tops snapping in the winter wind. The men in the back," Daniel wrote, "are tired and cramped after eleven hours on the road. The last wisecrack was made a hundred miles back. But one of them peers out, sees the name of the street and says, 'La Fayette, we're here.' The truck growls to a halt . . . The men dismount, a little stiff at first, light up cigarettes and start looking. They inspect the cornices of the Opera House, watch the crowds swirling past the Galeries Lafayette and eye the passing girls—always the girls . . ."

By spring, Daniel was back in London describing the city as the blackout restrictions were lifted, but before he could become adjusted to the light and tranquility he was sent to North Africa and back to the sound of gunfire and rioting; then from Egypt he went to Iran, arriving in Tabriz with two other journalists hours ahead of the Iranian Army that was to take over the city from a collapsing Soviet-backed Azerbaijanian rebel regime. As Daniel and the two others rode into town they were greeted by thousands of villagers lined along the road, and several sheep were sacrificed in their honor. The ceremony, the highest honor that a Persian can pay, consisted of beheading a sheep on one side of the road as the traveler approaches and carrying the head to the other side of the road; the traveler then passes between the body and the head.

The exotic sights and sounds, the headline makers and headhunters from the Middle East to Great Britain—this was Daniel's world for the next seven years, although now, in 1966, all those events and faces are, if not forgotten, rarely remembered by anyone except those who were there, like Daniel, watching twenty years ago in Dhahran as a fat roasted hump of young camel was set before King Ibn Saud; listening at midnight from his hotel in Jerusalem as the troops below with rifles shuffled through the sloping street near Zion Square; dancing and dining in Cairo at Shepheard's with a pretty English girl when King Farouk arrived and asked Daniel and the girl to join him for a drink and a discussion about things that now mean little. Then Daniel was back in London observing "an elderly cherub with a cigar almost as big as the butt end of a billiard cue"—Winston Churchill, one of the few names that survives the momentary madness that makes headlines; the others quickly die or fade—Naguib, Mossadegh, Klaus Fuchs. Men like Daniel go off to new names, new places, never getting *involved*, although sometimes they worry about the impermanence of their work and wonder where it will lead them.

Daniel would have liked to have become chief of the *Times'* London bureau, but Drew Middleton, suspected by a few New York editors of having a private line of communication with the publisher, Arthur Hays Sulzberger, got the job. Daniel was assigned to replace Middleton in Germany and, as an Anglophile, he could barely abide the Germans. His reporting was uninspired, sometimes noticeably disdainful: "BERLIN—In the cold, dirty slush of last night's snow a few thousand of Berlin's millions stood along Potsdamer Strasse today watching the custodians of Germany's destiny roll by in a fleet of limousines. They were typical Berliners, seedy, cynical and slangy . . ."

In New York, Catledge was having his troubles too. He had been separated from his wife in 1948 and was spending a good deal of time in Sardi's bar, so much in fact that his picture was soon hanging on the wall and his name was on the menu ("Veal Cutlet Catledge"); and his dream of bringing the power back to the managing editor's office in New York, of demoting the dukes, was very slow in materializing. Though Catledge had been Sulzberger's appointee, the publisher never did give him carte blanche—no editor gets that on the *Times*—and there were also rising up around Mr. Sulzberger many new young men who had a good deal to say about anything Catledge did, or tried to do.

One was Orvil Dryfoos, a friend of Reston's, a onetime Wall Street broker who, after marrying a Sulzberger daughter, became an assistant to the publisher and eventually, in 1961, would become the publisher himself. Another was Amory Howe Bradford, a tall, blond Yale man who had married Carol Warburg Rothschild, whose family knew the Sulzbergers. Bradford would also become very influential on the *Times*, and remain so until the early sixties.

James Reston was also a power, particularly after taking over in 1953 as chief of Krock's twenty-four-man Washington bureau, a concession quickly made when Reston contemplated quitting the *New York Times* for a better job on the *Washington Post*; and the most autonomous duke in the New York office, of course, was the Sunday editor, Lester Markel, who started at the paper in 1923 with a staff of only three editors, a secretary, and an office boy. By 1951 he had a staff of eighty-four, including fifty-eight editors, layout and picture crews, and special correspondents in Paris, London, and Washington.

And Turner Catledge, though he had become the No. 2 man under Edwin L. James in 1945, was no further along in 1951; James was ill much of the time, but he was still the managing editor and Catledge never crossed him, even though the veteran gossips around the office generally agreed that James was hardly Sulzberger's favorite person. James had been *Ochs's* managing editor, they pointed out, and Adolph Ochs—whose only daughter had married Arthur Hays Sulzberger in 1917—used to make remarks about Sulzberger's night life to James, observations that must have quietly amused James who, years before, had been privy to some of Adolph Ochs's nocturnal excursions through Paris and elsewhere.

When Ochs died in 1935 and Sulzberger became publisher, he was never entirely comfortable around James, it was said, although this might have been due to their difference in style—Sulzberger preferred the more sedate, subtle manners of his favorite city, London, while James responded to the frisky freedom of Paris and remained the boulevardier long after he ceased being the *Times'* chief correspondent there. In the New York office he dressed with a flair, kicked his polished shoes or rapped his cane against the elevator when it moved too slowly, placed bets with his book-maker who worked as a news clerk in the rear of the city room (the bookie remained there until, years after James's death, he was quietly transferred into the *Times'* financial-news department).

Through these years Catledge, waiting patiently and trying to keep his balance, never was entirely certain that he would succeed James; there was always the possibility that Reston might want the job; or perhaps Cyrus L. Sulzberger, the publisher's nephew who now had James's old Paris assign-ment as the *Times'* chief foreign correspondent. During the six years that Catledge was James's understudy he was exceedingly careful, provoking James's anger only once, and that was over James's son, Michel.

Michel James, born in France but educated at Princeton, was up for employment as a *Times* reporter at the suggestion of Cyrus Sulzberger, and Catledge later suspected a plot. Michel James, Catledge believed, would become a foreign correspondent under Cyrus Sulzberger (who then was virtually in charge of all *Times* foreign correspondents) and would serve as Sulzberger's hostage.

Catledge strongly opposed the hiring of Michel James. Edwin James became very angry. Michel James was hired and soon became a most in-teresting addition to the staff. He was a very thin, zany young man who dressed himself in very narrow, rather bizarre clothes, lived in Greenwich Village, and frequented the more far-out parties. He was also an excellent photographer, often of subjects that the *Times* never would have found fit to print.

As a writer he had talent, but as a foreign correspondent he ran up enormous expense accounts, would be incommunicado sometimes for days, weeks, and then might suddenly appear in Cambodia or Bonn or in Paris with a pet monkey on his back, a lively little animal that absolutely terrified the *Times* bureau chief in Paris, Harold Callender.

On a staff saturated with men who take themselves seriously at all times, too seriously sometimes, Michel James was a refreshing figure, but Catledge saw little humor in his presence on the *Times* for those years he remained. As to whether Michel James was of any use as a hostage, it was never possible to tell. For in December of 1951, Edwin L. James died. And Arthur Hays Sulzberger's memo on the bulletin board of the newsroom read:

> To the Staff: When death takes a valued member of an organization, it is always a sad occasion. Such it was with the passing of Mr. Edwin L. James. But the institution must go on, and I have today appointed Turner Catledge to the post of managing editor of the *Times* . . .

Now Catledge, while causing as little commotion as possible, began his campaign to centralize the paper, to bring friendly forces into his camp. In 1952 he promoted two men to the rank of assistant managing editor, Robert E. Garst and Theodore M. Bernstein. At the same time he tried to make it clear to both men, as clearly as he could without being offensive, that they would go no further, would never succeed him as the managing editor.

No objections were raised at the time, but in the years that followed, as Turner Catledge focused his attention elsewhere, Theodore Bernstein became increasingly powerful. Responding perhaps to Catledge's call for good writing, Theodore Bernstein established himself as the final arbiter of what was good. He had been an outstanding professor of journalism at Columbia University, then a dedicated *Times* deskman who in 1939 took charge of all war copy, and later he edited the Churchill memoirs for the *Times*, as well as those of Cordell Hull and General Walter Bedell Smith. As a person, Bernstein was warm and friendly, very approachable; with a pencil in his hand, however, he was cold and dogmatic, a strict believer in rules, especially *his* rules. From his office in the southeast corner of the city room, a section called the "bullpen" and populated by subordinate editors who shared most of his opinions on news and grammar, Bernstein, in addition to his many other duties, published a little paper called *Winners & Sinners* that was distributed to *Times*men in New York and throughout the world; it listed examples of their work, good and bad, that had appeared recently in the *Times*, and it also included a recitation of Mr. Bernstein's rules and comments. These were memorized by deskmen throughout the vast city room, and these men were held accountable by Bernstein for the maintenance of his principles; thus the deskmen, in the interest of a more readable and grammatical newspaper, gained new power with Bernstein as their mentor—he had become the *Times'* grammarian or, as *Encounter* magazine later suggested, its "governess."

Such a position, of course, made Bernstein a villain with those reporters who had their own ideas about writing. They charged that the deskmen, overreacting to Bernstein's rules, were merely hatchet men who deleted from stories the choicest phrases and gems of originality. Catledge did not become involved in the feud at this time. If Bernstein's men went too far they could always be checked, and the quicker pace of postwar life, the coming of television, the increased cost of news production, among other factors, required that the *Times* become a more tightly edited paper for faster reading. Also, *somebody* had to worry about the proper uses of "that" or "which," "whom" or "who," and so Catledge now concerned himself with other, more pressing problems, and there were many.

Ever since the beginning of World War II, when the workday in the city room was expanded so that the *Times* could publish the maximum amount of late-breaking news, there had been a lack of coordination between various editors of the "day side" and "night side"—neither knew what the other was up to, there was competition, intrigue. There was also throughout the *Times'* many departments—City, Science, Sports, Financial, a dozen more—a dangerous commitment to the traditional way of doing things. Editors in some of these departments would sometimes peek back at the *Times'* edition of exactly one year ago, would see how certain stories had been approached, laid out, written; then they would try to duplicate that day one year later.

The morale was low on the New York local staff. It had long been running a poor third in performance behind the prestigious Foreign staff, which often attracted away the best New York men, and the National staff, which was led by Reston's elite corps in Washington. (Reston, incidentally, at that time hired his own men—usually tall, tweedy men who were deceptively bright and were born and reared, preferably, some hundreds of miles from New York City.)

The Sports staff was sluggish, and Catledge decided that he would retire the Sports editor as soon as possible. The staff was sectioned off into little cliques and there was tension. There had even been a fight between the makeup man, Frank Blunk, and the slot man, Harry Heeren. Blunk had told Heeren to stop sending up copy for the first edition, there was no more room, and Heeren replied, "Don't you tell me when to cut off copy!"

"Com'on, Harry," Blunk had said, "the first edition's in, forget it."

"I will not forget it!"

"Well, if you don't keep your mouth shut, I'll hit you in the nose."

Heeren opened his mouth, Blunk hit him in the nose.

Heeren ran through the city room into the bullpen to make an official complaint to Bernstein. The next day Frank Blunk, standing in Catledge's office, explained that he had been trying for years to get a transfer to the writing staff, being weary of working indoors near Harry Heeren. So Catledge quickly acted; he made Blunk a reporter specializing in auto races, a plush job that would take him to Florida and Nassau much of the winter; and it confirmed for Blunk the notion that small men in big institutions frequently get what they want only after raising some hell.

The death of Anne O'Hare McCormick, the foreign-affairs columnist, opened up that busy job for Cyrus Sulzberger, and he no longer sought to influence the running of the *Times*' overseas bureaus. Catledge himself took trips abroad and spent time with correspondents, and he frequently was amazed at how well they lived, the number of servants they had, the size of their homes.

In Mexico he visited the young bureau chief, Sydney Gruson, who explained at the outset: "Okay, Turner, while you're here we can go off each morning and see people, and I'll make phone calls, and I'll pretend that this is the way I really work here. Or," Gruson said, eyes lighting up, "we can do what I really do here. I own five racehorses, I see them run two or three times a week, and I play golf three or four times a week. And, well, how do you want to do it, Turner?"

"Don't be silly," Catledge said, "we'll do it the way you always do it."

So during the next week they had a magnificent time. They went to several parties, they bet on Gruson's horses, losing every time, and went to the bullfights, where Gruson had arranged for a bull to be dedicated in honor of Catledge.

Ten days later, after Catledge had returned to New York, Gruson received word that his Mexican assignment was over. He was to report back to the New York office. Some months later he was assigned to Prague. Catledge maintained that his Mexico trip had nothing to do with it. (Gruson did extremely well during his assignment in Eastern Europe, and also in

Bonn and London; and he became, in 1965, the *Times'* foreign news editor.)

One of the major personnel problems facing Catledge in 1954 was finding a replacement in Russia for Harrison E. Salisbury. Salisbury, a tall and remote individualist—he was once fired as editor of the University of Minnesota daily newspaper for smoking in the library—had been the *Times*man in Moscow since 1949. He had worked long and hard under the most adverse conditions—the Stalin era, censorship—and yet Catledge had no other qualified *Times*man who wished to go to Moscow. Then Clifton Daniel volunteered.

Catledge was delighted. It confirmed for him many of the things he had come to accept about Daniel: in fact, Catledge had for the last two years been thinking of Clifton Daniel as a future executive, a possible successor, being impressed with Daniel's performance in the London bureau, both as an administrator and newsman, and Catledge also had been pleased with Daniel's attitude in accepting the Bonn assignment. Daniel was eleven years younger than Catledge, was an organization man who could operate within the corporate ego of the *Times*. And—he was a Southerner. Take away all that fancy English tailoring, that long wavy hair and courtly manner, and Daniel was what Catledge was—a country boy who said "sir" to his superiors, and had reverence for the Southern past and big-city dreams for the future.

So Clifton Daniel returned to New York to study Russian at Columbia University. One day after class he had lunch at Sardi's, checking his Russian first reader with the blonde in the cloakroom. He also took a trip down to Zebulon to see his parents and friends, and while in the Zebulon post office he was approached by the clerk, Whitley Chamblee, who leaned forward and whispered, "Did I hear you're going to *Russia*?"

After Daniel confirmed it, Whitley Chamblee asked, "I wonder, when you're there, if you would buy me one of those cuckoo clocks."

"Whitley, I don't believe they make cuckoo clocks in Russia," Daniel said. "They make them in Germany and Switzerland. But, well, if I find one, I'll send it to you."

A year later Clifton Daniel was in Geneva for the Big Four Conference. He had flown there from Moscow to join a team of *Times*men reporting the big story. While there he also bought a cuckoo clock and mailed it to the postman in Zebulon.

Daniel arrived in Moscow in the late summer of 1954, a vintage period in Russian news—Stalin only eighteen months dead, Krushchev emerging with a new party line that would include vodka toasts and receptions in the Great Kremlin Palace; at one reception, Daniel reported to the readers of the *Times*, "I was as close to Mr. Malenkov as this paper is to your nose."

His reporting in the *New York Times* was remarkable in that it captured not only the political rumblings but also the mood of the people: the audience at the Bolshoi and the barber in Kharkov; the athletes preparing for the Olympics, and the fashion models wearing designs of "socialist realism" in this land where "bosoms are still bosoms, a waist is a waist, hips are hips, and there is no doubt about what they are and where they are situated." He reported, too, how tipping—a "relic of the dark bourgeoisie past"—was a necessary reality despite government disapproval, and he also described the arrival of winter:

"This was Christmas morning in Russia, and a cruel snow-laden wind blowing straight out of the pages of Russian history and literature whipped across roofs and through the frozen streets of Moscow. At midnight the bells in the tower of Yelokhovskaya Cathedral in the northern quarter of the city set up an insistent clangor. The faithful of the Russian Orthodox Church—women tightly wrapped in shawls and men in fur-collared coats and caps—hastened through the churchyard to escape the icy bite of the wind."

Since Daniel was then the only permanent correspondent of a Western non-Communist newspaper in the Russian capital, he was able to pick his subjects at will and write them well and not have to contend with editorial second-guessing that would have come from New York had there been rival papers' men in Moscow focusing on government spokesmen with their endless pronouncements. And not being part of a pack, Daniel had to work harder than he ever had. He developed an ulcer and lost between thirty and forty pounds. In November of 1955, Turner Catledge, acting on orders from Arthur Hays Sulzberger—who had by this time received letters from *Times*men commenting on how bad Daniel had looked at the Big Four Conference in Geneva—ordered Daniel home immediately.

He returned, emaciated, but was not long in recovering, and soon was working in the New York office. He had been named *an* assistant to the foreign news editor, although nobody in the city room knew precisely what this meant, including possibly *the* foreign news editor. But it seemed obvious from the way Daniel moved around the room, and from the way the room moved around him, that he was not going to remain an assistant to the foreign news editor for very long.

Daniel's desk, which normally would have given a clue, was in a non-descript spot. It was on the south side of the room, where all the senior editors sit, but it was partially obscured by a post. It was also up a bit between two secretaries, equidistant from the Foreign editor and the "bull-pen." He also rarely remained seated. Usually he walked slowly around the big room, his glasses sometimes tucked like a tiara into the top of his silver hair. Sometimes he would stop, sit down, and chat with reporters or desk-men in the Science department, or in Sports, or Education, or Financial, or Society. Occasionally he would return to one of these departments for a whole week or two, sitting in various places, and conversing in a very casual, disarming way about the *New York Times*, and asking occasionally what they liked about working there, or did not like.

He was living at the Algonquin Hotel then, and was spotted at night also in Sardi's after the theater, and was once seen at the opera with a tall, striking brunette.

After they had gone twice more to the opera they became a "twosome" in Walter Winchell's column. The lady was mildly upset, partly because she felt that Daniel, a *Times* editor in a gossip column, might be very embarrassed, especially when their relationship had been so innocent: a drink, dinner, the opera, another drink perhaps, then home. Directly. A pleasant good night in front of the doorman. That was it.

She had met Clifton Daniel at a New York party prior to his leaving for Moscow, had received one postcard from him, and was now pleased to be seeing him again. And, hoping that he would not be angered by the Winchell item, she telephoned Daniel at the *Times*.

He could not have been nicer. He only laughed when the Winchell subject was brought up, and hardly seemed sorry about the item appearing— which, she later told a friend, "kind of surprised me."

Shortly after that, in March of 1956, she read in the newspapers the engagement announcement of Margaret Truman to Clifton Daniel. She wrote a note of congratulations to Daniel, and received in turn a note thanking *her* "for being such a fine cover-up for myself and Margaret."

The brunette was "devastated" by the note, and she neither spoke to nor saw Clifton Daniel again for two years. Now, looking back, she concedes that perhaps she was wrong to have reacted as she did: perhaps he was being "light" or "humorous."

Clifton Daniel met Margaret Truman in November 1955 at the New York home of Mrs. George Backer, a friend of Daniel's from the forties in London. Mrs. Backer's husband, the politically active New Yorker who was once publisher of the *New York Post*, was out of town, and so there were only Turner Catledge and Daniel for dinner, in addition to Madeleine Sherwood, widow of Robert Sherwood. After dinner, others came. Among them were Alan Campbell, who had been married to Dorothy Parker, and Mr. Campbell's date, Margaret Truman.

Margaret and Campbell had been to Edna Ferber's for dinner, and were merely stopping in, at Campbell's insistence, for a quick nightcap at the Backers. Mrs. Backer introduced Daniel to Margaret Truman.

To this day Daniel remembers very sharply the smallest details about her that night—her wonderful complexion, never suggested in her photographs, and the way she wore her hair, her shoes, the dark blue Fontana dress with the plunging neckline: Daniel recalling to a friend years later, "I looked down the neck of that dress and I haven't looked back since."

Soon, at the Backers, Daniel and Miss Truman were conversing in a corner, he telling her that if she, the daughter of a prominent political figure, had been reared in Russia she would be "practically unknown," because the politicians there shun publicity for their families. This interested her, and he continued to talk in his worldly way, and before she left he had made a date for lunch.

They were married in Independence, Missouri, on April 21, 1956. She was thirty-two, he was forty-three. The wedding, in Trinity Protestant Episcopal Church where she once sang in the choir, was witnessed by about fifty relatives and close friends and the maid and housekeeper from the Truman home. Most of those present were from the two small towns in which the bride and bridegroom grew up. The best man was Daniel's boyhood friend from Zebulon, John K. Barrow, Jr., a college roommate and fraternity brother who operated a big lumber business in Ahoskie, North Carolina. The ushers were George Backer and Turner Catledge.

Within the next five years Clifton Daniel moved steadily upward, becoming assistant to the managing editor in 1957, and *the* assistant managing editor in 1959. In this capacity he became a Catledge trouble-shooter and the author of many long, highly critical memos to the staff, which in turn became highly critical of him. One day in the city room Margaret Daniel, making an infrequent visit, was introduced to a reporter who said, "Oh, it's a pleasure meeting you, Mrs. Daniel, I *love* your father."

"What about my husband?" she asked.

"That," he said, forcing a smile, "I'll have to think about."

While the Catledge-Daniel influence was undoubtedly increasing during these years, it did not go unchallenged. Reston was still a singular power in Washington. During the steel strike in 1959 when the *Times'* top labor reporter, A. H. Raskin, who worked out of the New York office, appeared at the Washington bureau to continue his coverage of the developments—a presidential panel was about to hold hearings on a possible emergency injunction—Reston blocked him. The steel story had moved into the Washington area and Reston wanted one of his men, namely his own labor specialist, Joseph Loftus, to take over the story, and Loftus did. A. H. Raskin returned to New York. Turner Catledge, out of the office at the time, was angry when he learned of it and he made a loud interoffice speech about how the *Times* was now being run from Forty-third Street; but no one really wanted to have a showdown with Reston at this time.

Reston's close friend, Orvil Dryfoos, was then president of the New York Times Company and heir-apparent to his father-in-law; and the expected happened in 1961 when Arthur Hays Sulzberger, seventy years old and not in good health, made Orvil Dryfoos the publisher. While Dryfoos and Catledge shared a convincing cordiality and mutual respect, it was not to be compared with the warm affection that existed between Dryfoos and Reston. Reston, too, was the poet laureate of the paper, a man whose writing had a lyrical quality even when dealing with the more ponderous issues of the day; and his staff, fashioned in his own image, had unquestionably enhanced the prestige of the *Times.* Reston did not covet Catledge's job, such as it was, for he would probably lose more than he would gain; he would have to leave Washington for New York, a city he never liked, and he would have to give up his column, a thing he could probably never do.

For the column in the *New York Times* was the podium from which Reston could spread his Calvinist view of life throughout the land, thrilling thousands with his sound logic and wit, influencing scholars, students, and politicians, sometimes infuriating such presidents as Eisenhower, who once asked, "Who the hell does he think he is, telling me how to run the country?"

And so as long as Reston had his column and could run his bureau as he wished—a prerogative he thought reasonable since he was held responsible for its performance—he would remain in Washington, a reasonably happy man. And that is what he was for as long as Dryfoos lived. In the spring of 1963, at the age of fifty, Orvil Dryfoos died.

He died of a heart ailment shortly after the settlement of a 114-day New York newspaper strike, a tedious and strenuous period that, some of his friends insist, impaired his health. It was he who, at a crucial moment when negotiations seemed about to break up in angry recriminations, persuaded the chief negotiators to resume talks and submerge their hostility. Much of this hostility had been directed at Dryfoos's own colleague and adviser, Amory Bradford, the *Times'* general manager who was then chief spokesman for the New York publishers' committee with the union. In a remarkable example of independent journalism, the *New York Times*, in a long analysis published after the strike but before Dryfoos died, reported that Amory Bradford had brought "an attitude of such icy disdain into the conference rooms that the mediator often felt he ought to ask the hotel to send up more heat." This story by A. H. Raskin also characterized Bradford as an "aloof" man who operated on a "short fuse" and had called the Mayor's strike methods "foolish" and had become "sick and tired of the whole proceedings."

When Catledge read A. H. Raskin's story, he immediately called Dryfoos and asked him to look at it. Dryfoos said he would when it appeared in the *Times.* Catledge urged him to read it prior to publication. So Dryfoos took the story with him to Central Park, where he could read it alone near the lake, and Catledge remained in the office uncertain of Dryfoos's reaction and whether the story would ever be published. Later Dryfoos returned the story, telling Catledge to let it run.

When Amory Bradford saw a copy of Raskin's story, he became enraged and urged Dryfoos to have the story killed. Dryfoos replied that he did not feel it was his responsibility to censor the news. He knew that Catledge had absolute faith in Raskin's accuracy and the story would be published as planned.

At Orvil Dryfoos's funeral, attended by two thousand persons at Temple Emanu-El on Fifth Avenue in New York, Amory Bradford did not sit among the many *Times* editors near the front. He sat several rows back, and Harrison Salisbury, who has an eye for such things, immediately foresaw Bradford's resignation.

James Reston delivered the eulogy of Orvil Dryfoos. It was a beautifully composed portrait of the publisher, revealing touching insights into the man's mind and ideals. Reston recalled that in the city room on election night, 1960, Dryfoos was the first man to "sense that we had gone out on a limb for Kennedy too early and insisted that we reconsider. And again in 1961," Reston continued, "when we were on the point of reporting a premature invasion of Cuba, his courteous questions and wise judgment held us back."

This last point seemed to carry just the slightest sting for the New York editors. *They* had planned to play up the Bay of Pigs invasion plan, but Dryfoos, agreeing with Reston that it was not in the national interest, had the story toned down and had eliminated from it any phraseology stating that the invasion of Cuba was imminent. (Three years later, in June of 1966, after the power had shifted within the *Times*, Clifton Daniel would make a speech at the World Press Institute in Minneapolis that would get back a bit at Reston: Daniel would say that the Bay of Pigs operation "might well have been canceled and the country would have been saved enormous embarrassment if the *New York Times* and other newspapers had been more diligent in the performance of their duty," and he would also report President Kennedy's later concession to Turner Catledge: "If you had printed more about the operation you would have saved us from a colossal mistake.")

After the Dryfoos funeral there were weeks of intense guessing in the city room as to whom the next publisher would be. Various names were mentioned: John Oakes, the editorial writer whose late father, Ochs's brother, had changed the family name during World War I because of the Germanic flavor of "Ochs"; there was Ruth Sulzberger Golden, Arthur Hays Sulzberger's daughter who was then publisher of the *Chattanooga Times*, first published in 1878 by Adolph Ochs; there were individuals who were not part of the family, including James Reston; and there was Arthur Hays Sulzberger's thirty-seven-year-old son, Arthur Ochs Sulzberger, known by his nickname, "Punch," given him at home because his youngest sister was called Judy.

Punch Sulzberger was a charming and completely unostentatious young man, but many people around the newspaper seriously doubted that he was yet old enough or mature enough to take over the *New York Times*. As a young boy he had many problems in school, and his older sister Ruth, making light of it once in the *Times'* house organ, wrote: "Nearly every school in the vicinity of New York was graced with Punch's presence at one time or another. They were all delighted to have him, but wanted him as something other than a spectator."

He, too, was always amusing when recalling his days at Browning or Lawrence Smith or Loomis, or while he was tutoring at Morningside. But on rare occasions, though he tried to conceal it with his laughter and his casual manner, there was a hint of deep hurt, the dark memory of displeasure from his father. "They sent me to St. Bernard's, then based on the English school system, and I rebelled," he once said. "I was a natural left-hander, but I was made to write with my right. And the result even now is that I do a lot of flipping—instead of writing '197' I'll reverse it to '179.' Anyway, I was at St. Bernard's for maybe five or six years, and I still get those letters addressed 'Old Boy.'" Then, lips hardening, he added quietly, "I never gave them a penny."

He joined the Marines in 1943. He served in the Philippines and Japan, remembering fondly a certain tough Marine Corporal Rossides "who helped me grow up." After his release from the Marines in 1946 he entered Columbia ("my old man was on the board") and made the dean's list; and then during the Korean War he was recalled and made a lieutenant. By 1954, after a year on the *Milwaukee Journal* as a reporter, Punch Sulzberger came to the *New York Times* where, until the death of Orville Dryfoos, almost nobody in the city room thought, or knew, very much about him. He was just Punch, the smiling son of Arthur Hays Sulzberger, a dark curly-haired boy smoking a pipe, wearing a Paul Stuart suit, saying hello to everyone in the elevator, sometimes wandering through the newsroom and looking up at the walls inspecting the paint, or scrutinizing the air-conditioning ducts. Later in the afternoon, once the four-o'clock news conference was over, Punch would usually slip into a little room behind the managing editor's office and sit down and chat and have a few drinks with his very close friend, Turner Catledge.

Catledge and he had been friends for years, although there was nothing unusual about this; Catledge seemed to be friends with everybody for years—copyboys and senators, bellhops and bootleggers. And it seemed natural that Punch Sulzberger—who, like Catledge, had marital difficulties and was in no rush to get home—would wind up in Catledge's smoky little room at five o'clock drinking with Catledge and the other members of the "club": Joe Alduino, the comptroller, and Irvin Taubkin from Promotion, both of whom had marriage problems; and also Nat Goldstein, the circulation manager, whose wife accepted his "marriage" to the *Times* and never counted on his appearances at home.

Turner Catledge had a very paternal way with young Sulzberger without ever being condescending; he gave advice willingly, but Punch made his own decisions. Through the years their friendship deepened, and this at a time when many top *Times*men were merely polite to Punch. Even James Reston, when he would come flying into New York from Washington, would, after a quick handshake and hello, breeze past Punch into the office of the *Times*' publisher, Orvil Dryfoos. Everyone on the *Times*, seeing Dryfoos in apparent good health, expected that he would remain the chief executive through the 1980s, and hardly anyone expected that Punch, until then, would be anything but Punch.

Almost one month after Dryfoos's death, Punch Sulzberger became publisher of the *New York Times*. At thirty-seven, he was the youngest publisher the *Times* had ever had. His appointment was made known through a statement from his seventy-two-year-old father, the *Times*' chairman of the board. This statement also accepted, with regret, the resignation of Amory Bradford. "Amory Bradford has been a valuable source of strength and leadership in our organization," the statement read. "We are sorry he has decided to resign. He will be greatly missed."

Within Punch Sulzberger's first year as publisher, he devised the plans for the *Times*' most dramatic shakeup in history. His intent was to appoint Turner Catledge to the newly established office of executive editor, meaning that Catledge would have unquestioned authority over Lester Markel's Sunday department, over Reston's bureau in Washington, and over all *Times*men and *Times* bureaus at home and overseas. Markel would become "associate editor" and get his name on the *Times*' masthead, as would James Reston, still writing the column; both Markel and Reston would be consulted and respected on the paper, but neither of them would again have the power to challenge Catledge.

Markel's protests were vigorous, but he was then seventy, the Sunday editor for forty-one years. Sulzberger, while recognizing Markel's enormous contributions, insisted on replacing him with a judicious man named Daniel Schwarz, who had been an assistant to Markel since 1939. Most of Markel's staff welcomed the change. His autocratic rule had cracked the spirit of many writers and editors through the years; on occasions some had actually broken down and cried, others had gone off and written bad novels about him. "For all those years," one editor said, "Lester Markel was our great Jewish father-figure, and we were his sons—and he had a way of convincing us that we were always failing him."

Reston in Washington was different. His staff admired him and tried to identify with him; he was self-assured, very informal—even the office boys called him "Scotty"—and, when he spoke, there was something in the timbre of his wonderful distant voice, the words he slowly chose, the way he paused, that gave to almost everything he said the ring of instant history.

When some of his intimates on the bureau heard of Sulzberger's plan, they were shocked, but not surprised. Nothing from New York, no matter how preposterous, would surprise them, they said. Two years before, in 1962, Harrison Salisbury had been appointed the National editor. Since all stories written by *Times*men in bureaus around the nation, including the Washington bureau, had to go through the National editor's desk, Harrison Salisbury had the prerogative of pressuring Washington a bit; and he did. He had an obsession about suspecting plots and sinister deals in the American government, they said, and when these stories did not materialize they felt he thought they were vulnerable—soft on their sources, protecting their friends on Capitol Hill. Reston's men countercharged that Salisbury possessed a conspiratorial mind, the result of too much time spent covering the Communists in Russia—or, as one *Times*man in Washington put it: "Salisbury spent so many years watching who was standing next to Stalin that now *he's* standing next to Stalin!"

Yet Salisbury had continued to pepper the Washington bureau with memos, ideas, questions: Was there any Murchison money behind that Johnson deal? What was Abe Fortas *really* up to? Is it true, as rumored, that the State Department would recognize Mongolia? (The Washington men said that Salisbury had asked that last question so many times that the State Department probably will recognize Mongolia.)

It was Salisbury, they said, and probably Clifton Daniel, too, who made the decision to publish President Kennedy's S.O.B. remark in the *Times* during the administration's confrontation with the steel industry in April of 1962. Wallace Carroll of the Washington bureau had written in his story that President Kennedy had been enraged at the steel men's decision to raise prices across the board, had spoken unflatteringly of them, but Carroll did not attribute to Kennedy the direct quotation that would later appear in his story ("My father always told me that all business men were sons of bitches but I never believed it till now!"); it was the New York editors, tipped off by a news source they trusted, who identified these words as the president's. So Salisbury called up Carroll and told him to write an insertion that would include this quotation. Carroll said that *he* had not heard the president use such language. When Salisbury persisted, Carroll snapped back, "The hell with it—you write it in yourself!"

If James Reston had not been so busy at this time writing his column and running the bureau, trying also to keep in touch with his Washington contacts, including his family, he could have made a full-time career of fighting the editors in New York. But Reston was now approaching his middle fifties and was resigned to an attitude of give-and-take (with the ageless Arthur Krock muttering in the background that when *he* was bureau chief he took nothing from New York), and Reston might have continued along these lines had he not been informed of Punch Sulzberger's plan to centralize the *Times*' news operation with Catledge in charge of everything.

Reston reacted, and his friends in Washington and elsewhere rallied behind him, urging him to go to New York and make a pitch for the big job—not for himself, but in the interest of saving the *New York Times* from the destructive elements they saw encircling it. And if the executive editorship had been offered Reston, they later said, he would have taken it, even though it would have undoubtedly meant his leaving Washington to live in New York, and giving up his column. But the job was not offered. Other alternatives were made for Reston's coming to New York in a higher executive capacity, but these would not have checked the central order of things with Catledge at the top.

Reston, in his discussions with Sulzberger, tried other approaches, suggesting that the youthful publisher might be wise to surround himself not with older men but rather with the bright young men of his own generation—such men as Tom Wicker, Max Frankel, and Anthony Lewis (all of the Washington bureau). But Sulzberger by that time was already

committed to his plan for combining all the news elements under one senior editor, a plan that Catledge had been envisioning for twenty years.

With the cards so stacked, James Reston contemplated his resignation.
His bureau manager in Washington, Wallace Carroll—whom Dryfoos had
viewed as Markel's successor in the Sunday department—did resign in the
summer of 1963, becoming editor and publisher of the *Winston-Salem
Journal and Sentinel*. Carroll had been on the *New York Times* since 1955,
and his resignation did not carry with it the same emotional torment that
Reston's would have, because Reston, who had joined the paper in 1939,
had grown with it, earning and receiving from it national fame and more
literary freedom than any *Times*man before him or since.

Still Reston had immense pride, and he could not be submissive to New
York. Also he now had an offer from his close friend, Katharine Graham,
president of the Washington Post Company, whereby he would not only
continue as a syndicated columnist but would also have a hand at guid-
ing this paper up to perhaps a challenging position, as well as helping to
run the company's other publication, *Newsweek* magazine. He would receive enough money and stock benefits to guarantee that he and his family
would be quite rich. He thought it over, discussing it also with such friends
as Walter Lippmann. In the end, Reston turned it down. He could not
leave the *Times*.

So he continued with his column which, appearing on the editorial
page, did not make him answerable to the news department. Reston's
choice as successor, Tom Wicker, did get the job, although receiving be-
forehand a short briefing from Catledge on the new organizational chain of
command. Tom Wicker was then thirty-seven, a superb journalist whose
description from Dallas of the Kennedy assassination took up more than
a page of the *Times'* November 23, 1963, issue. A native of North Carolina, a graduate of the University of North Carolina, Wicker had once been
interviewed, while wearing a beard, by Clifton Daniel; he was not hired.
In 1960, without the beard, and having written six novels (three under a
pseudonym), Wicker went to see Reston; he was hired. Reston's two other
bright young men in Washington, Max Frankel and Anthony Lewis, were
not entirely joyful over Wicker's appointment as bureau chief. Frankel, the
diplomatic correspondent, remained on the bureau, however, resisting a
later temptation from *The Reporter* magazine. Anthony Lewis left Washington to take over the *Times'* London bureau, replacing Sydney Gruson,

who returned to New York as the Foreign editor, replacing Emanuel R. Freedman, who became an assistant managing editor. Harrison Salisbury, who vacated his National editor's job to a hustling Atlanta-born reporter named Claude Sitton, moved up to become *the* assistant managing editor, the third man, under Daniel and Catledge.

Before most of these changes had been made, Catledge had gone off to Tokyo to try to convince the *Times'* correspondent there, A. M. Rosenthal, to return home and become editor of the New York staff, which was then being rather rigidly run by a stout, ruddy man who had gone to Princeton, and by his assistant, a former colonel. Rosenthal, just over forty, had been considered by many to be the *Times'* best writer-reporter combination. His stories from Japan, and before that from Poland and India, were incisive and warm, very readable and sensitive to the nuances of politics and people. His story on a visit to Auschwitz is a journalistic classic: "And so there is no news to report from Auschwitz. There is merely the compulsion to write something about it, a compulsion that grows out of a restless feeling that to have visited Auschwitz and then turned away without having said or written anything would be a most grievous act of discourtesy to those who died here."

Rosenthal had been a reporter on the *New York Times* since 1944, while still an undergraduate at City College of New York. Though very anxious to become a foreign correspondent with his own country to cover, Rosenthal was unable to get such an assignment until 1954—not because he was unqualified before that, but rather because of an incident that occurred in 1948 while he was in Paris helping to cover the United Nations' General Assembly session there. Returning to his hotel room one day, he noticed that a twenty-dollar traveler's check had been removed from his bureau drawer. He angrily reported this to the concierge, hinting that if it were not returned he would deduct that amount from his bill. The concierge, equally angry, telephoned the *Times'* office in Paris and reported young Rosenthal's assertiveness to Cyrus Sulzberger.

Back in New York, Rosenthal continued to work in the United Nations bureau, being unable, though he often tried, to get his assignment changed for the next six years. Several years later, after he had achieved his stature as a correspondent and had won the Pulitzer Prize, Rosenthal was driving to Geneva with Cyrus Sulzberger. As they talked, Sulzberger, suddenly and out of context, brought up the hotel incident of 1948. He admitted, somewhat casually, that Rosenthal had been kept in New York all those years because he, Sulzberger, had wanted it that way. He explained that Rosenthal in those early days had seemed the sort who would cause problems. Rosenthal felt the tension building within himself now, in the car; he thought of all the frustrating years at the UN, and thought, too, that if Sulzberger's influence as an overseas duke had been continued into the fifties, he might have never gotten to be a correspondent. The recollection of this silly, little impulsive moment in a hotel, and the realization of the harsh consequences, caused Rosenthal now to feel such a whirling sensation of both nausea and fury that he could barely, just barely, control himself until they reached Geneva.

Turner Catledge, long before approaching Rosenthal in Tokyo about the New York editor's job, debated the logic of removing from the *Times* one of the bylines that readers looked for, and sticking that man behind a desk. The idea of doing this had originally been Theodore Bernstein's; Catledge became intrigued with it because it was, for the *Times*, a rather drastic move, somewhat insane. Rosenthal had no experience as an editor, had been away from New York for nearly a decade, and might be intimidated by the enormity of the job itself—yet the New York staff, Catledge felt, was lethargic, needed a real shot to get it going again, and maybe this drastic move would bring results.

Rosenthal was responsive to the idea, but he really wanted to do a column, "Asia," for the editorial page. Catledge hates columns. He calls them a "malignancy" and prefers a paper with just news, well-written news, no columns that allow reporters to sound off on days when they often have nothing to say. If Rosenthal would take this editor's job, Catledge said, selling it hard now, Rosenthal each day would have not just *one* byline— he'd have *forty* bylines, *fifty* bylines: each story by one of Rosenthal's men would represent part of him, *Rosenthal*, and the gratification each night, the challenge each morning, would be something Rosenthal could never imagine until he tried it.

While Catledge remained briefly in the Orient, Rosenthal spent a good deal of time with him, and revealed finally that he would give the job a try. Catledge was delighted. He looked forward to Rosenthal's finishing the Tokyo assignment and coming home. Later, before Catledge left for New York, he discussed other things with Rosenthal—among them the fact that there would be a new column in the paper after all—one by Russell Baker. Catledge tried not to look too deeply into Rosenthal's face—but he knew that, had he hurled a bucket of cow dung into it, Rosenthal's expression would have been about the same.

A casual visitor to the *New York Times* city room during these years, between 1962 through 1964, would never have guessed that there was then in progress an institutional power shift and struggle of more magnitude than any in the *Times'* history. The city room would seem as quiet as ever: rows and rows of gray-metal desks occupied by reporters speaking calmly into telephones; in other parts of the room, seated behind long curved tables, would be deskmen, heads down, heads up, gazing softly into space for a headline. The headline might concern murder, riots, rapes, war— but the deskman's contact with these problems would be with a pencil. Over his head, racing across the ceiling, but quietly, would be a mechanical snake curving and hooking its way forward, clutching between its tiny metal tentacles single pieces of paper; it would transport each piece from the glass-enclosed telegraph room, in the distance, through the city room, down a hall, then into a remote room behind the morgue and into the hand of a person seated behind the keyboard of a sturdy black machine. The only overpowering voice in this big newsroom would come from the silver microphone that rests on the desk of the Metropolitan editor—and is occasionally picked up by a clerk when asked to page a reporter: "Mr. Arnold, Metropolitan desk"; and Mr. Arnold, with a soft sigh, would get up from his desk and begin the walk up the aisle toward the big desk centered near the front of the room.

A casual reader of the *New York Times*, too, would have no idea that there would be going on then a quiet revolution. There would be small announcement stories inside the paper (reading as if *everybody* was being promoted)—and even big front-page stories announcing the appointment of Punch Sulzberger, or mourning the death of Orvil Dryfoos—but none would offer any insight into the ramifications.

During these same years, and continuing through 1966, the *New York Times* would publish several stories of other institutional revolutions within such places as the *Saturday Evening Post*, as well as print interpretive pieces on the events leading up to the demise of the *New York Mirror* in 1963 and the *Herald Tribune* in August of 1966; and the *Times* would spark its news columns, too, with in-depth stories about the CIA and the "black-power" battle, about Franklin D. Roosevelt's mistress and the New Left, and oral contraceptives.

Yet the more than seven hundred thousand daily readers of the *New York Times* would get only dull reporting couched in institutional phrases when it would come to the story of Turner Catledge's triumph—and the rise of Daniel—a story that headed the second section of the *Times* on September 2, 1964. The headline read: CATLEDGE NAMED EXECUTIVE EDITOR OF TIMES, and the small second lines banked underneath: *Market, Reston Raised to Associate Editors—Schwarz Sunday Chief; Daniel Managing Editor—Wicker Will Direct Washington Bureau.*

The *Times* story began: "Six major changes in editorial assignments for *The New York Times* were announced yesterday by Arthur Ochs Sulzberger, publisher."

The big office and the little back room that Catledge occupied as managing editor was taken over by Daniel; and Catledge moved into a big new office—with a *new* little back room. Instead of being entered from the city room, as was his old office, Catledge's present office is now reachable only through an outside hall: meaning that if Catledge might wish to step out the door thirty times a day and ascend to the fourteenth floor to see Punch Sulzberger, or if Sulzberger might wish to come down to the third floor thirty times a day to see Catledge, both men might do so without being watched by the city-room gossips.

When Clifton Daniel moved into Catledge's old office, which is thirty-five feet long and eighteen feet wide, he made dramatic changes in the decor. One of the first things he did was to convert Catledge's little room, which smacked of turn-of-the-century Tammany, into a tastefully appointed sitting room. On the walls are now hung photographs showing the Clifton Daniels at the White House with the Lyndon Johnsons, the Harry Trumans, the John F. Kennedys—these being but a sample of many such photographs that the Daniels have, a few of which, blurred, were taken by Jacqueline Kennedy.

Behind Clifton Daniel's sitting room there is a cozy bar and bathroom; only Daniel and Catledge, among the third-floor news editors, and Theodore Bernstein, have private offices with bathrooms. Bernstein, who is as conspicuously informal as Daniel is formal, likes, in his subtle way, to mock the much larger and grander office that Daniel occupies directly across the newsroom. When Daniel ordered for his floor a brand-new blue-black tweed rug, Bernstein requested (and received) for *his* floor a chunk of the old tattered Catledge rug that was being pulled up, possibly to be junked. While Daniel sits in his traditional English office that contains, in addition to his desk, a new oval conference table surrounded by eighteen Bank of England chairs, Theodore Bernstein sits, with his shirt sleeves rolled up to the elbow, on an old wooden chair behind a scratchy desk, upon which he writes with flawless grammar on the cheapest memo paper he can find.

In the two years that Clifton Daniel has been managing editor he admits to having raised his voice in anger only once, refusing further clarification. Others in the city room, however, believe his estimate to be on the conservative side, claiming to have heard Daniel locked in a quarrel with Theodore Bernstein on at least a half-dozen occasions—usually the result of Bernstein's having passed off an irreverent remark about one of Daniel's pet projects, most likely the women's page.

While Daniel has been instrumental in several of the *Times*' big changes for the better—the expanded coverage of cultural news, the more literate obituaries, the encouragement of flavor and mood in "hard news" stories that formerly would have been done in a purely routine way—he is more quickly credited with (or blamed for) the women's page.

Its critics say that the women's page gets too much space, and they particularly oppose the publication of lengthy stories by Charlotte Curtis, a five-foot fast-stepping blonde, describing the activities of wealthy wastrels from Palm Beach to New York at a time when most of America is moving toward the goals of a more egalitarian society. Miss Curtis, however, is rarely flattering to her subjects, though many may lack the wit to realize this—but what is more important about Miss Curtis's work is that Clifton Daniel likes to read it. The deskmen, therefore, rarely trim her stories, and she is extremely careful with her facts, knowing that should she make an error Daniel will surely catch her.

Some years ago, in a story on Princess Radziwill, she mentioned the Prince's nickname, "Stash," only to receive the next day a memo from Daniel noting that while it was pronounced "Stash," it was spelled "Stas." Having previously checked the spelling with Pamela Turnure, then secretary to Prince Radziwill's sister-in-law, Jacqueline Kennedy, Miss Curtis telephoned Mr. Daniel to inform him that he was wrong—it was spelled "Stash."

"On what authority?" he asked.

"The White House," she quickly answered.

"Well, when I knew him," Daniel said, "it was spelled S-t-a-s."

He hung up. She thought that was the end of it. But Daniel tracked the Prince down in Europe, and some months later Miss Curtis got another memo from Daniel—it was "Stas."

Another change on the *Times* during Daniel's early days as managing editor, one that nearly caused paroxysms of panic among the Old Guard in the city room, began with the arrival from Japan of A. M. Rosenthal, the new Metropolitan editor. A quick and vibrant man, dark-haired and wearing horn-rimmed glasses, rather short and seeming ten years younger than his forty years, Rosenthal's primary commitment was to the livelier coverage of New York, and he was not at all interested in the way the city room used to be run.

Previously, at least in the opinion of one reporter who had lived for years in Europe, the city room had been run somewhat along the lines of a Paris café. In the late afternoon, he noted, the reporters at their desks would lean back in their chairs, sip coffee, read the newspapers, and observe other people walking back and forth in front of them. There was always a card game at one of the desks, always a conventional gathering at another, and there was also a late-afternoon tranquility about the place that induced sleep. Some of the men and women who were having love affairs would, after the senior editors had disappeared into the 4 p.m. news conference, slip away to one of the hotels in the Times Square area, having only to remember to place an occasional precautionary call to a friend in the city room and to return before 6:20, for that was when the editor would stroll through the city room giving his traditional "good-night" to individuals on the early shift.

There had been a reporter named Albert J. Gordon who had once left for home at the end of the day without a "good-night"; later reached by phone he was told that the editor wished to discuss with him a most important matter—*now*, and in person. Gordon lived at an inconvenient distance from the office, and it was also then raining heavily, but he reappeared in the city room as soon as he could. There, wet and sullen, he stood for a few seconds in front of the City desk until the editor looked up and said, almost with a smile, "Good-night, Mr. Gordon."

In those days, too, there was a traditional method in assigning stories; the best local stories each morning were given to the front-row veterans, and the younger reporters near the back usually ended up with such stories as a water-main break in Yorkville or a small fire in Flushing, or were sent up to Watertown, New York, to cover the training activities of the Seventy-seventh Division, General Julius Ochs Adler's old outfit, a traditional "must" on the assignment sheet.

Younger New York reporters who wrote with a certain flair in those days were never completely trusted by their superiors in the city room, the assumption being that "writers" would compromise the facts in the interest of better literature; such staff men therefore usually were assigned to cover the weather or parades or the Bronx Zoo and the circus— where, if the quotes were brightened a bit, there was a reasonably good chance that the clowns and animals would not complain to the Letters department.

The arrival of A. M. Rosenthal, of course, changed all this. Now, suddenly, stories were not only supposed to be accurate and complete—but also "written." As a result some of the senior *Times*men, losing out to younger men who were superior writers, became embittered and helped spread the rumor that the new policy was to "fake" stories. And when Rosenthal would assign "project" stories that would perhaps require three or four days' research and would make greater demands on the reporter's ability to organize his facts and weave them with transition, there was the angry reaction from some that the newspaper was now a "magazine."

Even more unpopular than Rosenthal at this time was Rosenthal's hand-picked assistant, a lanky creative tower of tension named Arthur Gelb. The staff's main objection to Gelb was that he had too many "wild" ideas. Each morning, fresh off the train from Westchester, Gelb's tall, thin figure would come breezing into the city room with pockets packed with ideas—twenty ideas, thirty ideas: people to interview, tips to check, angles to investigate, grand "projects" that might take weeks to complete. Some of these ideas were brilliant, most had merit, a few *were* wild, all meant work, lots of work. So the less-ambitious *Times*men, whenever they saw Gelb getting up from his desk and about to look around, would head for the men's room, or to the dictionaries located behind posts.

Inevitably, most of Gelb's ideas went to the eager young men, and he employed an almost hypnotic manner in communicating his ideas to them. He would whisper. First he would put an arm around a young man, would walk him down the aisle, and then would whisper, very confidentially, hand over mouth, into the young man's ear—the inference being that this particular idea was so great that Gelb did not want to risk its being overheard by other reporters who would surely become envious. Finally, before the young reporter would leave the city room to embark on the assignment, Gelb would whisper again, "And remember, *there's a great deal of interest in this story.*" There was the barest hint that this idea might be Rosenthal's, or maybe even Daniel's or Catledge's, and the young reporter had better do his best. Then, after the reporter had gone, Gelb would have his arm around another young man, and again there would be the parting whisper: "And remember, *there's a great deal of interest in this story.*"

Rosenthal and Gelb—behind their backs they were occasionally called Rosencrantz and Guildenstern—would later read the stories as they came in, page by page, and would check to see that the touches and angles that they had requested were in the story. Then they would try to assure that the story was not overedited by one of Bernstein's deskmen; on occasion, in order to prevent the cutting of a certain paragraph or phrase, Rosenthal would carry the fight to Bernstein himself.

When Rosenthal was particularly pleased with the way a story had been done, the reporter would receive a congratulatory memo, and Rosenthal also pressured Daniel and Catledge into quickly producing big raises for certain of his favorites. One of his young stars was R. W. Apple, Jr., whose popularity with older *Times*men was hardly enhanced by the rumor that, after a few months on Rosenthal's staff, he was making $350 a week.

If so, he was earning it. An indefatigable young man with a round smiling face and a crew cut, the look of a slightly overweight West Point cadet, Apple was very gung-ho; he never stopped running, the perspiration showing through his shirt by 2 p.m., and he never dismissed one of Gelb's ideas without giving it a try. The result was that Apple got more good stories into the paper than anybody on Rosenthal's staff. This is not what bothered his older colleagues so much, for they soon recognized his ability to get a story and write it; what really unsettled them was Apple's incredible enthusiasm for *everything* he had been assigned to cover—a boring Board of Estimate hearing, a talk with the tax commissioner, a repetition of campaign speeches by Bobby Kennedy—and Apple's insistence, once he'd returned, on telling everybody in the city room about what he had seen or heard, or what had happened to him while on the story. Once, returning from the Democratic National Convention, Apple burst into the city room to report that Ethel Kennedy had sneaked up and pinched his behind on the boardwalk in Atlantic City.

Many other staff members, too, soon caught some of this enthusiasm, and the *Times'* coverage of the city was expanded to include lengthy investigative reports on New York's hospitals and its homosexuals, its interracial marriages and its bookmakers. One exclusive story about a screaming girl being murdered one night in Queens, while thirty-eight people heard her and did nothing, provoked many editorials and follow-up stories about New York's "inertia." (None considered the possibility that if New Yorkers did not have this built-in resistance to screams in the night, to screaming headlines and the loud forecasters of alarm and hate, there might only be mayhem in New York and political assassination: so perhaps human inertia, which permits some to die, allows others to live.)

Nevertheless the spark that Catledge had wanted in the city room was supplied by Rosenthal and Gelb, and one victim of all the chasing, writing, and rewriting was the late-afternoon card game. Another was the traditional "good-night," inasmuch as Rosenthal did not care when his reporters came and went, so long as they got the story. A third result was that the national and foreign staffs, once so superior to New York's, were now beginning to feel the pressure and competition for space on Page One.

Claude Sitton, the National editor, drove his staff harder, especially such reporters as Roy Reed, who was assigned to cover racial demonstrations in the South, Sitton's beat during his reporting days. After James Meredith had been shot in Mississippi, and a wire-service photograph of his prone body on the road was received in New York, Sitton grabbed the photo and scanned its edges closely, asking, "Where's Roy Reed?"

Tom Wicker in Washington became the target of Daniel's troubleshooter, Harrison Salisbury, and was chided for not producing enough front-page exclusives. Later there were discussions in New York about replacing Wicker as the bureau chief in Washington. This increased the animosity in Washington toward Salisbury and, to a lesser degree, Daniel—Salisbury being referred to as "Rasputin."

James Reston staunchly defended Wicker. But New York kept up its attack. There was not only the recurring theme that the Washington bureau was overly protective of its friends in government, but Wicker himself was blamed both for his running of the bureau and his performance as a reporter. He was just not coming up with big exclusive stories, they said, although failing to explain what specific big stories he was missing, nor how he was supposed to get exclusives that his own specialists were obviously not getting. The New York editors pointed out that Reston had come up with numerous exclusives during his younger days in Washington, but Reston quickly came back with the argument that Washington in those days was different—the war had just ended, it was a world of emerging nations, news was more easily gotten. Today, he said, Washington is pretty much a one-man town, Johnsonville, and if Wicker were the sort who was merely interested in protecting his own flank from New York's attack he could have focused each day on the President's movements and moods.

This volleying went back and forth between New York and Washington for more than a year, with some in the bureau contending that it was no more than New York's taking further vengeance on Washington, making Wicker pay for all the years of autonomy enjoyed by Reston and Krock.

But New York seemed committed to its decision to replace Tom Wicker as late as July of 1966. With the possible retirement of Arthur Krock, who would be eighty in November—though he seemed as nimble as when he joined the *Times* in 1927—there would be room on the editorial page for a column by Wicker.

Then, inexplicably, New York changed its plan. Perhaps cognizant of the low morale in Washington, perhaps unable to replace Wicker with an individual who could run the bureau better, the New York editors reversed themselves. Wicker now was told that he would remain as bureau chief *and* write a column. Wicker was pleased, but also weary of office politics. He did not want to remain the bureau chief if he had to be continuously bombarded by New York, and he communicated this to Catledge. If Wicker were to succeed as the bureau chief, he knew, he could not afford to be regarded in New York as just Reston's boy, or anybody else's boy. He had to be the actual choice of the New York editors, including Turner Catledge. When he put this notion up to New York, he was assured that he was New York's choice.

Suddenly there were new rumors in the New York city room. Salisbury was out. Rosenthal was sitting at Salisbury's desk. Gelb was at Rosenthal's desk. Rosenthal was Daniel's heir apparent. Where was Daniel? Where was Catledge? Who was running the store?

These rumors—prompted perhaps by Salisbury's going on a round-the-world reporting trip, and by his recently expressed desire to get back to writing after four years in the city room—continued throughout the summer.

It had been a wonderful summer for Clifton Daniel. His wife had delivered their fourth son; the *Times* was stronger than ever, unshaken by all the internal movement; and he, as its managing editor, was being recognized as something of a celebrity. He was included in the 1966 edition of *Current Biography*, and magazine writers made appointments to see him—no longer because he was married to a President's daughter, but because of his position at the helm of one of the few newspapers that seemed certain of survival.

As one being interviewed, however, he is not nearly so smooth as when he is conducting an interview. Once he kept a man from the *Saturday Evening Post* waiting for forty-five minutes. Then instead of merely apologizing for the delay, Daniel perhaps tried to make light of it—as he had years ago, possibly, in that note to the brunette lady he called a "fine cover-up" for his courtship with Margaret. Daniel's greeting to the magazine writer was, "If someone had kept *me* waiting for forty-five minutes when I was a reporter, I'd have gotten up and left." The man from the *Post* said nothing. But interviewers always get in the last word, and his article about the *Times* was hardly flattering to Daniel.

Mrs. Daniel, who has had so much more experience than her husband in such matters, will sometimes sit in when he is being interviewed at home; and one evening, after he had tossed off a remark that might have seemed conceited in print, she quickly edged forward on the sofa and warned, "Watch out, he'll print that."

"No, he won't print that," Daniel said, casually dismissing her fears.

"He *will*," she said, nodding.

"No, I won't," the magazine writer said. "Someday I may come to you for a job."

"Yes, and you'll not get one if you print that," Daniel said.

"He couldn't be less concerned," Margaret said.

"That's not true," the writer said.

"He couldn't be *less* concerned," Margaret repeated, more firmly, still shaking her head at what Daniel had said.

The most endearing thing about Daniel at home is his obvious delight in his four children. With them he is entirely relaxed, delightfully informal—a manner that seems beyond him in the office. On weekends he is seen often in Central Park with his older boys—Clifton Truman Daniel, nine, and William Wallace Daniel, seven—and whenever he makes airplane trips he usually checks the terminal's toy counters to see what he may buy to take home. In summertime the Daniels vacate their Park Avenue duplex for a house in Bedford, New York, and Daniel commutes to the *Times*. When he returns in the evening Margaret is waiting at the station, always parked in the same spot. When she sees him, she honks her horn. He comes over, perfectly pressed, not a hair out of place, and gets into the driver's seat as she slides over. He kisses her on the cheek. She begins to talk as he starts up the engine of a Chevrolet station wagon. Then he spins the car around, and they begin the drive home—a typical American couple.

He is, she says, somewhat like her father. Mr. Truman, though not known for it, was also something of a "dude"; while he is known for his Giv'em-Hell-Harry manner, Mr. Truman at home was reserved and he never swore. "The only cussing done at home was by my mother," Margaret said. Both men, she continues, are "very tough characters, in a nice way," adding, "I couldn't get along with a man that wasn't definite, tough." The two men are also very compatible, and when a writer visited Mr. Truman in Independence, Missouri, earlier this year about Clifton Daniel, Harry Truman's last words were the gentle warning: "You'd better write something nice about my son-in-law. He's a good boy, an ideal son-in-law. He's never done anything to embarrass me." Mr. Truman paused for a second, then said, "And I don't *think* I've done anything to embarrass him."

The Daniels occasionally take the children to visit the Trumans in Missouri, and Daniel himself often takes one or two of his boys to revisit Zebulon. Margaret is "terrified" of airplanes and avoids any trip that she can, but Daniel likes to fly, enjoying the comfort of first-class travel. He is in tune with the tidiness of terminals, the well-dressed people; he relishes the two drinks before dinner served by winsome stewardesses who appeal to him not only because of their good grooming and precise tailoring, their pleasant smiles and desire to please—but also because of their almost ritualistic movements as they bend to serve, so graceful and controlled. "They are America's geisha girls," he once observed, flying back to New York after a speech in the Midwest. Then he said, almost wistfully, "I never knew an airline stewardess. A few of them used to live in the building I was in years ago in London. I used to hear them at night. But I never knew one." Then he said, "Premier Ky's wife was once an airline stewardess." He thought for a second. "Very pretty."

The speeches that Daniel makes around the country, usually concerning the role of a free press, are delivered in his style of cool elegance, and are followed by questions from the audience. People are very curious about the *Times*, and many of them get from hearing and seeing Daniel a confirmation of their own ideas about the paper, its calm posture and pride in appearance, the respect for its tradition and the certainty of its virtue. They get from Daniel the image the institution has of itself, which is not necessarily all the reality beneath the surface. For there are other sides to the *Times*, other speeches made by *Times*men gathered at a Forty-third Street bar, or *Times*men talking to themselves in bed at 4 a.m., that reveal the frustration in working for a place so large, so solvent and sure—a fact factory where the workers realize the too-apparent truth: they are replaceable. The paper can get along without any of them. The executives like to deny it, and nobody likes to talk about it, but it is true.

And this truth evokes both sadness and bitterness in many who deeply love the paper, who have romanticized and personalized it, thought of it as some great gray goddess with whom they were having an affair—forgetting that no matter who they are, nor how well they have performed, they will soon be too old for her. She is ageless and they must yield to newer, younger men, and sometimes they are replaced as casually as light bulbs in a great movie marquee—changed automatically, though luminous as ever, once they reach a certain age; and this act does not go unnoticed by *Times*men still on the scene. They deplore the departure of older men such as Brooks Atkinson, who has not revisited the paper since; and William L. ("Atomic Bill") Laurence, the science writer; and the baseball writer, John Drebinger, who at his retirement party announced, after a few drinks, "Well, if I'd known retirement was so great, I'd have done it long ago," to which a *Times* executive responded, coolly, "Well, then, why did you give us so much trouble, John?"

Automation is everywhere, the complex problem shared by big business throughout the world, and yet at the *New York Times* there is the lingering notion that journalism is not a business, but a calling, and there is resentment in the city room on election night when a half-dozen machines are rolled in to do what the late Leo Egan used to do so well, predict the outcome; and there is vengeance among the ink-stained workers in the composing room for the increasing number of machines that can do everything better than men—except strike. There is irreverence in the city room for those items that promote communication without contact—the memos, the silver microphone on the City desk; and there is perhaps a realization among the high executives, too, that though the *Times* has long thrived on keeping "in touch," it has now grown to such enormity that it does not really know what is going on under its own roof. In the spring of 1966 there was the announcement in the *Times'* house organ that a team of trained psychologists, working under the auspices of an independent research organization, Daniel Yankelovich, Inc., would interview a "scientifically selected random sample" of *Times* employees in an effort "to determine how, in this large and varied organization, it can establish greater rapport with the men and women who work for it."

None of these intrafamilial matters are hinted at in any of the public speeches by Clifton Daniel or other executives; and the audiences who listen, and the subscribers who each day read the *Times*—and indeed, many who work for it, including the *Times'* editorial board—are not aware that there is any difference in what the *Times* seems to be, and what it is. The editorial writers, for example, continue to publish their lofty principles—they condemn congestion on city streets (ignoring the traffic jams caused at night by *Times* delivery trucks parked below); they lament the passing of landmarks, the demolition of historic buildings (not explaining why the newspaper sold its famous Times Tower building to Allied Chemical, nor why the celebrated electric-light sign that once rotated *Times* headlines around the building is now run by *Life* magazine). The *Times* is quick to denounce the suppression of news and ideas, even when such may be contrary to its own editorial policy, and yet in recent years its news department has refused to print anything by Herbert L. Matthews, who now sits rather quietly in room 1048 along a corridor of editorial writers. In 1963 Matthews revisited Cuba and Fidel Castro—who profited so greatly from Matthews's interviews prior to the revolution—and, upon his return, offered to write articles; but the news department refused. He had embarrassed the paper, he knows, and yet even now Matthews believes that Castro was not a Communist when the revolution began.

In the spring of 1966, Herbert Matthews returned to Cuba, again representing the *Times*' editorial board, not its news department; while there he reacquainted himself with Fidel Castro and Cuba, amassing twenty-five thousand words of notes. The news department again, upon his return to New York, declined his offer to write for it. So now Matthews writes anonymously for the *Times*' editorial page on Latin American affairs, including those in Cuba—about which he has often been critical; other than that, he devotes himself to his books and to his belief that history will finally absolve him. But at the age of sixty-six, he is not counting on a clearance during his own lifetime.

Clifton Daniel appears at the *New York Times* each morning around ten, having read all the newspapers including the *Wall Street Journal* and, until recently, *Women's Wear Daily.* His secretary, Pat, who greets him outside his office, is an extremely pretty young woman who dresses impeccably—he chose her himself, and one is not surprised. "I am interested," he admits, "in appearances," and this extends to not only individuals' grooming or clothes, but also to the manner in which they conduct their private lives. He objects to being described as "puritanical," indicating that it matters little to him if the whole staff of the *New York Times* is involved in a vast assortment of pleasurable pursuits, sexual or otherwise; he is concerned, however, with "appearances."

Daniel's day is a smoothly run schedule of exits and entrances by subordinate editors seeking his advice or affirmation, and by strangers seeking his confirmation prior to employment on the *Times.* He also reserves time, prior to the four-o'clock news conference in his office, to reread those portions of the *Times* that bothered him slightly, perhaps because of the vagueness of the wording; or the sense that the reporter was becoming *involved*, the unpardonable sin; or maybe there had been an error that would require a "Correction," always an upsetting item on his agenda.

As he read the paper on one balmy summer day in 1966 he did not notice the item at first; it was on Page 30, and it was printed in agate type deep within a list announcing the names of City College students who had received awards: and yet there it was: "BRETT AWARD to the student who has worked hardest under a great handicap—Jake Barnes."

To anyone who has read Hemingway's *The Sun Also Rises*, the references are clear: Lady Brett and the impotent hero who loves her, Jake Barnes. In the *Times*!

A. M. Rosenthal, whose deskmen had edited and checked the story, had not noticed it, either, until the next day, after it had run through all editions; and he learned of it through a phone call from *Newsweek* magazine, which thought it was very funny.

Rosenthal saw nothing funny about the item. He was immediately infuriated. If the young *Times* correspondent who had been assigned to the City College story had been guilty of deliberately inserting false information into the *Times*' news columns, there was no recourse but to fire him. Many years ago, A. J. Liebling, then employed as a deskman in the Sports department, had done something like this; instead of listing the correct name of the basketball referee in the agate box score, as was required, Liebling—who always experienced difficulty in getting the correspondents to remember to get the referee's name—would merely write, in place of the name, the Italian word *Ignoto*—"Unknown." Mr. Ignoto's name would appear on sometimes two, three, or even four basketball games a night—far too energetic and omnipresent a man to be believed for very long. When the prank became known, Liebling was fired, and he went on to use his imagination more wisely on the *New Yorker*.

The difficulty in the City College incident was that the correspondent who *might* have been guilty—Rosenthal had not yet called him—was Clyde Haberman, one of Rosenthal's favorites, a young man of twenty-one who reminded Rosenthal very much of himself: Haberman was skinny and driving, as Rosenthal had been twenty years ago when *he* was the City College correspondent, and Haberman had quickly demonstrated an ability to sense a story, then to write it well. In the eight months he had been the City College correspondent, Clyde Haberman had produced more than sixty pieces, a remarkable achievement for an individual whose beat was limited to one campus. Rosenthal also knew how dedicated Haberman was to journalism, how determined he seemed to be in making the grade on the *Times*; in no time at all, Rosenthal believed, Clyde Haberman would be recognized as one of the bright young men of the *New York Times*.

But if Haberman had inserted the Brett Award, Rosenthal knew, he would have to go. There was no chance of supporting a young man in this situation as Rosenthal had supported another man, a Negro named Junius Griffin, who had written for the *Times* about the existence of a "Blood

Brother" gang in Harlem, militant men trained in karate who would soon move on Manhattan if things did not get better. Immediately, in Harlem and throughout New York, there were angry denials about the veracity of the Blood Brothers—some people challenging the story as an exaggeration, others calling it an outright hoax. Rosenthal checked it, and even today claims that Junius Griffin was not writing fiction; but the *Times* was loudly criticized then by other newspapers and periodicals—an opportunity never missed when they think the *Times* is wrong—and Rosenthal himself was mocked by some of the Old Guard in the city room. The Blood Brother story, they said, was "Rosenthal's Bay of Pigs."

Clyde Haberman was in bed when Rosenthal called his home in the Bronx. Haberman had been awakened fifteen minutes before by a call from the City College publicity department saying it had been receiving inquiries about the "Brett Award." It was then, and only then, that Haberman remembered that he had forgotten to remove the humorous award, as he had intended, from the long list before turning it into the desk. The Brett Award had come into his head after an hour of boredom and drowsiness in having to type the long, unending list of prizes and awards that, Haberman was sure, nobody read. He gave an award to "Jake Barnes," then laughed and continued to type; later he became busy with something else, forgetting about Barnes and Lady Brett as he turned the story in—and it took the morning phone calls to remind him, first from the college press agent, then from Rosenthal himself.

"Clyde," Rosenthal began, softly, "did you see the City College prize list this morning?"

"Yes."

"Did you see a Brett Award?"

"Yes."

"How did that get there?"

"I, uh, guess I put it in," Clyde Haberman said, timidly, "in a moment of silliness."

"You did," Rosenthal said, slowly, the voice getting hard. "Well, that moment finished you in newspapers."

Haberman could not believe the words. His first reaction, as he later related it to a friend, was to be stunned by Rosenthal: "Finished with newspapers! He must be kidding! It isn't possible over an inane thing like this!"

Haberman got dressed, having been told by Rosenthal to appear in the city room immediately, but even as he rode the subway to Times Square, Haberman could not believe that he was finished at the *Times*. Rosenthal, who had learned from personal experience the importance of a second chance on the *Times*, Rosenthal, the author of that classic on the Warsaw ghetto—"So sentimental," Haberman had said, upon rereading it, "that you'd think he would be ashamed to expose such raw emotion"— Rosenthal was merely upset by the incident. Haberman knew him well enough to sense that Rosenthal regarded a joke on the *Times* to be a joke on him; yet he was confident, once the lack of malicious intent had been explained, that the mistake would pass and be forgotten.

It was noon when Haberman entered the city room. Nearly everybody was out to lunch. He walked up to the City desk and addressed a broad-shouldered gray-haired clerk named Charley Bevilacqua who had been there for years.

"Is Mr. Rosenthal in?" Haberman asked.

"Out to lunch," Bevilacqua said.

Haberman walked away, but Bevilacqua called after him, harshly, "You'd better stick around. He wants to talk to you."

Haberman wanted to whirl around and say, "No kidding, you idiot, why didn't someone tell me?", but being in no position to act offensively, he retreated meekly into the city room's rows and rows of empty desks, occupied only by the obituary writer, Alden Whitman; a reporter, Bernard Weinraub; and a young man on tryout, Steve Conn, a friend of Haberman's.

"Hey, Clyde," Conn said, laughing, "did you see that Brett Award in the paper today?"

Haberman admitted writing it, and Conn smacked a hand gently against his forehead and groaned, "Oh, *God.*"

Haberman took a seat in the middle of the city room to await Rosenthal's return from lunch. He focused on the silver microphone up ahead—a most intimidating gadget, he always thought, for most young men on the paper: they feared, after having turned in their story, the sight of the editor picking up the microphone and booming out their names, paging them to the City desk to explain their ambiguities or errors. Just from the sound from the microphone, Haberman knew, a young reporter could usually tell the mood of the editor: if the editor paged the reporter in a snappy, peremptory tone—"*Mr. Haberman!*" very quick—it meant that there was only a small question, one that the editor wished to hastily discuss so he could get on to other matters elsewhere; but if the editor languished on the sound of a young man's name—"*Mr. H a b e r m a n*"—then the editor's patience was thin, and the matter was very serious indeed.

Twenty-five minutes later Haberman saw Rosenthal walk into the city room, then stride toward his desk. Haberman lowered his head as he heard the microphone being picked up; it was the voice of Charley Bevilacqua, a low sad note of finality, "*Mr. H a b e r m a n.*"

Haberman got up and began the long walk up the aisle, passing the rows of empty desks, thinking suddenly of a course he had taken under Paddy Chayefsky in screenplay-writing, and wishing he had a camera panning the room to capture permanently the starkness of the scene.

"Sit down," Rosenthal said. Then, as he sat, Haberman heard Rosenthal begin, "You will never be able to write for this newspaper again."

Haberman now accepted the reality of it all, and yet made one final attempt at reminding Rosenthal of the work he had done from City College, the many exclusives and features, and Rosenthal cut him off: "Yes, and that's why you acted like a fool—I had backed you, and written memos about you, and you could have been on staff in a year or two . . . You made me look like a jackass. You made the *Times* look like a jackass."

Then, his voice softening and becoming sad, Rosenthal explained that the most inviolate thing the *Times* had was its news columns: People should be able to believe *every* word, and there would never be tolerance for tampering. Further, Rosenthal said, if Haberman were pardoned, the discipline of the whole staff would suffer—any one of them could err and then say, "Well, Haberman got away with it."

There was a pause, and in this time Rosenthal's voice shifted to yet another mood—hope for Haberman, not on the *Times* but somewhere else. Haberman had talent, Rosenthal said, and now it was a question of accepting the fact that it was all over with the Gray Lady and moving on determinedly to make the grade somewhere else.

Rosenthal talked with him for another five minutes, warmly and enthusiastically; then the two men stood up, and shook hands. Haberman walked back, shaken, to a desk to type out his resignation. Clifton Daniel knew what was going on; Rosenthal had conferred with him, and also with other editors in Daniel's office, and they all agreed to accept the resignation as soon as Haberman could type it out.

Having done so, and handed it in, Haberman was aware that other people in the city room were now watching him. He did not linger. He quickly left the city room and waited in the hall for an elevator, and was surprised to see the tall figure of Arthur Gelb running after him calling, "Clyde, wait."

Haberman had never particularly liked Gelb, having been influenced by the Old Guard's view; but now Gelb was deeply concerned only about Haberman, and he reassured the younger man that the world was not over, there were brighter days ahead. Haberman thanked him and was very moved by Gelb's concern.

Then Haberman rode the elevator down to the first floor, not pausing as he passed the stern statue of Adolph Ochs in the lobby, nor stopping to talk with the few friends he met coming through the revolving door. He would return to City College for his final session in the fall, and then after graduation worry about what would happen next. The next day there was a "Correction" in the *Times*, only a single paragraph, yet it reaffirmed that despite all the shifting and shuffling of people and ideas, there are some things that never change at the *Times*. The paragraph, written by Clifton Daniel, read:

In Wednesday's issue, *The New York Times* published a list of prizes and awards presented at the City College commencement. Included was a "Brett Award." There is no such award. It was put in as a reporter's prank. *The Times* regrets the publication of this fictitious item.

March 16, 1963

Memo: Harold Hayes
Subj: Expense acct for "Paris
      Review" crowd

From: Gay Talese

Saturday,Jan 12th	—Interview Harold Humes, cabs, lunch...........	$6.50
Sunday Jan 13th	—Harold Humes,Jack Gelber; cabs, lunch.......	$7.00
Wednesday,Jan 16th	—Donald Stewart, lunch,drinks (Gino's)......	$12.00
Thursday,Jan 17th	— Robert Silvers, drinks/lus;Patsy Matthiessen	$15.00
Friday, Jan 18th	—Harold Humes, dinner....	$10.00
Saturday,Jan 19th...	—Thomas H.Guinzburg, drinks.....	$5.00
Monday,Jan. 21—	—John P.C.Train...cabs, drinks...	$6.00
Tuesday, Jan.22	—George Plimpton....cabs, lunch	$7.00
Wednesday,Jan 23	" "	$8.00
Thurs,Jan 24...	—Peter Matthiessen,Geo Plimpton;lunch,drinks... Plus William Styron...incl drinks after........ (at Gino's)	$35.00
Friday,Jan 25....	—Breakfast with Styron...	$4.00
Sunday,January 27th ...	..Breakfast at Sherry Netherlands with Harry Kurnitz, PeterDuchin, Plimpton,Silvers.......	$10.00
Thursday,January 31....	—Breakfast with James Baldwin,cabs,etc.........	$6.00
Wednesday,January 30...	—Plimpton,Styron,Humes..lunch....	$13.00
Friday,February 1...	—Plimpton lunch,cabs,drinks..	$6.00
Satur ay,Feb 2 ..	—John P.C.Train, cabs...etc.	$3.00
Sunday ,Feb 3d	—Plimpton, cabs, drinks...	$4.50
Monday,Feb 4th ...	—Plimpton, drinks...	$3.00
Tuesday,Feb 5...	—Wm BPene du Bois, lunch....Plimpton....	$15.00
Wednesday,Feb 6th...	—Plimpton, drinks.....	$5.00
Thursday,Feb 7th..	—Plimpton, lunch...	$8.00
Monday,Feb 11th....	—Richard Seaver , cabs, drinks...	$4.50

Plus, incidentals: home fone,typewriter
             ribbons,etc................ $8.50

Total spent $200.00

Total advanced by
     Esquire............ $200.00

Amount owed Esquire   0
Amount owed Talese   0

EXPENSE ACCOUNT ACCRUED WITH THE *PARIS REVIEW*
CROWD WHILE WRITING "LOOKING FOR HEMINGWAY" IN 1963

Looking for Hemingway

> I remember very well the impression I had of Hemingway that first
> afternoon. He was an extraordinarily good-looking young man,
> twenty-three years old. It was not long after that that everybody
> was twenty-six. It became the period of being twenty-six. During
> the next two or three years all the young men were twenty-six years
> old. It was the right age apparently for that time and place.
>
> —GERTRUDE STEIN

EARLY IN THE FIFTIES another young generation of American
expatriates in Paris became twenty-six years old, but they were not
Sad Young Men, nor were they Lost; they were the witty, irreverent
sons of a conquering nation, and, though they came mostly from wealthy
parents and had been graduated from Harvard or Yale, they seemed endlessly delighted in posing as paupers and dodging the bill collectors, possibly because it seemed challenging and distinguished them from American
tourists, whom they despised, and also because it was another way of having fun with the French, who despised *them.* Nevertheless, they lived in
happy squalor on the Left Bank for two or three years amid the whores,
jazz musicians, and pederast poets, and became involved with people both
tragic and mad, including a passionate Spanish painter who one day cut
open a vein in his leg and finished his final portrait with his own blood.

In July they drove down to Pamplona to run from the bulls, and when
they returned they played tennis with Irwin Shaw at Saint-Cloud on a
magnificent court overlooking Paris—and, when they tossed up the ball
to serve, *there,* sprawled before them, was the whole city: the Eiffel Tower,

Sacré-Coeur, the Opéra, the spires of Notre Dame in the distance. Irwin Shaw was amused by them. He called them "The Tall Young Men."

The tallest of them, at six feet four inches, was George Ames Plimpton, a quick, graceful tennis player with long, skinny limbs, a small head, bright blue eyes, and a delicate, fine-tipped nose. He had come to Paris in 1952, at the age of twenty-six, because several other tall, young Americans—and some short, wild ones—were publishing a literary quarterly to be called the *Paris Review,* over the protest of one of their staff members, a poet, who wanted it to be called *Druids' Home Companion* and to be printed on birch bark. George Plimpton was made editor in chief, and soon he could be seen strolling through the streets of Paris with a long, woolen scarf flung around his neck, or sometimes with a black evening cape billowing from his shoulders, cutting a figure reminiscent of Toulouse-Lautrec's famous lithograph of Aristide Bruant, that dashing litterateur of the nineteenth century.

Though much of the editing of the *Paris Review* was done at sidewalk cafés by editors awaiting their turns on the pinball machine, the magazine nevertheless became very successful because the editors had talent, money, and taste, and they avoided using such typical little-magazine words as *zeitgeist* and *dichotomous,* and published no crusty critiques about Melville or Kafka, but instead printed the poetry and fiction of gifted young writers not yet popular. They also started a superb series of interviews with famous authors—who took them to lunch, introduced them to actresses, playwrights, and producers, and everybody invited everybody else to parties, and the parties have not stopped, even though ten years have passed; Paris is no longer the scene, and the Tall Young Men have become thirty-six years old.

They now live in New York. And most of the parties are held at George Plimpton's large bachelor apartment on Seventy-second Street overlooking the East River, an apartment that is also the headquarters for what Elaine Dundy calls "the Quality Lit Set," or what Candida Donadio, the agent, calls "The East Side Gang," or what everybody else just calls "the *Paris Review* Crowd." The Plimpton apartment today is the liveliest literary salon in New York—the only place where, standing in a single room on almost any night of the week, one may find James Jones; William Styron; Irwin Shaw; a few call girls for decoration; Norman Mailer; Philip Roth;

Lillian Hellman; a bongo player; a junkie or two; Harold L. Humes; Jack Gelber; Sadruddin Aga Khan; Terry Southern; Blair Fuller; the cast from *Beyond the Fringe*; Tom Keogh; William Pène du Bois; Bee Whistler Dabney (an artist who descends from Whistler's mother); Robert Silvers; and an angry veteran of the Bay of Pigs invasion; and a retired bunny from the Playboy Club; John P. C. Train; Joe Fox; John Phillips Marquand; and Robert W. Dowling's secretary; Peter Duchin; Gene Andrewski; Jean vanden Heuvel; and Ernest Hemingway's former boxing coach; Frederick Seidel; Thomas H. Guinzburg; David Amram; and a bartender from down the street; Barbara Epstein; Jill Fox; and a local distributor of pot; Piedy Gimbel; Dwight Macdonald; Bill Cole; Jules Feiffer; *and* into such a scene one wintry night earlier this year walked another old friend of George Plimpton's—Jacqueline Kennedy.

"Jackie!" George called out, opening the door to greet the First Lady and also her sister and brother-in-law, the Radziwills. Mrs. Kennedy, smiling broadly between gleaming earrings, extended her hand to George, whom she has known since her dancing-school days, and they chatted for a few seconds in the hallway while George helped her with her coat. Then, peeking into the bedroom and noticing a mound of overcoats piled higher than a Volkswagen, Mrs. Kennedy said, in a soft, hushed, sympathetic voice, "Oh, *George*—your *b e d!*"

George shrugged and then escorted them through the hall down three steps into the smoky scene.

"Look," said one hipster in the corner, "there's Lee Radziwill's sister!"

George first introduced Mrs. Kennedy to Ved Mehta, the Indian writer, and then slipped her skillfully past Norman Mailer toward William Styron.

"Why, hel*LO*, Bill," she said, shaking hands, "nice to see you."

For the next few moments, talking with Styron and Cass Canfield, Jr., Mrs. Kennedy stood with her back to Sandra Hochman, a Greenwich Village poetess, a streaked blonde in a thick woolly sweater and partially unzipped ski pants.

"I think," Miss Hochman whispered to a friend, tossing a backward nod at Mrs. Kennedy's beautiful white brocade suit, "that I am a bit *déshabillée.*"

"Nonsense," said her friend, flicking cigarette ashes on the rug. And, in truth, it must be said that none of the seventy other people in that room felt that Sandra Hochman's outfit contrasted unpleasantly with the First Lady's; in fact, some did not even notice the First Lady, and there was one who noticed her but failed to recognize her.

"My," he said, squinting through the smoke toward the elaborately teased coiffure of Mrs. Kennedy, "that *really* is the look this year, isn't it? And that chick has almost made it."

While Mrs. Kennedy conversed in the corner, Princess Radziwill talked with Bee Whistler Dabney a few feet away, and Prince Radziwill stood alone next to the baby grand piano humming to himself. He often hums to himself at parties. In Washington he is known as a great hummer.

Fifteen minutes later Mrs. Kennedy, expected soon at a dinner given by Adlai Stevenson, said good-bye to Styron and Canfield and, escorted by George Plimpton, headed for the steps toward the hall. Norman Mailer, who had meanwhile drunk three glasses of water, was standing by the steps. He looked hard at her as she passed. She did not return his glance.

Three quick steps, and she was gone—down the hall, her coat on, her long white gloves on, down two flights of steps to the sidewalk, the Radziwills and George Plimpton behind her.

"Look," squealed a blonde, Sally Belfrage, gazing down from the kitchen window at the figures below climbing into the limousine, "there's *George*! And *look* at that car!"

"What's so unusual about that car?" somebody asked. "It's only a Cadillac."

"Yes, but it's *black*, and so-o-o *un*chromed."

Sally Belfrage watched as the big car, pointed in the direction of another world, moved quietly away, but in the living room the party went on louder than before, with nearly everyone oblivious to the fact that the host had disappeared. But there was liquor to be consumed, and, besides, by just casting an eye over the photographs on the walls throughout the apartment, one could easily feel the presence of George Plimpton. One photograph shows him fighting small bulls in Spain with Hemingway; another catches him drinking beer with other Tall Young Men at a Paris café; others show him as a lieutenant marching a platoon of troops through Rome, as a tennis player for King's College, as an amateur prizefighter sparring with Archie Moore in Stillman's Gymnasium, an occasion during which the rancid smell of the gym was temporarily replaced by the musk of El Morocco and the cheers of Plimpton's friends when he scored with a solid jab—but it quickly changed to *"Ohhhhhhh"* when Archie Moore retaliated with a punch that broke part of the cartilage in Plimpton's nose, causing it to bleed and causing Miles Davis to ask afterward, "Archie, is that black blood or white blood on your gloves?" to which one of Plimpton's friends replied, "Sir, *that* is blue blood."

Also on the wall is Plimpton's rebab, a one-stringed instrument of goatskin that Bedouin tribesmen gave him prior to his doing a walk-on in *Lawrence of Arabia* during a dust storm. And above his baby grand piano—he plays it well enough to have won a tie-for-third prize on Amateur Night at the Apollo Theater a couple of years ago in Harlem—is a coconut sent him by a lady swimmer he knows in Palm Beach, and also a photograph of another girl, Vali, the orange-haired Existentialist known to all Left Bank concierges as *la bête,* and also a major-league baseball that Plimpton occasionally hurls full distance across the living room into a short, chunky, stuffed chair, using the same windup as when he pitched batting practice against Willie Mays while researching his book *Out of My League*, which concerns how it feels to be an amateur among pros—and which, incidentally, is a key not only to George Ames Plimpton but to many others on the *Paris Review* as well.

They are obsessed, so many of them, by the wish to know how the other half lives. And so they befriend the more interesting of the odd, avoid the downtown dullards on Wall Street, and dip into the world of the junkie, the pederast, the prizefighter, and the adventurer in pursuit of kicks and literature, being influenced perhaps by that glorious generation of ambulance drivers that preceded them to Paris at the age of twenty-six.

In Paris in the early fifties, their great white hope was Irwin Shaw because, in the words of Thomas Guinzburg, a Yale man then managing editor of the *Paris Review*, "Shaw was a tough, tennis-playing, hard-drinking writer with a good-looking wife—the closest thing we had to Hemingway." Of course, the editor in chief, George Plimpton, then as now, kept the magazine going, kept the group together, and set a style of romanticism that was—and is—infectious.

Arriving in Paris in the Spring of 1952 with a wardrobe that included the tails his grandfather had worn in the twenties, and which George himself had worn in 1951 while attending a ball in London as an escort to the future queen of England, he moved immediately into a tool shed behind a house owned by Gertrude Stein's nephew. Since the door of the shed was jammed, Plimpton, to enter it, had to hoist himself, his books, and his grandfather's tails through the window. His bed was a long, thin cot flanked by a lawn mower and garden hose, and was covered by an electric blanket that Plimpton could never remember to turn off—so that, when he returned to the shed at night and plopped into the cot, he was usually greeted by the angry howls of several stray cats reluctant to leave the warmth that his forgetfulness had provided.

One lonely night, before returning home, Plimpton took the walk through Montparnasse down the same streets and past the same cafés that Jake Barnes took after leaving Lady Brett in *The Sun Also Rises*. Plimpton wanted to see what Hemingway had seen, to feel what Hemingway had felt. Then, the walk over, Plimpton went into the nearest bar and ordered a drink.

In 1952 the *Paris Review*'s headquarters was a one-room office at 8 Rue Garancière. It was furnished with a desk, four chairs, a bottle of brandy, and several lively, long-legged Smith and Radcliffe girls who were anxious to get onto the masthead so that they might convince their parents back home of their innocence abroad. But so many young women came and went that Plimpton's business manager, a small, sharp-tongued Harvard wit named John P. C. Train, decided it was ridiculous to try to remember all their names, whereupon he declared that they should henceforth all be called by one name—"Apetecker." And the Apetecker alumnae came to include, at one time or another, Jane Fonda, Joan Dillon Moseley (daughter of Treasury Secretary Dillon), Gail Jones (daughter of Lena Horne), and Louisa Noble (daughter of the Groton football coach), a very industrious but forgetful girl who was endlessly losing manuscripts, letters, dictionaries. One day, after John P. C. Train received a letter from a librarian complaining that Miss Noble was a year overdue on a book, he wrote back:

Dear Sir:

I take the liberty of writing to you in my own hand because Miss L. Noble took with her the last time she left this office the typewriter on which I was accustomed to compose these messages. Perhaps

when she comes into your library you will ask if we might not have
this machine.
Subscription blank enclosed.
Yours faithfully,

J. P. C. Train

Since the *Paris Review*'s one-room office obviously was too small to
fulfill the staff's need for mixing business with pleasure, and since there
was also a limit to the number of hours they could spend at cafés, everybody would usually gather at 5 p.m. at the apartment of Peter and Patsy
Matthiessen on 14 Rue Perceval, where by that time a party was sure to be
in progress.

Peter Matthiessen, then fiction editor of the *Paris Review*, was a tall,
thin Yale graduate who as a youngster had attended St. Bernard's School in
New York with George Plimpton, and who now was working on his first
novel, *Race Rock*. Patsy was a small, lovely, vivacious blonde with pale blue
eyes and a marvelous figure, and all the boys of twenty-six were in love
with her. She was the daughter of the late Richard Southgate, onetime chief
of protocol for the State Department, and Patsy had gone to lawn parties
with Kennedy children, had chauffeurs and governesses, and, in her junior year at Smith, in 1948, had come to Paris and met Peter. Three years
later, married, they returned to Paris and acquired for twenty-one dollars
a month this apartment in Montparnasse that had been left vacant when
Peter's old girlfriend had gone off to Venezuela.

The apartment had high ceilings, a terrace, and lots of sun. On one wall
was a Foujita painting of a gigantic head of a cat. The other wall was all
glass, and there were large trees against the glass and wild growth crawling
up it, and visitors to this apartment often felt that they were in a monstrous
fishbowl, particularly by 6 p.m., when the room was floating with Dutch
gin and absinthe and the cat's head seemed bigger, and a few junkies would
wander in, nod, and settle softly, soundlessly in the corner.

This apartment, in the fifties, was as much a meeting place for the young
American literati as was Gertrude Stein's apartment in the twenties, and
it also caught the atmosphere that would, in the sixties, prevail at George
Plimpton's apartment in New York.

William Styron, often at the Matthiessens', describes their apartment in his novel *Set This House on Fire*, and other novelists there were John Phillips Marquand and Terry Southern, both editors on the *Paris Review*, and sometimes James Baldwin, and nearly always Harold L. Humes, a chunky, indefatigable, impulsive young man with a beard, beret, and a silver-handled umbrella. After being dismissed from MIT for taking a Radcliffe girl sailing several hours beyond her bedtime, and after spending an unhappy tour with the Navy making mayonnaise in Bainbridge, Maryland, Harold Humes burst onto the Paris scene in full rebellion.

He became a chess hustler in cafés, earning several hundred francs a night. It was in the cafés that he met Peter Matthiessen, and they both talked of starting a little magazine that would be the *Paris Review.* Before coming to Paris, Humes had never worked on a magazine, but had grown fond of a little magazine called *Zero,* edited by a small Greek named Themistocles Hoetes, whom everybody called "Them." Impressed by what Them had done with *Zero,* Humes purchased for $600 a magazine called the *Paris News Post,* which John Ciardi later called the "best fourth-rate imitation of the *New Yorker* I have ever seen," and to which Matthiessen felt condescendingly superior, and so Humes sold it for $600 to a very nervous English girl, under whom it collapsed one issue later. Then Humes and Matthiessen and others began a long series of talks on what policy, if any, they would follow should the *Paris Review* ever get beyond the talking and drinking stages.

When the magazine was finally organized, and when George Plimpton was selected as its editor instead of Humes, Humes was disappointed. He refused to leave the cafés to sell advertising or negotiate with French printers. And in the summer of 1952 he did not hesitate to leave Paris with William Styron, accepting an invitation from a French actress, Mme. Nénot, to go down to Cap Myrt, near Saint-Tropez, and visit her fifty-room villa that had been designed by her father, a leading architect. The villa had been occupied by the Germans early in the war. And so when Styron and Humes arrived they found holes in its walls, through which they could look out to the sea, and the grass was so high and the trees so thick with grapes that Humes's little Volkswagen became tangled in the grass. So they went on foot toward the villa, but suddenly stopped when they saw, rushing past them, a young, half-naked girl, very brown from the sun, wearing only handkerchiefs tied bikini-style, her mouth spilling with grapes. Screaming behind her was a lecherous-looking old French farmer whose grape arbor she obviously had raided.

"*Styron*," Humes cried, gleefully, "*we have arrived!*"

"Yes," he said, "we are *here!*"

More nymphets came out of the trees in bikinis later, carrying grapes and also half cantaloupes the size of cartwheels, and they offered some to Styron and Humes. The next day they all went swimming and fishing, and, in the evening, they sat in the bombed-out villa, a breathtaking site of beauty and destruction, drinking wine with the young girls who seemed to belong only to the beach. It was an electric summer, with the nymphets batting around like moths against the screen. Styron remembers it as a scene out of Ovid, Humes as the high point of his career as an epicurean and scholar.

George Plimpton remembers that summer not romantically but as it was—a long, hot summer of frustration with French printers and advertisers; and the other *Review* staff members, particularly John P. C. Train, were so annoyed at Humes's departure that they decided they would drop his name from the top of the masthead, where he belonged as one of the founders, down to near the bottom under "advertising and circulation."

When the first issue of the *Paris Review* came out, in the spring of 1953, Humes was in the United States. But he had heard what they had done to him, and, infuriated, he now planned his revenge. When the ship arrived at the Hudson River pier with the thousands of *Paris Reviews* that would be distributed throughout the United States, Harold Humes, wearing his beret and swearing, "*Le Paris Review c'est moi!*" was at the dock waiting for them; soon he had ripped the cartons open, and, with a rubber stamp bearing his name in letters larger than any on the masthead, he began to pound his name in red over the masthead of each issue, a feat that took several hours to accomplish and which left him, in the end, totally exhausted.

"But . . . but . . . how *c-o-u-l-d* you have *done* such a thing?" George Plimpton asked when he next saw Humes.

Humes was now sad, almost tearful; but, with a final flash of vengeance, he said, "I am damned well not going to get shoved around!"

Rages of this sort were to become quite common at the *Paris Review*. Terry Southern was incensed when a phrase in one of his short stories was changed from "don't get your crap hot" to "don't get hot." Two poets wished to dissect John P. C. Train when, after a French printer had accidentally spilled the type from one poem into another, and the two poems appeared as one in the magazine, Train *casually* remarked that the printer's carelessness had actually improved the work of both poets.

Another cause for chaos was the Paris police force, which seemed ever in pursuit of John Train's nocturnal squad of flying poster plasterers, a union of Yale men and Arab youths who ran through Paris at night sticking large *Paris Review* advertising posters on every lamppost, bus, and *pissoir* they could. The ace of the squadron, a tall Yale graduate named Frank Musinsky, was so impressive that John Train decided to name all the other young men "Musinsky"—just as he had previously named the girls "Apeteker"—which Musinsky considered quite an honor, even though his real name was not Musinsky. Musinsky acquired the name because his grandfather, whose surname was Supovitch (sic), had switched names in Russia many years ago with a countryman named Musinsky who, for a price, agreed to take Frank's grandfather's place in the Russian army.

Nobody knows what became of him in the Russian army, but Frank's grandfather came to the United States, where his son later prospered in the retail shoe business, and his grandson, Frank, after Yale and his tour with Train's flying squad, got a job in 1954 with the *New York Times*—and soon lost it.

He had been hired as a copyboy in the *Times* sports department and, as such, was expected to devote himself to running galley proofs and filling pastepots, and was not expected to be sitting behind a desk, feet propped up, reading Yeats and Pound and refusing to move.

One night an editor shouted, "Musinsky, without doubt you're the worst copyboy in the history of the *Times*," to which Musinsky, rising haughtily, snapped, "Sir, to quote e. e. cummings, whom I'm sure you have heard of, 'There is some shit I shall not eat.'" Frank Musinsky turned and left the *Times*, never to return.

Meanwhile, Frank's place in the Paris flying squad was taken by several other Musinskys—Colin Wilson was one—and they all helped to preserve the *Review*'s traditional irreverence for the bourgeoisie, the Establishment, and even for the late Aga Khan, who, after offering to give a $1,000 prize for fiction, then submitted his own manuscript.

The editor quickly snapped up his money, but just as quickly returned the manuscript, making it clear that his prose style was not what they were seeking, even though the Aga's own son, Sadruddin Khan, a Harvard friend of Plimpton's, had just become publisher of the *Paris Review*, an offer that George proposed and Sadruddin accepted rather impulsively one day when they both were running from the bulls at Pamplona—a moment during which George suspected, correctly, that Sadruddin might agree to just about anything.

As improbable as it may seem, what with all the Musinskys and Apeteckers flying this way and that, the *Paris Review* did very well, publishing fine stories by such younger writers as Philip Roth, Mac Hyman, Pati Hill, Evan Connell, Jr., and Hughes Rudd, and, of course, distinguishing itself most of all by its "Art of Fiction" interviews with famous authors, particularly the one with William Faulkner by Jean Stein vanden Heuvel and the one with Ernest Hemingway by Plimpton, which began in a Madrid café with Hemingway asking Plimpton, "You go to the races?"

"Yes, occasionally."

"Then you read *The Racing Form*," Hemingway said. "There you have the true Art of Fiction."

But as much as anything else, the *Paris Review* survived because it had money. And its staff members had fun because they knew that, should they ever land in jail, their friends or families would always bail them out. They would never have to share with James Baldwin the experience of spending eight days and nights in a dirty French cell on the erroneous charge of having stolen a bedsheet from a hotelkeeper, all of which led Baldwin to conclude that while the wretched round of hotel rooms, bad food, humiliating concierges, and unpaid bills may have been the "Great Adventure" for the Tall Young Men, it was not for him because, he said, "there was a real question in my mind as to which would end soonest, the Great Adventure or me."

The comparative opulence of the *Paris Review*, of course, made it the envy of the other little magazines, particularly the staff members of a quarterly called *Merlin*, some of whose editors charged the *Review* people with dilettantism, resented their pranks, resented that the *Review* would continue to be published while *Merlin*, which had also discovered and printed new talent, would soon fold.

In those days *Merlin*'s editor was Alexander Trocchi, born in Glasgow of a Scotch mother and Italian father, a very exciting, tall, and conspicuous literary figure with a craggy, satanic face, faun's ears, a talent for writing, and a powerful presence that enabled him to walk into any room and take charge. He would soon become a friend of George Plimpton, John Phillips Marquand, and the other *Review* people, and years later he would come to New York to live on a barge, and still later in the back room of the *Paris Review*'s Manhattan office, but eventually he would be arrested on narcotics charges, would jump bail, and would leave the United States with two of George Plimpton's Brooks Brothers suits. But he would leave behind a good novel about drug addiction, *Cain's Book,* with its memorable line: "Heroin is habit-forming . . . habit-forming . . . rabbit-forming . . . Babbitt-forming."

Alexander Trocchi's staff at *Merlin* in those days was made up largely of humorless young men in true rebellion, which the *Paris Review* staff was not; the *Merlin* crowd also read the leftist monthly *Les Temps Modernes* and were concerned with the importance of being *engagé.* Their editors included Richard Seaver, who was reared in the Pennsylvania coal-mine district and in whose dark, humid Paris garage *Merlin* held its staff meetings, and also Austryn Wainhouse, a disenchanted Exeter-Harvard man who wrote a strong, esoteric novel, *Hedyphagetica,* and who, after several years in France, is now living in Martha's Vineyard building furniture according to the methods of the eighteenth century.

While the entire *Merlin* staff was poor, none was so poor as the poet Christopher Logue, about whom it was said that once, when playing a pinball machine in a café, he noticed a ragged old peasant lady staring at a five-franc piece lying on the floor near the machine, but before she could pick it up Logue's foot quickly reached out and stomped on it. He kept his foot there while the old lady screamed and while he continued, rather jerkily, to hold both hands to the machine trying to keep the ball bouncing—and *did,* until the owner of the café grabbed him and escorted him out.

Sometime later, when Logue's girlfriend left him, he came under the influence of a wild Svengali character then living in Paris, a pale, waxen-faced South African painter who was a disciple of Nietzsche and his dictum "Die at the right time," and who, looking for kicks, actually encouraged Logue to commit suicide—which Logue, in his depressed state, said he would do.

Austryn Wainhouse, who had suspected that suicide was very much on Logue's mind, had spent the following week sitting outside of Logue's hotel each night watching his window, but one afternoon when Logue was late for a luncheon date with Wainhouse, the latter rushed to the poet's hotel and there, on the bed, was the South African painter.

"Where's Chris?" Wainhouse demanded.

"I am not going to tell you," the painter said. "You can beat me if you wish; you're bigger and stronger than I, and . . ."

"I *don't* want to beat you," Wainhouse shouted. It then occurred to him how ridiculous was the South African's remark since he (Wainhouse) was actually much smaller and hardly stronger than the painter. "Look," he said finally, "don't you leave here," and then he ran quickly to a café where he knew he would find Trocchi.

Trocchi got the South African to talk and admit that Christopher Logue had left that morning for Perpignan, near the Spanish border twelve hours south of Paris, where he planned to commit suicide in much the same way as the character in the Samuel Beckett story in *Merlin*, entitled "The End"—he would hire a boat and row out to sea, further and further, and then pull up the plugs and slowly sink.

Trocchi, borrowing 30,000 francs from Wainhouse, hopped on the next train for Perpignan, five hours behind Logue. It was dark when he arrived, but early the next morning he began his search.

Logue, meanwhile, had tried to rent a boat, but did not have enough money. He also carried with him, along with some letters from his former girlfriend, a tin of poison, but he did not have an opener, nor were there rocks on the beach, and so he wandered about, frustrated and frantic, until he finally came upon a refreshment stand where he hoped to borrow an opener.

It was then that the tall figure of Trocchi spotted him and placed a hand on Logue's shoulder. Logue looked up.

"Alex," Logue said, casually handing him the tin of poison, "will you open this for me?"

Trocchi put the tin in his pocket.

"*Alex,*" Logue then said, "what are *you* doing here?"

"Oh," Trocchi said lightly, "I've come down to embarrass you."

Logue broke down in tears, and Trocchi helped him off the beach, and then they rode, almost in total silence, back to Paris on the train.

Immediately George Plimpton and several others on the *Paris Review* who were very fond of Logue, and proud of Trocchi, raised enough money to put Christopher Logue on a kind of monthly allowance. Later Logue returned to London and published books of poetry, and his plays, *Antigone* and *The Lily-White Boys*, were performed at the Royal Court Theatre in London. Still later he began to write songs for the Establishment, London's satirical nightclub act.

After the Logue episode, which, according to George Plimpton, sent at least a half-dozen young novelists to their typewriters trying to build a book around it, life in Paris at the *Review* was once more happy and ribald—but, a year later with the *Review* still doing well, Paris slowly seemed to pall.

John P. C. Train, then managing editor, put a sign on his in-basket reading, "Please Do Not Put Anything In The Managing Editor's Box," and one day when a pleasant, blue-eyed Oklahoman named Gene Andrewski wandered in with a manuscript and mentioned that he had once helped produce his college humor magazine, John Train quickly handed him a beer and said, "How would you like to run this magazine?" Andrewski said he would think it over. He thought it over for a few seconds, looked around at everybody else drinking beer, and agreed to become a kind of Assistant Managing Editor in Charge of Doing Train's Job. "The main reason I took the job," Andrewski later explained, "was I wanted the freedom."

In 1956 Peter Duchin moved to Paris and lived on a barge on the Seine, and many *Paris Review* people made this their new headquarters. There was no water on the barge, and in the morning everybody had to shave with Perrier. But the attempt at merriment on the barge seemed futile because, by this time, most of the old crowd had left. Paris was, as Gertrude Stein suggested, the right place for twenty-six, but now most of them were thirty years old. And so they returned to New York—but not in the melancholy mood of Malcolm Cowley's exiles of the twenties, who were forced home during the early currents of the crash, but rather with the attitude that the party would now shift to the other side of the Atlantic. Soon New York was aware of their presence, particularly the presence of Harold L. Humes.

After taking over a large apartment on upper Broadway with his wife, his daughters, and his unclipped wirehair terrier, and installing seven telephones and a large paper cutter that had the cracking eighteenth-century sound of a guillotine, Humes lashed out with a series of ideas and tall deeds: He hit on a theory of cosmology that would jolt Descartes, finished a second novel, played piano in a Harlem jazz club, began to shoot a movie called *Don Peyote*, a kind of Greenwich Village version of *Don Quixote* starring an unknown from Kansas City named Ojo de Vidrio, whose girlfriend eventually grabbed the film and ran off with it. Humes also invented a paper house, an *actual paper house* that is waterproof, fireproof, and large enough for people to live in; he set up a full-sized model on the Long Island estate of George Plimpton's family, and Humes's corporation, which included some backers from the *Paris Review* crowd, insured Humes's brain for $1 million.

During the Democratic National Convention in 1960, Humes led a phalanx of screaming Stevensonians onto the scene after employing the gate-crashing techniques of the ancient armies of Athens. When back in New York he called for an investigation of the New York police force, whereupon the police commissioner called for an investigation of *Humes*—and discovered fourteen unpaid traffic tickets. Humes went to jail just long enough to be discovered by the commissioner of corrections, Anna Kross, who upon recognizing him behind bars said, "Why, Mr. Humes, what are *you* doing in *there?*" to which he responded with Thoreau's line to Emerson, "Why, Miss Kross, what are *you* doing out *there?*"

When released on bail that was produced by Robert Silvers, another *Paris Review* editor, Harold Humes was asked by newspaper reporters how he liked the cell, and he replied, once more after Thoreau, "In a time of injustice, the place for an honest man is in jail."

Robert Silvers, one of the few quiet editors on the *Review*, a man with no apparent vices except smoking in bed, had no place to stay when he returned from Paris, and so he temporarily occupied the guest room in George Plimpton's apartment on East Seventy-second Street, where he proceeded to burn many holes in the mattress. He then plugged up the holes with peach pits. George Plimpton did not object. Robert Silvers was an old friend, and, besides, the mattress did not belong to Plimpton. It belonged to a fashion model who had once occupied the apartment, and who surprised both Plimpton and Silvers one day with a letter asking if they would please send the mattress to her home in France. They did, pits and all, and, having heard no complaints, they both nurture some delight in the thought that somewhere in Paris, somewhere in the very chic apartment of a high-fashion model, there is a mattress stuffed with peach pits.

Fortunately for Plimpton, he did not have to buy a new mattress for his guest room because, at about that time, the *Paris Review*, which had an office in a tenement on Eighty-second Street, had been evicted; and so Plimpton took home the small bed that had been in the back room of the *Paris Review*'s office—a room that had been the locale of several parties that had reduced the premise to a collage of broken bottles, bent spoons, rats, and chewed manuscripts.

After the eviction from the tenement, the *Paris Review*'s New York office shifted to the unlikely and quiet borough of Queens, where, in a large home between Grand Central Parkway and a cemetery, Lillian von Nickern Pashaian, when she is not tending to her three children, canaries, and turtles, accepts manuscripts that are addressed to the *Paris Review* and forwards them for a reading to either Jill Fox in Bedford Village, New York, or to Rose Styron in Roxbury, Connecticut. If *they* like what they have read, they forward the manuscript to George Plimpton's apartment on Seventy-second Street, where, between all his other activities, he gives a final reading and decides whether or not it will be accepted. If it is accepted, the author usually becomes the recipient of a small check and all he can drink at the next Plimpton party.

A Plimpton party is often planned only a few hours before it begins. George will pick up the phone and call a few people. They, in turn, will call others. Soon there is the thunder of feet ascending the Plimpton staircase. The inspiration for the party may have been that Plimpton won a court-tennis match earlier that day at the Racquet and Tennis Club, or that one member of the *Paris Review* crowd has a book coming out (in which case the publisher is invited to share the expenses), or that a member has just returned to Manhattan from a trip—a trip that might have carried John P. C. Train, a financial speculator, to Africa, or Peter Matthiessen to New Guinea to live with Stone Age tribesmen, or Harold Humes to the Bronx to fight in court over a parking ticket.

And in giving so many parties, in giving out keys to his apartment, in keeping the names of old friends on the *Paris Review* masthead long after they have ceased to work for it, George Ames Plimpton has managed to keep the crowd together all these years, and has also created around himself a rather romantic world, a free, frolicsome world within which he, and they, may briefly escape the inevitability of being thirty-six.

It exudes charm, talent, beauty, adventure. It is the envy of the uninvited, particularly of some child-bearing Apeteckers in the suburbs who often ask, "When is that group going to settle down?" Some in the group have remained bachelors. Others have married women who like parties—or have been divorced. Still others have an understanding that, if the wife is too tired for a party, the husband goes alone. It is largely a man's world, all of them bound by their memories of Paris and the Great Adventure they shared, and it has very few exiles, although it has had some—one being the beautiful blonde who was very much on everyone's mind in Paris ten years ago, Patsy Matthiessen.

Patsy and Peter are divorced. She is now married to Michael Goldberg, an abstract painter, lives on West Eleventh Street, and moves in the little world of downtown intellectuals and painters. Recently she spent several days in a hospital after being bitten by the dog of the widow of Jackson Pollock. In her apartment she has a cardboard box full of snapshots of the *Paris Review* crowd of the fifties. But she remembers those days with some bitterness.

"The whole life seemed after a while to be utterly meaningless," she said. "And there was something very *manqué* about them—this going to West Africa, and getting thrown in jail, and getting in the ring with Archie Moore. . . . And *I* was a Stepin Fetchit in that crowd, getting them tea at four, and sandwiches at ten."

A few blocks away, in a small, dark apartment, another exile, James Baldwin, said, "It didn't take long before I really was no longer a part of them. They were more interested in kicks and hashish cigarettes than I was. I had already done that in the Village when I was eighteen or seventeen. It was a little boring by then.

"They also used to go to Montparnasse, where all the painters and writers went, and where I hardly went. And they used to go there and hang around at the cafés for hours and hours looking for Hemingway. They didn't seem to realize," he said, "that Hemingway was long gone."

A group of suave and wrinkle—proof women who call each other "dear"
or "dahling," and can speak in italics and curse in French, move
into Manhattan's Graybar Building each weekday morning, elevate to
the nineteenth floor, and then slip behind their desks at Vogue—a magazine
that has long been the supreme symbol of sophistication for every American
female who ever dreamed of being wooed by Balenciaga, shoed by Roger Vivier,
coiffed by Kenneth, or set free to swing from the Place Vendome in maiden-
form mink.

Not since Sappho has anybody worked up such a lather over women as
have the editors of Vogue. With almost every issue they present stunning
goddesses who seemingly become more perfect, more devasting with the flip
of each page. Sometimes the Vogue model is leaping across the page in
mocha-coloured silk, or piloting a teak-tipped ketch through the lesser
Antilles, or standing, Dior-length, in front of the Eiffel Tower as racy
Renaults buzz by—but never hit her—as she poses in the middle of the
street, one leg kicking, mouth open, teeth agleam, two gendarmes winking in
the background, all Paris in love with her and her dinner dress of mousseline
de soie with ripply panels.

-more-

FIRST DRAFT OF "VOGUELAND"

*Vogue*land

FROM *Esquire*, 1961

ACH WEEKDAY MORNING A group of suave and wrinkle-proof women, who call one another "dear" and "dahling," and can speak in italics and curse in French, move into Manhattan's Graybar Building, elevate to the nineteenth floor, and then slip behind their desks at *Vogue*—a magazine that has long been the supreme symbol of sophistication for every American female who ever dreamed of being frocked by Balenciaga, shod by Roger Vivier, coiffed by Kenneth, or set free to swing from the Arc de Triomphe in maiden-form mink.

Not since Sappho has anybody worked up such a lather over women as have the editors of *Vogue*. With almost every issue they present stunning goddesses who seemingly become more perfect, more devastating with the flip of each page. Sometimes the *Vogue* model is leaping across the page in mocha-colored silk, or piloting a teak-tipped ketch through the Lesser Antilles, or standing, Dior-length, in front of the Eiffel Tower as racy Renaults buzz by—but never hit her—as she poses in the middle of the street, one leg kicking, mouth open, teeth agleam, two gendarmes winking in the background, all Paris in love with her and her dinner dress of mousseline de soie.

At other times the *Vogue* model is wearing "never-out-of-season black" on the Queensboro Bridge with a white cat crawling up her back, a cat she presumably leaves home when she later jets down to Puerto Rico to lunch with Casals while being watched from the hills by native women holding naked children—women who smile at her, admire her silk tussah skirt ("Nantucket nipped"), love her as she spikes up the nine-hole course inside the fortress of old El Morro.

While these fashion models in *Vogue* are merely stupendous, the socialites photographed for that magazine are rich, beautiful, indefatigable, vivid, vital, brilliant, witty, serve on more committees than congressmen, know more about airplanes than Wolfgang Langewiesche, thrive on country air and yet are equally at home in the smart poker parlors of Cannes; they never age, fade, or get dandruff, and are also (in the words of *Vogue*'s battery of sycophantic caption writers) "amusable," "exquisite," "delicate," "fun," and "smashing."

In one *Vogue* issue, for instance, Mrs. Loel Guinness, photographed before she sashayed from Lausanne to Palm Beach, was described as "vivid, vital, amusing." And, in another issue, Mrs. Columbus O'Donnel possessed a "quick, amused sparkle," Queen Sirikit of Thailand was "amusable, exquisite," and the Countess of Dalkeith was "ravishing" and as effulgent as Lady Caroline Somerset—herself a "delicate moonbeam beauty." Mrs. Murray Vanderbilt, last year a "slender brunette with direct, heartbreaker eyes, and a soft, open laugh," this year is a "beauty with a strong sense of purpose"—her purpose being to fly to Paris to have her portrait painted by "jaunty, rakish" Kees Van Dongen on a Tuesday, and then fly back to New York the same night, "investing," as *Vogue* said, "only 23 hours, 45 minutes."

Should there be that extraordinary case when a celebrated woman in *Vogue* is not a "rare beauty"—as, for instance, when she is almost homely— she is then described as "wise" or "filled with wisdom" or reminiscent of heroines in exquisite, vital novels. Madame Helene Rochas "looks rather like the heroine of a novel by Stendhal." And, should *Vogue* make mention of a non-*Vogue* type, such as Ingrid Bergman, who spends little money in the cosmetic industry, she is credited with having a nose which is "rather generous."

The noses of *Vogue* heroines are usually long and thin, as are the noses of many *Vogue* editors—noses they can look down upon their generally shorter, younger, and less-sophisticated Condé Nast relatives at *Glamour* magazine, also located on the nineteenth floor of the Graybar Building. But it is usually quite simple to tell the two staffs apart because the *jeunes filles* at *Glamour*, in addition to possessing a high quota of noses that *Vogue* might dismiss as "eager, retroussé," are also given to wearing shirtdresses, college-girl circle pins, smiling in the elevator, and saying, "Hi." A *Vogue* lady once described the *Glamour* staff as "those peppy, Hi people."

One day a few years ago a wide-eyed, newly hired *Vogue* secretary went bouncing into an editor's office with a package, and said, "Hi"—at which the editor is supposed to have cringed, and finally snapped, "We don't say *that* around *here!*"

"Everyone at *Glamour* of course hopes to work her way up to the *Vogue* staff of grim vigilantes," says the writer Eve Marriam, once a fashion copy editor at *Glamour*. "But it rarely happens. *Vogue* has to be careful. The upcomer might use the word *cute* instead of *panche*; she might talk about giving a *party* instead of a *dinner*; or describe a suede coat 'for weekending with the station-wagon set' rather than 'for your country home.' Or talk of going to a jewelry store instead of a *bijouterie*. Most maladroit of all, she might talk in terms of a *best buy* rather than an *investment*, or a *coup*. Or refer to a *ballgown* as—one shudders to think of it—a *formal*."

One has only to leave the elevator and enter the nineteenth floor to experience a sudden sensation of being *in Vogue*. The floors are black and star-studded, and the spacious outer room is tastefully furnished with a "delicate, amusable" receptionist with a British accent—perchance in keeping with the magazine's policy of spelling many words the British way: *colour, honour, jewellery*, and *marvellous* (pronounced *MAA*-vellous!).

To the rear of the receptionist is a curved corridor leading to *Vogue*'s editorial offices. The first office, that of the Beauty Editor, smells of pomades and powders, rejuvenators and other fountains of youth. Beyond this point, and around a second curve, are a half-dozen offices of other editors, and dividing them is the large, noisy Fashion Room. From nine till five the Fashion Room and the offices around it throb with the shrill, exuberant voices of fifty women, the incessant ring of telephones, the blurred image of leggy silhouettes shooting past, their heels clacking with *élan*. In one corner, the Fabrics Editor picks at silk swatches; in another corner, near a window, the Shoe Editor ponders what's next in "smashing" footwear; in still another corner, the Model Procurer flips through a filing cabinet that contains such highly classified data on models as which will pose for corset ads, which have the best legs, which have clawlike fingers (ideal for modeling gloves), and which have small, pretty hands (ideal for making small, expensive perfume bottles seem larger).

From the nearby offices of an editor named Carol Phillips ("delicate, amusable, pure-profiled beauty") can be heard the well-bred titters and talk of other *Vogue* tastemakers who stand, arms akimbo, toes pointed out, in front of Mrs. Phillips's desk. Inevitably their chatter blends with the dialogue that ricochets through the corridor, making it at times most difficult for the Baron De Gunzburg, a senior fashion editor, to concentrate fully on the *London Times* crossword puzzle that a messenger fetches for him each morning from the out-of-town newsstand in Times Square. The Baron, who is called "Nickkee" by *Vogue* ladies, and who makes his 7s in the European-style 7, is a former dancer with a Russian ballet and a onetime actor in a German film called *The Vampire.* (In the film he played a poet who spent two weeks in a casket before getting a chance to murder the vampire; nowadays the Baron is rarely without a black tie, and it is said that once, while entering a Seventh Avenue elevator without specifying his choice of floors, he was immediately whisked up to the floor of a tailor who made uniforms for undertakers.)

Upstairs from the Baron, in one of the few offices occupied by *Vogue* on the twentieth floor, Feature Editor Allene Talmey, whom editorial director Frank Crowninshield once described as a "Soufflé of Crowbars," bats out her famous column "People Are Talking About"—a collection of items that she and other *Vogue* ladies are talking about, and think *everybody* should be talking about. She writes:

> PEOPLE ARE TALKING ABOUT . . . *the present need for the Greek word,* **bottologia,** *meaning much speaking, or vain repetitions, as used by St. Matthew (6:7)* . . .
>
> PEOPLE ARE TALKING ABOUT . . . *the christening presents given to the daughter of the great Austrian conductor, Herbert von Karajan* . . .
>
> PEOPLE ARE TALKING ABOUT . . . *Takraw, a game beautiful to watch* . . .
>
> PEOPLE ARE TALKING ABOUT . . . *hummingbirds* . . .
>
> PEOPLE ARE TALKING ABOUT . . . *the Eastern half of the world.*

While some of *Vogue*'s critics contend that the magazine's literary policy can be summed up with "When in Doubt, Reprint Colette," it must be said in *Vogue*'s behalf that it has printed work by some excellent writers, among them Marianne Moore, Jacques Barzun, Rebecca West, and Allene Talmey. And yet one of *Vogue*'s former art directors, the inimitable Dr. Mehemet Femy Agha, once said, "Although Allene is wonderful, I've often told her she's like a piano player in a whorehouse. She may be a very good piano player, but nobody goes there to hear music. Nobody buys *Vogue* to read good literature; they buy it to see the clothes."

Among the first to see the clothes is the Baron De Gunzburg, who, having finished the *London Times* crossword puzzle, is now in the Garment Center on Seventh Avenue reclining in a posh divan in the showroom of the clothier Herbert Sondheim, who is giving *Vogue* magazine a private preview of Sondheim's spring frocks. Sitting next to the Baron is another *Vogue* editor, Mildred Morton ("pure-profiled blonde with slightly bored, raised eyebrow").

"You are the first persons in the entire world to be seeing these," says Mr. Sondheim, a short, rather stout, gravel-voiced man who rubs his hands, smiles from ear to ear.

A moment later a blond model appears from behind the curtain, prances toward the Baron and Mrs. Morton, and coos, "Number 628."

The Baron writes down the style number in his Hermés leather notebook and watches her twirl around and then walk back through the curtain.

"That's pomecia," says Mr. Sondheim.

"Expensive?" asks Mrs. Morton.

"Pomecia cotton is about $2.50 a yard," Mr. Sondheim says.

"Number 648," says a second model, a brunette, who slithers past Mr. Sondheim, dips, then twirls around in front of the Baron De Gunzburg.

"Awfully smart," says the Baron, letting his fingers give the model's pomecia evening dress a professional pinch. "I just *love* the slashed coat."

Mrs. Morton raises her right eyebrow.

"Are you getting away this winter?" the Baron asks Mr. Sondheim.

"Probably," he says. "Palm Beach."

The Baron seems unimpressed.

"Number 624," announces the brunette model, appearing again with a flourish of frock, a dip, a spin.

"Wonderful texture, pomecia," Mr. Sondheim says, quickly getting businesslike again. "Furthermore, it doesn't crease."

"Like the other two better, don't you, Nick-*kee?*" asks Mrs. Morton.

The Baron is silent. The model twirls in front of him again, then stands with her back to him.

"What is your number?" the Baron asks, in a clipped British tone.

"*Numba* 639," she shoots back over her shoulder. The Baron writes it down and then watches the model disappear behind the curtain to the clatter of plastic hangers.

Five minutes later, Mr. Sondheim's collection has been shown, and the Baron gives him the style numbers of the dresses *Vogue* wishes to have photographed and shown exclusively. Mr. Sondheim is delighted to comply, for having clothes appear first in *Vogue's* editorial pages almost guarantees their successful sale.

It all started back on December 17, 1892, when "quiet, clubby" Arthur Baldwin Turnure (Princeton '76), husband of one of America's first lady golf bugs, founded *Vogue* magazine. By 1895 he had created a sensation by displaying in his magazine the dresses and underwear to be worn by Miss Consuelo Vanderbilt on the occasion of her marriage to the Duke of Marlborough.

In 1909 *Vogue* was purchased by Condé Nast, under whom it flourished as never before, and no other magazine in the fashion field has ever been able to challenge it. *Harper's Bazaar*, which has always been less conservative—"It goes one rhinestone too *far*," a *Vogue* lady explains— does not provide its readers with quite so much of what Mary McCarthy calls "Democratic snobbery."

Some years ago Miss McCarthy, who did a rather extensive study of women's fashion magazines for the *Reporter*, concluded that as one descended through the less chichi magazines—such as *Charm, Glamour, Mademoiselle*—one found more genuine solicitude for the reader and her problems—"The pain of being a B.G. (Business Girl), the envy of superiors, self-consciousness, awkwardness, loneliness, sexual fears, timid friendliness to the Boss, endless evenings with the mirror and the tweezers, desperate Saturday social strivings ('Give a party and ask *everyone* you know'), the struggle to achieve any identity in the dead cubbyhole of office life."

And in another study of female magazines, this one done in *Social Forces* by two sociologists, Bernard Barber of Barnard College and Lyle S. Lobel, then of Harvard, it was stated that while the symbols of prestige in *Vogue* were "sophistication and chic," these same symbols were scorned by the respectable, PTA-types on the *Ladies Home Journal*, where there "is a distaste for 'high style,' for what is 'daring' or 'unusual.'"

But above *Vogue's* ultrachic level, according to the sociologists, there looms an even more-envied class of women: the unfashionable "old money" rich.

"At this top-most level, where there is little need to compete for status through consumption," wrote Barber and Lobel, "women may even maintain a certain independence of current changeful 'fashion.' Their quality clothes can remain roughly the same for several years. . . . Even eccentric, like the old ladies on Beacon Street in Boston."

Describing the *Vogue* level, they continued: "In the social class just below the 'old money' families we find most of the 'high fashion,' Paris-conscious style leaders. Since they are aware of the class above, perhaps trying to gain entrance into it, these women seek to combine opulence with 'quiet elegance.' 'Fashion copy' for this group stresses the *pose* of assured distinction, effortless superiority, and inbred elegance."

Before *Vogue* magazine can display its pose of assured distinction and elegance, of course, it must summon its high-fashion models and have them photographed by fashion photographers, and on this particular afternoon *Vogue's* colour photography sitting was being held in the penthouse studio of the noted photographer Horst Horst, a marvellous spot overlooking the East River. In the studio, while Horst Horst adjusts his German, Japanese, and Swedish cameras, his Chinese houseboy tacks enormous sheets of balmy sky-blue cardboard to the wall, creating a summery background. In the middle of the floor, in front of a box of flowers, is a plush stool on which the model will sit. In the adjoining dressing room, *Vogue's* Mrs. Simpson, while awaiting the arrival of the model, Dorothea McGowan, does needlepoint from a Matisse pattern.

"I'd go mad, *mad* without this," Mrs. Simpson says of her needlepoint.

In another corner of the dressing room, *Vogue's* wardrobe mistresses press a half-dozen Galanos chiffon gowns that the model will wear. Finally, ten minutes later, Dorothea McGowan, a tall, pale girl, lunges in with her hair in curlers. Immediately she removes her coat, unhinges her hair, dashes for the mirror, and quickly begins to stroke her canvaslike facial skin with a Japanese paintbrush.

"Which shoes, Mrs. Simpson?" she asks.

"Try the red ones, dear," Mrs. Simpson says, looking up from Matisse.

"Let's go," calls Horst from the other room.

Within a few minutes, after expert facial painting, Dorothea transforms herself from the pale, gangling Brooklyn girl she had been upon entering the studio into a sophisticated ageless woman about to pose for her seventh *Vogue* cover. She walks confidently into the studio, stands fifteen feet in front of Horst, stretches her calf muscles, spreads her legs slightly, places hands on hips, and prepares for her love affair with the camera.

Horst Horst, hands caressing his tripod, crouches and is about to shoot when Mrs. Simpson, standing on the sidelines like a duenna, shouts, "Wait." And the trance is momentarily broken as Mrs. Simpson says, "Her nails look terrible."

"Do they?" asks Dorothea, no longer the confident woman but now again the girl from Brooklyn.

"Yes, do you have your nails with you?"

The model goes into the dressing room to put on her false nails and then returns in front of the camera. Mrs. Simpson, satisfied now, returns to her needlepoint in the next room, and the Chinese boy places a fan in front of Dorothea, blowing her chiffon dress into her thin, lean body.

Dorothea throws her head back.

"Oh, such a rich feeling when the fan blows," she titters.

"Do something with your leg," Horst says.

She bends it backward, opens her mouth. And Horst's camera goes *click*. Then she leans down against the stool, lips puckered. Horst goes *click*.

"Oh, that's good," Horst says. "Do it again" (click).

Dorothea smiles (click); opens her mouth (click); wider, a big *O* (click).

"Hat's coming off." She giggles.

"Just smile, don't grin," he says (click). "Make a long neck."

She stretches (click).

"That's my girl," he says (click).

"Yesss," he repeats slowly (click).

And now, without any directions from him, she automatically strikes different poses, each one punctuated with a click; her face now bitchy, now primed for love, now blazy-eyed, now as demure as a Vassar virgin's. And Horst all the while is saying, excitedly behind the camera, "Yesss" (click), "Yesss" (click), "Yesss" (click).

"What are these little flowers?" Dorothea asks finally, breaking out of the mood.

"Azaleas," Horst says, lighting a cigarette. Dorothea pulls off a large rhinestone ring from her right hand, places it on her left, and then says,

"You know, if you take a ring off one finger and put it on another finger, it still feels like you have it on the first finger."

Horst Horst looks at her in mild wonderment. Then Dorothea goes to change her dress. And the Chinese boy, built like a speed swimmer, turns off the fan and quickly changes the background from blue cardboard to pink. When Dorothea returns, Mrs. Simpson is back for another look.

"Dorothea," Mrs. Simpson says, "you have little hairs sticking out in the back of your neck."

"Oh?" Dorothea says, touching her neck.

Dorothea, turning toward the dressing room, notices the pink background, and her face becomes alive with anticipation.

"*Oh,*" she exclaims, "I have pink . . . pink, PINK!"

Last dance with the Gray Lady on W.43d
for: *The New York Observer,*
  by Gay Talese

When Arthur Gelb joined The New York Times as a copyboy
in 1944 the uniformed doormen wore white gloves, the desk editors
donned green eye shades, and reporters making phone calls from
the third-floor newsroom had to be connected by one of the dozen
female operators seated at the eleventh-floor switchboard (perhaps
the most vibrant center of gossip in all of New York) ; and up on
the fourteenth floor, adjoining the publisher's office, was a private
apartment visited on occasion by the publisher's mistress--*and*
there was also nearby a bedroom for the publisher's valet, a
gentleman of high moral character and undaunted discretion.

The Times' neo-Gothic nerve center at 229 West Forty-third
Street, whose finials, scallops and fleurs-de-lis were in accord with
young Arthur Gelb's vision of himself as an aspiring vassal in
House of Ochs, is now being moved in a figurative (if not physical
sense) sense from under Gelb's feet to a new location a few blocks
away, terminating his ties to where he has invested sixty-three
years of his working life and making him at eighty-three the most
persevering employee in the history of the paper.

Having risen from copyboy to reporter in 1947, and from
Metro editor in 1967 to Managing Editor in 1990, and thereafter a
fixture in the corporate hierarchy overseeing the paper's
scholarship programs and other forms of munificence, Gelb now

FIRST DRAFT OF "THE KINGDOM AND THE TOWER"

The Kingdom
and the Tower

FROM *The New York Observer*, 2007

W HEN ARTHUR GELB JOINED the *New York Times* as a copy-boy in 1944, the uniformed elevator men wore white gloves, the desk editors donned green eye shades, and reporters making phone calls from the third-floor newsroom had to be connected by one of the dozen female operators seated at the eleventh-floor switchboard (perhaps the most vibrant center of gossip in all of New York); and up on the fourteenth floor, adjoining the publisher's office, was a private apartment visited on occasion by the publisher's mistress—and there was also nearby a bedroom for the publisher's valet, a gentleman of high moral character and undaunted discretion.

The *Times'* citadel of communication, whose neo-Gothic finials, scallops, and fleurs-de-lis at 229 West Forty-third Street were in accord with young Arthur Gelb's vision of himself as an aspiring vassal in the House of Ochs, is now operational within the *Times'* recently occupied skyscraper on Eighth Avenue between Fortieth and Forty-first streets, thus terminating Mr. Gelb's ties to where he had invested sixty-three years of his working life and left him at his current age of eighty-three as the most enduring employee in the history of the paper.

Having risen from copyboy to reporter in 1947, and from Metro editor in 1967 to managing editor (1986 to 1990), and thereafter a fixture in the corporate hierarchy overseeing the paper's scholarship programs and other forms of munificence, Mr. Gelb now continues his relationship with the *Times* as a consultant and, for whatever it is worth in an age when the journalism he knew and practiced may be on the cutting edge of oblivion, he exists as the institution's éminence grise and one of its ceremonial hosts for such events as last Thursday evening's farewell party to the chateau of the Good Gray Lady on West Forty-third Street.

Hundreds of the paper's employees and their guests were invited to dance in the aisles and drink beer in the vacated third-floor area where Mr. Gelb had once overseen the Metro staff and where his present-day successor, Joe Sexton, a physically fit and bespectacled man of forty-seven who had a salt-and-pepper goatee and was wearing a light blue cotton shirt darkened with his perspiration, danced with such tireless vigor around the room that he got the attention of someone with a digital camera and, promptly, his picture was available around the globe via *Gawker* along with a written account of the event:

It was like Dorkfest 2007. The newsroom, filled with empty desks which were lousy with dustballs, contained about a hundred pizzas, 500 bottles of beer, and hundreds of journalists, editors and photogs sweating it out to the sounds . . . It was so crowded that it was nearly impossible to make the rounds, so some hopped up on the desks and filing cabinets and shimmied to the beat.

But the best was Joe Sexton, Metro Editor, who is always a relaxed, jovial presence in the newsroom, always encouraging social outings, and he's a huge hip-hop fan, so nobody could hold a candle to his moves. He was on that dance floor for at least a couple of hours, drenched in sweat.

Watching from the sidelines, with his facial expression suggesting benign noninvolvement, was Mr. Gelb in a suit and tie chatting with some of the *Times* veterans, myself included, with whom he had dined an hour earlier at Sardi's on West Forty-fourth Street, next to the rear entrance of the Times Building. At the dinner, Mr. Gelb had begun by expressing condolences over the deaths of such *Times*men as David Halberstam, R. W. Apple Jr., Sammy Solovitz (a pint-sized lifetime copyboy), and Abe Rosenthal, who had preceded Mr. Gelb as the Metro editor and whose leadership in the newsroom was often defined by the staff as a reign of terror.

Bernard Weinraub remembered being in the men's room one day when Abe Rosenthal walked in and asked, "Hey, Bernie, you think I'm losing weight?"

Mr. Weinraub regarded him momentarily, then replied, "No, Abe, I don't think you are."

"You son of a bitch!" Abe shouted, abruptly leaving the room.

The stunned young Bernard Weinraub soon hurried over to where Mr. Gelb was sitting and, after relating the incident, asked, "Arthur, is this the end of my career?"

"I'm not sure," responded Mr. Gelb.

Another reporter told a bathroom story regarding Michiko Kakutani, who, shortly after being hired as a cultural reporter, collapsed in tears and refused to leave the ladies' room for a half hour after being told that Rosenthal was critical of the clichés he found in her writing.

For no particular reason, certainly none having to do with Rosenthal, Joseph Lelyveld (former reporter and executive editor) made reference to the suicidal death of a venerable and zealously reliable staff member named Russell Porter, who one day left the Times Building and jumped out of his apartment window.

Many other recollections of shared experiences good and bad were exchanged by Mr. Gelb's twenty guests, and the digressions might have continued at length had he not interrupted everyone by saying: "C'mon, it's getting late—let's go to the party."

After leading the way out of Sardi's, he paused on the sidewalk to remove from his pocket a key that he said held special meaning. "This key was given to me many years ago by [then publisher] Punch Sulzberger and it provides a shortcut from Sardi's into the *Times*, meaning you don't have to walk all the way around the block to get in. Oh, I've used this key thousands of times, and now, on this night, I'll be using it for the last time."

He then inserted the key into the lock of a metal door that was a few steps above what had once been a loading dock for *Times* delivery trucks, and soon we were following Mr. Gelb through the mail room which was directly over where the huge printing presses used to function until this operation was transferred in 1997 to plants out of town. Still, as we passed one row of tanks, there was evidence of ink oozing out.

Following our ride on one of the back elevators up to the third floor, we immediately heard the loud music blaring from two self-powered Mackie speakers affixed to ten-foot-high tripods that overlooked the Metro desk, and the LP records spinning around on two turntables sequentially introduced us to the voices of James Brown ("Sex Machine"), Aretha Franklin ("Respect"), Michael Jackson ("Don't Stop 'Til You Get Enough"), Diana Ross ("I'm Coming Out"), Justin Timberlake ("SexyBack"), and the Temptations ("Ain't Too Proud to Beg"). In rhythm with all of this music was the redoubtable Joe Sexton, and within the crowds of other dancers and on-lookers—it was not easy to distinguish between them—were such newsroom notables as the executive editor, Bill Keller; a managing editor, John Geddes; and an assistant managing editor, William E. Schmidt.

It had been Mr. Schmidt's secretary, along with Mr. Sexton, who had arranged for the services of the disc jockey known professionally as "DJ Herbert Holler"—but as "Kenny" to his friends—and who rents himself out (along with his hundreds of vinyl records and his two-channel Rane mixer) for $1,000 an hour. While he refused to reveal his rate of pay from the *Times*, he did say that Mr. Keller did not want him to leave at their prearranged 10 p.m. exit.

"Can we get you to spin another hour?" Mr. Keller asked, but Kenny said, "I can't," explaining that he had another private party to go to down-town in the meatpacking district. "But," he added, "I'll put on one more long dance." He selected "Love Thang" by First Choice.

The evening was very successful, in the opinion of Charles Kaiser, a writer who had worked as a Metro reporter for the *Times* until 1980, hav-ing first gained Mr. Gelb's attention in the early 1970s when Mr. Kaiser was a Columbia student serving as a stringer. "What we saw in this place tonight was what you'd never have seen when I started as a reporter here in 1974," he said, adding, "You saw all these young people of color, and peo-ple of all kinds dancing with one another—men dancing with men, men dancing with women, women dancing with women—and it really reflects the fundamental change in the *Times* since Arthur Ochs Sulzberger Jr. be-came the publisher [in 1992]. When he started out here in the early 1980s as an assistant Metro editor, he figured out who all the gay reporters were, and then he took each of them to lunch, and one by one he said: 'I know you're gay—don't worry about it. When Abe Rosenthal leaves I'll make sure that the fact that you're gay will make no difference in your career.'"

After the music stopped, most people left the building; but others were free to roam around, and even wander up to the executive suite on the fourteenth floor, as I did, to get a final look at the exalted domestic quarters occupied many years ago by the publisher, the publisher's mistress, and the publisher's valet. Although the beds are gone, I assumed that what I saw was pretty much as things looked a half-century ago, notwithstanding the fact that there are draperies sprawled along the floor, and the ornate chandeliers were dislodged from the ceiling, and a few plush chairs, tables, and other furniture were scattered here and there and sometimes turned upside down. One object that remains in place, however, is an elegantly carved oak-wood grandfather's clock that stands about ten feet high and displays a medallion that marks it as a gift to Adolph S. Ochs from the citizens of Chattanooga, dated December 8, 1892. This was when Ochs was publisher of the *Chattanooga Times*, and the clock was presented to him four years before he left the South to take over the failing *New York Times*, whose founding editor, Henry J. Raymond, had introduced the *Times* in 1851 with offices downtown at 113 Nassau Street. The clock is still ticking perfectly. It will not be available to the auctioneers, having been claimed by Ochs's fifty-five-year-old great-grandson and present publisher, Arthur Ochs Sulzberger Jr.

While the interior of this building at 229 West Forty-third Street that the staff first inhabited in 1913 will soon be gutted by its new owner—an Israeli diamond billionaire named Lev Leviev who paid $525 million for the property, and might well convert the interior to profitable usage beyond anything imagined by the heirs of Ochs—the façade of the building will remain as it now is in accord with the building's landmark status.

The *Times*' new headquarters building on Eighth Avenue, a fifty-two-story "shimmering tower of transparent glass" (words by Paul Goldberger), has already received much welcoming attention from architectural critics and has elicited few negative comments from members of the staff, even though the top editors were more prestigiously endowed when they were at 229 West Forty-third—which is to say that in the old place anyone holding the rank of managing editor or above (be it Mr. Gelb, Rosenthal, or Mr. Sulzberger) had offices with private bathrooms. But not in the new place. Not even Mr. Sulzberger will have one, as he apparently wishes to convey his egalitarian sensibilities, whether they truly exist within him or not, and at the same time he emphasizes his paper's devotion to transparency by making it virtually impossible for any reporter or editor in this glass-walled emporium to enjoy a single moment of privacy—be it a furtive gesture of flirtatiousness expressed across the aisle toward a co-worker, or an upraised index finger in the face of an irascible colleague. But it behooves me not to enlarge upon my meanderings, for I have only briefly visited the new premises, having done so during the past weekend while accompanied by Mr. Gelb and two amiable *Times* escorts who deal harmoniously with Mr. Sulzberger.

Among the things that Mr. Gelb and I learned during our visit are the following:

- Of the building's 52 floors, only the lower 20 are being used by the newspaper, the rest being rentals.
- While there were less than 40 conference rooms in the old building, there are 113 conference rooms in this new one, giving me the impression that Mr. Sulzberger is inclined toward a talkier *Times* management.
- In the old building, especially when Mr. Gelb and I were employed there together during the 1960s, we routinely mingled and associated with multitudes of fellow employees who were members of the working class: We sat among ink-stained printers in the cafeteria, and we knew the first names of many of the *Times*' elevator men, the carpenters, the electricians, floor sweepers, and so on—nearly all of whom, I believe, took satisfaction in being affiliated with the *Times*, and in their neighborhoods this affiliation no doubt bestowed upon them a prideful identity. But now in the twenty-first-century *Times*, the employment is largely monocultural, and while blue-collar workers abound on the premises they lack the old-time sense of kinship because they are sent in by outside contractors.

In the lobby of the new building, as Mr. Gelb and I headed home and thanked our escorts for showing us around, I noticed a bronze statue of Adolph S. Ochs that had held the preeminent position in the lobby of Forty-third Street, but now in the new building it was positioned at an oblique angle behind the reception desk, with the statue's foundation wrapped in packing cloth, and the imperial gaze seemingly adrift.

"Where's that going to go?" I asked one of the escorts.

"We don't know yet," he replied.

PART III

The Offbeat Wonders

Journey Into the Cat Jungle

Tough, smart and loud, New York's 400,000 alley cats have their own class society. But all face the same problem—new buildings don't have garbage cans and back fences.

By GAY TALESE

AFTER years of going unsung (except for their own nightly arias on backyard fences), New York alley cats have made good on Broadway in the musical "Shinbone Alley." And it's about time. For, though the census just completed in the city completely overlooked them, there is an enormous population of stray cats, among whom are some of our most clamorously prominent residents. Nobody knows exactly how many stray mehitabels and Big Bills live here, but the American Feline Society, Inc., estimated the other day that there must be about 400,000.

When street traffic dwindles and most people are sleeping, some neighborhoods crawl with cats. They move quickly through the shadows of buildings; night watchmen, policemen, garbage collectors and other nocturnal wanderers see them — but never for very long. Usually hobo cats travel alone. A majority of them hang around the fish markets, in Greenwich Village and in the East and West Side neighborhoods where garbage cans abound. But no part of the city is without its strays. An all-night garage attendant on Fifty-fourth Street near Sixth Avenue counted twenty of them around the Ziegfeld Theatre early one morning last week. Troops of cats patrol the waterfront piers at night searching for rats. Subway track-walkers have discovered cats living in the darkness. They seem never to get hit by trains, though some are occasionally liquidated by the third rail. About twenty-five cats live seventy-five feet below the west end of Grand Central Terminal, are fed by the underground workers and never wander up into the daylight.

THE roving, independent, self-laundering cats of the streets live a life strangely different from that of the kept, apartment-house cats. Most are flea-bitten. Many die of food poisoning, exposure and malnutrition; their average life-span is two years, whereas stay-at-home cats live ten to twelve years or more. Last year the A. S. P. C. A. killed 107,307 street cats for whom no homes could be found.

"The street cat and the apartment cat are on two distinct social levels," says Robert Lothar Kendell, president of the American Feline Society. "Apartment cats are pampered, are much more timid than the strays. Normally they will have nothing to do with the strays — except the female apartment cat, who may sneak away during its mating season, looking for toms. There hardly ever is any feeling of loyalty in a cat relationship. Females are indiscriminate—one tom is the same as another. Later, the female

GAY TALESE, a Times staff writer, emerged without a scratch from the alleys of New York after gathering material for this article.

will go back to the apartment, sit around, watch television and forget all about the cats in the street."

According to both the city's cat-lovers, or ailurophiles, and cat-haters, or ailurophobes, alley cats are smarter, louder, more adjustable and certainly more alert than the apartment pets. Generally, alley cats never get as fat as pets, but some people who leave the back-fence arias swear that they have seen some "the size of small Shetland ponies." (In truth, the largest of alley cats rarely are more than a sinewy eighteen pounds.)

SOCIAL-CLIMBING in the cat world is not common. Street cats rarely acquire a better mailing address—out of choice. "As a rule, cats die within the blocks of their birth," said Mrs. Judith Scofield, a Gotham Cat Club official.

"They become attached to their section and don't leave it."

Some strays, however, have fortune thrust upon them. A flea-bitten, disheveled specimen picked up by the A. S. P. C. A. on the West Side was recently adopted by a wealthy woman; it now lives in a luxurious East Side apartment and will spend the summer at the lady's establishment on Long Island. The American Feline Society once moved two strays into the headquarters of the United Nations. "I heard that there were some rodents from Lake Success that had been shipped in with some U. N. filing cabinets," said Mr. Kendell. "So these cats went in and took care of things. The cats seemed happy at the U. N. One of them used to sleep on a Chinese dictionary."

In every neighborhood the strays are dominated by a "boss"—the largest, strongest tomcat. The boss' posi-

Latter-day mehitabel—Some of New York's most clamorously prominent residents are cats.

tion is secure so long as he can whip every other tom in the neighborhood. Some bosses stay in power for years—surviving the average stray by nine or ten lives. They usually have many scars, like Mickey, a grisly-looking cat that roams about the Corvan Garage in the mid-Fifties.

"For years, every cat in this block would run when they saw Mickey coming," said a workman at the garage. "He's fought everything—dogs, cats, taxicabs—and he's been bumped once or twice by the Cadillacs the chauffeurs park along here. That cat is afraid of nothing."

ANOTHER boss, on the waterfront in the Fifties, is cordially despised by that area's watchmen. "Just before Thanksgiving," one of them said, "a guy had his turkey wrapped up ready to take home. He left it on the desk for a minute and when nobody was looking that cat snuck in and made off with it."

Except for the boss, there is not much organization in the street-cat society. But within the group there are three "types"—wild cats, Bohemians and part-time grocery-store (or restaurant) cats.

The wild cat relies on an occasional loose garbage lid or on rats for food, and will have little or nothing to do with people—even those who would feed it. The most unkempt of strays, it has, says Arthur L. Amundsen, the A. S. P. C. A.'s assistant general manager, a recognizable "hard look—a wide-eyed, hunted expression; there's nothing docile about it."

The Bohemian, however, is more tractable. It does not run from people. Often, it is fed in the streets daily by sensitive cat-lovers (mostly women) who call the strays "little people," "angels" or "darlings," and are indignant when the objects of their charity are referred to as "alley cats."

SO punctual are most Bohemians at feeding time that one cat-lover has advanced the theory that cats can tell time. He cited a gray tabby that appears five days a week, precisely at 5:30 P. M., in an office building at Broadway and Seventeenth Street, where the elevator men feed it. "But I've never seen it on Saturdays and Sundays," he said. "It seems to know people don't work on those days."

The part-time grocery-store or restaurant cat, often a reformed Bohemian, eats well and keeps rodents away, but it prefers to spend the nights prowling in the streets. One grocer says his part-time cat comes and goes, using the store like a hotel. Despite the liberal working hours, such cats still assume most of the privileges of a related breed—the full-time, or wholly owned, stray grocery-store cat—including the right to sleep in the window. A reformed Bohemian at a Bleecker Street delicatessen some years ago used to hide behind *(Continued on Page 28)*

(Continued on Page 28)

THE NEW YORK TIMES MAGAZINE

MAGAZINE CLIPPING OF "JOURNEY INTO THE CAT JUNGLE"

Journey into the
Cat Jungle

FROM *The New York Times Sunday Magazine*, 1957

A FTER YEARS OF GOING unsung (except for their own nightly arias on backyard fences), New York alley cats have made good on Broadway in the musical "Shinbone Alley." And it's about time. For, though the census just completed in the city completely overlooked them, there is an enormous population of stray cats, among whom are some of our most clamorously prominent residents. Nobody knows exactly how many stray mehitabels and Big Bills live here, but the American Feline Society, Inc., estimated the other day that there must be about 400,000.

When street traffic dwindles and most people are sleeping, some neighborhoods crawl with cats. They move quickly through the shadows of buildings; night watchmen, policemen, garbage collectors and other nocturnal wanderers see them—but never for very long. Usually hobo cats travel alone. A majority of them hang around the fish markets, in Greenwich Village and in the East and West Side neighborhoods where garbage cans abound. But no part of the city is without its strays. An all-night garage attendant on Fifty-fourth Street near Sixth Avenue counted twenty of them around the Ziegfeld Theatre early one morning last week. Troops of cats patrol the waterfront piers at night searching for rats. Subway trackwalkers have discovered cats living in the darkness. They seem never to get hit by trains, though some are occasionally liquidated by the third rail. About twenty-five cats live seventy-five feet below the west end of Grand Central Terminal, are fed by the underground workers, and never wander up into the daylight.

• • •

The roving, independent, self-laundering cats of the streets live a life strangely different from that of the kept, apartment-house cats. Most are flea-bitten. Many die of food poisoning, exposure, and malnutrition; their average life-span is two years, whereas stay-at-home cats live ten to twelve years or more. Last year the A.S.P.C.A. killed 107,307 street cats for whom no homes could be found.

"The street cat and the apartment cat are on two distinct social levels," says Robert Lothar Kendell, president of the American Feline Society. "Apartment cats are pampered, and are much more timid than the strays. Normally they will have nothing to do with the strays—except the female apartment cat, who may sneak away during its mating season, looking for toms. There hardly ever is any feeling of loyalty in a cat relationship. Females are indiscriminate—one tom is the same as another. Later, the female will go back to the apartment, sit around, watch television and forget all about the cats in the street."

According to both the city's cat-lovers, or aelurophiles, and cat-haters, or aelurophobes, alley cats are smarter, louder, more adjustable, and certainly more alert than the apartment pets. Generally, alley cats never get as fat as pets, but some people who have been awakened in the middle of the night by back-fence arias swear that they have seen some "the size of small Shetland ponies." (In truth, the largest of alley cats rarely are more than a sinewy eighteen pounds.)

Social-climbing in the cat world is not common. Street cats rarely acquire a better mailing address—out of choice. "As a rule, cats die within the blocks of their birth," said Mrs. Judith Scofield, a Gotham Cat Club official. "They become attached to their section and don't leave it."

Some strays, however, have fortune thrust upon them. A flea-bitten, disheveled specimen picked up by the A.S.P.C.A. on the West Side was recently adopted by a wealthy woman; it now lives in a luxurious East Side apartment and will spend the summer at the lady's establishment on Long Island. The American Feline Society once moved two strays into the headquarters of the United Nations. "I heard that there were some rodents from Lake Success that had been shipped in with some U. N. filing cabinets," said Mr. Kendell. "So these cats went in and took care of things. The cats seemed happy at the U. N. One of them used to sleep on a Chinese dictionary."

In every neighborhood the strays are dominated by a "boss"—the largest, strongest tomcat. The boss's position is secure so long as he can whip every other tom in the neighborhood. Some bosses stay in power for years—surviving the average stray by nine or ten lives. They usually have many scars, like Mickey, a grisly-looking cat that roams about the Corvan Garage in the mid-Fifties.

"For years, every cat in this block would run when they saw Mickey coming," said a workman at the garage. "He's fought everything—dogs, cats, taxicabs—and he's been bumped once or twice by the Cadillacs the chauffeurs park along here. That cat is afraid of nothing."

Another boss, on the waterfront in the Fifties, is cordially despised by that area's watchmen. "Just before Thanksgiving," one of them said, "a guy had his turkey wrapped up ready to take home. He left it on the desk for a minute and when nobody was looking that cat snuck in and made off with it."

Except for the boss, there is not much organization in the street-cat society. But within the group there are three "types"—wild cats, Bohemians, and part-time grocery-store (or restaurant) cats.

The wild cat relies on an occasional loose garbage lid or on rats for food, and will have little or nothing to do with people—even those who would feed it. The most unkempt of strays, it has, says Arthur L. Amundsen, the A.S.P.C.A.'s assistant general manager, a recognizable "hard look—a wide-eyed, hunted expression; there's nothing docile about it."

The Bohemian, however, is more tractable. It does not run from people. Often, it is fed in the streets daily by sensitive cat-lovers (mostly women), who call the strays "little people," "angels," or "darlings," and are indignant when the objects of their charity are referred to as "alley cats."

So punctual are most Bohemians at feeding time that one cat-lover has advanced the theory that cats can tell time. He cited a gray tabby that appears five days a week, precisely at 5:30 p.m., in an office building at Broadway and Seventeenth Street, where the elevator men feed it. "But I've never seen it on Saturdays and Sundays," he said. "It seems to know people don't work on those days."

The part-time grocery-store or restaurant cat, often a reformed Bohemian, eats well and keeps rodents away, but it prefers to spend the nights prowling in the streets. One grocer says his part-time cat comes and goes, using the store like a hotel. Despite the liberal working hours, such cats still assume most of the privileges of a related breed—the full-time, or wholly non-stray, grocery-store cat—including the right to sleep in the window. A reformed Bohemian at a Bleecker Street delicatessen some years ago used to hide behind the door and chase away all other Bohemians looking for handouts.

The number of full-time cats, incidentally, has diminished greatly since the decline of the small food store and rise of the supermarket. With better rat-proofing methods, improved packaging of foods, and more sanitary conditions, chain stores like the A. & P. say they don't need cats. "There are over 400 A. & P. stores in the metropolitan New York area," said an executive, "and I'll bet not one of them keeps a cat full-time."

On the waterfront, however, the great demand for cats remains unchanged. Longshoremen occasionally tell stories of unhappy experiences with waterfront cats, and many hate cats—but they hate rats more. "Once we had a guy here who couldn't stand cats, and he got rid of them," said a workman on Pier 62, on Eleventh Avenue in the Twenties. "Well, within a day or so we started seeing rats all over the place. Every time you looked up you'd see a rat on a crate looking right down on you. They'd steal your lunch. Some of them seemed bigger than the cats."

And on Pier 95, in the Fifties, another man said: "Cats don't get much sleep around here. They can't. Rats would overrun them. We've had cases here where the rat has torn up the cat. But it doesn't happen often. These big toms around here are mean bastards. They usually don't eat rats, they just catch and kill them; sometimes they chew the rat's head, which is less tough than the body.

"During the strike in November, though, lots of cats weren't eating so well, since many of the men were away from the pier. And some of the toms went really mad. They attacked kittens. And a few of the cats were even snapping at people around here."

As for the stray cat's future in the city, it seems to be pretty much of a question mark. The unsettling factor (from the cat's point of view) is the continued rise of new buildings—with incinerators and without backyards all over New York.

"With the garbage can on the way out, and fewer and fewer backyards or fences, the alley cat seems to be in a bad way," said a city housing official. "But street cats are amazingly adjustable creatures. Like everyone else, they may soon move to the suburbs."

In focusing on the outward appearance of these individuals, it is not my
intention to divert attention from their genuine plight, nor to establish any
distinctions between them and the other unfortunates among them. On the contrary,
I am suggesting that the problems of urban destitution and despair are now increasing
to a degree that makes it often impossible to vitually identify the victims. The
victims in the streets are beginning to look like the rest of us. (Still, a formidable
language barrier exists between us and the downtrodden among us, along with a certain
amount of skepticism and cynicism on our parts toward some who do not to be truly
needy, to say nothing about the confusion many of us feel about t

Give money to bureaus who will keep
it them, sevedls...and ...How ...Do you give to the homeless, and risk it being siften
off by bureaucrats who are wlawyas the middle-...problem and the solution......
p foist themselves between the problem and the solution. I have no problem giving
a dollar into the palm of the Vietnamn Veter on...crippled "Vietnan Vetern on Second
Avenue who sits crippled beghind his sign, nor the elderly black man on the ...wisened
black man on the...steps around the corner...church steps...nor the woman in the
bask ...who h for years...practiatio. hav has made a permanent address ...within
a church on park Avenue.. ...on teh ste stone...columns of a church on Park AVenue.
..red-faced lady who has ...But I confess to have ......far less charity toward the
bl long blakzed hair...pallid compeltion...serene.....serenely behind her sign
nearby Tiffany...& Co., behind a sign seek ing conations toward her competion of
her master's degreed, and I have passed...now pass withoiut regret the tall young
boy...hyouth...in basket...who appraoched...aggressiven.ly.... they are g blib,
rehearsed. We can't tell the hustleers from the homeless....truly home. I and
my better side...cynical.....The sketpci within me...... The worst within me says,
"this bum should .. "This kjid .... "...the slam-dunk tactics..... The worst ...
The worst side of me ...is agnered by him, I tell him (never to his face) get a job!
The better side of me says that, for all I know, his "trauma" is no wo...as bad as the older
that this young man is not using the money for dope, or grass, but for his infant danguther/

The Homeless Woman
with Two Homes

FROM *New York Magazine*, 1989

S HE WAS A PETITE and attractive woman in her early forties, with delicate bones, blue eyes, and short curly blond hair; and although it was the coldest autumn afternoon in New York so far, she wore a light cotton frock and sandals, and her face retained the glow of a deep summer tan. I stood waiting next to her on a crowded corner at Lexington Avenue and Fifty-ninth Street, dividing my attention between her fine features and the fact that she was carrying over her shoulders two bulky bags, one plastic and one cloth, containing blankets and other items associated with people who sleep and beg in the streets.

The light changed. I crossed the street and continued on my way uptown. Bag ladies with appealing faces are not uncommon sights in New York. I have seen one such woman, an angular brunette in her late twenties, who, with the aid of a hairstylist and a change of wardrobe, could have blended in with those advertising scenarios by Ralph Lauren. I have seen many men, too, whose polite manner of solicitation and unshabby appearance have led me to wonder why they are where they are—panhandling in subways, curled up at night near subway gratings or within the doorways of boutiques and department stores.

By focusing on the outward appearance of such people, I do not mean to divert attention from their genuine plight, or to establish any distinction between them and the other unfortunate men and women who dwell, perhaps more convincingly, in the shadows of street life. On the contrary, I am suggesting that urban destitution and despair are now spreading to the degree that identifying their victims visually is often impossible. Increasingly, the victims in our streets are looking like the rest of us.

Still, a formidable language barrier separates us—along with some skepticism on our part as to who are the truly needy, and who are merely masqueraders pandering to our sympathies. And what of the small blond woman with whom I had stood moments before at the corner of Fifty-ninth Street and Lexington Avenue?

Now on Sixty-second Street, I turned around. I spotted her in the crowd a half-block behind me. I had never approached a destitute person so directly, but at this moment I did not hesitate.

"Can I help you?" I asked, prompting her to stop and look up. Her inquiring blue eyes examined me, but whatever conclusion she came to she kept to herself.

"Are you a homeless person?" I continued, hoping this awkward question conveyed more compassion than curiosity.

She shifted the weight of the bags on her shoulders and waited for the noisy bus to pass the curb toward its stop near the southwest corner.

"Yes," she said in a cultivated voice barely audible above the street sounds.

"How long have you been homeless?"

"Five months, or more," she said.

"And where do you sleep and eat?"

"There's a women's shelter downtown, but I usually sleep in the park or the streets."

"Aren't you worried about the danger?"

She did not reply.

"Don't you have any family or friends?"

"Yes," she said, after a pause. Then after a longer pause, she added, "I also have three children."

There was another bus now, and the commotion of pedestrians passing between us and around us, for we were blocking the narrow sidewalk that extended from the Korean market to the yellow-leafed tree rising out of a patch of curbside dirt littered with candy wrappings and bottle caps.

"How old are your children?"

"Eleven, ten, and eight."

"Who takes care of them?"

"My mother," she said. "And also my husband. He has a back problem from his job and is home a lot." She explained that her husband, a mechanic on oil trucks who usually earns more than $50,000 a year, and her mother (employed as an accountant in Manhattan) share the domestic chores within a "high-rancher" house in Queens. The homeless woman said that she and her husband bought the Queens residence for $85,000 when they married twelve years ago, but that it is worth an estimated four times that now. She and her husband also own a weekend house in the Pocono Mountains with six acres and a pond.

I stood listening without changing my expression. My experience as a young New York reporter decades ago prepared me to be astonished by virtually nothing. This woman before me was articulate and convincing. In her manner and appearance there was no hint of drug or alcohol abuse (she said she used neither); nor did her healthy, smooth complexion, bronzed from the months outdoors, suggest that she was a battered wife. "We argued in the last few years" was all that she would concede about her husband, and when I asked why she had left him, her response was, "I left because I didn't want to live that life anymore."

"Is what you have any better?" I interrupted. She did not reply.

"Look," I said, "I can give you money, but that's not going to help. How about a job? Did you ever hold a job?"

"Yes," she said. "I worked as a hairdresser. In Queens, until the second child was born, I even had my own salon."

"I know people in that business," I said. "If I get appointments, will you show up?"

"Yes."

I guided her toward a nearby telephone booth, but both phones were out of order. It was after 5 p.m. I was eager to reach my acquaintances before they left for the day. Taking a piece of paper out of my pocket and also some change, I jotted down my home number and told her to contact me from another booth within the hour, by which time I hoped to have arranged for the interviews. Before I left her on Lexington Avenue, I also asked for, and received without delay, the phone number of the home in Queens where she had lived as a wife and mother.

The managers of both Manhattan salons I called agreed to see her the following morning, and both were disposed to hiring her on trial. As I waited at home for the woman's call, I typed letters of introduction for her to give to them, together with their business locations. These I intended to place in her hands after she called to tell me where to meet her. But she did not call that night. Nor the next day.

Two days later, a Sunday afternoon, I telephoned the number in Queens. After a male voice identified himself as her husband, I told him how I had met her, and of the appointments awaiting her.

"She'll never keep those appointments," the husband assured me. "She doesn't want to work. She doesn't want to stay home with the children. All she wants is to be free and wander around."

"I'm dropping these letters off at your place today," I said, not seeking his permission. His wife had given me the address of the house.

What she had not given me was any insight into why she had left it.

It was a two-story building on a quiet tree-lined street in a residential neighborhood of tidy but fading lawns, and of new-model automobiles parked along curbs or driveways. The door was opened by a polite man in his late forties, who, after extending his hand, led me into a spacious living room and introduced me to his three children and the mother of his missing wife. The mother occupies the lower level of the house, which has a private entrance, kitchen, living room, bedroom, and bath; the children—two of whom wore braces that their father seemed proud to say he could afford—share the upper portion of the residence, which has three bedrooms, a large kitchen, and a living room and dining area in the rear. On the condition that the family name would not be published—the children claim their schoolmates do not know that their mother has left home—the husband and mother agreed to talk with candor.

"She called us from a phone booth," volunteered the eleven-year-old, "and we all cried and told her we wanted her to come home. She said she could come someday, but . . ."

"She disappeared a few times last year," the husband said, "but just for a few days at a time then. I asked her if she wanted a divorce, and she said no. We took her to psychiatrists, but they said there's nothing really wrong with her. They gave her some pills, which she took for a while, then stopped."

"Did you force her to stop working as a hairdresser?" I asked.

"At first, after the second baby, I said I wanted her home. But later I said for her to go back to work. We have enough money for someone to come in and help out. But the kids are almost old enough now and don't even need it."

The husband doubted that another man was a factor in her absence, adding that her choosing to live in the streets seemed to confirm this.

He would take her back, he said, but since he has little faith in her capacity to reconcile herself with him permanently, he has recently begun proceeding toward a divorce.

Her mother, whose blue eyes and features the missing woman carries with her, spoke sadly about the situation, but she seemed reluctant to unburden herself in the presence of the children and their father. A day later, however, at a table in the cafeteria of the building where she works, she was both forthcoming and tearful as she related her own biographical background and the formative years of her only child.

The mother is now sixty-two. She was born in 1926 in the German town of Delmenhorst, on the Weser River near Bremen. Her father, a factory worker, returned home injured from the Battle of Verdun of 1916, and the harsh penalties imposed upon the German nation for its part in the war seemed to linger in the grimness and penury of her girlhood surroundings from the thirties through the aftermath of the second German defeat, in World War II. Allied bombers hit the Bremen area, and although her home was not hit, she associates that period of her life with rubble, grief, and bitterness. In the final year of the war, 1945, she was sent with other young women to work in the countryside as a farm laborer, replacing the men at the front. During this time, she met a young German soldier and fell in love. Neither ever believed that they would have the funds or opportunity to settle down in marriage, and by 1946, he had drifted out of her life. And she was pregnant.

Her infant girl, born in the spring of 1946, was raised in the home of the child's grandparents, whose scornful attitude toward their unmarried daughter's having a child out of wedlock improved to, at most, resignation in the years to come. They were even relieved when, in 1953, their husbandless daughter met and married a heavy-drinking American merchant seaman, who subsequently provided the money that brought his bride and her seven-year-old daughter to the United States.

Except for the funds, he provided little else. He was in and out of seaports, and drunk when he returned home to their apartment in the Bronx. His wife finally divorced him after nearly seven years of marriage.

By holding two jobs—as a cleaning lady at night, a bookkeeper during the day—she supported herself and her daughter, and she eventually left the Bronx for a garden apartment in Astoria. Her daughter attended school there, and at seventeen she registered at a Manhattan training school for beauticians. A year later she was working in a salon in Woodside, and four years later, when the owner retired, she became the proprietor, with a down payment of three thousand dollars.

Still living with her mother, the daughter bought a new car, hired extra help for the thriving salon, and on two occasions confided to her mother that she was in love. But both relationships ended unhappily. One of her lovers borrowed her car one night, left it parked outside a tavern in Yorkville, and was not heard from again. Her mother seemed to be even more distressed by this than she was, and, in 1977, thinking that she was doing her daughter a good turn, the mother answered an ad placed in the *Staats Zeitung* (a German-language daily) by a man who wished to meet a respectable young woman.

"My daughter has a broken heart," the mother told him on the telephone.

"I also have a broken heart," he replied.

Without telling her daughter, she invited the man to dinner, but much to her relief and delight, the couple appeared to like each other at once. Though a mechanic, the man had clean fingernails, and in addition to earning between one thousand dollars and fifteen hundred dollars a week with overtime, he owned a sizable apartment house in Bensonhurst that was filled with Italian tenants who paid their rent on time.

The daughter's marriage in 1978 was followed by the purchase of the eighty-five-thousand-dollar two-family home (for which the daughter contributed fifty thousand dollars from her savings from the salon). With the birth of the second child, she sold the salon, but until two years ago, when she first began to disappear for days at a time, she did not seem to be disenchanted by her duties as a homemaker and mother.

During my one and only talk with her, a fortnight ago, the homeless woman indicated that she spends much of her time in the area of the South Street Seaport. It later occurred to me that this might remind her of the river that ran close to her girlhood home in Germany, and that the rubble that she doubtless passes during her excursions through the deteriorating sections of New York might evoke memories of postwar Bremen. It might even be inferred that her wayward course, if that is what it is, is following the path of the wandering soldier who sired her. But such are merely musings.

The reality is that her children, her mother, and her husband—those most intimately connected with her life—appear to be unable to help her. If they cannot, what can we expect of our government? And what is expected of us?

Being a homeless woman with two homes certainly marks her as unique in New York; but how truly unique is she among New Yorkers impelled to withdraw from their inherited place, or wishing to escape institutionalism—be it the institution of marriage or the institutions that we look to for detecting symptoms and providing solutions?

These mysterious people live among us each day, sleep at our doors, walk shoulder-to-shoulder with us in the streets. Yet, regrettably, we do not know them, and too many New Yorkers, with the donation of a few quarters daily, are able to buy their way out of whatever momentary concern or discomfort is caused by the presence of the homeless.

6. Rises 8 A.M.; 116th subway;
    thinks of "leads" "leads"
    subway stops; tile, black,
    white; tea at Gus; "lead"
    "Mao"...things he is work-
    ing...head spinning with
    leads...

V-

1. Alden everyman,anyman,
    nobody,Library Card No__;

2. Mild; tea-man; Pyrex drip-drip
    no sip for him, tea man,yes;
    whisky,no beer man; no cigs;
    pipe. click-click on teeth
    long gone,busted in a 1936
    alley,stone,sticks and fists,
    management goons.

    Alden near death many times:
    a) drowning. "pleasant."
3. b) fallen plaster, close.
    c) Denver auto slip,close.

    Medical writing. Scope.

4. Does own cooking; then down,
    after paper-reading, to sub'
    to think,contemplate,leads,leads;
    all that Picasso research, all the
    interviews, the trip suggestion ko'd;
    writing now, 8,000 words on Pablo P.

5. Yes, 8,000 wds, done in advance like
    Schweifer...but most of his big
    obits have been on deadline:
    -Fr.Devine
    -Adlai
    -TS Eliot
    -Courb'
    -Huber
    -Churchill (in adv;collaborate)

    leads, leads...Mao "...son of
    obscure..."; Picasso "the paint-
    er,the playwright"); Marlene
    ("Mrs. Steiber...sex,glamor..."):
    TS Eliot, got this lead in cab,
    ("out with a whimper")...Macavity
    missing,regrets to cats.

6. Buber-deadline, yes, "fraud-fear"
    ..Adlai--to lunch, to lunch.

    "I am many people," Alden sayeth.
    good,not great newsman;competent;
    -Rather old-fashioned music taste
    Bach ,Beethoven,oldmasters who
    live.....for chrissake.

7. Bridgeplayer; Daughter, problem.

8. Vivisection. Alden writes,but
    in event they don't die,obit
    is held, perhaps too long, must
    later be cut down to size.
    Vivisection. In "hell box"
    Type-remelted, into problems...
    of living.

    In "storage"--LBJ,Pope,Ahs,etc.
    written by writers now dead.

9. Alden's obit. Elegy for a
    literary grave-digger. Ode to an
    Obituary writer. No pix,plse,thnx.

FIRST DRAFT OF "MR. BAD NEWS"

Mr. Bad News

Let's talk of graves, of worms and epitaphs,
Make dust our paper and with rainy eyes
Write sorrow on the bosom of the earth.
Let's choose executors and talk of wills.

—SHAKESPEARE, *RICHARD II*

W INSTON CHURCHILL GAVE YOU your heart attack," the wife of the obituary writer said, but the obituary writer, a short and rather shy man wearing horn-rimmed glasses and smoking a pipe, shook his head and replied, very softly, "No, it was not Winston Churchill."

"Then T. S. Eliot gave you your heart attack," she quickly added, lightly, for they were at a small dinner party in New York and the others seemed amused.

"No," the obituary writer said, again softly, "it was not T. S. Eliot."

If he was at all irritated by his wife's line of questioning, her assertion that writing lengthy obituaries for the *New York Times* under deadline pressure might be speeding him to his own grave, he did not show it, did not raise his voice; but then he rarely does. Only once has Alden Whitman raised his voice at Joan, his present wife, a youthful brunette, and on that occasion he *screamed*. Alden Whitman does not recall precisely why he screamed. Vaguely he remembers accusing Joan of misplacing something around the house, but he suspects that in the end *he* was the guilty one. Though this incident occurred more than two years ago, lasting only a few seconds, the memory of it still haunts him—a rare occasion when he truly lost control; but since then he has remained a quiet man, a predictable man who early each morning, while Joan is asleep, slips out of bed and begins to make breakfast: a pot of coffee for her, one of tea for himself. Then he sits for an hour or so in his study smoking a pipe, sipping his tea, scanning the newspapers, his eyebrows raising slightly whenever he reads that a dictator is missing, a statesman is ill.

By midmorning he will dress in one of the two or three suits he owns and, looking briefly into a mirror, will tighten his bow tie. He is not a handsome man. He has a plain, somewhat round face that is almost always serious, if not dour, and it is topped by a full head of brown hair which, though he is fifty-two, is without a trace of gray. Behind his horn-rimmed glasses are small, very small, blue eyes that he douses with drops of pilocarpine every three hours for his case of controlled glaucoma, and he has a thick, reddish mustache beneath which protrudes, most of the day, a pipe held tightly between a full bridge of false teeth.

His real teeth, all thirty-two of them, were knocked out or loosened by three strong-arm men in an alley one night in 1936 in Alden Whitman's hometown, Bridgeport, Connecticut. He was twenty-three years old then, a year out of Harvard and full of verve, and his assailants apparently opposed opinions supported by Whitman. He bears no ill will toward those who attacked him, conceding they had their point of view, nor is he at all sentimental about his missing teeth. They were full of cavities, he says, a blessing to be rid of them.

After he is finished dressing, Whitman says good-bye to his wife, but not for long. She too works for the *Times*, and it was there, one spring day in 1958, that he spotted her walking through the large, noisy City Room on the third floor dressed in paisley and carrying an inky page proof down from the women's department on the ninth floor, where she works. After learning her name, he proceeded to send anonymous notes in brown envelopes up to her through the house mail, the first of which read, "You look ravishing in paisley," and was signed, "The American Paisley Association." Later he identified himself, and they dined on the night of May 13 at the Teheran Restaurant, on West Forty-fourth Street, and talked until the maître d' asked them to leave.

Joan was fascinated by Whitman, especially by his marvelous, magpie mind cluttered with all sorts of useless information: He could recite the list of popes backward and forward; knew the names of every king's mistress and his date of reign; knew that the Treaty of Westphalia was signed in

1648, that Niagara Falls is 167 feet high, that snakes do not blink; that cats attach themselves to places, not people, and dogs to people, not places; he was a regular subscriber to the *New Statesman, Le Nouvel Observateur,* to nearly every journal in the Out-of-Town Newsstand in Times Square, he read two books a day, he had seen Bogart in *Casablanca* three dozen times. Joan knew she had to see *him* again, even though she was sixteen years his junior and a minister's daughter, and he was an atheist. They were married on November 13, 1960.

After Whitman leaves his apartment, which is on the twelfth floor of an old brick building on West 116th Street, he walks slowly uphill toward the subway kiosk on Broadway. At this time of morning the sidewalk is rushing with youth—pretty Columbia co-eds in tight skirts clasping books to their breasts and walking quickly to class, young long-haired men distributing leaflets attacking American policies in Vietnam and Cuba—and yet this neighborhood near the Hudson River is also solemn with reminders of mortality: Grant's Tomb, the grave of St. Claire Pollock, the memorial statues to Louis Kossuth and Governor Tilden and Joan of Arc; the churches, the hospitals, the Fireman's Monument, the sign on the upper Broadway office building "The Wages of Sin is Death," the old-ladies' home, the two aging men who live near Whitman—a recently retired *Times* obituary writer and the *Times* obituary writer who retired before *him.*

Death is on Whitman's mind as he sits in the subway that now races downtown toward Times Square. In the morning paper he has read that Henry Wallace is not well, that Billy Graham has visited the Mayo Clinic. Whitman plans, when he arrives at the *Times* in ten minutes, to go directly to the newspaper's morgue, the room where all news clippings and advance obituaries are filed, and examine the "conditions" of the advance obituaries on Reverend Graham and former vice president Wallace (Wallace died a few months later). There are 2,000 advance obituaries in the *Times's* morgue, Whitman knows, but many of them, such as the ones on J. Edgar Hoover and Charles Lindbergh and Walter Winchell, were written long ago and now require updating. Recently, when President Johnson was in the hospital for gallbladder surgery, his advance obituary was brought up-to-the-minute; so was Pope Paul's before his trip to New York; so was Joseph P. Kennedy's. For an obituary writer there is nothing worse than to have a world figure die before his obituary is up-to-date; it can be a harrowing experience, Whitman knows, requiring that the writer become an instant historian, assessing in a few hours the dead man's life with lucidity, accuracy, and objectivity.

When Adlai Stevenson died suddenly in London in 1965, Whitman, who was just beginning his new assignment as the *Times*'s mortician and was anxious to make good, learned of it through a telephone call from Joan. Whitman broke into a cool sweat, slipped out of the City Room, went to lunch. He took the elevator up to the cafeteria on the eleventh floor. But soon he felt a soft tap on his shoulder. It was one of the metropolitan editor's assistants asking, "Will you be down soon, Alden?"

Whitman, his lunch finished, returned downstairs and was given a basket full of folders containing data on Adlai Stevenson. Then, carrying them to the back of the room, he opened them and spread them out on a table in the thirteenth row of the City Room, reading, digesting, making notes, his pipe tip tapping against his false teeth, *cluck-cluck*.

Finally, he turned, facing his typewriter. Soon, paragraph by paragraph, the words began to flow: "Adlai Stevenson was a rarity in American public life, a cultivated, urbane, witty, articulate politician whose popularity was untarnished by defeat and whose stature grew in diplomacy. . . ." It ran 4,500 words and would have gone longer had there been time.

Difficult as it was, it was not nearly so demanding as a 3,000-word deadline assignment he was given on Martin Buber, the Jewish philosopher, about whom he knew virtually nothing. Fortunately, Whitman was able to reach by telephone a scholar who was very familiar with Buber's teachings and life, and this, together with the clippings in the *Times*'s morgue, enabled Whitman to complete the job. But he was far from pleased with it, and that night Joan was constantly aware of the sound of his pacing up and down the floor of their apartment, drink in hand, and the words uttered in contempt and self-derision, "fraud . . . superficial . . . fraud." Whitman went to work the following day expecting to be criticized. But instead he was informed that there had been several congratulatory telephone messages from intellectuals around New York, and Whitman's reaction, far from relief, was to immediately suspect all those who had praised him.

The obituaries that leave Whitman untroubled are those that he is able to complete before the individual dies, such as the rather controversial one he did on Albert Schweitzer, which both paid tribute to "Le Grand Docteur" for his humanitarianism yet damned him for his lofty paternalism; and the one on Winston Churchill, a 20,000-word piece in which Whitman and several other *Times* men were involved and which was finished almost two weeks before Sir Winston's death. Whitman's obituaries on Father Divine, Le Corbusier, and T. S. Eliot *were* produced under deadline pressure but caused him no panic because he was quite familiar with the work and lives of all three, particularly Eliot, who had been the poet-in-residence at Harvard during Whitman's student days there. His obituary on Eliot began: "*This is the way the world ends / This is the way the world ends / This is the way the world ends / Not with a bang but a whimper,*" and it went on to describe Eliot as a most unlikely poetic figure, lacking "flamboyance or oddity in dress or manner, and there was nothing of the romantic about him. He carried no auras, cast no arresting eye and wore his heart, as nearly as could be observed, in its proper anatomical place."

It was while writing the Eliot obituary that a copyboy had dropped onto Whitman's desk a number of statements praising the poet's work, and one of these came from a fellow poet, Louis Untermeyer. When Whitman read Untermeyer's statement, he raised an eyebrow in disbelief. He had thought Louis Untermeyer was dead.

This is part of an occupational astigmatism that afflicts many obituary writers. After they have written or read an advance obituary about someone, they come to think of that person as being dead in advance. Alden Whitman has discovered, since moving from his copyreader's job to his present one, that in his brain have become embalmed several people who are *alive,* or were at last look, but whom he is constantly referring to in the *past* tense. He thinks, for example, of John L. Lewis as being dead and also E. M. Forster and Floyd Dell, Rudolf Hess and Rhode Island's former senator Green, Ruth Etting and Gertrude Ederle, among many others.

Furthermore, he admits that, after having written a fine advance obituary, his pride of authorship is such that he can barely wait for that person to drop dead so that he may see his masterpiece in print. While this revelation may mark him as something less than romantic, it must be said in his defense that he thinks no differently than most obituary writers; they are, even by City Room standards, rather special.

A former obituary writer for the *New York World-Telegram and Sun,* Edward Ellis, who is also the author of a book about suicides, admits that he enjoys seeing, from time to time, his old advance obituaries fulfilling their destiny in the *Telegram.*

At the Associated Press, Mr. Dow Henry Fonda announces with satisfaction that he is all set with up-to-date obituaries on Teddy Kennedy, Mrs. John F. Kennedy, John O'Hara, Grayson Kirk, Lammot du Pont Copeland, Charles Munch, Walter Hallstein, Jean Monnet, Frank Costello, and Kelso. The United Press International, which has a dozen four-drawer filing cabinets of "preparation stories"—including one on five-year-old John F. Kennedy, Jr. and the children of Queen Elizabeth—does not have any full-time death specialist but passes the corpse copy around, some of the best of it going to a veteran reporter named Doc Quigg about whom it has been said, with pride, that he can "smooth 'em out, make 'em sing."

An obituarian's traditional eagerness about breaking into print is not exclusively based on author's pride, according to one antique in the trade, but it is also a holdover perhaps from the days when editors did not pay their obituary writers, whom they often hired on a freelance basis, until the subject of the obit had died—or, as they sometimes phrased it in those days, "passed away," "departed from this Earth," "gone to his reward." Occasionally, while waiting, those in the City Room would form a so-called ghoul pool in which everybody would put up $5 or $10 and try to select from the list of advance obituaries the name of the person who would go first. Karl Schriftgiesser, the *Times*'s gravedigger about twenty-five years ago, recalls that some ghoul-pool winners in those days collected as much as $300.

There are no such pools in evidence around the *Times* today, but Whitman, for quite different reasons, does keep in his desk a kind of list of the living to whom he is giving *priority*. These individuals are included because he thinks their days are numbered, or because he believes their life's work is finished and sees no reason to delay the inevitable writing task, or because he merely finds the individual "interesting" and wishes to write the obituary in advance for his own enjoyment.

Whitman also has what he calls a "deferred list," which is composed of aging but durable world leaders, *monstres sacrés*, who are still in power or still making news in other ways, and to attempt a "final" obituary on such individuals not only would be difficult but would require continuous alterations or insertions in the future; so even if these "deferred" people may have out-of-date obituaries in the *Times* morgue—people like de Gaulle, Franco—Whitman still chooses to let them wait awhile for a final polishing. Whitman realizes of course that any or all of these "deferred" customers may suddenly tap out, but he also has candidates that he thinks will die sooner or remain out of the news longer, and so he continues to give priority to those *not* on his deferred list, and should he be wrong—well, he has been wrong before.

There are, naturally, some people that Whitman may *think* will soon die, and for whom he has already tucked away a final tribute in the *Times*'s morgue, that may *not* die for years and years; they may diminish in importance or influence in the world, perhaps, but they keep right on living. If this be the case—if the name dies before the man, as A. B. Housman would put it—then Whitman reserves the right to cut the obituary down. Vivisection. He is a precise, unemotional man. While death obsessed Hemingway and diminished John Donne, it provides Alden Whitman with a five-day-a-week job that he likes very much and he would possibly die sooner if they took the job away and put him back on the copydesk where he could no longer write about it.

And so each weekday morning, after riding the subway down to Times Square from his apartment on upper Broadway, Whitman anticipates another day at the *Times,* another session with men who are dead, men who are dying, or men who, if Whitman's guess is correct, will soon die. He arrives in the lobby of the Times Building usually at eleven, his soft rubber-soled shoes hardly making a sound against the glossy marble floor. In his mouth is his pipe, and in his left hand is a container of tea that he bought a moment ago across the street at a small lunch counter run by a large Greek whose face he has known for years, never his name. Whitman then elevates to the third floor, says good morning to the receptionist, swings into the City Room, says good morning to all the other reporters who sit behind their desks, rows and rows of desks, and they greet him in turn, they know him well, they are happy it is *he,* not they, who must write for the obituary page—a page that is read very carefully, they know, maybe *too* carefully by readers with a morbid curiosity, readers searching for clues to life, readers searching for vacant apartments.

Occasionally all reporters must do their share of the smaller obituaries, which are bad enough, but the long ones are hard work; they must be accurate and interesting, they must be infallible in their analysis, and will be later judged, as will the *Times,* by historians. And yet for the writer there is no glory, no byline, it being a policy of the newspaper to eliminate bylines from such stories, but Whitman does not care. Anonymity superbly suits him. He prefers being everyman, anyman, nobody—*Times* Employee No.

97353, Library Card No. 663 7662, the possessor of a Sam Goody Courtesy Card, the borrower of his mother-in-law's 1963 Buick Compact on sunny weekends, an eminently unquotable man, a onetime manager for the Roger Ludlowe High School football, baseball, and basketball teams who is now keeping toll for the *Times*. All day long while his colleagues are running this way and that, pursuing the here and now, Whitman sits quietly at his desk near the back, sipping his tea, dwelling in his strange little world of the half-living, the half-dead in this enormous place called the City Room.

It is a room as large as a football field, maybe twice as large, and it is lined with rows and rows of gray metal desks, all the same shade, each with a telephone held by reporters who are talking to their news sources about the latest rumors, tips, reports, allegations, threats, robberies, rapes, accidents, crises, problems, problems—it is a Problem Room, and from all over the world via cable, telex, telegram, ticker, or telephone the news reports on world problems are rocketed into this *one* room, hour after hour: disaster in the Danube, turmoil in Tanzania, peril in Pakistan, touchy Trieste, rumors in Rio, the Saigon scene, coups d'état, informed sources said, reliable sources said, African problems, Jewish problems, NATO, SEATO, Sukarno, Sihanouk—and Whitman sits, sipping tea, in the back of this room paying little attention to all this; he is concerned with the *final* fact.

He is thinking of the words he will use when these men, these problem makers, finally die. He is leaning forward behind his typewriter now, shoulders forward, thinking of the words that will, bit by bit, build the advance obituaries of Mao Tse-tung, of Harry S Truman, of Picasso. He is also contemplating Garbo and Marlene Dietrich, Steichen and Haile Selassie. On one piece of paper, from a previous hour's work, Whitman has typed: ". . . Mao Tse-tung, the son of an obscure rice farmer, died one of the world's most powerful rulers. . . ." On another piece of paper: ". . . At 7:09 p.m., April 12, 1945, a man few people had ever heard of became president of the United States. . . ." On still another piece: ". . . there was Picasso the painter, Picasso the faithful and faithless lover, Picasso the generous man, even Picasso the playwright. . . ." And, from an earlier day's notes: ". . . As an actress, Mrs. Rudolph Sieber was nondescript, her legs were by no means as beautiful as Mistinguett's, but Mrs. Sieber as Marlene Dietrich was for years an international symbol of sex and glamour. . . ."

Whitman is not satisfied with what he has written, but he goes over the words and phrases with care, and then he pauses and thinks aloud, *Ah, what a wonderful collection of photographs will appear on the* Times' *obituary page when the great Steichen dies.* Then Whitman reminds himself that he must not forget to purchase the issue of the *Saturday Review* with its fine cover story on the white-haired British communications tycoon Baron Roy Thomson, now seventy years old. This story may soon come in handy. Another man of interest, Whitman says, is the noted humorist Frank Sullivan, who lives in Saratoga Springs, New York. A few days ago Whitman telephoned one of Mr. Sullivan's close friends, the playwright Marc Connelly, and almost began with, "You *knew* Mr. Sullivan, didn't you?" But he caught himself and said, instead, that the *Times* was "bringing its files up-to-date"—yes, that is the phrase—on Frank Sullivan and could a lunch be arranged with Mr. Connelly so that Mr. Whitman could learn something of Mr. Sullivan? A lunch was arranged. Next Whitman hopes to go up to Saratoga Springs and discuss the life of Marc Connelly over lunch with Mr. Sullivan.

When Whitman goes to concerts, as he so often does, he cannot resist looking around the hall and observing the distinguished members in the audience about whom he might be particularly curious someday soon. Recently, at Carnegie Hall, he noticed that one of the spectators seated up ahead was Arthur Rubinstein. Quickly, Whitman lifted his opera glasses and brought Mr. Rubinstein's face into sharp focus, noticing the expression around the eyes, the mouth, the soft gray hair, and noticing, too, when Rubinstein stood up at intermission, how surprisingly short he was.

Whitman made notes on such details, knowing that someday they would help bring life to his work, knowing that masterful obituaries, like fine funerals, must be planned well in advance. Churchill himself had arranged his own funeral; and the relatives of Bernard Baruch, before he died, visited the Frank E. Campbell Funeral Chapel to arrange the details; and now Baruch's son, though in apparent good health, has done the same thing—as has a little charwoman who recently purchased a mausoleum for more than $6,000 and had her name put on it, and now every month or so she travels up to the cemetery in Westchester County to get a look at it.

"Death never takes a wise man by surprise," wrote La Fontaine, and Whitman agrees and keeps his "files up-to-date," although he never permits any man to read his own obituary; as the late Elmer Davis said, "A man who has read his own obituary will never be quite the same again."

Several years ago, after a *Times* editor had recovered from a heart attack and returned to the office, the reporter who had done the editor's obituary showed it to him so that any errors or omissions might be corrected. The editor read it. That evening he had another heart attack. Ernest Hemingway, on the other hand, thoroughly enjoyed reading the newspaper accounts of his death during a plane crash in Africa. He had the newspaper clippings pasted up in a thick scrapbook and claimed to begin each day with "a regular morning ritual of a glass of cold champagne and a couple of pages of obituaries." Elmer Davis had twice been erroneously reported as having died in catastrophes, and while he conceded that "to turn up alive after you have been reported dead is an unwarrantable imposition on your friends," he nonetheless denied the rumor and was "more generally believed than is usually the case when people have to contradict something that the papers have said about them."

Some newspapermen, possibly not trusting their colleagues, have written their own advance obituaries and inconspicuously slipped them into the morgue to await the proper moment. One of these advance obituaries, written by a *New York Daily News* reporter named Lowell Limpus, appeared under his own by-line in that newspaper in 1957 and began: "This is the last of the 8,700 or more stories I've written to appear in the *News*. It must be the final one because I died yesterday. . . . I wrote this, my own obituary, because I know more about the subject than anybody else and I'd rather have it honest than flowery. . . ."

While the obituary page might have once been sodden with sentimentality, it is rarely so today except in that italicized column of death notices that usually appears on the right-hand side of the page above the flowered ads of the undertakers. The relatives of the deceased pay to have these notices published, and in them every dead man is invariably described as a "loving" father, a "beloved" husband, a "dear" brother, an "adored" grandfather, or a "revered" uncle. All the names of the dead are listed in alphabetical order and set in capital letters and bold type so that the casual reader may scan them quickly, like the baseball scores, and it is the rare reader that ponders over them. One such rarity is a seventy-three-year-old gentleman named Simon de Vaulchier.

Mr. de Vaulchier, a retired research librarian, was for a brief period a kind of professional reader of the obituary pages of New York's metropolitan dailies. And he compiled for the Jesuit magazine *America* the research for a study in which it was observed, among other things, that most of the dead in the *New York Post* were Jewish, most of those in the *New York World-Telegram and Sun* were Protestant, most of those in the *Journal-American* were Catholic. A rabbi added a footnote, after reading the survey, to the effect that they *all* seemed to die for the *Times*.

If one is to believe only what one reads in the *Times*, however, then the individuals with the highest fatality rate are chairmen of the board, Mr. de Vaulchier noted. Admirals usually got longer obits than generals in the *Times*, he continued, architects did better than engineers, painters did better than other artists and always seemed to die in Woodstock, New York. Women and Negroes hardly ever seemed to die.

Obituary writers never die. At least Mr. de Vaulchier said he has never read such an obituary in a newspaper, although early last year on the occasion of Whitman's heart attack he came quite close.

After Whitman had been taken to Knickerbocker Hospital in New York, a reporter in the City Room was assigned to "bring the files on him up-to-date." Whitman, since recovering, has never seen this advance obituary, nor does he expect to, but he imagines that it ran seven or eight paragraphs in length and, when it is finally used, will begin something like this:

"Alden Whitman, a member of the *New York Times* staff who wrote obituary articles on many of the world's notable personalities, died suddenly last night at his home, 600 West 116th Street, of a heart attack. He was fifty-two years old...."

It will be very factual and verifiable, he is sure, and will record that he was born on October 27, 1913, in Nova Scotia and was brought to Bridgeport by his parents two years later; that he was twice married, had two children by the first wife, was active in the New York Newspaper Guild, and that in 1956 he, among other newsmen, was questioned by Senator James O. Eastland about his Leftist activities. The obituary will possibly list the schools he attended but will not mention that during his elementary years he skipped *twice* (to his mother's delight; she was a schoolteacher, and this happy event did her reputation with the school board no harm); it will list his places of employment but will not report that in 1936 he got his teeth knocked out, nor that in 1937 he nearly drowned while swimming (an experience he found highly pleasant), nor that in 1940 he came within an inch of being crushed by part of a falling parapet; nor that in 1949 he lost control of his automobile and skidded helplessly to the very edge of a mountain in Colorado; nor that in 1965, after surviving his coronary thrombosis, he repeated what he had been saying most of his life: There is no God; I do not fear death because there is no God; there will be no Judgment Day.

"But what will happen to you then, after you die, Mr. Whitman?"

"I have no soul that is going anywhere," he said. "It is simply a matter of bodily extinction."

"If you had died during your heart attack, what, in your opinion, would have been the first thing your wife would have done?"

"She would first have seen to it that my body was disposed of in the way that I wanted," he said. "To be cremated without fuss or fanfare."

"And then what?"

"Then, after she'd gotten to that, she would have turned her attention to the children."

"And then?"

"Then, I guess, she would have broken down and had a good cry."

"Are you sure?"

Whitman paused.

"Yes, I would assume so," he said finally, puffing on his pipe. "This is the formal outlet for grief under such circumstances."

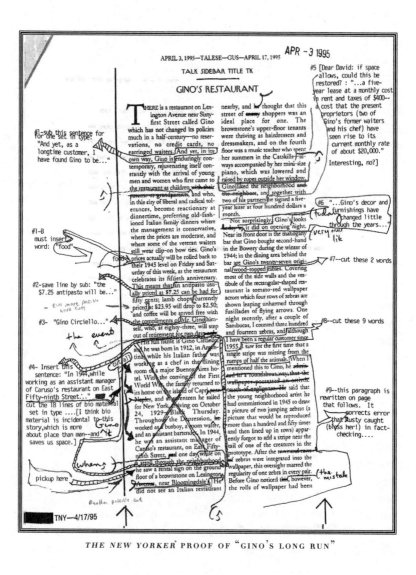

THE NEW YORKER PROOF OF "GINO'S LONG RUN"

Gino's Long Run

FROM *The New Yorker*, 1995

T HERE IS A RESTAURANT on Lexington Avenue near Sixty-first Street called Gino, which has not changed its policies much in a half century—no reservations, no credit cards, no earringed waiters. And yet, as a long-time customer, I have found Gino to be enduringly contemporary, rejuvenating itself constantly with the arrival of young men and women who first came to the restaurant as children and now, in this city of liberal and radical tolerances, become reactionary at dinnertime, preferring old-fashioned Italian family dinners where the management is conservative, the prices are moderate, and some of the veteran waiters still wear clip-on bow ties. Gino's food prices will actually be rolled back to their 1945 level on Friday and Saturday of this week, as the restaurant celebrates its fiftieth anniversary. This means that the $7.25 antipasto will be 60¢; lamb chops at $23.95 will drop to $2.50; and coffee will be served free with the compliments of Gino himself, whose full name is Gino Circiello, and who, at eighty-three, will step out of retirement for a two-day event.

In 1944, while working as an assistant manager of Caruso's restaurant on East Fifty-ninth Street, Gino saw a rental sign on the ground floor of a brownstone on Lexington Avenue near Bloomingdale's. He did not see an Italian restaurant nearby, and thought that this street of shoppers was an ideal place for one. The brownstone's upper-floor tenants were thriving as hairdressers and dressmakers, and on the fourth floor was a music teacher who spent her summers in the Catskills, always accompanied by her mini-size piano, which was lowered and raised by ropes outside her window. Gino liked the neighborhood and the neighbors, and, together with two partners, he signed a five-year lease at a monthly cost in rent and taxes for four hundred dollars—a cost that the present proprietors (two of Gino's former waiters and his chef) have seen rise to a current monthly rate of about twenty thousand dollars.

Fittingly, the restaurant's décor and furnishings have changed little through the years. Near its front door is the mahogany bar that Gino bought on the Bowery during the winter of 1945; in the dining area behind the bar are Gino's twenty-seven original tables. Covering most of the sidewalls and the vestibule of the rectangular restaurant is tomato-red wallpaper across which four rows of zebras are shown leaping unharmed through fusillades of flying arrows. One night recently, after a couple of Sambucas, I counted three hundred and fourteen zebras, and I saw for the first time that a single stripe was missing from the rumps of half the animals.

When I mentioned this to Gino, he admitted in a roundabout way that the wallpaper possessed an artistic touch of negligence. He explained that after the restaurant was forced to close briefly in the 1970s, owing to a kitchen fire, he had the wallpaper remade by a young designer, and the designer somehow failed to copy a stripe near the tail of the smaller of a pair of zebras that were the prototypes for all the zebras in the pattern. This oversight was repeated throughout, marring the regularity of one zebra in every pair. Before Gino noticed the mistake, however, the rolls of paper had been glued to his restaurant's walls. And, in true Gino tradition, he decided against changing anything. Several years later, when the wallpaper again was replaced, because its colors were faded and its texture was deteriorating, the pattern was repeated in conformity with the past—with a tomato-red background and with half the zebras missing a stripe.

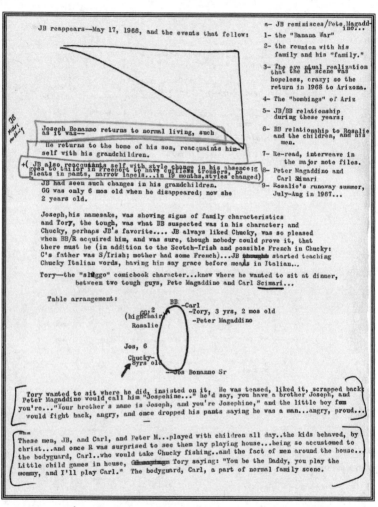

JB reappears--May 17, 1966, and the events that follow:

a- JB reminisces/Pete Magaddino...

1- the "Banana War"

2- the reunion with his family and his "family."

3- The eventual realization that the AZ scene was hopeless, crazy; so the return in 1968 to Arizona.

4- The "bombings" of Ariz

5- JB/BB relationship during these years;

6- BB relationship to Rosalie and the children, and his men.

7- Re-read, interweave in the major note files.

8- Peter Magaddino and Carl Simari

9- Rosalie's runaway summer, July-Aug in 1967...

JB Where nothing

Joseph Bonanno returns to normal living, such as it was--

He returns to the home of his son, reacquaints himself with his grandchildren.

+(JB also reacquaints self with style change in his absence; goes to tailor in Freeport to have cuffless trousers, no pleats in pants, narrow lapels...in 19 months, styles changed)

JB had seen such changes in his grandchildren. GG was only 6 mos old when he disappeared; now she 2 years old.

Joseph, his namesake, was showing signs of family characteristics and Tory, the tough, was what BB suspected was in his character; and Chucky, perhaps JB's favorite.... JB always liked Chucky, was so pleased when BB/R acquired him, and was sure, though nobody could prove it, that there must be (in addition to the Scotch-Irish and possible French in Chucky: C's father was S/Irish; mother had some French)...JB thought started teaching Chucky Italian words, having him say grace before meals in Italian...

Tory--the "sluggo" comicbook character...knew where he wanted to sit at dinner, between two tough guys, Pete Magaddino and Carl Scimari...

Table arrangement:

```
                        BB-Carl
          GG, 2          -Tory, 3 yrs, 2 mos old
       (highchair)       -Peter Magaddino
        Rosalie

        Jos, 6

        Chucky-
        6 yrs old
                    Jos Bonanno Sr
```

Tory wanted to sit where he did, insisted on it. He was teased, liked it, scrapped back; Peter Magaddino would call him "Josephine..." he'd say, you have a brother Joseph, and you're..."Your brother's name is Joseph, and you're Josephine," and the little boy would fight back, angry, and once dropped his pants saying he was a man...angry, proud...

These men, JB, and Carl, and Peter M...played with children all day..the kids behaved, by christ...and once R was surprised to see them lay playing house...being so accustomed to the bodyguard, Carl..who would take Chucky fishing..and the fact of men around the house... Little child games in house, Chucky Tory saying: "You be the Daddy, you play the mommy, and I'll play Carl." The bodyguard, Carl, a part of normal family scene.

AUTHOR'S REMEMBRANCE OF THE SEATING ARRANGEMENT AT JOE BONANNO'S DINNER TABLE

The Kidnapping of
Joe Bonanno

FROM *Esquire*, 1971

KNOWING THAT IT IS possible to see too much, most doormen in New York have developed an extraordinary sense of selective vision: they know what to see and what to ignore, when to be curious and when to be indolent—they are most often standing indoors, unaware, when there are accidents or arguments in front of their buildings, and they are usually in the street seeking taxicabs when burglars are escaping through the lobby. Although a doorman may disapprove of bribery and adultery, his back is invariably turned when the superintendent is handing money to the fire inspector or when a tenant whose wife is away escorts a young woman into the elevator—which is not to accuse the doorman of hypocrisy or cowardice but merely to suggest that his instinct for uninvolvement is very strong, and to speculate that doormen have perhaps learned through experience that nothing is to be gained by serving as a material witness to life's unseemly sights or to the madness of the city. This being so, it was not surprising that on the night when the reputed Mafia chief, Joseph Bonanno, was grabbed by two gunmen in front of a luxury apartment house on Park Avenue near Thirty-sixth Street, shortly after midnight on a rainy Tuesday in October, the doorman was standing in the lobby talking to the elevator man and saw nothing.

It all happened with dramatic suddenness: Bonanno, returning from a restaurant, stepped out of a taxicab behind his lawyer, William P. Maloney, who ran ahead through the rain toward the canopy. Then the gunmen appeared from the darkness and began pulling Bonanno by the arms toward an awaiting automobile. Bonanno struggled to break free but he could not. He glared at the men, seeming enraged and stunned—not since Prohibition had he been so abruptly handled, and then it had been by the police when he had refused to answer questions; now he was being prodded by men from his own world, two burly men wearing black coats and hats, both about six feet tall, one of whom said: "Com'on, Joe, my boss wants to see you."

Bonanno, a handsome gray-haired man of fifty-nine, said nothing. He had gone out this evening without bodyguards or a gun, and even if the avenue had been crowded with people he would not have called to them for help because he regarded this as a private affair. He tried to regain his composure, to think clearly as the men forced him along the sidewalk, his arms numb from their grip. He shivered from the cold rain and wind, feeling it seep through his gray silk suit, and he could see nothing through the mist of Park Avenue except the taillights of his taxicab disappearing uptown, and could hear nothing but the heavy breathing of the men as they dragged him forward. Then, suddenly from the rear, Bonanno heard the running footsteps and voice of Maloney shouting: "Hey, what the hell's going on?"

One gunman whirled around, warning, "Quit it, get back!"

"Get out of here," Maloney replied, continuing to rush forward, a white-haired man of sixty waving his arms in the air, "that's my client!"

A bullet from an automatic was fired at Maloney's feet. The lawyer stopped, retreated, ducking finally into the entrance of his apartment building. The men shoved Bonanno into the back seat of a beige sedan that had been parked on the corner of Thirty-sixth Street, its motor idling. Bonanno lay on the floor, as he had been told, and the car bolted toward Lexington Avenue. Then the doorman joined Maloney on the sidewalk, arriving too late to see anything, and later the doorman claimed that he had not heard a shot.

Bill Bonanno, a tall, heavy, dark-haired man of thirty-one whose crew cut and button-down shirt suggested the college student that he had been in the 1950s, but whose moustache had been grown recently to help conceal his identity, sat in a sparsely furnished apartment in Queens listening intently as the telephone rang. But he did not answer it.

It rang three times, stopped, rang again and stopped, rang a few more times and stopped. It was Labruzzo's code. Frank Labruzzo was in a telephone booth a few blocks away signaling that he was on his way back to the apartment. On arriving at the apartment house, Labruzzo would repeat the signal on the downstairs doorbell and the younger Bonanno would then press the buzzer releasing the lock. Bonanno would then wait, gun in hand, looking through the peephole of the apartment to be sure that it was Labruzzo getting out of the elevator. The furnished apartment the two men shared was on the top floor of a brick building in a middle-class neighborhood, and since their apartment door was at the end of the hall they could observe everyone who came and went from the single self-service elevator.

Such precautions were being taken not only by Bill Bonanno and Frank Labruzzo but by dozens of other members of the Joseph Bonanno organization who for the last few weeks had been hiding out in similar buildings in Queens, Brooklyn, and the Bronx. It was a very tense time for all of them. They knew that at any moment they could expect a confrontation with rival gangs trying to kill them or with government agents trying to arrest them and interrogate them about the rumors of violent plots and vendettas now circulating through the underworld. The government had recently concluded, largely from information obtained through wiretapping and electronic bugging devices, that even the top bosses in the Mafia were personally involved in this internal feud and that Joseph Bonanno, a powerful don for thirty-three years, was in the middle of the controversy. He was suspected by other dons of excessive ambition, of seeking to expand at their expense, and perhaps over their dead bodies, the influence that he already had in various parts of New York, Canada, and the Southwest. The recent elevation of his son, Bill, to the No. 3 position in the Bonanno organization was also regarded with alarm and skepticism by a few leaders of other gangs as well as by some members of Bonanno's own gang of about three hundred men in Brooklyn.

The younger Bonanno was considered something of an eccentric in the underworld, a privileged product of prep schools and universities, whose manner and methods, while not lacking in courage, conveyed some of the reckless spirit of a campus activist. He seemed impatient with the system, unimpressed with the roundabout ways and Old World finesse that are part of Mafia tradition. He said exactly what was on his mind, not altering his tone when addressing a mafioso of superior rank, and not losing his sense of youthful conviction even when speaking the dated Sicilian dialect he had learned as a boy from his grandfather in Brooklyn. The fact that he was six-feet-two and more than two hundred pounds, and that his posture was erect and his mind very quick, added to the formidability of his presence and lent substance to his own high opinion of himself, which was that he was the equal or superior of every man with whom he was associating except for possibly one, his father. When in the latter's company, Bill Bonanno seemed to lose some of his easy confidence and poise, becoming more quiet, hesitant, as if his father were severely testing his every word and thought. He seemed to exhibit toward his father a distance and formality, taking no more liberties than he would with a stranger. But he was also very attentive to his father's needs and seemed to take great pleasure in pleasing him. It was obvious that he was awed by his father, and, while he no doubt had feared him and perhaps still did, he also worshiped him.

During the last few weeks he had never been very far from Joseph Bonanno's side, but last night, knowing that his father wished to dine alone with his lawyers and that he planned to spend the evening at Maloney's place, Bill Bonanno passed a quiet evening at the apartment with Labruzzo watching television, reading the newspapers, and waiting for word. Without knowing exactly why, he was mildly on edge. Perhaps one reason was a story he had read in the *Daily News* reporting that life in the underworld was becoming increasingly perilous and claiming that the older Bonanno had recently planned the murder of two rival dons, Carlo Gambino and Thomas (Three Finger Brown) Luchese, a scheme that supposedly failed because one of the triggermen had betrayed Bonanno and had tipped off one of the intended victims. Even if such a report were pure fabrication, being based possibly on the FBI's wiretapping of low-level Mafia gossip, the publicity given to it was of concern to the younger Bonanno because he knew that it could intensify the suspicion that indeed did exist among the various gangs that ran the rackets (which included numbers games, bookmaking, loan-sharking, prostitution, smuggling, and enforced protection), and the publicity could also inspire the outcry of the politicians, provoke the more vigilant pursuit of the police, and result in the issuing of more subpoenas by the courts.

The subpoena was now dreaded more in the underworld than before because of a new federal law requiring that a suspected criminal, if picked up for questioning, must either testify if given immunity by the court or possibly face a sentence for contempt. This made it imperative for the men of the Mafia to remain inconspicuous if wishing to avoid subpoenas every time there were newspaper headlines, and the law also impeded the Mafia leaders' direction of their men in the street because the latter, having to be very cautious and often detained by their caution and evasiveness, were not always where they were supposed to be at the appointed hour to do a job, and they were also frequently unavailable to receive, at designated telephone booths at specific moments, prearranged calls from headquarters seeking a report on what had happened. In a secret society where precision was important, the new problem in communications was grating the already jangled nerves of many top mafiosi.

The Bonanno organization, more progressive than most partly because of the modern business methods introduced by the younger Bonanno, had solved its communications problem to a degree by its bell-code system and also by the use of a telephone-answering service. It was perhaps the only gang in the Mafia with an answering service. The service was registered in the name of a fictitious Mr. Baxter, which was the younger Bonanno's code name, and it was attached to the home telephone of one member's maiden aunt who barely spoke English and was hard of hearing. Throughout the day various key men would call the service and identify themselves through agreed-upon aliases and would leave cryptic messages confirming their safety and the fact that business was progressing as usual. If a message contained the initials "IBM"—"Suggest you buy more IBM"—it meant that Frank Labruzzo, who had once worked for IBM, was reporting. If the word "monk" was in a message it identified another member of the organization, a man with a tonsured head who often concealed his identity in public under a friar's robe. Any reference to a "salesman" indicated the identity of one of the Bonanno captains who was a jewelry salesman on the side; and "flower" alluded to a gunman whose father in Sicily was a florist. A "Mr. Boyd" was a member whose mother was known to live on Boyd Street in Long Island, and reference to a "cigar" identified a certain lieutenant who was never without one. Joseph Bonanno was known on the answering service as "Mr. Shepherd."

One of the reasons that Frank Labruzzo had left the apartment that he shared with Bill Bonanno was to telephone the service from a neighborhood coin box and also to buy the early edition of the afternoon newspaper to see if there were any announcements or developments of special interest. As usual, Labruzzo was accompanied by the pet dog that shared their apartment. It had been Bill Bonanno who had suggested that all gang members in hiding keep dogs in their apartments, and while this had initially made it more difficult for the men to find rooms, since some landlords objected to pets, the men later agreed with Bonanno that the presence of a dog not only made them more alert to sounds outside their doors but a dog was also a useful companion to have when going outside for a walk—a man with a dog aroused very little suspicion in the street.

Bonanno and Labruzzo also happened to like dogs, which was one of the many things that they had in common, and it contributed to their compatibility in the small apartment. Frank Labruzzo was a calm, easy-going, somewhat stocky man of fifty-three with glasses and graying dark hair; he was a senior officer in the Bonanno organization and also a member of the immediate family—Labruzzo's sister, Fay, was Joseph Bonanno's wife and Bill Bonanno's mother, and Labruzzo was close to the son in ways that the father was not. There was no strain or stress between these two, no competitiveness or problems of vanity and ego. Labruzzo, not terribly ambitious for himself, not driven like Joseph Bonanno nor restless like the son, was content with his secondary position in the world, recognizing the world as a very much larger place than either of the Bonannos seemed to think that it was.

Labruzzo had attended college and had engaged in a number of occupations, but he had pursued none for very long. He had, in addition to working for IBM, operated a dry-goods store, sold insurance, and had been a mortician. Once he had owned, in partnership with Joseph Bonanno, a funeral parlor in Brooklyn near the block of his birth in the center of a neighborhood where thousands of immigrant Sicilians had settled at the turn of the century. It was in this neighborhood that the elder Bonanno had courted Fay Labruzzo, daughter of a prosperous butcher who had manufactured wine during Prohibition. The butcher had been proud to have Bonanno as a son-in-law even though the wedding date, in 1930, had had to be postponed for thirteen months due to a gangland war involving hundreds of newly arrived Sicilians and Italians, including Bonanno, who were continuing the provincial discord transplanted to America but originating in the ancient mountain villages that they had abandoned in all but spirit. These men had brought with them to the New World their old feuds and customs, their traditional friendships and fears and suspicions, and they not only consumed themselves with these things but they also influenced many of their children, sometimes their children's children—and among the inheritors were such men as Frank Labruzzo and Bill Bonanno, who now, in the middle 1960s, in the age of space and rockets, were fighting a feudal war.

It seemed both absurd and remarkable to the two men that they had never escaped the insular ways of their parents' world, a subject that they had often discussed during their many hours of confinement, discussing it usually in tones of amusement and unconcern, although with regret at times, even bitterness. Yes, we're in the wagon-wheel business, Bonanno had once sighed, and Labruzzo had agreed—they were modern men, lost in time, grinding old axes; and this fact was particularly surprising in the case of Bill Bonanno: he had left Brooklyn at an early age to attend boarding schools in Arizona, where he had been reared outside the family, and had learned to ride horses and brand cattle, had dated blond girls whose fathers owned ranches; and he had later, as a student at the University of Arizona, led a platoon of ROTC cadets across the football field before each game to help raise the American flag prior to the playing of the national anthem. That he could have suddenly shifted from this campus scene in the Southwest to the precarious world of his father in New York was due to a series of bizarre circumstances that were perhaps beyond his control, perhaps not. Certainly his marriage had been a step in his father's direction, a marriage in 1956 to Rosalie Profaci, the pretty dark-eyed niece of Joseph Profaci, the millionaire importer who was also a member of the Mafia's national commission.

Bill Bonanno had first met Rosalie Profaci when she was a young student attending a convent school in upstate New York with his sister. At that time he had had a girlfriend in Arizona, a casual American girl with a flair for freedom; while Rosalie was appealing, she also was demure and sheltered. That the young couple would meet again and again, during summer months and holidays, was largely due to their parents, who were very close, and whose approval was bestowed in subtle but infectious ways whenever Rosalie and Bill would converse or merely sit near to one another in crowded rooms. At one large family gathering months before the engagement, Joseph Bonanno, taking his twenty-one-year-old daughter Catherine aside, asked her privately what she thought of the likelihood that Bill would marry Rosalie. Catherine Bonanno, an independent-minded girl, thought for a moment, then said that while she was extremely fond of

Rosalie personally she did not feel that Rosalie was right for Bill. Rosalie lacked the strength of character to accept him for what he was and might become, Catherine said, and she was about to say something else when, suddenly, she felt a hard slap across her face, and she fell back, stunned, confused, then had burst into tears as she ran, having never before seen her father so enraged, his eyes so fiery and fierce. Later he had tried to comfort her, to apologize in his way, but she remained aloof for days although she understood as she had not before her father's desire for the marriage. It was a wish shared by Rosalie's father and uncle. And it would be fulfilled the following year, an event that Catherine Bonanno would regard as a marriage of fathers.

The wedding, on August 18, 1956, had been extraordinary. More than three thousand guests had attended the reception at the Astor Hotel ballroom in New York following the church wedding in Brooklyn, and no expense had been spared in embellishing the occasion. Leading orchestras had been hired for the dancing, and the entertainment included the singing of the Four Lads and Tony Bennett. Pan American Airways was engaged to fly in thousands of daisies from California because that flower, Rosalie's favorite, was then unavailable in New York. A truckload of champagne and wine had been sent as a gift by a distributor in Brooklyn. The guest list, in addition to the legitimate businessmen and politicians and priests, included all the top men of the underworld. Vito Genovese and Frank Costello were there, having requested and received inconspicuous tables against the wall. Albert Anastasia was there, it being a year before his murder in the Park Sheraton Hotel barbershop, and so was Joseph Barbara, whose barbecue party for nearly seventy mafiosi at his home in Apalachin, New York, three weeks after the murder, would be discovered by the police and would result in national publicity and endless investigations. Joseph Zerilli had come with his men from Detroit, and so had the Chicago delegation led by Sam Giancana and Tony Accardo. Stefano Magaddino, the portly old don from Buffalo, cousin of Joseph Bonanno, had been given an honored table in front of the dais, and seated near to him were other relatives or close friends of the Bonannos and Profacis. All of the twenty-four semi-independent organizations that formed the national syndicate had been represented at the wedding, meaning that there were men from New England to New Mexico, and the group from Los Angeles alone had totaled almost eighty.

• • •

Bill Bonanno, smiling next to his bride on the dais, toasting the guests and being toasted in turn, had often wondered during the evening what the FBI would have done had it gotten its hands on the guest list. But there had been little chance of that since the list, in code, had been in the careful custody of Frank Labruzzo and his men who had been posted at the door to receive the guests and to escort them to their tables. There had been no intruders on that night, nor had there been a great deal of public concern over the Mafia in 1956, the Kefauver hearings of 1951 having been forgotten, and the Apalachin fiasco being one year away. And so the wedding and reception had proceeded smoothly and without incident, with Catherine Bonanno as the maid of honor and Joseph Bonanno, elegant in his cutaway, had presided over the gathering like a medieval duke, bowing toward his fellow dons, dancing with the women, courtly and proud.

After the reception, during which the bridal couple had received in gift envelopes about $100,000 in cash, they had flown to Europe for a honeymoon. They had stayed for a few days at the Ritz Hotel in Paris, then at the Excelsior in Rome, receiving special attention in each place and having been ushered quickly through customs at the airport. Later they had flown to Sicily, and as the plane slowly taxied toward the terminal building in Palermo, Bill Bonanno noticed that a large crowd had gathered behind the gate and that a number of carabinieri were among them, standing very close to Bonanno's aging bald-headed uncle, John Bonventre, who seemed rather grim and tense. Bill Bonanno's first thought was that Bonventre, who had once served in the United States as an under-boss in the Bonanno organization, was about to be deported from his native Sicily, to which he had gone the year before to retire, having taken with him from America a lifetime's supply of toilet paper, preferring it to the coarse brands produced in Sicily. As the plane had stopped, but before the door had opened, a stewardess stood to ask that Mr. and Mrs. Bonanno please identify themselves. Slowly, Bill Bonanno had raised his hand. The stewardess had then asked that the couple be the first to leave the plane.

Walking down the ramp into the hot Sicilian sun, mountains rising in the distance behind sloping villages of tan stone houses, Bonanno had sensed the crowd staring at him, moving and murmuring as he got closer. The old women were dressed in black, the younger men had fixed dark expressions, children were milling everywhere, and the statuesque cara-binieri, flamboyantly dressed and brandishing gleaming silver swords, stood taller than the rest. Then the uncle, Bonventre, bursting with a smile of recognition, had run with arms outstretched toward the bridal couple, and the crowd had followed, and suddenly the Bonannos had been sur-rounded by clutching kissing strangers, and Rosalie, blushing, had tried without success to conceal the awkwardness she had felt in the center of swarming unrestrained affection. Her husband, however, had seemed to enjoy it thoroughly, reaching out with his long arms to touch everyone that he could, leaning low to be embraced by the women and children, basking in the adoration and salutations of the crowd. The carabinieri had watched impassively for a few moments, then had stepped aside, clearing a path that led toward a line of illegally parked automobiles waiting to take the couple to the first of a series of celebrations that would culminate with a visit on the following day to Castellammare del Golfo, the town in western Sicily where Joseph Bonanno had been born and where earlier Bonannos had long ruled as *uomini rispettati*—men of respect.

Rosalie had hoped that they would also visit her father's birthplace, a town just east of Palermo called Villabate, but her husband, without ever explaining why, indicated that this was impossible. Moments after he had landed at Palermo his uncle had whispered a message just received from the United States from the elder Bonanno insisting that the couple avoid Villabate. A number of friends and distant relatives of the Profacis still living in Villabate were then struggling with a rival gang for control over certain operations, and there had already been seven murders in the last ten days. It was feared that the enemies of Profaci's friends in Villabate might seek revenge for their dead upon Bill Bonanno or his wife, and al-though Rosalie had persisted in her request to see Villabate, her husband had managed to avoid the trip after making endless excuses and offer-ing a busy itinerary of pleasant distractions. He had also been relieved that Rosalie had not questioned, nor had even seemed to notice, the quiet group of men that followed them everywhere during their first day of sight-seeing in Palermo. These men, undoubtedly armed, were serving as bodyguards for the Bonanno couple, even sitting outside the couple's hotel door at night to guarantee that no harm would come to them in Sicily.

The journey to Castellammare del Golfo, sixty miles west of Palermo, had been the high point of the Sicilian visit for Bill Bonanno. As a boy he had seen framed photographs of his father's town hanging on the walls at home, and he had later noted references to it in history books and travel guides, although the references had been very brief and superficial—it was as if the writers, with few exceptions, had quickly driven through the town without stopping, being perhaps intimidated by one published report, claiming that 80 percent of Castellammare's adult male population had served time in prison.

There was no social stigma attached to this, however, because most of the local citizens regarded the law as corrupt, representing the will of invaders who had long sought to control the islanders, and exploit the land through conqueror's law. The history of Castellammare, as with most of Sicily, had been turbulent for centuries, and Bonanno had remembered reading that the island had been conquered and reconquered no less than sixteen times—by Greeks, Saracens, and Normans, by Spaniards, Germans, and English, by various combinations and persuasions ranging from Holy Crusaders to Fascists: they had all come to Sicily and did what men do when away from home, and the history of Sicily was a litany of sailors' sins.

As the caravan of cars had arrived at Castellammare, having driven for two hours along narrow mountain roads above the sea, Bonanno felt a sudden sense of familiarity with the landscape that was beyond mere recognition from pictures; he felt united with all that he had imagined for years, all that he had heard as a boy from the reminiscing men gathered around his father's dinner table on Sunday afternoons. The town was actually quite beautiful, a tranquil fishing village built along the bottom of a mountain, and at the very tip of the land, on a jagged rocky edge splashed by waves, stood the old stone castle that had given the town its name.

The castle, built many centuries ago by the Saracens or Aragons, no one was absolutely certain, had served as the town's lookout post for spotting invading ships; but now it was a decaying structure of no purpose, and the elder Bonanno and the other men had recalled playing in it as boys.

Near the castle, along the small beach, were the fishermen, weatherworn and ruddy, wearing black berets; they had been pulling in their nets as the Bonanno party had passed but had been too busy to notice the line of cars. In the town square, near a church built four hundred years ago, were many men walking slowly, arm in arm, making many gestures with their hands. The stone houses, most of them two or three stories high with balconies in front, were arranged in tight rows along narrow cobbled roads over which was heard the clacking sounds of donkeys pulling colorfully painted wagons between the motor traffic. Here and there, sunning themselves in front of their doors, had been groups of women, the unmarried ones seated with their backs to the street, possibly following a fashion inherited a thousand years ago when the Arabs had occupied Sicily.

In front of one particularly well-constructed house, on Corso Garibaldi, a crowd had gathered. When the procession of cars had been spotted, the people had stepped up to the curb, waiting. They were about thirty in number, dressed in dark clothes except for the children, one of whom held a bouquet of flowers. They had been standing in front of the home where Joseph Bonanno had been born, and the arrival of his son had been regarded as a historical event. An indication of the Bonanno family status in Castellammare had been the fact that the ceremony surrounding Joseph Bonanno's baptism in 1905 had marked the end of a shooting war between the local mafiosi and those in the neighboring village of Alcamo; and when Joseph Bonanno's father, Salvatore Bonanno, had died in 1915, he had been buried in the most prominent plot at the base of the mountain.

After the bridal couple had been greeted by, and had disentangled themselves from, the embracing crowds, and had had coffee and pastry with their cousins and compari, they had gone to the cemetery; and Bill Bonanno, standing before a large gravestone that exhibited a proud picture of a man with a handlebar moustache, had sensed something more about his own father's relationship to the past. The eyes looking out from the gravestone were penetrating and dark, and Bill Bonanno could readily accept what he had heard of his grandfather's persuasive power, although he found it difficult to believe that this authoritative-looking photograph was of a man who had died at thirty-seven. His grandfather seemed to be a tall man, lean and tall unlike Sicilians; although the Bonannos were not Sicilians by origin. They had lived hundreds of years ago in Pisa, according to Joseph Bonanno, but had left rather hastily following a dispute with the ruling family. Joseph Bonanno, who kept a family coat-of-arms hanging in his home in the United States, a shield decorated with a panther, had compiled a history of his ancestry that claimed kinship with Charles Bonanno, engineer of the leaning Tower of Pisa.

After Bill Bonanno had returned from his honeymoon, in September of

1956, he had urged his father to visit Castellammare. And a year later, the elder Bonanno had done so. But the pleasant experiences of that trip had been curtailed by negative events that had followed in 1957, and had continued to follow into the 1960s. There had been the publicity attached to the Anastasia murder and the Apalachin meeting, and then there had been the Senate testimony of Joseph Valachi, the Mafia defector, who had identified Joseph Bonanno as his sponsoring godfather and as the leader of one of New York's five "families," as well as a member of the nine-man national commission. Finally, in 1963, there had been the dissension within Bonanno's organization, internal differences between a few old friends who had left Castellammare forty years before. And now, in October of 1964, hiding in the apartment, Bill Bonanno, the son, was a partner in the tension and intrigue.

He was tired of it, but there was little he could do. He had not seen Rosalie or his four young children in several days, and he wondered about their welfare and wished that his relationship with his in-laws, the Profacis, had not declined as it had in recent years. He and Rosalie had now been married for eight years, and much had happened since their honeymoon, too much, and he hoped that he could successfully repair the damage done. What was required, he felt, was a new start, a second attempt in another direction, and he had thought that they were moving toward this earlier this year, in February, when they had moved into their new home, a ranch-type house on a quiet tree-lined street in East Meadow, Long Island. They had finally left Arizona, a state that Rosalie had come to hate for a number of reasons, not the least of which was a certain woman in Phoenix, and they had come east to live for a few months in the mansion of Rosalie's uncle, Joe Magliocco, in East Islip, Long Island, prior to getting their own home. The time spent at Magliocco's place had been hectic, not only for them but for their children.

The mansion was on a sprawling estate protected by high walls and trees, by watchdogs and gunmen. Joe Magliocco, a muscular fat man of three hundred pounds, had taken over the Profaci operation, including its control over the Italian lottery in Brooklyn, after the death in 1962 of Joseph Profaci. (Rosalie's father, Salvatore Profaci, was also dead at this point, having been killed before her wedding due to an explosion he had caused while working on an engine in his motorboat.) Magliocco, an impulsive man who lacked great organizational ability, had also inherited many problems when he took over, the worst of which had been an internal revolt by younger members led by the Gallo brothers. The dissension caused by the Gallo faction, among other issues, was still unresolved when Rosalie and Bill Bonanno had moved in with Magliocco in 1963, and they had sensed that things were becoming almost desperate for Magliocco in the late summer and fall of that year—men were coming and going at odd hours, the dogs were on constant alert, and Magliocco was rarely without his bodyguard even when walking short distances through his estate.

One morning in December, as the Bonanno's two-year-old son, Joseph, was crawling through the dining room, he reached between the china closet and the wall, and pulled the trigger of a rifle that had been left standing there. The rifle blast blew a hole in the ceiling, hitting through the upper floor not far from where Magliocco lay sleeping. The fat man bolted out of bed, yelling; and Rosalie, who had been feeding her newly born infant in another part of the house, began to scream. The big house suddenly vibrated with a flurry of bodies running in panic, chasing and shouting—until the little boy was discovered downstairs, sitting on the rug wearing his red pajamas, stunned but safe, with a smoking rifle at his feet. Two weeks later, Joe Magliocco died of a heart attack.

On hearing Frank Labruzzo ringing the downstairs bell, Bill Bonanno pressed the buzzer and then watched through the peephole of the apartment door. He saw Labruzzo step out of the elevator with newspapers under his arm, and he could tell by the pale expression on Labruzzo's face that something had gone wrong.

Labruzzo said nothing as he entered the apartment. He handed the papers to Bonanno. On the front page of every one, in large headlines at the very top, was the news:

JOE BANANAS—CALL HIM DEAD
JOE BONANNO IS KIDNAPPED BY 2 HOODS IN NEW YORK
MOB KIDNAPS JOE BANANAS
FBI JOINS KIDNAPPER SEARCH

Bill Bonanno felt feverish and dizzy. He sank finally into a chair, his mind racing with confusion and disbelief. The headlines, large letters spreading across the entire page, more prominent than the war in Vietnam and the social revolution in America, seemed to be screaming at him and demanding a reply, and he wanted to react quickly, to run somewhere to do something violent, hating the feeling of being helpless and trapped. But he forced himself to sit and methodically read every paragraph. Most of the newspaper articles suggested that Joseph Bonanno was already dead, possibly encased in concrete and resting in a river. There was some speculation that he was perhaps being held hostage until he made certain concessions, and there was finally a theory that the kidnapping was a hoax arranged by Joseph Bonanno himself as a way of avoiding an appearance before a Federal grand jury meeting in Manhattan later in the week.

The younger Bonanno discounted this last point as absurd. He was convinced that his father had intended to appear before this grand jury as he had before others in the past—revealing nothing, of course, but at least appearing and pleading his innocence or seeking refuge in his constitutional rights. Bill Bonanno also did not believe that his father would have attempted anything so tricky as a staged kidnapping without first consulting with Labruzzo and himself.

He watched Labruzzo pacing back and forth through the room like a caged animal. Labruzzo still had said nothing. Normally very calm, he seemed at this moment very nervous and fearful. Finally aware that he was being observed, Labruzzo turned and, as if trying to reestablish his position as a cool man under pressure, said, almost casually, "Look, if it's true that he's dead, there is nothing we can do about it."

"If it's true," Bonanno replied, "they're going to be looking for us next."

Labruzzo was again silent. Bonanno got up to turn on the television set and radio for late news. He wondered if the location of their apartment was known to outsiders, and he also tried to figure out which men from his own organization might have collaborated in his father's capture, feeling certain that it had been handled partly from the inside. How else would they have known that Joseph Bonanno had planned to spend the night at Maloney's place? Everything had been so neatly done, the two gunmen appearing on Park Avenue just as the elder Bonanno had stepped out of a cab, and Maloney, having gotten out first, running ahead through the rain and not seeing anything until after it had happened. Although these suspicions were later to be proved unfounded and Bill was to come to feel guilty about them, he even thought Maloney might have been part of the deal.

Because Bill Bonanno, like his father, was suspicious of most lawyers. Lawyers were servants of the court, part of the system, which meant they could never be trusted entirely—or they were crime buffs, men who enjoyed being on the fringe of the gangsters' world, were fascinated no doubt by the occasional glimpses they got into the secret society. Sometimes they even became involved in Mafia intrigue, giving advice to one don or another, and shifting sides as the odds changed—it was a kind of game with them.

And no matter which faction won or lost, the lawyers survived. They lived to accompany their clients to the courthouse as photographers took pictures, and they later made statements to the press—they were a privileged clique, highly publicized, highly paid, often crooked but rarely caught; they were the untouchables. Bonanno remembered having heard years ago of how the Mafia dons had complained among themselves about the exorbitant fees charged by certain lawyers after the police had raided the Apalachin conference. A few dons claimed to have paid about $50,000 each for their legal defense, and since much of this had been paid in cash, as the lawyers had requested, the mafiosi could only guess at the amount on which no taxes had been paid. While Bonanno knew that Maloney was not this sort of lawyer, he nevertheless suspected the worst until future evidence proved otherwise; he was a lawyer, after all—and they lived off other people's misery.

As for the men who had provided the muscle in the kidnapping, Bonanno assumed that they had had the prior approval of the Mafia's national commission, which had recently suspended Joseph Bonanno from its membership. He also assumed that they had acted under the personal direction of the Mafia boss in Buffalo, the senior member of the commission, seventy-three-year-old Stefano Magaddino, his father's cousin and former friend from Castellammare. The apparent bitterness on Magaddino's part toward his father was a subject often discussed within the Bonanno organization in 1963 and 1964. It was believed to be based partly on the fact that Magaddino, whose territory extended from western New York into the Ohio Valley and included links with Canadian racketeers in Toronto, had felt threatened by Joseph Bonanno's ambitions in Canada. For decades the Bonanno organization had worked in partnership with a group of mafiosi in Montreal, sharing most profitably in the importation of untaxed alcohol as well as in gambling and other illegal activities, including the control of the pizza trade and various protection rackets in Montreal's large Italian community. In 1963, when Joseph Bonanno went to Montreal and later applied for Canadian citizenship, Magaddino interpreted this as further evidence that Bonanno's Canadian interests were going to extend into Magaddino's territory, and the latter was overheard one day complaining of Bonanno: "He's planting flags all over the world!"

Even though Bonanno's petition for Canadian citizenship was denied and was followed by his expulsion, Magaddino's suspicions had persisted. It was a feeling not based on any one issue, Bonanno's men believed, but was inspired by a combination of fear and jealousy. They remembered Magaddino's dark mood on the night of Bill Bonanno's wedding reception in 1956, how he had stood near the dais surveying the great gathering of mafiosi who had come from all parts of the nation out of respect for Joseph Bonanno, and Magaddino had said in a loud voice to a man at his table: "Look at this crowd. Who the hell's going to be able to talk to my cousin now? This will go to his head."

Bill Bonanno also had sensed how little Magaddino had thought of him, and how upset the Buffalo boss had become when the elder Bonanno had sanctioned his elevation to No. 3 man in the Bonanno organization and had overlooked a member that Magaddino considered more worthy of promotion—namely, Magaddino's own brother-in-law, Gasper Di Gregorio. Di Gregorio had been a member of the Bonanno organization for thirty years, and until recent months Bill Bonanno had believed that Di Gregorio was one of his father's most loyal followers. He was a quiet, unassuming gray-haired man of fifty-nine who ran a coat factory in Brooklyn and was virtually unknown to the FBI; born in Castellammare, he had fought alongside the elder Bonanno in the famous Brooklyn gang war of 1930, and a year later he had been the best man when Joseph Bonanno had married Fay Labruzzo. He was also Bill Bonanno's godfather, a friend and adviser during the younger Bonanno's years as an adolescent and student, and it was difficult for Bonanno to figure out when and why Di Gregorio had decided to pull away from the Bonanno organization and lure others with him. Di Gregorio had always been a follower, not a leader, and Bill Bonanno could only conclude that Magaddino had finally succeeded after years of effort to use Di Gregorio as the dividing wedge in the Bonanno organization. Di Gregorio had taken with him perhaps twenty or thirty men, perhaps more—Bill Bonanno could only guess, for there was no easy way to know who stood where at this point. Maybe fifty of the three-hundred-man Bonanno family had defected in the last month, influenced by the commission's decision to suspend the elder Bonanno and encouraged by Magaddino's assurance that the commission would protect them from reprisals by Bonanno loyalists.

No matter what the situation was, Bill Bonanno knew that he could only wait. With his father gone, perhaps dead, it was important that he remain alive to deal with whatever had to be done. To venture outdoors at this point would be foolish and maybe suicidal. If the police did not spot him, Magaddino's men might. So Bonanno tried to suppress the fury and the despair that he felt and to resign himself to the long wait with Labruzzo. The phone was ringing now, the third code call in the last five minutes—the captains were reporting in from other apartments, available for any message he might wish to leave with the answering service. He would call it in a few moments to let them know that he was all right.

It was noon. Through the Venetian blinds he could see that it was a dark, dreary day. Labruzzo was sitting at the kitchen table drinking coffee, the dog at his feet. The pantry was well stocked with canned goods and boxes of pasta, and there was plenty of meat and sauce in the refrigerator. Bonanno, a fair cook, would now have lots of practice. They could exist here easily for several days. Only the dog would miss the outdoors.

Bonanno and Labruzzo lived in confinement for nearly a week, sleeping in shifts with their guns strapped to their chests, and being visited at night by the few men they trusted. One of these was a captain named Joe Notaro. He had been close to the Bonannos for years, and was respected for his sound judgment and caution. But on his first visit to the apartment, Notaro admitted with regret and embarrassment that he had probably been indirectly responsible for the elder Bonanno's capture.

He recalled that on the day of the kidnapping he had been sitting in his car discussing Joseph Bonanno's plans for the evening with another officer, speaking in a tone loud enough to be heard by the driver. Notaro's driver was a meek little man who had been with the organization for a number of years, and had never been taken very seriously by the members. As Notaro was later astonished to discover, the driver was then working as an informer for the Di Gregorio faction. The driver had apparently held a grudge against the organization ever since one of the captains had taken away his girlfriend, and Joseph Bonanno had been too preoccupied at the time with other matters to intercede on the driver's behalf. The fact that the offending captain had later been sentenced to a long jail term on a conspiracy charge in a narcotics case had not soothed the driver's wounded ego. After Bonanno's capture, the driver had disappeared, and Notaro had just learned that he was now driving for Di Gregorio's group.

Among other bits of information picked up by Notaro and his fellow officers from their sources around town—from bookmakers and loan sharks, from the men who work in nightclubs and in related businesses linked socially to the underworld—was that Joseph Bonanno was not yet dead and was being held by Magaddino's men at a farm somewhere in the Catskill Mountains in upstate New York. The FBI and the police were reported to be concentrating their efforts in that area, and had also visited Bonanno's home in Tucson and were keeping watch on the late Joe Magliocco's mansion, considering it an ideal hideaway because of its protective walls and the private dock. As for the status of the organization, Bonanno's officers believed that more than two hundred men were still loyal and that their morale was very high. Most of the men were remaining indoors, the officers said, and were sleeping in shifts and doing their own cooking in their apartments and rented rooms. Bonanno and Labruzzo were told that at one apartment the men had complained at dinner the previous evening that the spaghetti had a metallic taste—they later learned that the cook, while vigorously stirring the meat sauce, had knocked his pistol out of his chest holster into the pot.

With each visit the officers brought the latest papers, and Bonanno and Labruzzo could see that the kidnapping episode was continuing to receive enormous coverage. Pictures of the younger Bonanno had appeared in several papers, and there was speculation that he, too, had been taken by his father's enemies, or that he was hiding in New York or Arizona, or that he was in the protective custody of federal agents. When a reporter had telephoned FBI headquarters to verify this last item, an agency spokesman had refused to comment.

The headline writers were having fun with the story, Bonanno could see—YES, WE HAVE NO BANANAS—and reporters were also keeping a close watch on his wife and children at home in East Meadow, Long Island. One paper described Rosalie as leaning out of a window to reply to a reporter, in a "trembling voice," that she knew nothing of her husband's whereabouts, and her eyes were said to be "red-rimmed" as if she had been crying. Another newspaper, describing her as very pretty and shy, said she had spent part of the afternoon in a beauty parlor. A third paper reported that Bonanno's seven-year-old son, Charles, while playing on the sidewalk in front of the house, had been approached by a detective asking questions about his father; but the boy had replied that he knew nothing. Bill Bonanno was very pleased.

He had trained his children well, he thought. He had cautioned them, as his own father had once cautioned him, to be careful when speaking with strangers. He did not want his children to be curt or disrespectful to anyone, including the police, but he warned them to be on guard when asked about matters pertaining to their home or parents, their relatives or the friends of relatives. He had also conveyed to his children his disapproval of tattletales. If they saw their brothers, sisters, or cousins doing something wrong, he had said, it was improper for them to go talebearing to adults, adding that nobody had respect for a stool pigeon, not even those who gained by such information.

Sitting quietly in the apartment, after Notaro had left and Labruzzo was sleeping, Bonanno remembered an incident earlier in the year when his advice to his children had seemed to boomerang. The family had been spending the day at a relative's home in Brooklyn, and during the afternoon one of the aunts had complained that the little wagon she kept in the backyard for hauling laundry had been taken, and that the children, who had been playing with it earlier, had claimed not to know who had taken it out of the yard. Bonanno had then approached the children, lining them up for questioning; and when none had given any information about the wagon, he had said in a forceful tone that he was going to take a walk around the block, and that when he returned he wanted to see the wagon in the yard where it had been. He did not care who had taken it, there would be no punishment; he just wanted it back. After his walk, Bonanno returned to the yard. The children were out of sight, but the wagon had reappeared.

While Bonanno was not overly concerned about his children's welfare during his absence, knowing Rosalie's capabilities as a mother, he was worried about the loneliness and anxiety that she would undoubtedly feel each night after the four children had gone to sleep. Her mother, who lived forty-five minutes away in Brooklyn, would certainly visit; but Mrs. Profaci did not drive a car, and it would not be easy for her to arrange transportation. Her relatives, as well as most relatives on the Bonanno side of the family, were hesitant about appearing at Bill Bonanno's home, fearing the publicity and the police investigation that might follow. Bonanno's sister, Catherine, who feared neither publicity nor the police, would have been a great comfort to Rosalie but she lived in California with her husband and young children.

Bonanno's mother was probably in Arizona, or else living in seclusion with friends; and his nineteen-year-old brother, Joseph Jr., was a student at Phoenix College. Knowing Joseph, he doubted that he was attending classes very often. Joseph was the wild one of the family, a drag racer, a bronco rider, a nonconformist who was so thoroughly undisciplined that he could never become a member of the organization, Bill Bonanno felt sure. The elder Bonanno had been on the run during much of his younger son's adolescence, dodging the Kefauver committee or the McClellan committee or some other investigation or threat; and Joseph Jr. had been left under the supervision of his mother, who could not control him. In any case, Joseph Jr. was now in Phoenix, and Rosalie was in Long Island, and Bill Bonanno only hoped that she could manage things alone and not crack under the continued pressure that she had been forced to face in recent years.

He knew that Rosalie would probably be surprised if she knew his thoughts at this moment, having heard her accuse him so often of caring only about "those men" and never about her. But he sincerely was concerned about her, and was also aware of a certain guilt within himself which would be hard for him to admit, at least to a wife. That he loved her, he had no doubt, but the responsibilities that he felt toward his father's world, and all that had happened to him because of it, had destroyed a part of him, perhaps the better part. He knew that he could not justify much of what he had done with regard to Rosalie since their marriage, nor would he try. To himself he saw it all as a temporary escape from the tight terrifying world that he had inherited, an indulgence to his restlessness between the brief moments of action and interminable hours of boredom, the months of waiting and hiding and the machinations attached to the most routine act, like making a telephone call or answering a doorbell—in such a strange and excruciating world, he had done some damnable things, but now he could only hope that his wife would concentrate on the present, forgetting the past temporarily. He hoped that she would efficiently run the home, borrowing money from her relatives if necessary, and not become overly embarrassed by what she read in the newspapers, saw on television, or heard in the street. This was asking a lot, he knew, particularly since she had not really been prepared as a girl for the life she was now leading. He remembered her description of how her family had sought to protect her from reality, and how accustomed she had become as a girl to finding holes in the newspapers around the house, sections cut out where there had been photographs or articles dealing with the activities of the Profaci organization.

His homelife as a boy had been different. His father had never seemed defensive about any aspect of his life, seeming only proud and self-assured. The elder Bonanno had somehow suggested the nature of his life so gradually and casually, at least to Bill, that the ultimate realization of it was neither shocking nor disillusioning; although as a boy Bonanno had noticed his father's rather odd working hours. His father seemed either to be home all day and out at night, or to be at home constantly for weeks and then gone for weeks. It was very irregular, unlike the routines of the fathers of the boys with whom Bill had first gone to school on Long Island. But he was also aware that his father was a busy man, involved in many things, and at first this awareness satisfied his curiosity about his father, and seemed to explain why his father kept a private office in the house.

During this period of Bill Bonanno's life, in the 1940s, his father had a cheese factory in Wisconsin, coat factories and a laundry in Brooklyn, and a dairy farm in Middletown, New York, on which were forty head of cattle and two horses, one named after Bill and the other after Catherine. The family's home was in Hempstead, Long Island, a spacious two-story red brick Tudor-style house with lovely trees and a garden, not far from East Meadow, where Rosalie and Bill now lived. The family had moved to Hempstead from Brooklyn in 1938, and Bill had attended school in Long Island for four years, until a serious ear infection, a mastoid condition that had required operations, had led to his being transferred to schools in the dry climate of Arizona. His father had selected a boarding school in Tucson and would come to Arizona with his wife to visit Bill for the entire winter, renting an apartment there at first, later buying a house; and within four or five years Bill gradually became aware of the many men who frequently visited his father there, men who seemed very respectful and deferential. These were many of the same men that he had remembered seeing around the house as a boy in Long Island; and he also recalled a particular cross-country automobile trip that the Bonanno family had taken years before, when Bill was about eight years old, traveling from New York to California, visiting the Grand Canyon and other sites, and in every large city in which they stopped his father had seemed to know numbers of people, very friendly men who had made a great fuss over Bill and his sister.

After Bill Bonanno had gotten his driver's license, which was obtainable at sixteen in Arizona, his father had sometimes asked him to meet certain men arriving at the Tucson train station or the airport, men whom Bill knew very well now and had become fond of—they were like uncles to him. When he eventually began to recognize these same men's photographs in newspapers and magazines, and to read articles describing them as thugs and killers, he concluded, after a brief period of confusion and doubt, that the newspapers were uninformed and very prejudicial. The characterization of the men in the stories bore little resemblance to the men that he knew.

Perhaps his first personal involvement with his father's world occurred at Tucson High School, in 1951, on a day when he was called out of class and told to report to the principal's office. The principal seemed upset as he asked, "Bill, are you in any kind of trouble with the law?"

"No," Bonanno had said.

"Well, there are two men from the FBI in my outer office," the principal said, adding, "Look, Bill, you don't have to talk to them if you don't want to."

"I have nothing to hide," he said.

"Would you prefer that I be present?"

"Sure, if you want to."

The principal led Bill Bonanno into the outer office and introduced him to the agents, who asked if he knew anything about the disappearance and possible murder of the Mafia boss Vincent Mangano. Bill Bonanno said that he knew nothing about it. He had heard that name before, but it had been in connection with James Mangano, who had an asthmatic daughter and had rented the Bonanno's Tucson home one summer when they were away. The agents took notes, asked a few more questions, then left. Bill

Bonanno returned to his classroom, somewhat shaken. He felt the eyes of the other students on him, but he did not face anyone as he took his seat, although he felt separated from his classmates in a way he had not felt before.

It was a feeling, he was sure, that Rosalie had never had as a girl, and he even wondered if she had it now. She seemed totally unaware and naïve about his world. While he occasionally interpreted this as self-protectiveness on her part, a determination to ignore what she disapproved of, he also believed sometimes that his wife was genuinely remote from reality, as if her parents had really fulfilled their ambition to separate Rosalie from the embarrassing aspects of their own past. But this could not be entirely true, for if they had really wished to separate her from themselves they would never have condoned her marriage to him.

Still, for whatever reason, his wife's quality of detachment irritated him at times, and he hoped that now, following his father's disappearance, she would respond to the emergency and do nothing foolish or careless. He hoped, for example, that when she left their house with the children she would remember to lock the front and back doors, and would be certain that all the windows were securely bolted. He was worried that FBI men, posing as burglars, would break into the house and infest the interior with electronic bugs. They often did this, he had heard; they would enter a house and overturn a few pieces of furniture, and plow through the bureau drawers and closets, giving the impression that they were thieves looking for valuables, but what they really were doing was installing bugs. Once the agents got into a house, he knew, it was nearly impossible to detect their little handiwork, conceding that in this area the FBI was very creative and clever. He knew of a case in which the agents had even bugged a house before the carpenters had finished building it. It had happened to Sonny Franzese, an officer in the Profaci organization; the agents had apparently gone to the construction site of Franzese's new home in Long Island after the workmen had left for the day, inserting bugs into the framework and foundation. Franzese later wondered why the agents knew so much about him.

Bill Bonanno kept an electronic debugging device in his closet at home, a kind of plastic divining rod with an antenna that was supposed to vibrate when sensing bugs, but he was not sure how trustworthy it was. If the agents did get into his house, he was sure that they could find some things that would serve as evidence against him. They would find a few rifles in the garage, and pistols in his bedroom bureau. They might find a false identification card or two, and various drivers' licenses and passports. They would discover his vast collection of quarters, several dollars' worth neatly packed in long thin plastic tubes that fit into the glove compartment of his car, and were used for long-distance calls at telephone booths. The agents would probably help themselves to the excellent Havana cigars that he remembered having left on the top of his bedroom bureau, in a jar that also contained Q-tips cotton swabs on sticks that he used for draining his left ear in the morning, the infected ear that had gotten him to Arizona, where he wished he was at this moment. The agents might be interested in some of the books in his library, which included three books on the FBI and all the books about the Mafia, including ones by Senators Kefauver and McClellan; and several other books that he suspected would be over the agents' heads—the Churchill volumes, books by Bertrand Russell, Arthur Koestler, Sartre, and the poetry of Dante; but there was one book that they would surely like to thumb through: the large photo album of his wedding. The album, which consisted of several photographs of the reception, including the crowded ballroom scene at the Astor, would identify most of the distinguished guests; and what the album failed to reveal, the movie film of the wedding, packed in a tin can at the bottom of a bookshelf, would reveal. There was more than two thousand feet of home-movie film on the wedding, and he and Rosalie had enjoyed looking at it from time to time during the past eight years. The wedding event, the extravagance and splendor of it, had probably marked the high point of Joseph Bonanno's life, the pinnacle of his prestige; and a social historian of the underworld, should one ever exist, might describe the event as the "last of the great gangster weddings," coming before the Apalachin exposure and other vexations had put an end to such displays.

One of the things that had most fascinated Bill Bonanno about the film, after he had seen it three or four times, was what it revealed about the caste-consciousness of the mafiosi who had attended, and no doubt the FBI would be equally interested if it could review the film. By observing the way that a mafioso dressed, one could determine his rank within the organization. The lower-echelon men, Bonanno had noticed, all wore white dinner jackets to the wedding, while the middle-level men, the lieutenants and captains, wore light-blue dinner jackets. The top men, the dons, all were dressed in black tuxedoes; except, of course, the principal males in the wedding party, who wore cutaways.

On November 5, which was Bill Bonanno's thirty-second birthday, and was fifteen days after the elder Bonanno's disappearance, five of the Bonanno officers decided that they had had all the confinement they could stand—they needed a short vacation. Bill Bonanno agreed. It did not appear that their enemies planned an armed confrontation at this time, not with so many police on the alert, and Bonanno also welcomed a change of scenery. He had sent word to Rosalie through one of his men that he was alive. He had said no more than that, nor did Rosalie expect more. The question facing Bonanno now was where to go to find rest and relaxation and not attract attention. He and his men could not fly south because the airports were too well patrolled and, even with their disguises, they might be spotted. He also did not want to venture too far from New York because there was always the chance of some new development concerning his father. They would have to use their cars, traveling at night; and after a few hours of thought, Bonanno decided that they should visit the ski country of New England. None of the men had ever been on skis, nor did they intend to try. They merely wished to experience again the act of movement, to travel over open roads in the brisk outdoors, to clear their minds, recharge the batteries of their cars and walk their dogs away from the repressive environment of New York.

They left that evening within the first hour of darkness. Two men to a car, they planned to meet at a large motel near Albany. Bonanno's green Cadillac was parked a block away, under a lamplight. He approached it slowly and carefully, alert for any movement or sound around the car or along the dark street. Labruzzo followed several feet behind, holding the dog on a leash with his left hand and keeping his right hand free for his gun.

Lowering a suitcase to the ground, Bonanno walked around the car, which was covered with dust and a few fallen leaves. He examined the front fenders and the hood for fingerprints, as he always did before unlocking the door, in an attempt to detect the planting of bombs within the vehicle. Confident that the car had not been touched since he had left it, he got in and turned on the ignition. The car started up immediately, which did not surprise him, for he had always maintained it to perfection, changing the batteries and other engine parts long before they had ceased to function properly. Relaxing in the cold soft leather seats waiting for Labruzzo, he felt a renewed sense of appreciation for the car, its powerful engine idling quietly, its gleaming dashboard adorned with a stereo. It was a big comfortable car for a tall heavy man of his size, and he guessed that his weight had increased by eight or ten pounds during the last few weeks of tension and confinement. He was probably 235 pounds, and he felt it. Leaning toward the rear-view mirror, he saw that he bore little resemblance to his recent newspaper photographs. His face was heavier; and with his beard, his plain-glass horn-rimmed glasses, and the hat that he wore as part of his disguise, he imagined that he looked like a jazz musician.

After Labruzzo had deposited the dog in the back seat, and the gun under the front seat, the two men began the slow ride through the side streets of Queens that Bonanno knew so well. Within a half hour they were rolling smoothly on the highway, saying very little as they listened to the stereo, the lights of the city behind them. Bonanno was delighted to be leaving New York. He had never liked the city very much, and recently he had come to hate it. He had often wondered why so many mafiosi, men with roots in the sunny agrarian lands of Southern Europe, had settled in this cold polluted jungle crowded with cops and nosy newsmen, with hazards of every conceivable nature.

The Mafia bosses in the South, or in the Far West, in places like Boulder, Colorado, undoubtedly lived a much better life than any of the five dons with organizations centered in New York City. The don in Colorado probably owned a trucking business or a little nightclub and, with only ten or twelve men under his command, ran a few gambling parlors or a numbers racket on the side. He worked regular hours, probably played golf every afternoon, and had time in the evening for his family. His sons would graduate from college, becoming business executives or lawyers, and would know how to steal legally.

The five dons in New York each commanded forces of between 250 and 500 men, meaning that approximately two thousand mafiosi—40 percent of the national membership of five thousand—were in New York fighting the traffic and one another. The New York dons never felt secure no matter how much power they had. Why did they remain? Bonanno knew the answer, of course; New York was where the big money was. It was the great marketplace, the center of everything. Each day a million trucks came rolling into or out of New York—it was a hijacker's paradise, a town of tall shadows, sharp angles, and crooked people from top to bottom. Most New Yorkers, from the police to the prostitutes, were on the take or on the make. Even the average citizens seemed to enjoy breaking the law, or beating the system in some way. Part of the success of the numbers racket, which was the Mafia's most lucrative source of income, was that it was illegal. If the lawmakers would legitimize numbers betting, it would hurt business because it would deprive customers of that satisfactory sense of having beaten the system, of having outwitted the police and the august judiciary, with the mere placing of a bet. It was the same satisfactory sense that people got forty years ago when they dealt with their bootlegger, or were admitted into an all-night speakeasy.

New York was also a marvelous place in which to hide. One could get lost in the crowds of New York, could blend in with the blurring sights, movement, shadows, and confusion. People tended to mind their own business in New York, to remain uninvolved with the affairs of their neighbors, and this was a great asset for men in hiding. Bonanno knew that one of his father's captains, a man named Joseph Morale, had been hiding from Federal authorities for twenty years, and was still in circulation, living most of the time at his home in a neighborhood of nondescript houses in Queens. Morale came and went at odd hours, never following a predictable routine, and his family had been trained in ways that would not expose him by word or act.

Bonanno's father had once concealed himself for more than a year in Brooklyn, during the gangland discord of 1929 to 1930, a time when a rival boss had issued a "contract" for his death. Bill Bonanno was sure that if his father were alive now he could hide indefinitely in New York because he possessed the necessary discipline to do so. Discipline was the main requirement. Disguises and hideaways, false identification cards and loyal friends were important, but individual discipline was the essential factor, combining the capacity to change one's routine, to adjust to solitude, to remain alert without panicking, to avoid the places and people that had frequently been visited in the past. When his father had gone into hiding in 1929, a time when he had been actively courting Fay Labruzzo, he had suddenly and without explanation stopped appearing at her home. She had heard nothing from him for several months and assumed that their engagement had been terminated. Then one of her brothers-in-law noticed that the window shades of the building directly opposite the

Labruzzo home, on Jefferson Street in Brooklyn, had been down for a long time; and later he saw the glimmer of rifle barrels poised behind the small opening at the bottom of the shades, obviously waiting for Bonanno to appear in front of the Labruzzo home.

Bill Bonanno was confident that, if he had to, he could hide in New York for a very long time. He believed that he had discipline, that he would not panic if the search parties were getting close, that he had a certain talent for elusiveness. Even now, driving at night on the New York State Thruway, obeying the speed limit, he was aware of every car that followed him, the arrangements of their headlights in his rearview mirror. Whenever he passed a car he observed its body style, the license plate, tried to get a look at the driver, and his alertness intensified whenever a car behind him gained speed to pass. He tried to maintain a certain distance between himself and the others, shifting lanes or reducing speed when necessary. Since he had carefully studied the road map prior to the trip, as he did before every trip, he knew the exits, the detours, the possible routes of escape.

Whenever he planned to remain in a single town or certain area for a few days, he familiarized himself not only with the streets but also with the hill formations and arrangements of trees along certain roads that might temporarily obscure his car as he drove it from the view of drivers behind him. He actually charted out zones of obscurity into which he would drive when he felt he was being followed, particularly places where the road dipped or curved and was joined by an alternate route.

Whenever he sensed that he was being tailed in Long Island, for example, he led his possible pursuers into Garden City, where he was intimately familiar with several short curving roads that linked with other roads, and he knew several places where the roads dipped, then rose, then dipped again, stretches where his car vanished from sight for several seconds if his followers were keeping at a subtle distance. He also knew about seven ways to get into and out of Garden City, and anyone who followed him into that city, be it Federal agents or unfriendly *amici*, was almost sure to lose him.

Another reason that Bonanno had confidence in his ability to hide was that loneliness did not bother him. He had adjusted to it as a young teenager in Arizona when he had lived alone in a motel room, later in his parents' home, each year between fall and winter while his parents were in New York—an arrangement made necessary by his eviction at the age of fifteen from his boarding-school dormitory because one day he had led a group of classmates, who were supposed to be visiting a museum, into a film house showing the controversial *Forever Amber*. He remembered how embittered he had become by the punishment, which permitted him to attend classes but had prohibited his remaining on campus at night. He had also been surprised by his father's lack of influence with the headmaster, who had accepted generous gifts from the Bonannos in the past, including large shipments of cheese for the school from the factory in Wisconsin, and also butter when it was scarce because of World War II rationing. His parents, remaining in New York because of his father's activities, could do nothing after the eviction but arrange for him to stay at the Luna Motel, which was close to a bus stop where Bill could get a ride to school.

In angry response to his punishment, Bill had withdrawn his horse from the school's stable. He had kept the animal in a yard behind the motel. The horse and a miniature Doberman pinscher, the same type of dog that was in his car now as he drove upstate, had been his main companions during those months his parents were away, and he had become very independent and self-reliant. Each morning he got himself up, made his own breakfast. He had spent many evenings alone in the motel room listening to the radio. He remembered the sound of the fast-talking Garry Moore on the Jimmy Durante show, and the reassuring voice of Dr. Christian. Occasionally at sunset he would take long rides on his horse through the Arizona desert, passing the ranches of the rich, the smoking mud huts of the Zuñi tribesmen, the dusty wranglers and bronco riders who nodded toward him as he passed.

He had first ridden a horse as a three-year-old boy in Long Island, riding on weekends with his father and the other men. Many of Bonanno's men were superb horsemen, having ridden as small boys in Sicily where horses and donkeys were the main means of transportation; and Bill had many photographs of himself galloping with the mafiosi on weekends through the woods in Long Island. His father had insisted from the beginning that he ride a full-sized horse, not a pony, and his pride in his equestrianism compensated to a degree for his lack of achievement as an athlete when he got to high school.

It was not his ear ailment so much as his parents' travel schedule that limited his participation in organized sports. He had wanted to join the football team at Tucson High School, but he was with his parents in New

York when football practice began in August. In the winter and spring, when his parents were in Arizona, he spent considerable time with his father after school hours. His life had been one of extremes: he had either been entirely alone, or he had been encircled by his family and his father's friends. There had been times when he had wanted to escape the extremities, and not long after his eviction from the dormitory he had taken some money and run away. He had boarded a bus for New York, a five-day journey, and on arriving at the terminal on Forty-third Street off Broadway he had taken another bus upstate to the family farm in Middletown, which was very close to where he was driving at this moment on the New York State Thruway, and he was tempted now to pull off the main road and briefly revisit the farm that his father had since sold. He resisted the temptation, however, although he continued to think about his visit to the farm many years ago, remembering how upset the farmers had been when he had arrived, saying that his father had telephoned and had just flown to Tucson in an attempt to find him.

Within a few days the elder Bonanno had arrived at the farm, angry at first, but then his anger had subsided. He admitted that he had also run away at fifteen, in Sicily, and he thought that perhaps such experiences were part of a boy's growing up. He nevertheless talked his son into returning to school in Tucson, where a new yellow jeep would await him.

Once back in Arizona, Bill also arranged to visit a doctor. He had had stomach pains sporadically during the year, and after a medical examination it had been determined that he had an ulcer.

By most people's definition, the trip made by Bonanno, Labruzzo, and the other men through New York State into New England would hardly qualify as a vacation: it consisted largely of driving hundreds of miles each day and remaining in motels at night, watching television and talking among themselves.

After Albany they drove through Bennington, Vermont, and continued on up to Burlington along Lake Champlain. They then headed east into New Hampshire, then south two days later into Massachusetts. The travel route was charted each morning by one of the men who was a native New Englander, and they met each night at predestined places before they registered, in pairs, at separate motels which were close to one another and had suites with kitchenettes.

They shopped for groceries at local stores and, after walking the dogs, gathered at night in Bonanno's suite where the cooking was done. Bonanno had brought with him in his attaché case various spices and herbs and also a paperback edition of James Beard's cookbook. Each night he cooked and the other men cleaned up afterward. He was impressed with the modernization of motels since his boyhood days at the Luna—in addition to the streamlined kitchenettes there were the ice-making machines, body vibrators installed in beds, wall-to-wall carpeting, color television, and cocktail lounges that provided room service.

The most relaxing part of the trip for Bonanno was the act of driving, moving for dozens of miles without pausing for a traffic jam or even a signal light, and observing the tranquility of small towns and imagining the peaceful existence of those who occupied them. Occasionally he passed cars driven by young people with skis strapped onto the roofs and college emblems stuck to the windows, and also the Greek letters of fraternities that he could identify, and he was constantly reminded of how far he had drifted from the campus life he had known a decade ago.

It had been a very gradual drifting, occurring so slowly over a period of years that he did not really know when he had crossed the border into his father's world. During most of his college career, which had begun in the summer of 1951 and had extended irregularly through 1956, he had lived a kind of dual existence. At certain times, particularly when his father seemed to be at odds with other bosses or to be hounded by Federal agents, he had felt both a desire and a responsibility to stand by his father, to lend verbal and emotional support even though his father had not requested it, saying instead that he wanted Bill to remain in school concentrating on his studies. And there were times when Bill's interests had seemed to be centered entirely around the campus—he attended classes punctually, joined student groups, supported the football team. He was gregarious and generous, was popular with his classmates; and he always had a car and a girl.

But as a student he had limited powers of concentration, seeming to lose interest in subjects that he could not quickly master. He had grown accustomed in high school to making the grade with a minimum of effort because of his superior education in boarding school, but in college this advantage did not exist and he was also distracted quite often by an increasing awareness of his father and by the many conflicts that he was recognizing in himself. While he did not want to inherit his father's problems, did not want to be identified with gangsterism and to suffer the social ostracism resultant from exposure in the press, he also did not want to separate himself from his father's circumstances, nor to feel apologetic or defensive about his name, particularly since he did not believe that his father was guilty of crimes against society, feeling sometimes that the reverse was true, society was using such men as Joseph Bonanno to pay for the widespread sins in the system. In any case, no matter how damaging the consequences might be to himself, he could not turn against his father, nor did he really want to. His emotional link with his father was very strong, exceeding the normal bond of filial fidelity—it was more intense, more unquestioning, there was a unity in the tension shared and a certain romanticism about the risks and dangers involved, and there was also a kind of religious overtone in the relationship, a combination of blind faith and fear, formality and love. The many long periods of separation had in a strange way drawn them closer, had made each visit an event, a time of reunion and rejoicing; and during their months apart Bill's youthful imagination and memory had often endowed his father with qualities approximating a deity, so impressive, absolute, and almost foreign had the elder Bonanno been in person.

Joseph Bonanno was handsome in ways both strong and serene, having soft brown eyes, a finely etched face, and a benign expression that was evident even in photographs taken by the police. Considering that police photographers and the tabloid cameramen were rarely flattering, and usually made all Mafia suspects appear to be grim and sinister, Bill thought it remarkable that his father had seemed gracious and composed in nearly every one of the hundreds of news photos and police posters that had been displayed in recent years, including the latest ones circulated since his disappearance. Never let anyone know how you feel, Joseph Bonanno had told his son, and Bill had tried to follow the advice, remembering an occasion years ago when he had accepted an invitation to appear on Alumni Day at his old boarding school and how, after he had delivered a pleasant little speech to the students expressing the hope that his own children might one day benefit from the school's fine principles, he had walked across the stage, smiling, and had shaken the hand of the headmaster who had evicted him from the campus.

During the drive through New England he remembered several incidents from his past that had seemed inconsequential when they had occurred, but now in retrospect they revealed the double life he had led as a boy, the private battles he had fought without knowing he was fighting. He knew then only that his life was dominated by a soft-spoken man in silk suits who arrived in Arizona each winter from New York to end the loneliness, speaking in oracles, offering ancient remedies for contemporary ailments. He remembered his father directing him into the desert sun each afternoon to sit on a chair and tilt his head in such a way as to expose his left ear to the heat, saying that it would stop the draining; and it had. He remembered a summer day in Long Island when his sister had badly cut her leg while climbing a fence, and how his father had carried her into the house, had placed her on a table, and had squeezed lemon juice into her leg, massaging it in a slow special way that had not only stopped the bleeding but, after the wound had healed, had left no scar. He recalled how his father had arranged with a judge to free him without penalty after he had been caught speeding without a license when he was thirteen; and he remembered being extricated from other situations, too, boyish pranks or minor crimes during his hot-rodding days in high school, which was when he had become curious and even intrigued by his father's world.

He had wondered how he would measure up to the men around his father. He had heard them sometimes speaking casually about the danger they faced, or the jails that might await them, and he wondered if he would have been so calm in such circumstances.

The idea of jail had both worried and fascinated him in those days, and he remembered as a high-school student how he had once been arrested. He and a group of boys had been at a football game, behaving boisterously throughout the afternoon. Their pushing, shouting, and tossing of paper cups had so irritated other spectators that the police had finally evicted them from the stadium and charged them with disorderly conduct. They had spent the night in jail, an experience that Bill had found interesting during the first hour, but then it had quickly palled. And yet he realized that his offensive behavior had been deliberate, he had really wanted to end up in jail, and he was also somewhat satisfied later that he had remained cool and controlled during confinement.

News of the incident had not reached his father, although his teachers had learned of it and been disappointed and surprised. Unlike some boys in the junior class, Bill Bonanno was not thought of as troublesome or rebellious. He was regarded as a student leader; he was president of the student anti-liquor club, an organizer of the blood drive, an editor on the magazine. He did not smoke cigarettes, having one day promised an elderly woman he had met in a café, a tubercular recuperating in Tucson, that he would avoid the habit. After asking for his pledge in writing on a paper napkin, she handed him a five-dollar bill, and he had kept his word along with the money and napkin from that day on.

But despite the appearance of propriety and leadership in high school, there were nights when he indulged his restlessness by traveling with a gang of Mexican youths who specialized in stealing Cadillac hubcaps and other auto accessories that could be resold to used-car dealers, junkyards, or individual motorists. Some gang members became involved in the summer of 1950 with an older group of gunrunners along the Mexican border, a risky and exciting operation that appealed to Bill Bonanno, but he could not pursue it because he had to go east with his parents in June.

He remembered that trip as a strange, tense journey of long silences and new insights into his father's way of life. He had expected that his father would let him drive much of the way through Arizona into Texas and onward toward New York, as his father had done during previous June trips to New York for the summer; but on this occasion in 1950 his father would not relinquish the wheel, and, in addition to his mother and baby brother, there was one of his father's men in the car. The route his father followed was different from what had been familiar in the past; they drove through El Paso and Van Horn, avoiding the customary visit to Dallas, and then remained for two days in Brownsville, Texas, where other men had arrived to speak with his father. He remembered while stopping for the night in St. Louis that his mother and father had not registered together at the hotel; the elder Bonanno and his companion had taken one room, and Mrs. Bonanno and the two sons shared a suite elsewhere in the hotel. They left St. Louis in the middle of the night and drove before daybreak toward Wisconsin, not along the usual roads toward New York.

Through June and most of July they remained in Wisconsin, living in motels or cabins near the lakes north of Green Bay, not arriving in New York until the end of July. Then they settled in a house on the north shore of Long Island, living almost in seclusion except for the visits of men. It was a mournful summer in which conversations seemed leveled to a whisper, and dinner was served each night without the usual clattering of plates or rattling of silver. Bill had asked no questions. But he knew what was happening—his father and many of his father's friends were feeling the pressure of the Kefauver committee, and they were trying to avoid subpoenas that would summon them to testify before the Senate and the television cameras.

Although the main target of the committee was Frank Costello, whose appearance was marked by his ill temper under the hot lights as the cameras focused on his nervously tapping fingertips, there were other names mentioned in the press each day with which Bill Bonanno was personally familiar. Joseph Profaci was prominently cited on the Senate crime charts, and so was Joseph Magliocco. While Joseph Bonanno was also mentioned, he had not received great attention, and he had successfully avoided an appearance before the investigators. Nevertheless, Bonanno was deeply disturbed by the publicity he did get, it being the first time in years that he had been openly associated with organized crime. He was especially upset because the exposure had introduced his daughter to the charges against him, and Catherine, who was then sixteen, had broken down and cried for days. But the revelation did not diminish her affection for him. She, like Bill, was filled with compassion and actually felt closer to her father than she had before.

After that summer Bill had left New York to begin his final term at Tucson High. Borrowing a company car from the Bonanno cheese factory, and accompanied by a school friend, he drove quickly across the country, loving the buoyant sense of escape he felt behind the wheel, and he arrived in Arizona a week before classes began. Then he drove an additional thousand miles alone to San Antonio to visit a girl he was fond of, the sister of a classmate from his boarding-school days. Her father, an industrialist in Michigan, raised polo ponies, and Bill remembered riding them during the visit, galloping over the turf imagining the good life of men in white helmets and jodhpurs, swinging mallets through the sky.

But his final year in high school dragged on listlessly, the single memorable event being his father's graduation gift, a new Chevrolet Bel Air hardtop. He began at the University of Arizona that June, contemplating a degree in prelaw, but soon he switched to agricultural engineering, believing it would provide a useful background for the day when he would inherit part of his father's share in a large cotton farm north of Tucson. On reaching twenty-one, he would have in his own name not only land but certain income-producing properties that his father, a skillful real-estate speculator, had acquired since coming to Arizona. Bill looked forward to earning his own money, for his father had always been tight about allowances, an inconsistent trait in an otherwise generous man. It was typical of his father to buy him a new car but to provide so little spending money that Bill was usually out of gas.

As a result Bill had been compelled to take part-time jobs after school hours, which was what his father had wanted; the elder Bonanno abhorred idleness, and one of his favorite expressions was: The best way to kill time is to work it to death. Bill had begun working during his early teens, and during his college days he worked at night at a drive-in hamburger stand, where he met a pretty blond waitress, a divorcée with whom he had his first sexual affair.

Prior to this time his experience had consisted largely of heavy petting with such girls as the one in San Antonio, and quick ejaculations into a town tart who had first seduced him in the projection room of the Catalina movie house in Tucson on a day no film was being shown. Although he had had opportunities with other girls, and could have used his parents' home, he had never taken full advantage of their many absences. He had been somewhat puritanical in those days, incapable of sex in his mother's linen, and he had not even held parties there with his young friends because there was the possibility that outsiders might snoop through his father's things.

The affair with the divorcée had been conducted at her apartment, continuing for more than a year without his parents' knowledge. While there had never been talk of marriage he was very possessive of her, and he had become infuriated when he heard that she had dated in his absence a jockey who was in Arizona for the racing season. The fear of losing her, the first girl he thought he had ever truly had, and the shocking realization that she could make love to him and then date other men, had filled him with fury and despair. For the first time in his life he recognized his capacity for violence.

He remembered waiting for her in the apartment, then seeing her walking up the path with two tiny men, both tailored to the toes in an expensive but flashy way, their small sun-tanned faces drawn tight across their cheekbones. As she opened the door, laughing at something one of them had said, Bill had stepped forward, towering over them, shouting. When one of the men yelled back, Bill had grabbed him and shook him, then began to slap him hard against the wall as the girl screamed and the other jockey ran.

Soon the police had arrived to arrest Bill for assault. Later, however, perhaps through his father's influence, the case against him was dismissed.

The end of the romance was part of a depressing year in general. He was doing poorly in college; the girl in San Antonio informed him that she was going steady with a Texas football star; and then his father suffered a heart attack, and left Tucson to recuperate in a quiet spot near La Jolla, California. Bill was again alone in the house through the winter and spring, and through another session of summer school.

He spent part of the summer at an ROTC camp, preparing for a commission in the Army. He had adapted easily to the routine of military discipline, and he was soon promoted to drill sergeant in the cadets' elite unit, the Pershing Rifles. On the firing range he was a superb marksman with a rifle or pistol, having had previous target practice at boarding school, and being on familiar terms with guns since his boyhood days, when he noticed them bulging from beneath the jackets of men who came to visit. But it was after leaving New York for Arizona that he had become most aware of guns, seeing them carried openly and casually by people in cars or on horseback, by ranchers, wranglers, and Indians, and he sometimes felt that he was on the set of a cowboy film. And he liked the feeling.

He also liked the clothes, becoming quickly accustomed to wearing boots, hip-hugging pants, and string ties, and his father had done the same in Arizona. So had some of his father's men during their extended visits, although the fatter ones had always looked uncomfortable and comical in these clothes, their Western buckles lost under their bellies. Nevertheless a kinship of sorts probably did exist between these men and the legendary American cowboy, Bill thought, impressed by the similarity between the tales of the old West and certain stories he had heard as a boy involving gun battles between mounted mafiosi in the hills of western Sicily. He had heard that his grandmother in Castellammare had sometimes packed a pistol in her skirts, a kind of Ma Barker, and the Sicilians of that region today still honor the memory of the bandit Giuliano, a leader of a gang of outlaws who shared what they had stolen with the poor.

Although Giuliano was a hero in western Sicily he might easily be regarded elsewhere as a common thief—it depended largely on one's point of view, and the same could be said when appraising the life of any man, the activities of any group, the policies of any nation. If Bill Bonanno had learned anything from reading the memoirs of great statesmen and generals it was that the line between what was right and wrong, moral or immoral, was often very thin indeed, with the final verdict being written by the victors. When he had gone to ROTC camp, and later into military service with the Army Reserve, he had been trained in the technique of legal killing. He had learned how to use a bayonet, how to fire an M-1 rifle, how to adjust the range finder of a cannon in a Patton tank. He had memorized the United States military code, which in principle was not so dissimilar from the Mafia's, emphasizing honor, obedience, and silence if captured. And if he had gone into combat and had killed several North Koreans or Chinese Communists he might have become a hero. But if he killed one of his father's enemies in a Mafia war, where buried in the issues were the same mixture of greed and self-righteousness found in all the wars of great nations, he could be charged with murder.

In the Mafia today were many American veterans of World War II, one being a decorated infantryman who became Joseph Bonanno's bodyguard. This veteran wore a metal plate in his forehead and had several scars on his body as a result of combat against the Germans. He had fought in the North African campaign and also participated in the invasion of Sicily in which the Americans employed local mafiosi as intelligence agents and underground organizers against the Nazi and Fascist forces. Many such agents were rewarded with lawful authority by the Allies after the war, a fact documented in many books about the Mafia that Bill Bonanno had read; some of them became the mayors of towns and officials in the regional government because of their strong anti-fascism and hatred of Mussolini. During the Fascist regime in Italy, Mussolini had sponsored a campaign of terror against the Mafia, torturing many Mafia suspects, and without a fair trial killing many more. When Mussolini himself had been captured and killed, Bill remembered the satisfied reaction of his father and his father's friends. His father had been forced out of Sicily during his days as a student radical because he had opposed certain Fascist policies, and as a result he had settled in the United States. Otherwise he might have remained in his native land, and Bill wondered what it would have been like if he, too, had been born and had remained in Castellammare. Perhaps life might have been better. Perhaps it would have been worse.

Although the trip through New England taken by Bill Bonanno, Frank Labruzzo, and the other men was pleasantly uneventful and restful, there gradually developed within Bonanno a slight nagging feeling that he could not explain. It was as if he had forgotten something, was ignoring an obligation, compromising a trust, was somehow failing to fulfill all that his father might have expected of him. Whatever it was, he reasoned that it must be relatively unimportant, otherwise he would have no difficulty in defining it; and yet it continued to bother him as he drove south along Massachusetts Bay, then headed west toward Concord.

It was getting dark. Soon he and Labruzzo would be stopping at a motel where they would be joined later by the other men for dinner. They had now been on the road for a week, and during that time there had been nothing in the newspapers or on the radio indicating that the situation had changed in New York. The gangs were apparently still remaining out of sight. There had been no message on Bonanno's answering service requiring an immediate response. The government's search for his father had revealed no clues. Some police officials believed that Joseph Bonanno was still hiding in the Catskills, others believed that he was dead. Bill did not know what to believe, and during the last few days he had managed not to think too much about it. Maybe that was what had been bothering him. He did not know.

After dinner he wandered off by himself to walk the dog along a narrow dirt road near the highway, leaving the men seated around the television set in his suite. They were watching a crime series called *The Untouchables*, which was based loosely on the Mafia and had angered many Italo-Americans around the nation because the scriptwriters tended to give Italian names to the gangster roles. But the real-life gangsters enjoyed watching the show, Bonanno knew, although they appreciated it on a different level than the producers had intended. The gangsters saw this show, along with such other ones as *The F.B.I.* series and *Perry Mason*, as broad comedy or satire. They laughed at lines that were not intended to be funny; they mocked the dim-witted caricatures of themselves; they hooted and jeered the characters representing the FBI or the police, turning television-watching into a kind of psychodrama. They mostly seemed to enjoy the *Perry Mason* series, whose murder mysteries they could usually solve before the second commercial, and whose courtroom scene at the end of each show—a scene in which a prime suspect always collapses under cross-examination and jumps to his feet proclaiming his guilt—they found ridiculously amusing.

Returning to the motel, uncomfortably cold and unaccustomed to the Eastern climate after so many winters in Arizona, Bill Bonanno thought of Rosalie and the children, wishing that he could call them. If only Rosalie were reachable at a phone that was not tapped, he would call her at this moment; and as he thought about this he slowly became excited—he was clarifying what it was that had been bothering him.

He recalled a conversation with his father four months ago, in late July, immediately after the elder Bonanno had been evicted from Montreal and had returned to the United States. At that time Joseph Bonanno had recounted his legal hassle with the Canadian immigration authorities, the frustration of appearing all day in the Montreal courthouse and then not being able to reach Bill at night to talk freely on an untapped phone; and he said that should they ever again be separated for an extended period, they should have some system that would permit them to communicate. Joseph Bonanno had then devised a plan—a workable system, Bill had thought at the time, but during the hectic months that followed, culminating in his father's disappearance, Bill had forgotten all about his father's proposal. Now, on this November night in Massachusetts, it had come back to him.

The plan specified that, if they lost contact without explanation, Bill was to go to a particular telephone booth in Long Island on each Thursday evening, at eight o'clock sharp, until the elder Bonanno was able to call him there. The booth was located next to a diner on Old Country Road between Hicksville and Westbury, and Joseph Bonanno had kept a record of that number as he had of dozens of other booths that he had used in the past, at prearranged times, to speak with one of his men. This specific booth was selected for his son because it was not far from Bill's home, and because it had not been used so often in the past that it was likely to be under police surveillance. The booth was also chosen because there was a second telephone booth near it that could be used if the first was busy.

Excitedly, entering the motel, Bill announced to the other men that he was returning to New York early the next morning. He explained the reason, adding that the next day, November 12, was a Thursday. But the men thought it highly unlikely that the elder Bonanno would call; even if he were alive and unharmed, and had not forgotten his arrangement of four months ago, he would probably be too cautious or otherwise unable to make the call, they said. Bill, however, would not be discouraged. If his father were alive, he would make the call, Bill said. If he did not make it this Thursday, then he would make it next Thursday, or the Thursday after that, and Bill said he would be there every time, just in case, until he was convinced that his father was dead. He also pointed out, in a low tone that seemed almost self-accusatory, that when they had left New York a week ago, on the night of November 5, it had been a Thursday, and perhaps he had already missed one of his father's calls.

So it was agreed that they would return to New York. The other men were to go directly to their apartments, informing the subordinates that they were back in town, while Bonanno and Labruzzo would go on to Long Island.

They arrived in New York shortly before 7 p.m., the distant skyline glowing softly in the early-evening light, the last of the commuter traffic moving swiftly out of the city. At a quarter to eight, Bonanno and Labruzzo arrived at the diner on Old Country Road. They turned into the parking lot, stopping near the booth. It was glass-paneled and trimmed in green aluminum, and it was empty. They sat in the car for a few minutes, the motor running, the headlights off. Then, at five before eight, Bonanno got out, walked into the booth, and stood waiting.

He was relieved that the coin slot was not covered with the familiar yellow sticker reading "out of order"; and after depositing a coin and getting the reassuring sound of a dial tone, he replaced the receiver. The condition of coin-box phones was of vital importance to him and the other men, and he knew how infuriated they had all been at one time or another by malfunctioning phones, and they had sworn vengeance on the petty thieves who tamper with outdoor phones. Whenever they discovered one that was jammed or broken into, they reported it to the telephone company, and later checked back at the booth to be certain that the repairs had been made and also to be sure that the number had not been changed. If it had been, they recorded the new number on a private list they kept in their cars—a list containing not only the telephone numbers and booth locations, but also an identifying number that distinguished one booth from another. These last numbers were memorized by the Bonanno men as faithfully as baseball fans memorized the numbers on the backs of players, and the system had greatly reduced the organization's communications problem in recent years—it had enabled the elder Bonanno, for example, to use his home telephone, which was tapped, to call his son's home, where the phone was also tapped, and to engage his son in a folksy conversation in Sicilian dialect into which he slipped two numbers that indicated he wished to speak privately with Bill: the first number identified the locale of the booth that Bill was to go to, the second established the hour that Bill was to be there. Then, before the appointed hour, Joseph Bonanno would leave his home and go to a booth, would dial his son at the other booth, and they would speak freely without worrying about being tapped.

This system was similar to what Joseph Bonanno had proposed in July, except Bill had been told then to go automatically to booth No. 27—the one near the diner—each Thursday at 8 p.m. and to wait, as he was now waiting on this night in November. He felt chilly and cramped within the four glass walls that pressed him from all sides. He must go on a diet, he thought; he was becoming too large for phone booths. Raising his left arm, he looked at his watch, a diamond-studded gold one given him months ago by a few of his father's men. It was 7:59.

The silence in the booth was becoming intense, reminding him of boyhood moments waiting in a confessional, fretful seconds before the stern priest slapped open the sliding screen. At eight o'clock his senses were so sharp and expectant that he could almost hear ringing sounds piercing deep within his mind's ear and, looking down at the green plastic instrument, he searched for the slightest sign of vibration. But it hung motionless, quiet in its cradle.

He looked through the glass doors, seeing the parked car with Labruzzo behind the wheel. Labruzzo sat perfectly still, but the dog was jumping in the back, paws against the closed window. Bonanno then heard sounds coming from behind him—three men were leaving the diner, talking and laughing, getting into a station wagon. They did not look in his direction. Soon they were gone. He waited. Finally, he looked at his watch.

It was eight-four. It was all over for tonight, he thought. If his father did not call on the dot, he would not call at all. He also knew that his father would not want him to linger and possibly attract attention. So he reluctantly pulled open the door of the booth and walked slowly toward the car. Labruzzo flashed on the headlights. They drove in silence back to the apartment in Queens.

The rest of the week, and the weeks that followed through November into December, were for the most part monotonous. Bonanno and Labruzzo resumed housekeeping in their hideaway. They ventured out at night, remaining indoors during the day. They spoke with the men, read the papers, listened to the radio, learned very little.

On Thursday, however, their mood changed. Each Thursday was the high point of their week; it began in the morning with a sense of anticipation and it heightened during the late afternoon, building with each mile of the trip to the booth. The trip was taking on a strange, almost mystical meaning for Bonanno and Labruzzo—it was becoming an act of faith, a test of fidelity; and the booth, too, a solitary glowing structure in the vacant darkness, was approached almost reverentially. They drove slowly up to it, neither man speaking. Then Bill, after getting out of the car, would stand in the bright enclosure for two minutes—from 7:59 to 8:01. Conceding the silence, he would step out, betraying no emotion as he walked to the car. There was always another Thursday ahead, another visit to be made to the telephone booth that might finally link them to the hidden world of Joseph Bonanno.

The longer the government search continued without a trace of his father or the discovery of a bullet-riddled body, the more encouraged Bill Bonanno became. It was now six weeks since the disappearance; and if the elder Bonanno had been killed, that fact would presumably have already been circulated through the underworld by his father's ecstatic rivals, or it would at least have been hinted at in Mafia gossip. But so far the speculation about Bonanno's death had been largely limited to the newspapers, whose information came from the government, which was no doubt becoming embarrassed by its inability to find Bonanno after so much searching.

The younger Bonanno was also now encouraged by his own efforts during his father's absence. Quickly recovering from the initial shock, he had assumed the responsibility of trying to hold the organization together by eluding his potential captors and by demonstrating always a sense of confidence and optimism. In spite of his youth, he believed that he was now accepted by most of the men as their interim leader, their attitude toward him having changed considerably from what it had been when he first joined the outfit in the mid-fifties as "J.B.'s kid," and when the respect shown him had been in deference to the name. Aware of that situation, his father had contemplated denying him a place in the "family" and having him join the organization headed by Albert Anastasia. Anastasia, a close friend of Joseph Profaci, had come to know Bill during the latter's summer vacations from college, occasionally taking him to the Copacabana, and he would have eagerly found a spot for him. It might have been very advantageous for Anastasia to have done so, for it might have fostered closer ties with both the Bonanno and Profaci groups and perhaps ultimately formed a tight three-family alliance that could have dominated the two larger gangs in New York, one headed by Vito Genovese, the other by Thomas Luchese.

But Joseph Bonanno finally decided that he wanted his son with him, sensing perhaps the Mafia hierarchy's growing dissatisfaction with Anastasia, an autocratic and ambitious man with a tendency to overstep his boundaries—a tendency that would cost him his life. So Bill Bonanno, having quit college without a degree, followed in his father's path, although he straddled two worlds for a while—operating legitimate businesses in Arizona, including a wholesale food market and real estate trading, while being affiliated with the Bonanno organization, whose small Southwestern branch was involved in bookmaking and other illegal gambling activities.

Bill did not enjoy his involvement with his father's world during these years; he had no objection to it on moral grounds, but rather resented his lowly status among his father's men. Whether Bill was in New York or Arizona, his father gave him little to do, and he invariably dismissed all of Bill's suggestions promptly and without deliberation. His father seemed to be constantly second-guessing him, questioning him, and Bill had resented it.

He remembered one occasion when he had fought back, losing his temper completely and screaming uncontrollably at his father; and he remembered the look of surprise and shock on his father's face, the speechless astonishment. The elder Bonanno had apparently never been shouted at before in such an unrestrained manner, and he did not know how to react, at least toward his own son. Bill had quickly tried to pass over the situation, saying, "Look, I was born to lead, not to follow." After a pause, his father had replied with quiet firmness: "Before you can lead, you must learn to follow."

After that, Bill had managed to control his temper in front of his father, and although he did not refrain from disagreeing in private when he felt justified, he learned to follow orders. When he was told to be at a certain place at a certain time, he was there at the precise moment, remaining until he was instructed to leave. He remembered one morning when he had driven his father to a drugstore and had been told to wait outside. He waited for one hour, then a second hour. Then he left the car and looked into the drugstore and saw his father seated at a booth talking with another man, drinking coffee. Bill returned to the car, continuing to wait. The afternoon passed, extending into early evening. Finally, twelve hours after his father had entered the drugstore, he walked out. He nodded toward Bill, but did not apologize or explain what had taken so long.

Now, years later, looking back on that incident and similar incidents, Bill realized how his father had tested his patience and discipline, seeing how he would respond to a condition that was so necessary and common in the organization and yet was so unnatural to most restless men—waiting. In Bill's case, however, waiting had been no problem. He had spent most of his life waiting, especially for his father, waiting as a young teenager in Arizona for his father's reappearances each winter, as expectantly and hopefully as he was waiting now. His past had prepared him for the present, he thought, and he believed that he was now truly disciplined, capable of withstanding the worst that might come along, and this possibility pleased him very much.

On Thursday evening, December 17, Bill Bonanno and Frank Labruzzo paid their weekly visit to the phone booth on Long Island. It was the sixth consecutive Thursday that they had gone there. In a week it would be Christmas Eve, and on the way to the booth the two men wondered aloud if the holiday truce would be observed by the various gangs this year as it had been in the past. Under normal circumstances, it would be—all organization members would temporarily forget their differences until after January 1; but since the Bonanno loyalists were technically suspended from the national union, neither Bill nor Frank Labruzzo knew for sure whether the holiday policy would now be followed with regard to their people. They would have to anticipate the worst, they decided, and so both men assumed that they would not be spending Christmas with their wives and children.

At 7:55 p.m., they pulled into the parking lot near the diner and parked a few feet away from the booth. It was a very cold night, and Bill, turning off the radio, sat waiting in the car with the window partly open. The sky was dark and cloudy; the only reflection came from the big neon sign above the diner. There were three cars parked in front of the diner, and except for a few customers seated at the counter and an elderly couple at a table, it was empty. The food must be terrible, Bill thought, for the diner had never seemed busy during any of his visits, although he conceded the possibility that it had a late trade, maybe truck drivers, which might explain the large parking lot. Many people thought that places patronized by truckers must be serving good food, but Bill believed that the opposite was probably true. He had eaten at hundreds of roadside places during his many motor trips across the country, and most of the time he had observed the truckmen eating chicken soup and salted crackers, and he was willing to bet that most of them suffered from nervous stomachs and hemorrhoids.

He looked at his watch. It was exactly eight o'clock. He and Labruzzo sat silently as the seconds ticked away. He was about to conclude that it was another uneventful Thursday. Then, the telephone rang.

Bill slammed against the door, bounced out of the car, ran into the booth with such force that it shook. Labruzzo ran after him, pressing against the glass door that Bill had pulled shut.

Bill heard a woman's voice, very formal, sounding far away—it was the operator repeating the number, asking if it corresponded to the telephone number in the booth.

"Yes," Bill replied, feeling his heart pounding, "yes, it is."

He heard muffled sounds from the other end, then silence for a second, then the sound of coins being dropped into the slot, quarters, six or seven quarters gonging—it was long distance.

"Hello, Bill?"

It was a male voice, not his father's, a voice he did not recognize.

"Yes, who is this?"

"Never mind," the man replied, "just listen to me. Your father's okay. You'll probably be seeing him in a few days."

"How do I know he's okay?" Bill demanded, suddenly aggressive.

"Where the hell do you think I got this number from?" The man was now irritated. Bill calmed down.

"Now look," the man continued, "don't make waves! Everything's okay. Just sit back, don't do anything, and don't worry about anything."

Before Bill could respond, the man had hung up.

• • •

The excitement, the ecstasy that Bill Bonanno felt was overwhelming, and during the drive back to Queens he heard the conversation again and again, and he repeated it to Labruzzo. Your father's okay, you'll probably be seeing him in a few days. Bill was so happy that he wanted to go to a bar and have a few drinks in celebration, but both he and Labruzzo agreed that despite the good news they should remain as careful and alert as they had been before. They would follow the advice of the man on the telephone, would sit back and wait; in a few days Joseph Bonanno would reappear to make the next move.

Although, in the interest of efficiency, Bill thought that some preparation for his father's return was necessary; he felt, for example, that his father's attorney, William P. Maloney, should be informed immediately of this latest development. Bill reasoned that Maloney would be his father's chief spokesman after the reappearance, an event that would undoubtedly cause a circus of confusion and complex legal maneuvering in the courthouse, and Maloney would have to plan the elder Bonanno's strategy before the latter's interrogation by the Federal grand jury. Bill also felt a touch of guilt with regard to Maloney, about whom he had been so suspicious after the incident on Park Avenue. The veteran lawyer had been forced to appear on five or six occasions since then before the grand jury to defend himself against government implications that he was somehow involved in the kidnapping incident, and Bill imagined that Maloney's reputation as a lawyer might have suffered as a result. So, on the following day, Bill Bonanno drove to a telephone booth and called Maloney's office.

"Hi, Mr. Maloney, this is Bill Bonanno," he said, cheerfully, picturing the old man jumping out of his chair.

"Hey," Maloney yelled, "where are you? Where's your dad?"

"Hold on," Bonanno said, "take it easy. Go to a phone outside your office, to one of the booths downstairs, and call me at this number." He gave Maloney the number. Within a few minutes the lawyer had called back, and Bonanno recounted all that he had been told the night before.

But Maloney was dissatisfied with the brevity of the details. He wanted more specific information. He wondered on what day the elder Bonanno would appear, where he would be staying, how he could be reached now and through whom? Bill said he did not know anything other than what he had already told, adding that as soon as he knew more he would contact Maloney at once. When Maloney persisted with more questions, Bonanno cut him off. He had to run, he said. He hung up.

He returned to the apartment. Labruzzo had arranged for certain men to be there that evening, having already informed them of the news. The pace was quickening, there was activity, anticipation, and Bill Bonanno was confident that soon a few things would be resolved, soon he and the other men might get some relief from the wretched routine of hiding. The reappearance of his father should stabilize the organization to a degree and lessen the uncertainty. His father had undoubtedly come to some terms with his captors, or he would not be alive, and so the next hurdle was the government. His father would appear before the Federal grand jury, and Bill and the other men who were sought would probably do the same. They would come out of hiding, would accept their subpoenas, and, after consultation with their lawyers, would present themselves in court. If their answers displeased the judge, they might be sentenced to jail for contempt, but at this juncture they had few alternatives. Their terms could be for a month, a year, or more; but it would not be intolerable so long as some stability had been reestablished within the organization, and perhaps their status had been restored in the national society. Hopefully they would not enter prison as underworld outcasts. Their existence behind bars was much more pleasant when they were known to be members in good standing; they were accorded a respect not only by the other prisoners, but also by the prison guards and certain other workers, men for whom favors could be done on the outside. The "man of respect" serving time also knew that during his confinement he need not worry about his wife and children; they were being looked after by organizational representatives, and if they required help they received it.

While Bill Bonanno sat in the living room of the apartment reading the afternoon papers, Labruzzo took a nap, undisturbed by the noise from the television. It was too early for the evening news, and neither man had paid much attention during the last few hours to the series of quiz shows, soap operas, or comedies that monopolized the screen.

Suddenly, there was an interruption of the program—the announcement of a special news bulletin. Bill Bonanno looked up from his newspaper, waited. He expected to hear that war was declared, Russian bombers were on the way. Instead he heard the announcer say: Mafia leader Joseph

Bonanno, who was kidnapped and believed to have been killed by rival mobsters in October, is alive. Bonanno's attorney, William Power Maloney, made the announcement today. Maloney also said that his client would appear before the Federal grand jury investigating organized crime, at 9 a.m. on Monday, and . . .

Bill Bonanno sat stunned. Labruzzo came running in to watch. Bonanno began to swear quietly. Maloney had not only called a press conference, but had also identified him as the source of the information. Bonanno buried his head in his hands. He felt heat racing through his body, his sweat rising and seeping through his shirt. He knew he had made a horrible mistake in talking to Maloney in the first place, then in not swearing him to secrecy. Now he did not know what was ahead for his father. He recalled the words of the man on the phone saying don't make waves . . . don't do anything. And, stupidly, he had done it. He had possibly ruined everything, for the announcement would make Page One all over the country, would drive the elder Bonanno deeper into hiding, and it would intensify on a grand scale the investigation, activating those agents who had been lulled into thinking that Joseph Bonanno was dead.

The television set displayed a picture of Maloney, then a picture of the Park Avenue apartment house, and suddenly Bill was sick of the whole episode—and, reaching for a heavy glass ashtray on a nearby table, he threw it hard at the set, hitting the screen squarely in the center. It exploded like a bomb. Thousands of tiny pieces of glass sprayed the room, tubes popped, wires curled and burned in varicolored flame, sparks flared in several directions—a remarkable little fireworks show of self-destruction was playing itself out within the twenty-one-inch screen, and Bonanno and Labruzzo watched with fascination until the interior of the set had nearly evaporated into a smoldering hole of jagged edges and fizzling filament.

PART IV

The City's Crooners

GAY TALESE

Saturday, July 30, 2011

Managing Editor's office
re: Expense Account of Gay Talese

The New Yorker
4 Times Square
New York, NY 10036

Attn: Ms Pam McCarthy

Dear Pam:
    I am currently doing research on two stories that
Susan Morrison hopes to publish this fall: One is on singer
Tony Bennett; the other on the Yankees's baseball manager,
Joe Girardi.

    I am doing both at the same time, although I think Susan
wants to publish the Bennett one first, and so I have a late
August deadline.

    Both of these stories require travel, which of course means
spending money, and, although I keep careful records as you know,
we both know that you must scrutinize my record of spending and
perhaps there are items or costs I've listed that you'd like to
discuss. All I can do it tell you what I've spent, and give you
evidence, and after that you decide what is acceptable to you.
When I travel long distance, I go business class, although I'm
told your policy is coach. In this expense account I'm sending
to you today, you'll note that I traveled biz-class from Newark
Airport to Las Vegas, and my one-way ticket on Continental cost
$1,141.00, as you can see on Page 1 of my statement.
    But you'll also note that I did not list the cost of my
flight from Vegas to Denver; nor the flight from Denver back to
Teterboro on July 27th--because I accepted Tony Bennett's offer
to join him and his band and other staffers on his private jet.
And so I traveled free. This allowed me access to Tony Bennett
(sitting across from him on the plane) that I could not get in
Vegas or Denver, where his time was devoted to his rehearsals and
performances.

    Still, does my acceptance of his generosity violate New Yorker
policy? I don't know the rules and ethics of your magazine because
I have not been in this situation before. When I traveled with the
opera singer last year, we traveled together on a commercial flight
and, since she was going biz-class, I of course did likewise.

109 EAST 61ST STREET
NEW YORK, NEW YORK 10065
TEL: 212-832-7959
FAX: 212-753-3820

(more)

LETTER FROM THE AUTHOR CONCERNING *THE NEW YORKER*'S
EXPENSE ACCOUNT POLICY WHILE REPORTING FOR "HIGH NOTES"

High Notes

FROM *The New Yorker*, 2011

O N   A   B R I G H T   S U N D A Y   afternoon shortly after one o'clock in Manhattan, a few days before his eighty-fifth birthday, which he would modestly acknowledge on August 3 by dining at a neighborhood restaurant on the East Side with his wife, Susan—who, within a few weeks, would be celebrating her own, forty-fifth birthday—Tony Bennett was standing behind a microphone at the Avatar Studios, on West Fifty-third Street, rehearsing a few lines from "The Lady Is a Tramp" while awaiting the presence of Lady Gaga.

Lady Gaga was expected to arrive at two o'clock, with her hairdresser, her makeup artist, her creative director, her vocal coach, her producer, her security guards, and others who know her by her pre-fame name, Stefani Germanotta; and then, after she had warmed up, she would join Bennett in singing "The Lady Is a Tramp," the final recording for his latest album of duets, "Duets II," which will be released by RPM Records/Columbia on September 20. It is a sequel to his 2006 Grammy Award–winning album, and sixteen other singers had already collaborated with him. They included John Mayer ("One for My Baby"), Carrie Underwood ("It Had to Be You"), Queen Latifah ("Who Can I Turn To?"), Mariah Carey ("When Do the Bells Ring for Me?"), Aretha Franklin ("How Do You Keep the Music Playing?"), Willie Nelson ("On the Sunny Side of the Street"), Andrea Bocelli ("Stranger in Paradise"), and Amy Winehouse ("Body and Soul"). Bennett and Winehouse had sung together in London in March, four months before her death, in July, at twenty-seven, following years of familiarity with drugs and alcohol.

Over dinner a couple of weeks before the session with Lady Gaga, Bennett told me that he had been concerned about Winehouse's well-being when he spent time with her in London. He said, "I wanted to tell her that she needed to shape up or she could end up destroying herself." In August, he appeared on the MTV Video Music Awards in a special tribute to Winehouse, saying, "She was a true jazz artist in the tradition of Ella Fitzgerald and Billie Holiday." After the broadcast, he told a reporter, "What I wanted to do, I wanted to stop her. I wanted to tell her that many years ago I was naughty also with some drugs." He went on, "Woody Allen's manager at the time"—Jack Rollins—"said he knew Lenny Bruce, and he said one sentence that changed my life. He said, 'He sinned against his talent.' I wanted to tell her that."

As a few dozen people gathered within the glass-enclosed control room anticipating Lady Gaga's appearance, Bennett was standing alone on a white platform, in the center of the studio. He had on a hand-tailored Brioni tux with a red pocket square, a white shirt, and a black tie that had been a gift from his drummer, and he was singing the introductory verse to "The Lady Is a Tramp," the Rodgers and Hart show tune from their 1937 musical, "Babes in Arms":

I've wined and dined on Mulligan stew and never wished for turkey
as I hitched and hiked and grifted, too, from Maine to Albuquerque.

He then turned toward his musical director, Lee Musiker, a sharp-featured, energetic, dark-haired man of fifty-five, who sat behind a grand piano, a few yards away. "Let me ask you something," Bennett began, in his characteristically soft and deferential manner. "Can you go up another key?"

"You want me to raise it up more?" Musiker asked.

Bennett nodded. And, as Musiker's fingers moved with accelerated energy along the keyboard, Bennett appeared to be more contented as he again sang the opening lines of the intro:

I've wined and dined on Mulligan stew
and never wished for turkey.

After he had satisfactorily rehearsed the next eight lines of the intro, which he planned to sing alone on the record before participating with Lady Gaga in the duet, he decided to rest his voice for a while. She was due in about half an hour.

"I did my scales today," he said, as he stepped down from the platform. Bennett practices scales for fifteen to twenty minutes every day, singing along to a small tape recorder that plays a cassette of exercises created by his longtime teacher, the late Pietro D'Andrea. Once, I heard Bennett say, "The first day you don't do the scales, you know. The second day, the musicians know. The third day, the audience knows."

At Avatar, he popped a dime-size yellow lozenge into his mouth and headed over to the control room to spend some time with his guests and family members, including Susan, who is often with him when he sings.

A week earlier, she had flown with him and his quartet to concerts in Reno, Las Vegas, and Denver, three of nearly a hundred appearances he makes every year around the nation and overseas; and she intends to be in the audience on Sunday evening, September 18, when he and his quartet are scheduled to present a few dozen of his favorite songs from the stage of the Metropolitan Opera House. But, no matter where Tony Bennett is featured, what he sings and how he sings have pretty much remained the same for most of his more than sixty years as an entertainer. As his friend Count Basie once reminded him, "Why change an apple?"

Susan began dating Bennett in 1985, on the eve of his fifty-ninth birthday, when she was eighteen. Her mother, Marion Crow, a fourth-generation native of the San Francisco Bay Area—and a devotee of Bennett's music since her student days at the Convent of the Sacred Heart, in the early fifties—had introduced Susan to the singer five years earlier. Marion and her husband, Dayl Crow—a broker with Merrill Lynch who had been a fighter pilot in Korea—were vacationing in Las Vegas, accompanied by their daughter. After they had seen Bennett's show, they bumped into each other outside the venue, and Marion initiated the introduction. Susan shyly shook hands with the singer but was quickly put at ease by his graciousness.

Marion and Dayl had first met Bennett in New York many years before, in 1966. Dayl Crow was in the city on business and was staying with Marion at the Plaza. After she read that Bennett was booked at the Copacabana, she asked Dayl to get tickets. While they were having a drink at their table before the show, a young woman photographer stopped by and offered to take their picture.

"Yes," Marion replied, "but only if Tony Bennett is in it."

Soon the photographer returned to say that Bennett would see them in his dressing room before the performance, and it was there that he posed with them. Marion was two months pregnant with Susan. Forty-one years later, after she married Tony Bennett, in 2007, Susan explained to a reporter, "It was a prenatal influence that led me to him."

Their marriage, in a civil ceremony in New York, at which Mario and Matilda Cuomo were the principal witnesses, had been preceded by a twenty-four-year courtship, owing to Bennett's prolonged and contentious separation from his second wife, Sandra, with whom he has two daughters—Johanna, born in 1969, and Antonia, in 1974. He retains a warm relationship with both. Antonia, a singer, often travels with him and his musicians, opens his shows, and occasionally does a few numbers with him onstage, including a Sondheim song, "Old Friends."

Bennett's marriage, in 1952, to his first wife, Patricia, ended more amicably; and Patricia and Tony's two sons, Danny, born in 1954, and Daegal, a year later, are both professionally engaged in their father's career and were among those waiting for Lady Gaga. Danny, a well-proportioned six-footer who boxes in a gym about three times a week, is Bennett's manager. He has hazel eyes, a receding hairline, and an engaging demeanor not lacking in self-assurance. His somewhat shorter but equally fit brother, Daegal, who has inherited their father's green eyes and Roman nose, is in charge of sound.

Daegal—commonly called Dae, pronounced "day"—has his own recording studio, in Englewood, New Jersey. Earlier in the week, a seventeen-piece orchestra had met there to prerecord the music that would soon flow through the system at Avatar and blend in with Tony Bennett's and Lady Gaga's voices as they sang into their microphones. Dae believed it was more efficient to have the orchestra complete its work in the New Jersey studio, where the acoustics were ideal and which afforded the Bennett organization some flexibility when coping with the tight schedules imposed by most of the high-profile singers it sought for the duets.

Dae knew that Lady Gaga's time was very limited. As he waited for her to arrive at Avatar, he seemed unable to relax, sitting in the rear of the control room. When his father waved in his direction, Dae failed to notice him, because he was focusing on the console, a black soundboard about five feet wide and lined vertically and horizontally with rows of illuminated knobs (green, red, yellow, amber) that alternately cast slight reflections upon his forehead.

Danny Bennett was standing behind him, looking through the big window at a documentary film crew wheeling a camera along tracks laid on the studio floor near the white platform. Also in the control room, close to the doorway, were two longtime friends of Bennett's—seventy-year-old Leonard Riggio, the chairman of Barnes & Noble, and seventy-one-year-old Joseph Segreto, who owns a restaurant called Eleven 79, in New Orleans, and first met Bennett in Las Vegas in 1961, when Segreto was a roadie for a band from Philadelphia that was playing in the lounge of the Sahara.

Both Segreto and Riggio were smartly attired, and Susan, who has blond hair and brown eyes, stood talking with them. She was wearing orange linen pants with a yellow-and-white-striped short-sleeved shirt and sandals.

As Bennett joined them, Segreto patted him on the back and complimented him on how well he had sung the intro. Bennett smiled but changed the subject to Lady Gaga, whom he recalled meeting in early May when they had each performed at a charity event for the Robin Hood Foundation at the Javits Convention Center. He also met her mother and father that night, he said, as well as a young man who had told him, "I'm her boyfriend, so you'd better watch out."

The others laughed. Segreto shook his head. "She's big," he said.

"She's going to be bigger than Elvis Presley," Bennett said.

He went on to describe Lady Gaga as being enormously talented not only as a singer but as a dancer and a pianist—and he suggested that, at the same time, under all her makeup and marketing, she was just a normal human being, "a sweet little Italian-American girl who studied at NYU."

Bennett and his friends stood talking near the door for the next fifteen minutes, discussing, among other things, his upcoming show at the Metropolitan Opera. That reminded Riggio of a story about Luciano Pavarotti doing a book signing at Barnes & Noble.

"There were five thousand people lined up outside," Riggio said.

Bennett let out a low whistle.

"So we go inside the store, and Pavarotti, you know, he is signing slow, and talking to people, and the people are giving him pictures, and other books, to sign, and I feel bad for the people outside, so I'm saying, 'Only one book!' and I'm trying to move it. So Pavarotti looks at me, and he smacks me in the face, and he goes, 'Mind-a your own-a business-a!'"

Everybody laughed, and Bennett offered his own Pavarotti story.

He said, "I remember Sinatra once asked Pavarotti, 'How do you sing a soft high note?' and Pavarotti replied, 'You keep-a your mouth closed!'"

Conversation turned to Bennett's forthcoming visit to New Orleans, where he will join Riggio and Riggio's wife, Louise, in celebrating the completion of the 101st house built under the auspices of the couple's nonprofit foundation, Project Home Again in New Orleans, which has provided furnished housing, without cost, to low- and moderate-income families wishing to reestablish themselves in the city following Hurricane Katrina. Bennett said that he and his quartet would entertain the Riggios and the other celebrants there on November 11, and Segreto promised to cook something special at his restaurant. Segreto has developed a warm relationship with the couple ever since they launched their foundation, and Leonard Riggio has acknowledged it by naming one of his many race-horses, a two-year-old thoroughbred, Mr. Segreto.

"How about that, Tony?" Riggio called out, as Segreto took a little bow.

"That's nice," Bennett replied, and gave his signature smile. He then conceded being a frequenter of racetracks back in the seventies, when he lived in Los Angeles, and he remembered one day when he went to the track at the invitation of Cary Grant.

"All the women were just fainting as he's walking," Bennett recalled. "All the women in the boxes fainting. Cary Grant, you know. So I said, 'You come here often?' 'Yes,' he said. 'I own the track.'"

"He owns it?" Segreto exclaimed, in his gravelly voice.

"He owns it," Bennett repeated.

"Probably Fred Astaire paid for it," Segreto said, "because he used to go betting with two hands. Who bet more on horses than two guys, friends of yours, Mickey Rooney and Fred Astaire?"

"I didn't know that," Bennett said.

"Fred Astaire was at the track all the time," Segreto went on. Then Segreto mentioned the name of a woman who was once involved with Astaire, a woman whom Bennett was also acquainted with, and Bennett thought for a moment and then said, in a lowered voice, "She messed him up."

"Oh sure, she messed him up," Segreto declared knowingly. "But he was such a great fan of the races."

Lee Musiker approached Bennett from behind and asked, "You want to do a couple of warmups before she arrives?"

"OK," he said. With a little nod toward Susan and his friends, he turned and headed back into the studio, where he soon resumed his earlier position on the white platform. While Musiker began playing the piano, Bennett, microphone in hand, began to sing, without full voice, the first lines of the duet he would soon record:

She gets too hungry for dinner at eight,
Loves the theater but she never comes late.

On the music stand in front of him, in case he forgot the lyrics to "The Lady Is a Tramp," there were three sheets of paper on which were printed, in large letters, triple-spaced, every word of the song—approximately forty lines that he and Lady Gaga would alternately deliver, with her words printed in red and his in black.

GAGA: I never bother with people I hate . . .
BENNETT: Doesn't dig crap games with barons and earls . . .
GAGA: I won't go to Harlem in ermine and pearls
    I won't dish the dirt with the rest of those girls

But before he had completed his second run-through of the tune, his attention was drawn to the sounds of a crowd of newly arrived people—who, having exited the freight elevator, had proceeded down a hall in the direction of the control room, led by Lady Gaga, a slender young woman with aquamarine bobbed hair. She wore dark glasses, a long black lace gown that you could see through, and, over it, a sleeveless black leather motorcycle jacket, unzipped, with studs on the lapels. A silver buckle dangled from a belt that flapped along her right thigh as she ran gleefully toward Bennett.

"Hello, Tony!" she called out, her arms extended.

"Oh, great!" he exclaimed, stepping down from the platform to embrace her as she removed her dark glasses, revealing a small scimitar-shaped stroke of eyeliner beside each of her eyes, extending back toward the temple, resembling a couple of anchovies. As Musiker rose from the piano bench to shake hands with her, Dae and Danny were on their way down from the control room to review the recording procedure. When she removed her leather jacket, and Bennett tried to assist her, she good-naturedly shoved him away, saying, "No, that's OK. Don't you hold a thing." She dangled the jacket in the air until a young man hastened into the studio to take it and carry it to her dressing room.

Lady Gaga stood silently near the piano for a few seconds, looking around the studio and up at the ceiling, which was thirty-five feet at its highest point. She was tugging at the waist of her black lace gown, which she said had been designed by Tom Ford. The gown was so long that several inches of it swept along the floor, and had twisted around her ankles. It was impossible to see the shoes she was wearing, but underneath the lace dress she had on what looked like a black bikini.

"I love the way you wrap that skirt," Bennett said finally. "It's fabulous."

"I thought I'd give a little twist for you, Tony," she said.

Bennett was eager to tell her a story. "I've got to tell you that when my wife and I exercise we look out our window at a synagogue right across the street." He said that some men were working hard erecting a scaffolding there. "And then I noticed that, on the side of their truck, in big letters, the word 'Gaga' was painted!"

"Working so hard!" she said, and laughed.

Danny Bennett came up and introduced himself, and then pointed out his brother.

"Such an honor to meet you, wow, hello," she began, and then she asked some questions, such as "Do we both use the same mic?" (no, there was one for each singer) and "Should I use headphones?" Dae explained that his father did not want headphones, after which she turned to Bennett and said, "I love that you don't want them."

"Beautiful gown" was his reply.

"Thank you," she responded. "I wore it for you. The whole thing, head to toe, as in 'What would Tony want?'"

"Great," he continued, his bronzed face creased with its almost permanent smile.

She then asked Danny Bennett whether or not there was a limit on the rehearsal time before they began the recording.

"As many times as you want to rehearse it, or do it—anything," Danny said. "Everyone's really flexible here."

"Great," she said. "Thank you," and then in a loud voice she said, "Test," and proceeded on her own, without the accompaniment of the prerecorded music, to sing, "That's why this chick is a tramp."

Bennett laughed.

Then she corrected herself. "That's why the lady is a tramp," she sang, pronouncing the last word "tray-amp."

She was having fun, inflecting a slight Southern redneck intonation and a bit of "Guys and Dolls" spirit into the music of Rodgers and Hart: the words "I never bother with people I hate" she sang as "Eye-ha never bother with people I hay-yate."

Bennett joined in: "Doesn't dig crap games, with barons and earls."

When she followed with "I won't go to Harlem in ermine and pearls," she pronounced the words as "oimens" and "poils."

"Oh, I'm so nervous!" she said.

"No, it's terrific," he said.

"If I tap out, you can just tell 'em that it was all planned."

"Sounds great," he responded.

Then, after they had laughed through the rest of the song, she turned to him and asked, "What was it like with the girls?"

He looked at her quizzically.

"Do they always get this way around you?"

When he failed to answer, she continued, "Do they always get really nervous and stand there sweating and blushing?"

Among those joining in the laughter were Susan and the others in the control booth, who now included members of Lady Gaga's troupe and also her vocal coach, a gray-haired, bespectacled man of sixty-six named Don Lawrence, who first heard her sing when she was thirteen, and whose clients have included Mick Jagger, Christina Aguilera, Whitney Houston, Bono, and Jon Bon Jovi.

Danny Bennett, who had been sitting near Don Lawrence, returned to the studio carrying a newspaper clipping from the Yonkers *Record*, dated August 26, 1951, bearing the headline GIRLS "GAGA" AS TONY CROONS A HIT. The article displayed a photograph of a youthful, dark-haired Tony Bennett in a tuxedo surrounded by four smiling young female fans; the caption explained that he had just serenaded them with one of his all-time hit tunes, "Because of You."

Lady Gaga began reading the article aloud, standing next to Bennett. "Girls 'gaga' as Tony croons a hit," she read, and moving closer to him she said, "See, I told you. You make women do that. Look what you did! . . . Oh, Tony, I would have been chasing you around. Oh, Tony, do you die when you read that?"

"Oh, you're right," Susan Bennett replied, her voice echoing through the speaker in the control room. "Gotta keep the girls off him."

"Keep Gaga off!" Lady Gaga corrected her, before turning to somebody on her staff and requesting a drink. A young man scurried into the studio carrying a glass of whiskey. Bennett watched as she took a sip. Then she announced, "Now that I've had a little bit to drink, I'm not so nervous." Again she turned to Bennett.

"Do women do that around you, too?" she persisted.

"What's that?" he asked.

"Do they just knock 'em back, just so they can be in your presence?" she asked. He grinned.

"Yes, they all do," she answered for him. "We're all very nervous around him." She took another swallow, holding the glass in one hand and the microphone in the other.

Dae's voice was heard over the speaker in the control room, asking, "All set?"—meaning, in effect, Shall we finally get to work?

"I'm all set," Lady Gaga said. Then she added, "Hey, Tony."

"Yes?"

"I missed you, baby."

Suddenly, the brassy up-tempo sound of the orchestra filled the studio, and immediately it was accompanied by the two singers' voices:

BENNETT: She gets too hungry for dinner at eight,
  Loves the theatre but she never comes late.
GAGA: Eye-ha never bother with people I hay-yate.

They smoothly got through the song, taking a little more than two minutes, and after the conclusion Dae Bennett, in the control room, said, "OK, that sounds really good. We just need to do some inserts on the end, and we'll have everything."

"OK," Bennett said.

"Great," Gaga replied.

But then Bennett went on, "I think we should do it a couple more times, I really do, and get whatever's good there." He turned to Lady Gaga: "Is that all right with you?"

She agreed, saying, "We're having a good time."

She looked around at some of the guests standing in the hallway and the control room, and, seeing the dapper Leonard Riggio, and Joe Segreto in his seersucker suit, white shirt, blue-knit tie, and white shoes, she said to Bennett, "You know, all my friends—you have to meet them sometime, they're always in three-piece suits, with beautiful hats on. They like to go out and pretend like it's the fifties."

"Right," Bennett said. They agreed to do another take.

Gaga said, "I'm going to give it a little more character."

He started singing again, and when they finished she said, "It's like our third date now!"

Over the next half hour, they did six more takes, some with scatting, all of them acceptable to Bennett's sons, in the control room, but at the conclusion of each take neither Bennett nor Lady Gaga wanted the duet to end.

"Oh, fun!" she exclaimed, after yet another take. "We can do this all day?"

"Yes, I liked it," he said.

"Shall we do one more?" she asked.

"Whatever we want," he said. "We can do it till we're very happy with it."

"Oh, let's keep having fun. I'm having a good time."

"Good."

"Is your musical director happy?"

"So far," Dae Bennett replied over the speaker.

"Everybody's happy," Lady Gaga declared. "Happy faces!" she loudly announced, adding, "I've never done this without headphones. It's so liberating." She took another sip of whiskey.

For a different take, they decided to improvise some lyrics.

When Gaga burst out, "I like the Yankees," Bennett followed with "and Jeter's just fine."

Lady Gaga interrupted. "Maybe I should pick another Yankee. Posada's my favorite. But is he not playing anymore?"

Somebody shouted that he'd been benched.

"Makes me sad," Lady Gaga said, then improvised a new line: "I miss Posada!"

When they finally decided that there was a limit to their alacrity, and their duet was done for the day, they were called upon to do a short taped interview for the documentary film, which Danny was overseeing.

"Was it OK?" Lady Gaga asked Bennett, as they stepped off the platform.

"Aw, c'mon. It's the best thing that ever happened."

"I can't wait. I'm going to cry so hard when it comes out."

With Bennett and Lady Gaga sitting side by side in front of a camera, a staff member named Sylvia Weiner asked her to recount some of her feelings about working with Tony Bennett.

Lady Gaga replied that, when she knew she'd be recording a duet with him, first she decided she would have to change her wardrobe: "Well, I have to meet Mr. Bennett! What do I wear? Do I look classy? Do I look elegant? Do I look sexy? I don't know what he likes. So I tried a couple of different outfits on, and then I just ran out there, and"—turning toward him as she spoke—"I met your beautiful wife. It was wonderful."

"Well," Weiner went on, "tell us why 'Lady Is a Tramp' lent itself so well for your duet."

Lady Gaga thought for a moment, and then replied, "Well, 'cause I'm a tramp. And," she went on, gesturing at Bennett, "he knows it."

She laughed.

But he shook his head.

"I know that you're a lady," he said, emphatically. "Playing a tramp."

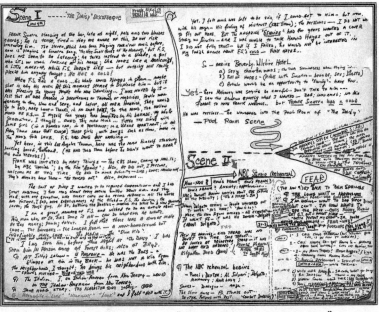

AUTHOR'S OUTLINE FROM "FRANK SINATRA HAS A COLD"

Frank Sinatra Has a Cold

FROM *Esquire*, 1966

F RANK SINATRA, HOLDING A glass of bourbon in one hand and a cigarette in the other, stood in a dark corner of the bar between two attractive but fading blondes who sat waiting for him to say something. But he said nothing; he had been silent during much of the evening, except now in this private club in Beverly Hills he seemed even more distant, staring out through the smoke and semidarkness into a large room beyond the bar where dozens of young couples sat huddled around small tables or twisted in the center of the floor to the clamorous clang of folk-rock music blaring from the stereo. The two blondes knew, as did Sinatra's four male friends who stood nearby, that it was a bad idea to force conversation upon him when he was in this mood of sullen silence, a mood that had hardly been uncommon during this first week of November, a month before his fiftieth birthday.

Sinatra had been working on a film that he now disliked, could not wait to finish; he was tired of all the publicity attached to his dating the twenty-year-old Mia Farrow, who was not in sight tonight; he was angry that a CBS television documentary of his life, to be shown in two weeks, was reportedly prying into his privacy, even speculating on his possible friendship with Mafia leaders; he was worried about his starring role in an hour-long NBC show entitled *Sinatra—A Man and His Music*, which would require that he sing eighteen songs with a voice that at this particular moment, just a few nights before the taping was to begin, was weak and sore and uncertain. Sinatra was ill. He was the victim of an ailment so common that most people would consider it trivial. But when it gets to Sinatra it can plunge him into a state of anguish, deep depression, panic, even rage. Frank Sinatra had a cold.

Sinatra with a cold is Picasso without paint, Ferrari without fuel—only worse. For the common cold robs Sinatra of that uninsurable jewel, his voice, cutting into the core of his confidence, and it affects not only his own psyche but also seems to cause a kind of psychosomatic nasal drip within dozens of people who work for him, drink with him, love him, depend on him for their own welfare and stability. A Sinatra with a cold can, in a small way, send vibrations through the entertainment industry and beyond as surely as a president of the United States, suddenly sick, can shake the national economy.

For Frank Sinatra was now involved with many things involving many people—his own film company, his record company, his private airline, his missile-parts firm, his real-estate holdings across the nation, his personal staff of seventy-five—which are only a portion of the power he is and has come to represent. He seemed now to be also the embodiment of the fully emancipated male, perhaps the only one in America, the man who can do anything he wants, anything, can do it because he has money, the energy, and no apparent guilt. In an age when the very young seem to be taking over, protesting and picketing and demanding change, Frank Sinatra survives as a national phenomenon, one of the few prewar products to withstand the test of time. He is the champ who made the big comeback, the man who had everything, lost it, then got it back, letting nothing stand in his way, doing what few men can do: he uprooted his life, left his family, broke with everything that was familiar, learning in the process that one way to hold a woman is not to hold her. Now he has the affection of Nancy and Ava and Mia, the fine female produce of three generations, and still has the adoration of his children, the freedom of a bachelor, he does not feel old, he makes old men feel young, makes them think that if Frank Sinatra can do it, it can be done; not that they could do it, but it is still nice for other men to know, at fifty, that it can be done.

But now, standing at this bar in Beverly Hills, Sinatra had a cold, and he continued to drink quietly and he seemed miles away in his private world, not even reacting when suddenly the stereo in the other room switched to a Sinatra song, "In the Wee Small Hours of the Morning."

It is a lovely ballad that he first recorded ten years ago, and it now inspired many young couples who had been sitting, tired of twisting, to get up and move slowly around the dance floor, holding one another very close. Sinatra's intonation, precisely clipped, yet full and flowing, gave a deeper meaning to the simple lyrics—"In the wee small hours of the morning/while the whole wide world is fast asleep/you lie awake, and think about the girl . . ."—it was like so many of his classics, a song that evoked loneliness and sensuality, and when blended with the dim light and the alcohol and nicotine and late-night needs, it became a kind of airy aphrodisiac. Undoubtedly the words from this song, and others like it, had put millions in the mood, it was music to make love by, and doubtless much love had been made by it all over America at night in cars, while the batteries burned down, in cottages by the lake, on beaches during balmy summer evenings, in secluded parks and exclusive penthouses and furnished rooms, in cabin cruisers and cabs and cabanas—in all places where Sinatra's songs could be heard were these words that warmed women, wooed and won them, snipped the final thread of inhibition and gratified the male egos of ungrateful lovers; two generations of men had been the beneficiaries of such ballads, for which they were eternally in his debt, for which they may eternally hate him. Nevertheless here he was, the man himself, in the early hours of the morning in Beverly Hills, out of range.

The two blondes, who seemed to be in their middle thirties, were preened and polished, their matured bodies softly molded within tight dark suits. They sat, legs crossed, perched on the high barstools. They listened to the music. Then one of them pulled out a Kent and Sinatra quickly placed his gold lighter under it and she held his hand, looked at his fingers: they were nubby and raw, and the pinkies protruded, being so stiff from arthritis that he could barely bend them. He was, as usual, immaculately dressed. He wore an oxford-gray suit with a vest, a suit conservatively cut on the outside but trimmed with flamboyant silk within; his shoes, British, seemed to be shined even on the bottom of the soles. He also wore, as everybody seemed to know, a remarkably convincing black hairpiece, one of sixty that he owns, most of them under the care of an inconspicuous little gray-haired lady who, holding his hair in a tiny satchel, follows him around whenever he performs. She earns four hundred dollars a week. The most distinguishing thing about Sinatra's face are his eyes, clear blue and alert, eyes that within seconds can go cold with anger, or glow with affection, or, as now, reflect a vague detachment that keeps his friends silent and distant.

Leo Durocher, one of Sinatra's closest friends, was now shooting pool in the small room behind the bar. Standing near the door was Jim Mahoney, Sinatra's press agent, a somewhat chunky young man with a square jaw and narrow eyes who would resemble a tough Irish plain-clothesman if it were not for the expensive continental suits he wears and his exquisite shoes often adorned with polished buckles. Also nearby was a big, broad-shouldered two-hundred-pound actor named Brad Dexter who seemed always to be thrusting out his chest so that his gut would not show.

Brad Dexter has appeared in several films and television shows, displaying fine talent as a character actor, but in Beverly Hills he is equally known for the role he played in Hawaii two years ago when he swam a few hundred yards and risked his life to save Sinatra from drowning in a riptide. Since then Dexter has been one of Sinatra's constant companions and has been made a producer in Sinatra's film company. He occupies a plush office near Sinatra's executive suite. He is endlessly searching for literary properties that might be converted into new starring roles for Sinatra. Whenever he is among strangers with Sinatra he worries because he knows that Sinatra brings out the best and worst in people—some men will become aggressive, some women will become seductive, others will stand around skeptically appraising him, the scene will be somehow intoxicated by his mere presence, and maybe Sinatra himself, if feeling as badly as he was tonight, might become intolerant or tense, and then: headlines. So Brad Dexter tries to anticipate danger and warn Sinatra in advance. He confesses to feeling very protective of Sinatra, admitting in a recent moment of self-revelation: "I'd kill for him."

While this statement may seem outlandishly dramatic, particularly when taken out of context, it nonetheless expresses a fierce fidelity that is quite common within Sinatra's special circle. It is a characteristic that Sinatra, without admission, seems to prefer: All the Way; All or Nothing at All. This is the Sicilian in Sinatra; he permits his friends, if they wish to remain that, none of the easy Anglo-Saxon outs. But if they remain loyal, then there is nothing Sinatra will not do in turn—fabulous gifts, personal kindnesses, encouragement when they're down, adulation when they're up. They are wise to remember, however, one thing. He is Sinatra. The boss. Il Padrone.

I had seen something of this Sicilian side of Sinatra last summer at Jilly's saloon in New York, which was the only other time I'd gotten a close view of him prior to this night in this California club. Jilly's, which is on West Fifty-second Street in Manhattan, is where Sinatra drinks whenever he is in New York, and there is a special chair reserved for him in the back room against the wall that nobody else may use. When he is occupying it, seated behind a long table flanked by his closest New York friends—who include the saloonkeeper, Jilly Rizzo, and Jilly's azure-haired wife, Honey, who is known as the "Blue Jew"—a rather strange ritualistic scene develops. That night dozens of people, some of them casual friends of Sinatra's, some mere acquaintances, some neither, appeared outside of Jilly's saloon. They approached it like a shrine. They had come to pay respect. They were from New York, Brooklyn, Atlantic City, Hoboken. They were old actors, young actors, former prizefighters, tired trumpet players, politicians, a boy with a cane. There was a fat lady who said she remembered Sinatra when he used to throw the *Jersey Observer* onto her front porch in 1933. There were middle-aged couples who said they had heard Sinatra sing at the Rustic Cabin in 1938 and "We knew then that he really had it!" Or they had heard him when he was with Harry James's band in 1939, or with Tommy Dorsey in 1941 ("Yeah, that's the song, 'I'll Never Smile Again'—he sang it one night in this dump near Newark and we danced . . ."); or they remembered that time at the Paramount with the swooners, and him with those bow ties. The Voice; and one woman remembered that awful boy she knew then—Alexander Dorogokupetz, an eighteen-year-old heckler who had thrown a tomato at Sinatra and the bobby-soxers in the balcony had tried to flail him to death. Whatever became of Alexander Dorogokupetz? The lady did not know.

And they remembered when Sinatra was a failure and sang trash like "Mairzy Doats," and they remembered his comeback and on this night they were all standing outside Jilly's saloon, dozens of them, but they could not get in. So some of them left. But most of them stayed, hoping that soon they might be able to push or wedge their way into Jilly's between the elbows and backsides of the men drinking three-deep at the bar, and they might be able to peek through and see him sitting back there. This is all they really wanted; they wanted to see him. And for a few moments they gazed in silence through the smoke and they stared. Then they turned, fought their way out of the bar, went home.

Some of Sinatra's close friends, all of whom are known to the men guarding Jilly's door, do manage to get an escort into the back room. But once they are there they, too, must fend for themselves. On the particular evening, Frank Gifford, the former football player, got only seven yards in three tries. Others who had somehow been close enough to shake Sinatra's hand did not shake it; instead they just touched him on the shoulder or sleeve, or they merely stood close enough for him to see them and, after he'd given them a wink of recognition or a wave or a nod or called out their names (he had a fantastic memory for first names), they would then turn and leave. They had checked in. They had paid their respects. And as I watched this ritualistic scene, I got the impression that Frank Sinatra was dwelling simultaneously in two worlds that were not contemporary.

On the one hand he is the swinger—as he is when talking and joking with Sammy Davis, Jr., Richard Conte, Liza Minelli, Bernice Massi, or any of the other show-business people who get to sit at the table; on the other, as when he is nodding or waving to his paisanos who are close to him (Al Silvani, a boxing manager who works with Sinatra's film company; Dominic Di Bona, his wardrobe man; Ed Pucci, a three-hundred-pound former football lineman who is his aide-de-camp), Frank Sinatra is Il Padrone. Or better still, he is what in traditional Sicily have long been called *uomini rispettati*—men of respect: men who are both majestic and humble, men who are loved by all and are very generous by nature, men whose hands are kissed as they walk from village to village, men who would personally go out of their way to redress a wrong.

Frank Sinatra does things personally. At Christmas time, he will personally pick dozens of presents for his close friends and family, remembering the type of jewelry they like, their favorite colors, the sizes of their shirts and dresses. When a musician friend's house was destroyed and his wife was killed in a Los Angeles mud slide a little more than a year ago, Sinatra personally came to his aid, finding the musician a new home, paying whatever hospital bills were left unpaid by the insurance, then personally supervising the furnishing of the new home down to the replacing of the silverware, the linen, the purchase of new clothing.

The same Sinatra who did this can, within the same hour, explode in a towering rage of intolerance should a small thing be incorrectly done for him by one of his paisanos. For example, when one of his men brought him a frankfurter with catsup on it, which Sinatra apparently abhors, he angrily threw the bottle at the man, splattering catsup all over him. Most of the men who work around Sinatra are big. But this never seems to intimidate Sinatra nor curb his impetuous behavior with them when he is mad. They will never take a swing back at him. He is Il Padrone.

At other times, aiming to please, his men will overreact to his desires:

when he casually observed that his big orange desert jeep in Palm Springs seemed in need of a new painting, the word was swiftly passed down through the channels, becoming ever more urgent as it went, until finally it was a command that the jeep be painted now, immediately, yesterday. To accomplish this would require the hiring of a special crew of painters to work all night, at overtime rates; which, in turn, meant that the order had to be bucked back up the line for further approval. When it finally got back to Sinatra's desk, he did not know what it was all about; after he had figured it out he confessed, with a tired look on his face, that he did not care when the hell they painted the jeep.

Yet it would have been unwise for anyone to anticipate his reaction, for he is a wholly unpredictable man of many moods and great dimension, a man who responds instantaneously to instinct—suddenly, dramatically, wildly he responds, and nobody can predict what will follow. A young lady named Jane Hoag, a reporter at *Life*'s Los Angeles bureau who had attended the same school as Sinatra's daughter, Nancy, had once been invited to a party at Mrs. Sinatra's California home at which Frank Sinatra, who maintains very cordial relations with his former wife, acted as host. Early in the party Miss Hoag, while leaning against a table, accidentally with her elbow knocked over one of a pair of alabaster birds to the floor, smashing it to pieces. Suddenly, Miss Hoag recalled, Sinatra's daughter cried, "Oh, that was one of my mother's favorite . . ."—but before she could complete the sentence, Sinatra glared at her, cutting her off, and while forty other guests in the room all stared in silence, Sinatra walked over, quickly with his finger flicked the other alabaster bird off the table, smashing it to pieces, and then put an arm gently around Jane Hoag and said, in a way that put her completely at ease, "That's okay, kid."

Now Sinatra said a few words to the blondes. Then he turned from the bar and began to walk toward the poolroom. One of Sinatra's other men friends moved in to keep the girls company. Brad Dexter, who had been standing in the corner talking to some other people, now followed Sinatra.

The room cracked with the clack of billiard balls. There were about a dozen spectators in the room, most of them young men who were watching Leo Durocher shoot against two other aspiring hustlers who were not very good. This private drinking club has among its membership many actors, directors, writers, models, nearly all of them a good deal younger than Sinatra or Durocher and much more casual in the way they dress for the evening. Many of the young women, their long hair flowing loosely below their shoulders, wore tight, fanny-fitting Jax pants and very expensive sweaters; and a few of the young men wore blue or green velour shirts with high collars and narrow tight pants, and Italian loafers.

It was obvious from the way Sinatra looked at these people in the poolroom that they were not his style, but he leaned back against a high stool that was against the wall, holding his drink in his right hand, and said nothing, just watched Durocher slam the billiard balls back and forth. The younger men in the room, accustomed to seeing Sinatra at this club, treated him without deference, although they said nothing offensive. They were a cool young group, very California-cool and casual, and one of the coolest seemed to be a little guy, very quick of movement, who had a sharp profile, pale blue eyes, blondish hair, and squared eyeglasses. He wore a pair of brown corduroy slacks, a green shaggy-dog Shetland sweater, a tan suede jacket, and Game Warden boots, for which he had recently paid sixty dollars.

Frank Sinatra, leaning against the stool, sniffling a bit from his cold, could not take his eyes off the Game Warden boots. Once, after gazing at them for a few moments, he turned away; but now he was focused on them again. The owner of the boots, who was just standing in them watching the pool game, was named Harlan Ellison, a writer who had just completed work on a screenplay, *The Oscar*.

Finally Sinatra could not contain himself.

"Hey," he yelled in his slightly harsh voice that still had a soft, sharp edge. "Those Italian boots?"

"No," Ellison said.

"Spanish?"

"No."

"Are they English boots?"

"Look, I donno, man," Ellison shot back, frowning at Sinatra, then turning away again.

Now the poolroom was suddenly silent. Leo Durocher, who had been poised behind his cue stick and was bent low, just froze in that position for a second. Nobody moved. Then Sinatra moved away from the stool and walked with that slow, arrogant swagger of his toward Ellison, the hard tap of Sinatra's shoes the only sound in the room. Then, looking down at Ellison with a slightly raised eyebrow and a tricky little smile, Sinatra asked: "You expecting a storm?"

Harlan Ellison moved a step to the side. "Look, is there any reason why you're talking to me?"

"I don't like the way you're dressed," Sinatra said.

"Hate to shake you up," Ellison said, "but I dress to suit myself."

Now there was some rumbling in the room, and somebody said, "Com'on, Harlan, let's get out of here," and Leo Durocher made his pool shot and said, "Yeah, com'on."

But Ellison stood his ground.

Sinatra said, "What do you do?"

"I'm a plumber," Ellison said.

"No, no, he's not," another young man quickly yelled from across the table. "He wrote *The Oscar.*"

"Oh, yeah," Sinatra said, "well, I've seen it, and it's a piece of crap."

"That's strange," Ellison said, "because they haven't even released it yet."

"Well, I've seen it," Sinatra repeated, "and it's a piece of crap."

Now Brad Dexter, very anxious, very big opposite the small figure of Ellison, said, "Com'on, kid, I don't want you in this room."

"Hey," Sinatra interrupted Dexter, "can't you see I'm talking to this guy?"

Dexter was confused. Then his whole attitude changed, and his voice went soft and he said to Ellison, almost with a plea, "Why do you persist in tormenting me?"

The whole scene was becoming ridiculous, and it seemed that Sinatra was only half-serious, perhaps just reacting out of sheer boredom or inner despair; at any rate, after a few more exchanges Harlan Ellison left the room. By this time the word had gotten out to those on the dance floor about the Sinatra-Ellison exchange, and somebody went to look for the manager of the club. But somebody else said that the manager had already heard about it—and had quickly gone out the door, hopped in his car, and drove home. So the assistant manager went into the poolroom.

"I don't want anybody in here without coats and ties," Sinatra snapped.

The assistant manager nodded, and walked back to his office.

It was the morning after. It was the beginning of another nervous day for Sinatra's press agent, Jim Mahoney. Mahoney had a headache, and he was worried but not over the Sinatra-Ellison incident of the night before.

At the time Mahoney had been with his wife at a table in the other room, and possibly he had not even been aware of the little drama. The whole thing had lasted only about three minutes. And three minutes after it was over, Frank Sinatra had probably forgotten about it for the rest of his life—as Ellison will probably remember it for the rest of his life: he had had, as hundreds of others before him, at an unexpected moment between darkness and dawn, a scene with Sinatra.

It was just as well that Mahoney had not been in the poolroom; he had enough on his mind today. He was worried about Sinatra's cold and worried about the controversial CBS documentary that, despite Sinatra's protests and withdrawal of permission, would be shown on television in less than two weeks. The newspapers this morning were full of hints that Sinatra might sue the network, and Mahoney's phones were ringing without pause, and now he was plugged into New York talking to the *Daily News*'s Kay Gardella, saying: "That's right, Kay . . . they made a gentleman's agreement to not ask certain questions about Frank's private life, and then Cronkite went right ahead: 'Frank, tell me about those associations.' That question, Kay—out! That question should never have been asked . . ."

As he spoke, Mahoney leaned back in his leather chair, his head shaking slowly. He is a powerfully built man of thirty-seven; he has a round, ruddy face, a heavy jaw, and narrow pale eyes, and he might appear pugnacious if he did not speak with such clear, soft sincerity and if he were not so meticulous about his clothes. His suits and shoes are superbly tailored, which was one of the first things Sinatra noticed about him, and in his spacious office opposite the bar is a red-muff electrical shoe polisher and a pair of brown wooden shoulders on a stand over which Mahoney can drape his jackets. Near the bar is an autographed photograph of President Kennedy and a few pictures of Frank Sinatra, but there are none of Sinatra in any other rooms in Mahoney's public-relations agency; there once was a large photograph of him hanging in the reception room but this apparently bruised the egos of some of Mahoney's other movie-star clients and, since Sinatra never shows up at the agency anyway, the photograph was removed.

Still, Sinatra seems ever present, and if Mahoney did not have legitimate worries about Sinatra, as he did today, he could invent them—and, as worry aids, he surrounds himself with little mementos of moments in the past when he did worry. In his shaving kit there is a two-year-old box of sleeping tablets dispensed by a Reno druggist—the date on the bottle marks the kidnapping of Frank Sinatra, Jr. There is on a table in Mahoney's office a mounted wood reproduction of Frank Sinatra's ransom note written on the aforementioned occasion. One of Mahoney's mannerisms, when he is sitting at his desk worrying, is to tinker with the tiny toy train he keeps in front of him—the train is a souvenir from the Sinatra film *Von Ryan's Express*; it is to men who are close to Sinatra what the PT-109 tie clasps are to men who were close to Kennedy—and Mahoney then proceeds to roll the little train back and forth on the six inches of track; back and forth, back and forth, click-clack-click-clack. It is his Queeg-thing.

Now Mahoney quickly put aside the little train. His secretary told him there was a very important call on the line. Mahoney picked it up, and his voice was even softer and more sincere than before. "Yes, Frank," he said. "Right . . . right . . . yes, Frank . . ."

When Mahoney put down the phone, quietly, he announced that Frank Sinatra had left in his private jet to spend the weekend at his home in Palm Springs, which is a sixteen-minute flight from his home in Los Angeles. Mahoney was now worried again. The Lear jet that Sinatra's pilot would be flying was identical, Mahoney said, to the one that had just crashed in another part of California.

On the following Monday, a cloudy and unseasonably cool California day, more than one hundred people gathered inside a white television studio, an enormous room dominated by a white stage, white walls, and with dozens of lights and lamps dangling: it rather resembled a gigantic operating room. In this room, within an hour or so, NBC was scheduled to begin taping a one-hour show that would be televised in color on the night of November 24 and would highlight, as much as it could in the limited time, the twenty-five-year career of Frank Sinatra as a public entertainer. It would not attempt to probe, as the forthcoming CBS Sinatra documentary allegedly would, that area of Sinatra's life that he regards as private. The NBC show would be mainly an hour of Sinatra singing some of the hits that carried him from Hoboken to Hollywood, a show that would be interrupted only now and then by a few film clips and commercials for Budweiser beer. Prior to his cold, Sinatra had been very excited about this show; he saw here an opportunity to appeal not only to those nostalgic, but also to communicate his talent to some rock-and-rollers—in a sense, he was battling the Beatles. The press releases being prepared by Mahoney's agency stressed this, reading: "If you happen to be tired of kid singers wearing mops of hair thick enough to hide a crate of melons . . . it should be refreshing, to consider the entertainment value of a video special titled *Sinatra—A Man and His Music.*"

But now in this NBC studio in Los Angeles, there was an atmosphere of anticipation and tension because of the uncertainty of the Sinatra voice. The forty-three musicians in Nelson Riddle's orchestra had already arrived and some were up on the white platform warming up. Dwight Hemion, a youthful sandy-haired director who had won praise for his television special on Barbra Streisand, was seated in the glass-enclosed control booth that overlooked the orchestra and stage. The camera crews, technical teams, security guards, Budweiser ad men were also standing between the floor lamps and cameras, waiting, as were a dozen or so ladies who worked as secretaries in other parts of the building but had sneaked away so they could watch this.

A few minutes before eleven o'clock, word spread quickly through the long corridor into the big studio that Sinatra was spotted walking through the parking lot and was on his way, and was looking fine. There seemed great relief among the group that was gathered; but when the lean, sharply dressed figure of the man got closer, and closer, they saw to their dismay that it was not Frank Sinatra. It was his double. Johnny Delgado.

Delgado walks like Sinatra, has Sinatra's build, and from certain facial angles does resemble Sinatra. But he seems a rather shy individual. Fifteen years ago, early in his acting career, Delgado applied for a role in *From Here to Eternity.* He was hired, finding out later that he was to be Sinatra's double. In Sinatra's latest film, *Assault on a Queen,* a story in which Sinatra and some fellow conspirators attempt to hijack the *Queen Mary,* Johnny Delgado doubles for Sinatra in some water scenes; and now, in this NBC studio, his job was to stand under the hot television lights marking Sinatra's spots on the stage for the camera crews.

Five minutes later, the real Frank Sinatra walked in. His face was pale, his blue eyes seemed a bit watery. He had been unable to rid himself of the cold, but he was going to try to sing anyway because the schedule was tight and thousands of dollars were involved at this moment in the assembling of the orchestra and crews and the rental of the studio. But when Sinatra, on his way to his small rehearsal room to warm up his voice, looked into the studio and saw that the stage and orchestra's platform were not close together, as he had specifically requested, his lips tightened and he was obviously very upset. A few moments later, from his rehearsal room, could be heard the pounding of his fist against the top of the piano and the voice of his accompanist, Bill Miller, saying, softly, "Try not to upset yourself, Frank."

Later Jim Mahoney and another man walked in, and there was talk of Dorothy Kilgallen's death in New York earlier that morning. She had been an ardent foe of Sinatra for years, and he became equally uncomplimentary about her in his nightclub act, and now, though she was dead, he did not compromise his feelings. "Dorothy Kilgallen's dead," he repeated, walking out of the room toward the studio. "Well, guess I got to change my whole act."

When he strolled into the studio the musicians all picked up their instruments and stiffened in their seats. Sinatra cleared his throat a few times and then, after rehearsing a few ballads with the orchestra, he sang "Don't Worry About Me" to his satisfaction and, being uncertain of how long his voice could last, suddenly became impatient.

"Why don't we tape this mother?" he called out, looking up toward the glass booth where the director, Dwight Hemion, and his staff were sitting. Their heads seemed to be down, focusing on the control board.

"Why don't we tape this mother?" Sinatra repeated.

The production stage manager, who stands near the camera wearing a headset, repeated Sinatra's words exactly into his line to the control room: "Why don't we tape this mother?"

Hemion did not answer. Possibly his switch was off. It was hard to know because of the obscuring reflections the lights made against the glass booth.

"Why don't we put on a coat and tie," said Sinatra, then wearing a high-necked yellow pullover, "and tape this . . ."

Suddenly Hemion's voice came over the sound amplifier, very calmly: "Okay, Frank, would you mind going back over . . ."

"Yes, I would mind going back," Sinatra snapped.

The silence from Hemion's end, which lasted a second or two, was then again interrupted by Sinatra saying, "When we stop doing things around here the way we did them in 1950, maybe we . . ." and Sinatra continued to tear into Hemion, condemning as well the lack of modern techniques in putting such shows together; then, possibly not wanting to use his voice unnecessarily, he stopped. And Dwight Hemion, very patient, so patient and calm that one would assume he had not heard anything that Sinatra had just said, outlined the opening part of the show. And Sinatra a few minutes later was reading his opening remarks, words that would follow "Without a Song," off the large idiot-cards being held near the camera. Then, this done, he prepared to do the same thing on camera.

"*Frank Sinatra Show*, Act 1, page ten, Take 1," called a man with a clapboard, jumping in front of the camera—clap—then jumping away again.

"Did you ever stop to think," Sinatra began, "what the world would be like without a song? . . . It would be a pretty dreary place . . . Gives you something to think about, doesn't it? . . ."

Sinatra stopped.

"Excuse me," he said, adding, "Boy, I need a drink."

They tried it again.

"*Frank Sinatra Show*, Act 1, page ten, Take 2," yelled the jumping guy with the clapboard.

"Did you ever stop to think what the world would be like without a song? . . ." Frank Sinatra read it through this time without stopping. Then he rehearsed a few more songs, once or twice interrupting the orchestra when a certain instrumental sound was not quite what he wanted. It was hard to tell how well his voice was going to hold up, for this was early in the show; up to this point, however, everybody in the room seemed pleased, particularly when he sang an old sentimental favorite written more than twenty years ago by Jimmy Van Heusen and Phil Silvers—"Nancy," inspired by the first of Sinatra's three children when she was just a few years old.

> *If I don't see her each day*
> *I miss her . . .*
> *Gee what a thrill*
> *Each time I kiss her*

As Sinatra sang these words, though he has sung them hundreds and hundreds of times in the past, it was suddenly obvious to everybody in the studio that something quite special must be going on inside the man, because something quite special was coming out. He was singing now, cold or no cold, with power and warmth, he was letting himself go, the public arrogance was gone, the private side was in this song about the girl who, it is said, understands him better than anybody else, and is the only person in front of whom he can be unashamedly himself.

Nancy is twenty-five. She lives alone, her marriage to singer Tommy Sands having ended in divorce. Her home is in a Los Angeles suburb and she is now making her third film and is recording for her father's record company. She sees him every day; or, if not, he telephones, no matter if it be from Europe or Asia. When Sinatra's singing first became popular on radio, stimulating the swooners, Nancy would listen at home and cry. When Sinatra's first marriage broke up in 1951 and he left home, Nancy was the only child old enough to remember him as a father. She also saw him with Ava Gardner, Juliet Prowse, Mia Farrow, many others, has gone on double dates with him . . .

She takes the winter
And makes it summer . . .
Summer could take
Some lessons from her

Nancy now also sees him visiting at home with his first wife, the former Nancy Barbato, a plasterer's daughter from Jersey City whom he married in 1939 when he was earning twenty-five dollars a week singing at the Rustic Cabin near Hoboken.

The first Mrs. Sinatra, a striking woman who has never remarried ("When you've been married to Frank Sinatra . . ." she once explained to a friend), lives in a magnificent home in Los Angeles with her younger daughter, Tina, who is seventeen. There is no bitterness, only great respect and affection between Sinatra and his first wife, and he has long been welcome in her home and has even been known to wander in at odd hours, stoke the fire, lie on the sofa, and fall asleep. Frank Sinatra can fall asleep anywhere, something he learned when he used to ride bumpy roads with band buses; he also learned at that time, when sitting in a tuxedo, how to pinch the trouser creases in the back and tuck the jacket under and out, and fall asleep perfectly pressed. But he does not ride buses anymore, and his daughter Nancy, who in her younger days felt rejected when he slept on the sofa instead of giving attention to her, later realized that the sofa was one of the few places left in the world where Frank Sinatra could get any privacy, where his famous face would neither be stared at nor cause an abnormal reaction in others. She realized, too, that things normal have always eluded her father: his childhood was one of loneliness and a drive toward attention, and since attaining it he has never again been certain of solitude. Upon looking out the window of a home he once owned in Hasbrouck Heights, New Jersey, he would occasionally see the faces of teenagers peeking in; and in 1944, after moving to California and buying a home behind a ten-foot fence on Lake Toluca, he discovered that the only way to escape the telephone and other intrusions was to board his paddle boat with a few friends, a card table, and a case of beer, and stay afloat all afternoon. But he has tried, insofar as it has been possible, to be like everyone else, Nancy says. He wept on her wedding day, he is very sentimental and sensitive . . .

"What the hell are you doing up there, Dwight?"

Silence from the control booth.

"Got a party or something going on up there, Dwight?"

Sinatra stood on the stage, arms folded, glaring up across the cameras toward Hemion. Sinatra had sung "Nancy" with probably all he had in his voice on this day. The next few numbers contained raspy notes, and twice his voice completely cracked. But now Hemion was in the control booth out of communication; then he was down in the studio walking over to where Sinatra stood. A few minutes later they both left the studio and were on the way up to the control booth. The tape was replayed for Sinatra. He watched only about five minutes of it before he started to shake his head. Then he said to Hemion: "Forget it, just forget it. You're wasting your time. What you got there," Sinatra said, nodding to the singing image of himself on the television screen, "is a man with a cold." Then he left the control booth, ordering that the whole day's performance be scrubbed and future taping postponed until he had recovered.

Soon the word spread like an emotional epidemic down through Sinatra's staff, then fanned out through Hollywood, then was heard across the nation in Jilly's saloon, and also on the other side of the Hudson River in the homes of Frank Sinatra's parents and his other relatives and friends in New Jersey.

When Frank Sinatra spoke with his father on the telephone and said he was feeling awful, the elder Sinatra reported that he was also feeling awful: that his left arm and fist were so stiff with a circulatory condition he could barely use them, adding that the ailment might be the result of having thrown too many left hooks during his days as a bantamweight almost fifty years ago.

Martin Sinatra, a ruddy and tattooed little blue-eyed Sicilian born in Catania, boxed under the name of "Marty O'Brien." In those days, in those places, with the Irish running the lower reaches of city life, it was not uncommon for Italians to wind up with such names. Most of the Italians and Sicilians who migrated to America just prior to the 1900s were poor and uneducated, were excluded from the building-trades unions dominated by the Irish, and were somewhat intimidated by the Irish police, Irish priests, Irish politicians.

One notable exception was Frank Sinatra's mother, Dolly, a large and very ambitious woman who was brought to this country at two months of age by her mother and father, a lithographer from Genoa. In later years Dolly Sinatra, possessing a round red face and blue eyes, was often mistaken for being Irish, and surprised many at the speed with which she swung her heavy handbag at anyone uttering "Wop."

By playing skillful politics with North Jersey's Democratic machine, Dolly Sinatra was to become, in her heyday, a kind of Catherine de Medici of Hoboken's third ward. She could always be counted upon to deliver six hundred votes at election time from her Italian neighborhood, and this was her base of power. When she told one of the politicians that she wanted her husband to be appointed to the Hoboken Fire Department, and was told, "But, Dolly, we don't have an opening," she snapped, "Make an opening."

They did. Years later she requested that her husband be made a captain, and one day she got a call from one of the political bosses that began, "Dolly, congratulations!"

"For what?"

"Captain Sinatra."

"Oh, you finally made him one—thank you very much."

Then she called the Hoboken Fire Department.

"Let me speak to Captain Sinatra," she said. The fireman called Martin Sinatra to the phone, saying, "Marty, I think your wife has gone nuts." When he got on the line, Dolly greeted him:

"Congratulations, Captain Sinatra!"

Dolly's only child, christened Francis Albert Sinatra, was born and nearly died on December 12, 1915. It was a difficult birth, and during his first moment on earth he received marks he will carry till death—the scars on the left side of his neck being the result of a doctor's clumsy forceps, and Sinatra has chosen not to obscure them with surgery.

After he was six months old, he was reared mainly by his grandmother. His mother had a full-time job as a chocolate dipper with a large firm and was so proficient at it that the firm once offered to send her to the Paris office to train others. While some people in Hoboken remember Frank Sinatra as a lonely child, one who spent many hours on the porch gazing into space, Sinatra was never a slum kid, never in jail, always well-dressed. He had so many pants that some people in Hoboken called him "Slacksey O'Brien."

Dolly Sinatra was not the sort of Italian mother who could be appeased merely by a child's obedience and good appetite. She made many demands on her son, was always very strict. She dreamed of his becoming an aviation engineer. When she discovered Bing Crosby pictures hanging on his bedroom walls one evening, and learned that her son wished to become a singer too, she became infuriated and threw a shoe at him. Later, finding she could not talk him out of it—"He takes after me"—she encouraged his singing.

Many Italo-American boys of his generation were then shooting for the same star—they were strong with song, weak with words, not a big novelist among them: no O'Hara, no Bellow, no Cheever, nor Shaw; yet they could communicate bel canto. This was more in their tradition, no need for a diploma; they could, with a song, someday see their names in lights . . . Perry Como . . . Frankie Laine . . . Tony Bennett . . . Vic Damone . . . but none could see it better than Frank Sinatra.

Though he sang through much of the night at the Rustic Cabin, he was up the next day singing without a fee on New York radio to get more attention. Later he got a job singing with Harry James's band, and it was there in August of 1939 that Sinatra had his first recording hit—"All or Nothing at All." He became very fond of Harry James and the men in the band, but when he received an offer from Tommy Dorsey, who in those days had probably the best band in the country, Sinatra took it; the job paid $125 a week, and Dorsey knew how to feature a vocalist. Yet Sinatra was very depressed at leaving James's band, and the final night with them was so memorable that, twenty years later, Sinatra could recall the details to a friend: "The bus pulled out with the rest of the boys at about half-past midnight. I'd said good-bye to them all, and it was snowing, I remember. There was nobody around and I stood alone with my suitcase in the snow and watched the taillights disappear. Then the tears started and I tried to run after the bus. There was such spirit and enthusiasm in that band, I hated leaving it."

But he did—as he would leave other warm places, too, in search of something more, never wasting time, trying to do it all in one generation, fighting under his own name, defending underdogs, terrorizing top dogs. He threw a punch at a musician who said something anti-Semitic, espoused the Negro cause two decades before it became fashionable. He also threw a tray of glasses at Buddy Rich when he played the drums too loud.

Sinatra gave away $50,000 worth of gold cigarette lighters before he was thirty, was living an immigrant's wildest dream of America. He arrived suddenly on the scene when DiMaggio was silent, when paisanos were mournful, were quietly defensive about Hitler in their homeland. Sinatra became, in time, a kind of one-man Anti-Defamation League for Italians in America, the sort of organization that would be unlikely for them because, as the theory goes, they rarely agreed on anything, being extreme individualists: fine as soloists, but not so good in a choir; fine as heroes, but not so good in a parade.

When many Italian names were used in describing gangsters on a television show, *The Untouchables*, Sinatra was loud in his disapproval. Sinatra and many thousands of other Italo-Americans were resentful as well when a small-time hoodlum, Joseph Valachi, was brought by Bobby Kennedy into prominence as a Mafia expert, when indeed, from Valachi's testimony on television, he seemed to know less than most waiters on Mulberry Street. Many Italians in Sinatra's circle also regard Bobby Kennedy as something of an Irish cop, more dignified than those in Dolly's day, but no less intimidating. Together with Peter Lawford, Bobby Kennedy is said to have suddenly gotten "cocky" with Sinatra after John Kennedy's election, forgetting the contribution Sinatra had made in both fundraising and in influencing many anti-Irish Italian votes. Lawford and Bobby Kennedy are both suspected of having influenced the late President's decision to stay as a house guest with Bing Crosby instead of Sinatra, as originally planned, a social setback Sinatra may never forget. Peter Lawford has since been drummed out of Sinatra's "summit" in Las Vegas.

"Yes, my son is like me," Dolly Sinatra says, proudly. "You cross him, he never forgets." And while she concedes his power, she quickly points out, "He can't make his mother do anything she doesn't want to do," adding, "Even today, he wears the same brand of underwear I used to buy him."

Today Dolly Sinatra is seventy-one years old, a year or two younger than Martin, and all day long people are knocking on the back door of her large home asking her advice, seeking her influence. When she is not seeing people and not cooking in the kitchen, she is looking after her husband, a silent but stubborn man, and telling him to keep his sore left arm resting on the sponge she has placed on the armrest of a soft chair. "Oh, he went to some terrific fires, this guy did," Dolly said to a visitor, nodding with admiration toward her husband in the chair.

Though Dolly Sinatra has eighty-seven godchildren in Hoboken, and still goes to that city during political campaigns, she now lives with her husband in a beautiful sixteen-room house in Fort Lee, New Jersey. This home was a gift from their son on their fiftieth wedding anniversary three years ago. The home is tastefully furnished and is filled with a remarkable juxtaposition of the pious and the worldly—photographs of Pope John and Ava Gardner, of Pope Paul and Dean Martin; several statues of saints and holy water, a chair autographed by Sammy Davis, Jr. and bottles of bourbon. In Mrs. Sinatra's jewelry box is a magnificent strand of pearls she had just received from Ava Gardner, whom she liked tremendously as a daughter-in-law and still keeps in touch with and talks about; and hung on the wall is a letter addressed to Dolly and Martin: "The sands of time have turned to gold, yet love continues to unfold like the petals of a rose, in God's garden of life . . . may God love you thru all eternity. I thank Him, I thank you for the being of one. Your loving son, Francis."

Mrs. Sinatra talks to her son on the telephone about once a week, and recently he suggested that, when visiting Manhattan, she make use of his apartment on East Seventy-second Street on the East River. This is an expensive neighborhood of New York even though there is a small factory on the block, but this latter fact was seized upon by Dolly Sinatra as a means of getting back at her son for some unflattering descriptions of his childhood in Hoboken.

"What—you want me to stay in your apartment, in that dump?" she asked. "You think I'm going to spend the night in that awful neighborhood?"

Frank Sinatra got the point, and said, "Excuse me, Mrs. Fort Lee."

After spending the week in Palm Springs, his cold much better, Frank Sinatra returned to Los Angeles, a lovely city of sun and sex, a Spanish discovery of Mexican misery, a star land of little men and little women sliding in and out of convertibles in tense tight pants.

Sinatra returned in time to see the long-awaited CBS documentary with his family. At about 9 p.m. he drove to the home of his former wife, Nancy, and had dinner with her and their two daughters. Their son, whom they rarely see these days, was out of town.

Frank, Jr., who is twenty-two, was touring with a band and moving cross country toward a New York engagement at Basin Street East with the Pied Pipers, with whom Frank Sinatra sang when he was with Dorsey's band in the 1940s. Today Frank Sinatra, Jr., whom his father says he named after Franklin D. Roosevelt, lives mostly in hotels, dines each evening in his nightclub dressing room, and sings until 2 a.m., accepting graciously, because he has no choice, the inevitable comparisons. His voice is smooth and pleasant, and improving with work, and while he is very respectful of his father, he discusses him with objectivity and in an occasional tone of subdued cockiness.

Concurrent with his father's early fame, Frank, Jr. said, was the creation of a "press-release Sinatra" designed to "set him apart from the common man, separate him from the realities: it was suddenly Sinatra, the electric magnate, Sinatra who is supernormal, not superhuman but supernormal. And here," Frank, Jr. continued, "is the great fallacy, the great bullshit, for Frank Sinatra is normal, is the guy whom you'd meet on a street corner. But this other thing, the supernormal guise, has affected Frank Sinatra as much as anybody who watches one of his television shows, or reads a magazine article about him . . .

"Frank Sinatra's life in the beginning was so normal," he said, "that nobody would have guessed in 1934 that this little Italian kid with the curly hair would become the giant, the monster, the great living legend . . . He met my mother one summer on the beach. She was Nancy Barbato, daughter of Mike Barbato, a Jersey City plasterer. And she meets the fireman's son, Frank, one summer day on the beach at Long Branch, New Jersey. Both are Italian, both Roman Catholic, both lower-middle-class summer sweethearts—it is like a million bad movies starring Frankie Avalon . . .

"They have three children. The first child, Nancy, was the most normal of Frank Sinatra's children. Nancy was a cheerleader, went to summer camp, drove a Chevrolet, had the easiest kind of development centered around the home and family. Next is me. My life with the family is very, very normal up until September of 1958 when, in complete contrast to the rearing of both girls, I am put into a college-preparatory school. I am now away from the inner family circle, and my position within has never been remade to this day . . . The third child, Tina. And to be dead honest, I really couldn't say what her life is like."

The CBS show, narrated by Walter Cronkite, began at 10 p.m. A minute before that, the Sinatra family, having finished dinner, turned their chairs around and faced the camera, united for whatever disaster might follow. Sinatra's men in other parts of town, in other parts of the nation, were doing the same thing. Sinatra's lawyer, Milton A. Rudin, smoking a cigar, was watching with a keen eye, an alert legal mind. Other sets were watched by Brad Dexter, Jim Mahoney, Ed Pucci; Sinatra's makeup man, "Shotgun" Britton; his New York representative, Henri Gine; his haberdasher, Richard Carroll; his insurance broker, John Lillie; his valet, George Jacobs, a handsome Negro who, when entertaining girls in his apartment, plays records by Ray Charles.

And like so much of Hollywood's fear, the apprehension about the CBS show all proved to be without foundation. It was a highly flattering hour that did not deeply probe, as rumors suggested it would, into Sinatra's love life, or the Mafia, or other areas of his private province. While the documentary was not authorized, wrote Jack Gould in the next day's *New York Times*, "it could have been."

Immediately after the show, the telephones began to ring throughout the Sinatra system conveying words of joy and relief—and from New York came Jilly's telegram: WE RULE THE WORLD!

The next day, standing in the corridor of the NBC building where he was about to resume taping his show, Sinatra was discussing the CBS show with several of his friends, and he said, "Oh, it was a gas."

"Yeah, Frank, a helluva show."

"But I think Jack Gould was right in the *Times* today," Sinatra said. "There should have been more on the man, not so much on the music . . ."

They nodded, nobody mentioning the past hysteria in the Sinatra world when it seemed CBS was zeroing in on the man; they just nodded and two of them laughed about Sinatra's apparently having gotten the word "bird" on the show—this being a favorite Sinatra word. He often inquires of his cronies, "How's your bird?"; and when he nearly drowned in Hawaii, he later explained, "Just got a little water on my bird"; and under a large photograph of him holding a whiskey bottle, a photo that hangs in the home of an actor friend named Dick Bakalyan, the inscription reads: "Drink, Dickie! It's good for your bird." In the song "Come Fly with Me," Sinatra sometimes alters the lyrics—"Just say the words and we'll take our birds down to Acapulco Bay."

Ten minutes later Sinatra, following the orchestra, walked into the NBC studio, which did not resemble in the slightest the scene here of eight days ago. On this occasion Sinatra was in fine voice, he cracked jokes between numbers, nothing could upset him. Once, while he was singing "How Can I Ignore the Girl Next Door," standing on the stage next to a tree, a television camera mounted on a vehicle came rolling in too close and plowed against the tree.

"Kee-rist!" yelled one of the technical assistants.

But Sinatra seemed hardly to notice it.

"We've had a slight accident," he said, calmly. Then he began the song all over from the beginning.

When the show was over, Sinatra watched the rerun on the monitor in the control room. He was very pleased, shaking hands with Dwight Hemion and his assistants. Then the whiskey bottles were opened in Sinatra's dressing room. Pat Lawford was there, and so were Andy Williams and a dozen others. The telegrams and telephone calls continued to be received from all over the country with praise for the CBS show. There was even a call, Mahoney said, from the CBS producer, Don Hewitt, with whom Sinatra had been so angry a few days before. And Sinatra was still angry, feeling that CBS had betrayed him, though the show itself was not objectionable.

"Shall I drop a line to Hewitt?" Mahoney asked.

"Can you send a fist through the mail?" Sinatra asked.

He has everything, he cannot sleep, he gives nice gifts, he is not happy, but he would not trade, even for happiness, what he is . . .

He is a piece of our past—but only we have aged, he hasn't . . . we are dogged by domesticity, he isn't . . . we have compunctions, he doesn't . . . it is our fault, not his . . .

He controls the menus of every Italian restaurant in Los Angeles; if you want North Italian cooking, fly to Milan . . .

Men follow him, imitate him, fight to be near him . . . there is something of the locker room, the barracks about him . . . bird . . . bird . . .

He believes you must play it big, wide, expansively—the more open you are, the more you take in, your dimensions deepen, you grow, you become more what you are—bigger, richer . . .

"He is better than anybody else, or at least they think he is, and he has to live up to it."—Nancy Sinatra

"He is calm on the outside—inwardly a million things are happening to him."—Dick Bakalyan

"He has an insatiable desire to live every moment to its fullest because, I guess, he feels that right around the corner is extinction."—Brad Dexter

"All I ever got out of any of my marriages was the two years Artie Shaw financed on an analyst's couch."—Ava Gardner

"We weren't mother and son—we were buddies."—Dolly Sinatra

"I'm for anything that gets you through the night, be it prayer, tranquilizers or a bottle of Jack Daniel's."—Frank Sinatra

Frank Sinatra was tired of all the talk, the gossip, the theory—tired of reading quotes about himself, of hearing what people were saying about him all over town. It had been a tedious three weeks, he said, and now he just wanted to get away, go to Las Vegas, let off some steam. So he hopped in his jet, soared over the California hills across the Nevada flats, then over miles and miles of desert to the Sands and the Clay-Patterson fight.

On the eve of the fight he stayed up all night and slept through most of the afternoon, though his recorded voice could be heard singing in the lobby of the Sands, in the gambling casino, even in the toilets, being interrupted every few bars however by the paging public address: "Telephone call for Mr. Ron Fish, Mr. Ron Fish . . . with a ribbon of gold in her hair . . . Telephone call for Mr. Herbert Rothstein, Mr. Herbert Rothstein . . . memories of a time so bright, keep me sleepless through dark endless nights."

Standing around in the lobby of the Sands and other hotels up and down the strip on this afternoon before the fight were the usual prefight prophets: the gamblers, the old champs, the little cigar butts from Eighth Avenue, the sportswriters who knock the big fights all year but would never miss one, the novelists who seem always to be identifying with one boxer or another, the local prostitutes assisted by some talent in from Los Angeles, and also a young brunette in a wrinkled black cocktail dress who was at the bell captain's desk crying, "But I want to speak to Mr. Sinatra."

"He's not here," the bell captain said.

"Won't you put me through to his room?"

"There are no messages going through, miss," he said, and then she turned, unsteadily, seeming close to tears, and walked through the lobby into the big noisy casino crowded with men interested only in money.

Shortly before 7 p.m., Jack Entratter, a big gray-haired man who operates the Sands, walked into the gambling room to tell some men around the blackjack table that Sinatra was getting dressed. He also said that he'd been unable to get front-row seats for everybody, and so some of the men—including Leo Durocher, who had a date, and Joey Bishop, who was accompanied by his wife—would not be able to fit in Frank Sinatra's row but would have to take seats in the third row. When Entratter walked over to tell this to Joey Bishop, Bishop's face fell. He did not seem angry; he merely looked at Entratter with an empty silence, seeming somewhat stunned.

"Joey, I'm sorry," Entratter said when the silence persisted, "but we couldn't get more than six together in the front row."

Bishop still said nothing. But when they all appeared at the fight, Joey Bishop was in the front row, his wife in the third.

The fight, called a holy war between Muslims and Christians, was preceded by the introduction of three balding ex-champions, Rocky Marciano, Joe Louis, Sonny Liston—and then there was "The Star-Spangled Banner" sung by another man from out of the past, Eddie Fisher. It had been more than fourteen years ago, but Sinatra could still remember every detail: Eddie Fisher was then the new king of the baritones, with Billy Eckstine and Guy Mitchell right with him, and Sinatra had been long counted out. One day he remembered walking into a broadcasting studio past dozens of Eddie Fisher fans waiting outside the hall, and when they saw Sinatra they began to jeer, "Frankie, Frankie, I'm swooning, I'm swooning." This was also the time when he was selling only about thirty thousand records a year, when he was dreadfully miscast as a funny man on his television show, and when he recorded such disasters as "Mama Will Bark," with Dagmar.

"I growled and barked on the record," Sinatra said, still horrified by the thought. "The only good it did me was with the dogs."

His voice and his artistic judgment were incredibly bad in 1952, but even more responsible for his decline, say his friends, was his pursuit of Ava Gardner. She was the big movie queen then, one of the most beautiful women in the world. Sinatra's daughter Nancy recalls seeing Ava swimming one day in her father's pool, then climbing out of the water with that fabulous body, walking slowly to the fire, leaning over it for a few moments, and then it suddenly seemed that her long dark hair was all dry, miraculously and effortlessly back in place.

With most women Sinatra dates, his friends say, he never knows whether they want him for what he can do for them now—or will do for them later. With Ava Gardner, it was different. He could do nothing for her later. She was on top. If Sinatra learned anything from his experience with her, he possibly learned that when a proud man is down a woman cannot help. Particularly a woman on top.

Nevertheless, despite a tired voice, some deep emotion seeped into his singing during this time. One particular song that is well remembered even now is "I'm a Fool to Want You," and a friend who was in the studio when Sinatra recorded it recalled: "Frank was really worked up that night. He did the song in one take, then turned around and walked out of the studio and that was that . . ."

Sinatra's manager at that time, a former song plugger named Hank Sanicola, said, "Ava loved Frank, but not the way he loved her. He needs a great deal of love. He wants it twenty-four hours a day, he must have people around—Frank is that kind of guy." Ava Gardner, Sanicola said, "was very insecure. She feared she could not really hold a man . . . twice he went chasing her to Africa, wasting his own career . . ."

"Ava didn't want Frank's men hanging around all the time," another friend said, "and this got him mad. With Nancy he used to be able to bring the whole band home with him, and Nancy, the good Italian wife, would never complain—she'd just make everybody a plate of spaghetti."

In 1953, after almost two years of marriage, Sinatra and Ava Gardner were divorced. Sinatra's mother reportedly arranged a reconciliation, but if Ava was willing, Frank Sinatra was not. He was seen with other women. The balance had shifted. Somewhere during this period Sinatra seemed to change from the kid singer, the boy actor in the sailor suit, to a man. Even before he had won the Oscar in 1953 for his role in *From Here to Eternity*, some flashes of his old talent were coming through—in his recording of "The Birth of the Blues," in his Riviera-nightclub appearance that jazz critics enthusiastically praised; and there was also a trend now toward LPs and away from the quick three-minute deal, and Sinatra's concert style would have capitalized on this with or without an Oscar.

In 1954, totally committed to his talent once more, Frank Sinatra was selected *Metronome's* "Singer of the Year," and later he won the UPI disc-jockey poll, unseating Eddie Fisher—who now, in Las Vegas, having sung "The Star-Spangled Banner," climbed out of the ring, and the fight began.

Floyd Patterson chased Clay around the ring in the first round, but was unable to reach him, and from then on he was Clay's toy, the bout ending in a technical knockout in the twelfth round. A half hour later, nearly everybody had forgotten about the fight and was back at the gambling tables or lining up to buy tickets for the Dean Martin-Sinatra-Bishop nightclub routine on the stage of the Sands. This routine, which includes Sammy Davis, Jr. when he is in town, consists of a few songs and much cutting up, all of it very informal, very special, and rather ethnic—Martin, a drink in hand, asking Bishop: "Did you ever see a Jew jitsu?"; and Bishop, playing a Jewish waiter, warning the two Italians to watch out "because I got my own group—the Matzia."

Then after the last show at the Sands, the Sinatra crowd, which now numbered about twenty—and included Jilly, who had flown in from New York; Jimmy Cannon, Sinatra's favorite sports columnist; Harold Gibbons, a Teamster official expected to take over if Hoffa goes to jail—all got into a line of cars and headed for another club. It was three o'clock. The night was young.

They stopped at the Sahara, taking a long table near the back, and listened to a baldheaded little comedian named Don Rickles, who is probably more caustic than any comic in the country. His humor is so rude, in such bad taste, that it offends no one—it is too offensive to be offensive. Spotting Eddie Fisher among the audience, Rickles proceeded to ridicule him as a lover, saying it was no wonder that he could not handle Elizabeth Taylor; and when two businessmen in the audience acknowledged that they were Egyptian, Rickles cut into them for their country's policy toward Israel; and he strongly suggested that the woman seated at one table with her husband was actually a hooker.

When the Sinatra crowd walked in, Don Rickles could not be more delighted. Pointing to Jilly, Rickles yelled: "How's it feel to be Frank's tractor? . . . Yeah, Jilly keeps walking in front of Frank clearing the way." Then, nodding to Durocher, Rickles said, "Stand up, Leo, show Frank how you slide." Then he focused on Sinatra, not failing to mention Mia Farrow, nor that he was wearing a toupee, nor to say that Sinatra was washed up as a singer, and when Sinatra laughed, everybody laughed, and Rickles pointed toward Bishop: "Joey Bishop keeps checking with Frank to see what's funny."

Then, after Rickles told some Jewish jokes, Dean Martin stood up and yelled, "Hey, you're always talking about the Jews, never about the Italians," and Rickles cut him off with, "What do we need the Italians for—all they do is keep the flies off our fish."

Sinatra laughed, they all laughed, and Rickles went on this way for nearly an hour until Sinatra, standing up, said, "All right, com'on, get this thing over with. I gotta go."

"Shaddup and sit down!" Rickles snapped. "I've had to listen to you sing . . ."

"Who do you think you're talking to?" Sinatra yelled back.

"Dick Haymes," Rickles replied, and Sinatra laughed again, and then Dean Martin, pouring a bottle of whiskey over his head, entirely drenching his tuxedo, pounded the table.

"Who would ever believe that staggering would make a star?" Rickles said, but Martin called out, "Hey, I wanna make a speech."

"Shaddup."

"No, Don, I wanna tell ya," Dean Martin persisted, "that I think you're a great performer."

"Well, thank you, Dean," Rickles said, seeming pleased.

"But don't go by me," Martin said, plopping down into his seat, "I'm drunk."

"I'll buy that," Rickles said.

By 4 a.m. Frank Sinatra led the group out of the Sahara, some of them carrying their glasses of whiskey with them, sipping it along the sidewalk and in the cars; then, returning to the Sands, they walked into the gambling casino. It was still packed with people, the roulette wheels spinning, the crapshooters screaming in the far corner.

Frank Sinatra, holding a shot glass of bourbon in his left hand, walked through the crowd. He, unlike some of his friends, was perfectly pressed, his tuxedo tie precisely pointed, his shoes unsmudged. He never seems to lose his dignity, never lets his guard completely down no matter how much he has drunk, nor how long he has been up. He never sways when he walks, like Dean Martin, nor does he ever dance in the aisles or jump up on tables, like Sammy Davis.

A part of Sinatra, no matter where he is, is never there. There is always a part of him, though sometimes a small part, that remains Il Padrone. Even now, resting his shot glass on the blackjack table, facing the dealer, Sinatra stood a bit back from the table, not leaning against it. He reached under his tuxedo jacket into his trouser pocket and came up with a thick but clean wad of bills. Gently he peeled off a one-hundred-dollar bill and placed it on the green-felt table. The dealer dealt him two cards. Sinatra called for a third card, overbid, lost the hundred.

Without a change of expression, Sinatra put down a second hundred-dollar bill. He lost that. Then he put down a third, and lost that. Then he placed two one-hundred-dollar bills on the table and lost those. Finally, putting his sixth hundred-dollar bill on the table, and losing it, Sinatra moved away from the table, nodding to the man, and announcing, "Good dealer."

The crowd that had gathered around him now opened up to let him through. But a woman stepped in front of him, handing him a piece of paper to autograph. He signed it and then he said, "Thank you."

In the rear of the Sands' large dining room was a long table reserved for Sinatra. The dining room was fairly empty at this hour, with perhaps two dozen other people in the room, including a table of four unescorted young ladies sitting near Sinatra. On the other side of the room, at another long table, sat seven men shoulder-to-shoulder against the wall, two of them wearing dark glasses, all of them eating quietly, speaking hardly a word, just sitting and eating and missing nothing.

The Sinatra party, after getting settled and having a few more drinks, ordered something to eat. The table was about the same size as the one reserved for Sinatra whenever he is at Jilly's in New York; and the people seated around this table in Las Vegas were many of the same people who are often seen with Sinatra at Jilly's or at a restaurant in California, or in Italy, or in New Jersey, or wherever Sinatra happens to be. When Sinatra sits to dine, his trusted friends are close; and no matter where he is, no matter how elegant the place may be, there is something of the neighborhood showing because Sinatra, no matter how far he has come, is still something of the boy from the neighborhood—only now he can take his neighborhood with him.

In some ways, this quasi-family affair at a reserved table in a public place is the closest thing Sinatra now has to home life. Perhaps, having had a home and left it, this approximation is as close as he cares to come; although this does not seem precisely so because he speaks with such warmth about his family, keeps in close touch with his first wife, and insists that she make no decision without first consulting him. He is always eager to place his furniture or other mementos of himself in her home or his daughter Nancy's, and he also is on amiable terms with Ava Gardner. When he was in Italy making *Von Ryan's Express*, they spent some time together, being pursued wherever they went by the paparazzi. It was reported then that the paparazzi had made Sinatra a collective offer of $16,000 if he would pose with Ava Gardner; Sinatra was said to have made a counter offer of $32,000 if he could break one paparazzi arm and leg.

While Sinatra is often delighted that he can be in his home completely without people, enabling him to read and think without interruption, there are occasions when he finds himself alone at night, and not by choice. He may have dialed a half-dozen women, and for one reason or another they are all unavailable. So he will call his valet, George Jacobs.

"I'll be coming home for dinner tonight, George."

"How many will there be?"

"Just myself," Sinatra will say. "I want something light, I'm not very hungry."

George Jacobs is a twice-divorced man of thirty-six who resembles Billy Eckstine. He has traveled all over the world with Sinatra and is devoted to him. Jacobs lives in a comfortable bachelor's apartment off Sunset Boulevard around the corner from Whisky a Go Go, and he is known around town for the assortment of frisky California girls he has as friends—a few of whom, he concedes, were possibly drawn to him initially because of his closeness to Frank Sinatra.

When Sinatra arrives, Jacobs will serve him dinner in the dining room. Then Sinatra will tell Jacobs that he is free to go home. If Sinatra, on such evenings, should ask Jacobs to stay longer, or to play a few hands of poker, he would be happy to do so. But Sinatra never does.

This was his second night in Las Vegas, and Frank Sinatra sat with friends in the Sands' dining room until nearly 8 a.m. He slept through much of the day, then flew back to Los Angeles, and on the following morning he was driving his little golf cart through the Paramount Pictures movie lot. He was scheduled to complete two final scenes with the sultry blond actress Virna Lisi, in the film *Assault on a Queen*. As he maneuvered the little vehicle up the road between the big studio buildings, he spotted Steve Rossi, who, with his comedy partner, Marty Allen, was making a film in an adjoining studio with Nancy Sinatra.

"Hey, Dag," he yelled to Rossi, "stop kissing Nancy."

"It's part of the film, Frank," Rossi said, turning as he walked.

"In the garage?"

"It's my Dago blood, Frank."

"Well, cool it," Sinatra said, winking, then cutting his golf cart around a corner and parking it outside a big drab building within which the scenes for *Assault* would be filmed.

"Where's the fat director?" Sinatra called out, striding into the studio that was crowded with dozens of technical assistants and actors all gathered around cameras. The director, Jack Donohue, a large man who has worked with Sinatra through twenty-two years on one production or other, has had headaches with this film. The script had been chopped, the actors seemed restless, and Sinatra had become bored. But now there were only two scenes left—a short one to be filmed in the pool, and a longer and passionate one featuring Sinatra and Virna Lisi to be shot on a simulated beach.

The pool scene, which dramatizes a situation where Sinatra and his hijackers fail in their attempt to sack the *Queen Mary*, went quickly and well. After Sinatra had been kept in the water shoulder-high for a few minutes, he said, "Let's move it, fellows—it's cold in this water, and I've just gotten over one cold."

So the camera crews moved in closer, Virna Lisi splashed next to Sinatra in the water, and Jack Donohue yelled to his assistants operating the fans, "Get the waves going," and another man gave the command, "Agitate!" and Sinatra broke out in song, "Agitate in rhythm," then quieted down just before the cameras started to roll.

Frank Sinatra was on the beach in the next situation, supposedly gazing up at the stars, and Virna Lisi was to approach him, toss one of her shoes near him to announce her presence, then sit near him and prepare for a passionate session. Just before beginning, Miss Lisi made a practice toss of her shoe toward the prone figure of Sinatra sprawled on the beach. As she tossed her shoe, Sinatra called out, "Hit me in my bird and I'm going home."

Virna Lisi, who understands little English and certainly none of Sinatra's special vocabulary, looked confused, but everybody behind the camera laughed. She threw the shoe toward him. It twirled in the air, landed on his stomach.

"Well, that's about three inches too high," he announced. She again was puzzled by the laughter behind the camera.

Then Jack Donohue had them rehearse their lines, and Sinatra, still very charged from the Las Vegas trip, and anxious to get the cameras rolling, said, "Let's try one." Donohue, not certain that Sinatra and Lisi knew their lines well enough, nevertheless said okay, and an assistant with a clapboard called, "419, Take 1," and Virna Lisi approached with the shoe, tossed it at Frank lying on the beach. It fell short of his thigh, and Sinatra's right eye raised almost imperceptibly, but the crew got the message, smiled.

"What do the stars tell you tonight?" Miss Lisi said, delivering her first line, and sitting next to Sinatra on the beach.

"The stars tell me tonight I'm an idiot," Sinatra said, "a gold-plated idiot to get mixed up in this thing . . ."

"Cut," Donohue said. There were some microphone shadows on the sand, and Virna Lisi was not sitting in the proper place near Sinatra.

"419, Take 2," the clapboard man called.

Miss Lisi again approached, threw the shoe at him, this time falling short—Sinatra exhaling only slightly—and she said, "What do the stars tell you tonight?"

"The stars tell me I'm an idiot, a gold-plated idiot to get mixed up in this thing . . ." Then, according to the script, Sinatra was to continue, "Do you know what we're getting into? The minute we step on the deck of the *Queen Mary*, we've just tattooed ourselves," but Sinatra, who often improvises on lines, recited them: "Do you know what we're getting into? The minute we step on the deck of that mother's-ass ship . . ."

"No, no," Donohue interrupted, shaking his head, "I don't think that's right."

The cameras stopped, some people laughed, and Sinatra looked up from his position in the sand as if he had been unfairly interrupted.

"I don't see why that can't work . . ." he began, but Richard Conte, standing behind the camera, yelled, "It won't play in London."

Donohue pushed his hand through his thinning gray hair and said, but not really in anger, "You know, that scene was pretty good until somebody blew the line . . ."

"Yeah," agreed the cameraman, Billy Daniels, his head popping out from around the camera, "it was a pretty good piece . . ."

"Watch your language," Sinatra cut in. Then Sinatra, who has a genius for figuring out ways of not reshooting scenes, suggested a way in which the film could be used and the "mother" line could be recorded later. This met with approval. Then the cameras were rolling again, Virna Lisi was leaning toward Sinatra in the sand, and then he pulled her down close to him. The camera now moved in for a close-up of their faces, ticking away for a few long seconds, but Sinatra and Lisi did not stop kissing, they just lay together in the sand wrapped in one another's arms, and then Virna Lisi's left leg just slightly began to rise a bit, and everybody in the studio now watched in silence, not saying anything until Donohue finally called out:

"If you ever get through, let me know. I'm running out of film."

Then Miss Lisi got up, straightened out her white dress, brushed back her blond hair, and touched her lipstick, which was smeared. Sinatra got up, a little smile on his lips, and headed for his dressing room.

Passing an older man who stood near a camera, Sinatra asked, "How's your Bell & Howell?"

The older man smiled.

"It's fine, Frank."

"Good."

In his dressing room Sinatra was met by an automobile designer who had the plans for Sinatra's new custom-built model to replace the $25,000 Ghia he has been driving for the last few years. He also was awaited by his secretary, Tom Conroy, who had a bag full of fan mail, including a letter from New York's mayor John Lindsay; and by Bill Miller, Sinatra's pianist, who would rehearse some of the songs that would be recorded later in the evening for Sinatra's newest album, *Moonlight Sinatra.*

While Sinatra does not mind hamming it up a bit on a movie set, he is extremely serious about his recording sessions; as he explained to a British writer, Robin Douglas-Home: "Once you're on that record singing, it's you and you alone. If it's bad and gets you criticized, it's you who's to blame—no one else. If it's good, it's also you. With a film it's never like that; there are producers and scriptwriters, and hundreds of men in offices and the thing is taken right out of your hands. With a record, you're it . . ."

But now the days are short
I'm in the autumn of the year
And now I think of my life
As vintage wine
From fine old kegs

It no longer matters what song he is singing, or who wrote the words— they are all his words, his sentiments, they are chapters from the lyrical novel of his life.

Life is a beautiful thing
As long as I hold the string

When Frank Sinatra drives to the studio, he seems to dance out of the car across the sidewalk into the front door; then, snapping his fingers, he is standing in front of the orchestra in an intimate, airtight room, and soon he is dominating every man, every instrument, every sound wave. Some of the musicians have accompanied him for twenty-five years, have gotten old hearing him sing "You Make Me Feel So Young."

When his voice is on, as it was tonight, Sinatra is in ecstasy, the room becomes electric, there is an excitement that spreads through the orchestra and is felt in the control booth where a dozen men, Sinatra's friends, wave at him from behind the glass. One of the men is the Dodgers' pitcher Don Drysdale ("Hey, Big D," Sinatra calls out, "hey, baby!"); another is the professional golfer Bo Wininger; there are also numbers of pretty women standing in the booth behind the engineers, women who smile at Sinatra and softly move their bodies to the mellow mood of his music:

Will this be moon love
Nothing but moon love
Will you be gone when the dawn
Comes stealing through

After he is finished, the record is played back on tape, and Nancy Sinatra, who has just walked in, joins her father near the front of the orchestra to hear the playback. They listen silently, all eyes on them, the king, the princess; and when the music ends there is applause from the control booth, Nancy smiles, and her father snaps his fingers and says, kicking a foot, "Ooba-deeba-boobe-do!"

Then Sinatra calls to one of his men. "Hey, Sarge, think I can have a half a cup of coffee?"

Sarge Weiss, who had been listening to the music, slowly gets up.

"Didn't mean to wake ya, Sarge," Sinatra says, smiling.

Then Weiss brings the coffee, and Sinatra looks at it, smells it, then announces, "I thought he'd be nice to me, but it's really coffee . . ."

There are more smiles, and then the orchestra prepares for the next number. And one hour later, it is over.

The musicians put their instruments into their cases, grab their coats, and begin to file out, saying good-night to Sinatra. He knows them all by name, knows much about them personally, from their bachelor days, through their divorces, through their ups and downs, as they know him. When a French-horn player, a short Italian named Vincent DeRosa, who has played with Sinatra since the Lucky Strike "Hit Parade" days on radio, strolled by, Sinatra reached out to hold him for a second.

"Vicenzo," Sinatra said, "how's your little girl?"

"She's fine, Frank."

"Oh, she's not a little girl anymore," Sinatra corrected himself, "she's a big girl now."

"Yes, she goes to college now. USC."

"That's great."

"She's also got a little talent, I think, Frank, as a singer."

Sinatra was silent for a moment, then said, "Yes, but it's very good for her to get her education first, Vicenzo."

Vincent DeRosa nodded.

"Yes, Frank," he said, and then he said, "Well, good-night, Frank."

"Good-night, Vicenzo."

After the musicians had all gone, Sinatra left the recording room and joined his friends in the corridor. He was going to go out and do some drinking with Drysdale, Wininger, and a few other friends, but first he walked to the other end of the corridor to say good-night to Nancy, who was getting her coat and was planning to drive home in her own car.

After Sinatra had kissed her on the cheek, he hurried to join his friends at the door. But before Nancy could leave the studio, one of Sinatra's men, Al Silvani, a former prizefight manager, joined her.

"Are you ready to leave yet, Nancy?"

"Oh, thanks, Al," she said, "but I'll be all right."

"Pope's orders," Silvani said, holding his hands up, palms out.

Only after Nancy had pointed to two of her friends who would escort her home, and only after Silvani recognized them as friends, would he leave.

The rest of the month was bright and balmy. The record session had gone magnificently, the film was finished, the television shows were out of the way, and now Sinatra was in his Ghia driving out to his office to begin coordinating his latest projects. He had an engagement at the Sands, a new spy film called *The Naked Runner* to be shot in England, and a couple more albums to do in the immediate months ahead. And within a week he would be fifty years old . . .

Life is a beautiful thing
As long as I hold the string
I'd be a silly so-and-so
If I should ever let go

Frank Sinatra stopped his car. The light was red. Pedestrians passed quickly across his windshield but, as usual, one did not. It was a girl in her twenties. She remained at the curb staring at him. Through the corner of his left eye he could see her, and he knew, because it happens almost every day, that she was thinking, It looks like him, but is it?

Just before the light turned green, Sinatra turned toward her, looked directly into her eyes waiting for the reaction he knew would come. It came and he smiled. She smiled and he was gone.

PART V

The Land Grabbers

Dr. Nicholas Bartha | Upper East Side City Scape | Vincent Astor | Kermit Roosevelt | Theodore Roosevelt

Original Brownstone Steps | Dr. Paul Mantia | Brian Sugrue | 36E 62nd Links Club NYC

Hugh Gaine | John Mason | Mary Mason Jones | Mary Manon Jones House 1 E 57th St

Dr. Bartha's Brownstone | Bartha Brownstone in smokey ruins | 34 East 62nd Street rubble

CAST OF CHARACTERS IN "DR. BARTHA'S BROWNSTONE"

Dr. Bartha's Brownstone

FROM *Bartleby and Me*, 2023

I

RISING WITHIN THE CITY of New York are about one million buildings. These include skyscrapers, apartment buildings, brownstones, bungalows, department stores, shopping malls, bodegas, auto-repair shops, schools, churches, hospitals, day-care centers, and homeless shelters.

Also spread through the city's approximately 302 square miles of space are more than 19,000 vacant lots, one of which suddenly became vacant many years ago—at 34 East 62nd Street, between Madison and Park Avenues—when the unhappy owner of a brownstone at that address blew it up (with him in it) rather than sell his cherished nineteenth-century high-stoop Neo-Grecian residence in order to pay the court-ordered sum of $4 million to the woman who had divorced him three years earlier.

This man was a physician of sixty-six named Nicholas Bartha. He was a hefty, bespectacled, gray-haired six-footer of formal demeanor and a slight foreign accent. He had been born in Romania in 1940 to resourceful parents—his father Catholic, his mother half Jewish—whose home and gold-mining enterprise were confiscated first by the Nazis and later by the Soviets, prompting Dr. Bartha to vow, many decades later, after a New York judge had favored his ex-wife in the divorce case, and after a deputy sheriff had ordered him to vacate 34 East 62nd Street: "I am not going to let anybody evict me as the Communists did in Romania, in 1947." He added: "The courts in N.Y.C. are the fifth column."

In July of 2006, shortly before he set off the explosion from which he would not recover, he addressed his former wife, Cordula, in a suicide note found in his computer: "You always wanted me to sell the house and I always told you, 'I will leave this house only if I am dead.'"

"He just snapped," said his lawyer, Ira Garr, referring to Dr. Bartha's response to the sheriff's eviction notice. "It was overwhelming for him because, well, he had come to this country with nothing. For many years his parents and he had scraped together the money to buy the town house. This was his American dream, a personification of 'I'm an American, I've made it in America. I own a piece of valuable property in a valuable neighborhood. And I want to live in this place.' This home was his mistress."

He had been living alone for a few years in his fourteen-room, five-floor residence. It had arch-topped windows and an ornamental wrought-iron double door that overlooked a nine-step stone staircase that at the sidewalk level had a pair of newel posts topped by globe-shaped finials. It was the oldest building on the block, constructed in 1882. It stood between the elite golf-devotee Links Club, built in 1917, and the sixteen-story Cumberland House co-op that in 1958 had replaced a number of demolished properties, including one house that had been lived in for a while by Theodore Roosevelt when he supervised the city's police department, between 1895 and 1898.

In fact two of Roosevelt's sons, Theodore Jr. and Kermit, would become frequent visitors, between the 1920s and 1940s, of the brownstone that Dr. Bartha would own in the 1980s. Beginning in 1927, within the building's parlor floor, there existed a secret club of about two dozen prominent men that included, along with TR's sons, the banker Winthrop W. Aldrich, the philanthropist William Rhinelander Stewart, the mining expert Oliver Dwight Filley, the naturalist C. Suydam Cutting, the chief justice of the New York County Supreme Court, Frederic Kernochan, as well as others who had an interest in international affairs and, in many cases, a working experience in Allied intelligence during World War I. The leader of the group was the real-estate magnate Vincent Astor, who was very interested in espionage and, while on ocean cruises in his private yacht, had often provided the United States government with data he had collected.

Drawing upon the archival papers of Vincent Astor, Kermit Roosevelt, and a few of their friends, the history professor and author Jeffery M.

Dorwart—writing in the *Quarterly Journal of the New York State Historical Association*, in 1981—described Astor's group as an "espionage ring" made up of well-born volunteers who were detached from government funding and directives and met on a monthly basis for dinner and conversation "in a nondescript apartment at 34 E. 62nd Street in New York City, complete with an unlisted telephone and mail drop."

The members referred to the site simply as "The Room," Professor Dorwart wrote, and "when members returned from their series of world travels, they reported their observations to The Room," which resembled an intelligence office, "albeit in an informal and somewhat romanticized manner."

Professor Dorwart, who taught history at the Rutgers University campus in Camden, New Jersey, wrote that although Franklin D. Roosevelt was not on The Room's roster, "he knew every member well through Groton, Harvard and New York society, business and social connections," and Dorwart pointed out that such Room regulars as Vincent Astor, Judge Kernochan, and William Rhinelander Stewart "were with Roosevelt in Miami in February 1933 when an assassin narrowly missed killing the president-elect."

Stansfield Turner, the onetime director of the Central Intelligence Agency, mentioned in his 2005 memoir, *Burn Before Reading*, that FDR had dispatched Vincent Astor and Kermit Roosevelt into the Pacific on Astor's yacht in 1938 in the hopes of discovering data about Japanese installations. "It appears that Astor had a thrilling adventure," Turner wrote, "but did not return with any ground-breaking intelligence . . . Astor, though, was a director of the Western Union Telegraph Company, which allowed him to provide FDR with the text of sensitive telegrams and cables. And he had a number of bankers in his 'Room' who allowed him to gather intelligence on transfers of funds. Roosevelt's directions to Astor are not on record, but Astor's messages to Roosevelt suggest that FDR fully approved of these questionable activities."

Dr. Bartha knew that his brownstone had once sheltered The Room, according to his close friend and colleague Dr. Paul J. Mantia. He said that Bartha had learned about it after a writer doing research had arrived one day to explain the story and then seek permission to see the parlor floor, claiming that it had historical significance.

Although the building's rental apartments from earlier times had been converted by Bartha into a single-family residence when he moved in, he nevertheless welcomed and guided his visitor through the spacious entranceway, with its high ceiling, rotunda, antique mirrors, and marble fireplace; and he soon warmed to the idea, encouraged by his guest, that they were following in the footsteps of Astor's social register spies. Later, Bartha smilingly hinted to Dr. Mantia that the space might someday serve as a museum.

The two doctors met in 1991 while working nights in the emergency room of Bronx Lebanon Hospital. At fifty-one, Bartha was fifteen years older than Paul Mantia, a slender, blue-eyed Brooklyn-born physician with glasses and an amiable and deferential manner that contrasted with Bartha's strong personality; but the latter's uncompromisingly high medical standards and ready guidance turned Mantia into his lifelong admirer, emulator, and filial presumptive. Whenever Bartha would telephone Mantia at home and his wife answered, she would call out to her husband: "Your father's on the phone!"; and Paul Mantia, who at thirteen had lost his father to a heart attack, would immediately drop whatever he was doing and take the call.

"Bartha was a great doctor," he said, explaining that physicians in emergency rooms are forced to deal with patients they do not know, patients that sometimes can barely speak due to their injuries or other illnesses; and yet somehow, through a combination of perspicacity and perseverance, Bartha could swiftly and accurately diagnose the situation and then prepare a written report upon which other doctors, perhaps those waiting in intensive care units, knew from experience that they could rely. "Whenever Dr. Bartha finished with a patient, everything was clear, everything was done, nothing was incomplete," Mantia said. "He was scrupulously thorough."

In 2001, after being friends and medical associates for ten years, Nicholas Bartha and Paul Mantia opened a private practice on the sidewalk level at 34 East 62nd Street; and from then on, during the last five years of Bartha's life, during brief but frequent conversations between patients' daytime appointments, and during equally brief late-night dinners in hospital cafeterias, Paul Mantia came to know more and more, little by little, about this serious, privately sad, but never sentimental man who was his mentor.

II

Nicholas Bartha was born in Romania to parents of Hungarian ancestry. Although his family identified itself as Catholic, his maternal grandfather was a rabbi. As a child during World War II he remembered hiding with others in caves belonging to gold-mining families, some of them Jewish, all hoping to elude the Iron Guard's anti-Semitic, ultra-nationalist political henchmen during this period when Romania was allied with Nazi Germany.

Later, when the Nazis retreated, the Russians quickly moved into Romania to create more misery. Nicholas could recall seeing horse-drawn carriages bearing the dead bodies of those who had challenged the Communists in 1946. In the early 1950s, his father spent two years in prison on charges, never proven, that he was hoarding gold somewhere in the hills of the Carpathian Mountains not far from where he had operated his mine, before it was nationalized.

Although Nicholas managed to finish high school, he was banned from attending college as a medical student because of his father's political problems. In October of 1956, while listening to Radio Free Europe and Voice of America, he was heartened to hear of the Hungarian Revolution in Budapest; but weeks later the uprising was crushed, two hundred thousand Hungarians became refugees, and the Soviets regained their dominance.

During these years Nicholas was working in factories and operating lathe machines—cutting, sanding, grooving, and drilling with such proficiency that by 1960 he had gained enough favor to be allowed to enter medical school in the northwestern Romanian city of Cluj. But in 1963, after both parents were imprisoned for nine months, again charged with hoarding gold, Nicholas was expelled from medical school—and the frustration and despair that he then felt would remain with him forever. In fact, hours before destroying his brownstone in 2006, in the suicide note he emailed to a number of people—including his attorney, Ira Garr; his computer teacher, Alejandro Justo; his best friend, Paul Mantia; and his worst friend and ex-wife, Cordula—there were references to his feelings shaped by World War II and the Cold War years in his native Romania.

- I hope there will be a memorial built in the memory of Eastern Europeans who were betrayed at Yalta by Pres. Roosevelt . . . [who] sent back a boat with Jewish refugees to Europe to be exterminated.
- The Romanians did the right thing to Nicolae Ceausescu [a reference to the 1960s Communist leader who, together with his wife, was executed by a firing squad in 1989].
- I am not good material to be a slave. I rebel easily.

He fled Romania in March of 1964. He was then twenty-four. A friendly source within the Romanian security service had told him that his arrest was imminent, saying that because his imprisoned parents were not satisfying their jailors he would soon be held hostage. On March 15, Nicholas Bartha arrived in Israel. He remained there for nine months, living and working on a kibbutz and studying Hebrew. In December he moved on to Italy after learning that his parents, recently released from jail, had relocated in Rome, assisted by a relative who was a priest at the Vatican.

After six months in Rome, Nicholas and his parents applied for a parolee visa to enter the United States, and this was granted in late June of 1965. They settled in an apartment in Rego Park, Queens, where Nicholas found work on the assembly line of the Bulova Watch Company in Queens, producing gadgets for timing devices and receiving the minimum wage of $1.98 an hour. His mother, Ethel, got a job in a beauty salon and his father, Janos, became a cook at the Plaza Hotel in Manhattan.

A year later Nicholas quit Bulova, where his advancement was stalled due to his not being a citizen, so he found work in Queens at the Astra Tool and Instrument Manufacturing Company, soon earning $5.00 an hour and saving every penny. In his personal journal he noted that he always walked to work, never bought a car, and, though tempted, never paused on his way to work to have breakfast at International House of Pancakes on Northern Boulevard.

In 1967, he obtained a Green Card and also was accepted as a medical student at the University of Rome. During the next seven years, while attending medical school, Nicholas would return each summer to live with his parents in Rego Park and resume working as a lathe machinist at Astra Tool, receiving several raises along the way.

By this time, he had become a U.S. citizen, and in the spring of 1974 he graduated from medical school. He had also been having a year-long love affair with a young woman he had met as a fellow student at the University of Rome. Her name was Cordula Hahn.

She was a petite, soft-spoken, plain, but cheerful thirty-year-old brunette who had earned a PhD in German literature and later worked as an editorial assistant in an Italian publishing firm. She had lived in Italy for fourteen years, arriving there as a teenager in 1960 from the Netherlands with her parents.

The latter had been wartime Czechoslovakian refugees who had left their Nazi-occupied homeland in 1938 for the Netherlands, settling in the village of Bilthoven, an affluent community about twenty miles east of Amsterdam. Cordula was born there in 1942. Cordula's father was Catholic, her mother Jewish, and, even though she converted to Catholicism, she was forced to publicly identify with her Jewish background by wearing a star on her clothing during the years when the Germans ruled over the Netherlands.

In Italy, Cordula's academic and well-to-do parents found contentment and social acceptance—although, in 1973, they experienced and expressed disappointment in Cordula's choice of a boyfriend. For reasons never made clear to Nicholas, her parents disapproved of him, and, not one to forget a slight, he held a grudge against them thereafter.

In 2002, while testifying in the divorce trial, he mentioned the lack of warmth existing between him and his mother-in-law; and in his 2006 suicide note, he described with a condemning eye the paternal side of Cordula's family. He wrote that her father was a left-wing Bohemian German born of a fascist family, adding that *his* father "was a social climber who married the daughter of an attorney in Carlsbad."

But in spite of her parents' misgivings about Nicholas, she followed him from Rome to the United States in 1974 after he had completed medical school; and for the next three years, though still not married, she lived with him in the rent-free basement apartment of the multi-family home in Rego Park, Queens, that Nicholas and his parents, pooling their resources, had purchased seven years earlier, in 1967, for $63,000, just before he had first left for medical school. The Bartha trio had acquired the building with a $20,000 down payment and mortgage of $43,000.

In 1974, at Elmhurst General Hospital in Queens, Nicholas began serving a two-year internship, followed by a one-year residency, while Cordula, who spoke five languages, was employed in Manhattan within the cultural section of the consulate-general of the Netherlands, which had also arranged for her visa.

But in 1977 she became pregnant. Nicholas would have preferred an abortion, but she insisted on having a child—which would be a daughter, Serena, born seven months after the couple became married in a civil ceremony in Queens. They then moved from their basement dwelling into an upper-floor apartment in the Bartha building, contributing $200 a month toward the family fund for household maintenance, matching the monthly rent of the tenants they had replaced.

In December of 1978, Cordula had a second daughter, Johanna. As a result, Nicholas felt more pressure to increase his income, which he did by accepting extra hours at hospitals for extra pay. But he was less frequently at home, and when he was he got little sleep in the crowded space he now shared with the two children and his heavily burdened and unhappy wife. Cordula complained of loneliness and abandonment. In Nicholas's 2006 suicide note, his ten-page long farewell manifesto that he emailed to several people, he referred back to his first early years of regret in being married to Cordula:

> Cordula developed post partum depression and later became
> psychotic after she had two daughters. She refused treatment. In 1980
> I was going to divorce her [but] changed my mind because of the
> children.

In 1980 Nicholas and his parents, again pooling their resources, bought the Manhattan brownstone at 34 East 62nd Street for $395,000, with a cash down payment of $199,699. It was Nicholas who had encouraged their move to Manhattan.

His friend Dr. Paul Mantia remembered hearing him describe the thrill of standing in front of the fountain at Grand Army Plaza on 59th Street one afternoon, with the Plaza hotel behind him and the entrance to Central Park not far away, and him thinking: *This is where I want to live someday.*

III

Even before the family had moved into the brownstone it was decided that Nicholas, his wife, and their two daughters would live on the upper two floors, his parents on the floor below, and the parlor floor would be used only as a spacious entranceway, a prideful *piano nobile*. On the sidewalk level of the brownstone, where in later years Nicholas and Paul Mantia would establish their private practice, Nicholas's mother, Ethel, planned a beauty salon.

Indeed, it was a business that would succeed almost immediately—serving such clients as the wife of actor Anthony Quinn, who came in to have her hair shampooed, and the television personality Barbara Walters, who had her legs waxed. But in or around 1990, a little more than a year after Ethel's salon had opened, it was shut down following complaints in the neighborhood that the street was not zoned for such a commercial enterprise.

Although Nicholas and his parents had first bought the brownstone in 1980, it actually took them more than five years to move in. This was due not only to the time-consuming remodeling and reconstruction work—new roof, new floors, new interior staircase, new bathrooms, new third-floor tile terrace and additional wall crumbling and dusty preparatory work involved in converting a century-old brownstone into a single-family dwelling (which it had been for decades until one of the owners during the postwar years had turned it into a rental building)—but the Bartha family was also forced to buy out or wait out the ensconced tenants whose leases had not yet expired or who otherwise refused to leave.

In fact, the leaseholders of the brownstone's ten apartments hired a lawyer to try to block the Bartha family's intentions to evict them. The organizer of the tenants' group was an audacious and frequent party giver in his midfifties named Joseph Conlin, who rented both apartments on the parlor floor (a total of six rooms, two kitchens, two bathrooms) for an almost bargain-priced $850 per month, and, as the president of a concert-management company, he had grown accustomed to using his vast living space for entertaining such opera star clients as Maria Callas, Carlo Bergonzi, and Renata Tebaldi.

Even though he lived part of the time in Palm Beach, Florida—where he also led an active social life, was a noted ballroom dancer, and sometimes hosted parties on a 360-foot-long, four-mast sailing cruise ship called the *Sea Cloud*, which had originally been built in 1931 for Marjorie Merriweather Post, the General Foods heiress—he was determined not to be deprived of his modestly priced fancy address on Manhattan's Upper East Side without challenging the Bartha family in civil court.

Mr. Conlin's most supportive collaborator in opposing the Barthas was an attractive blue-eyed, caramel-blond divorcée in her early thirties named Monika Barbier, who occupied the two-and-a-half-room rear apartment on the third floor for an affordable $400 a month. Like Mr. Conlin, she became attached to, and possessive of, her residency in this exclusive neighborhood, having previously shifted frequently from place to place in less desirable areas of the city.

Her apartment at 34 East 62nd Street had a sizable living room, a separate bedroom, a full-sized kitchen, and also contained fine furniture including such costly antiques as an ornate armchair, a chest of drawers, and a rolltop desk marked as being built in 1867. Ms. Barbier had purchased these pieces from a tenant who had moved out of 3R voluntarily in early 1979: Carolyn Jo Finklehoffe, the recent widow of the producer and screenwriter Fred F. Finklehoffe, who had written a number of films starring Judy Garland and Mickey Rooney.

Ms. Barbier, divorced in 1977 from a Frenchman named Jean-Marie Barbier, had been born Monika Wegener near Berlin in 1942 but spent much of her adult life in Paris before settling in New York following the marital breakup, and she was fluent in the three languages. Currently employed as the executive assistant to the president of a German educational TV network with offices in midtown Manhattan, she had earlier worked in the city as a travel agent, a designer's assistant with a women's sportswear company, and a showroom model in the Garment Center.

She had lived alone in a cramped $200-a-month studio apartment at 307 West 29th Street that, because it was located within a noisy and dirty neighborhood, one in which she often felt unsafe at night, she believed was overpriced. And yet she also appreciated living within a section of the city that teemed daily with the energy and diversity of people walking in or out of Penn Station, or Madison Square Garden, or the popular bar at the Egyptian Gardens tavern, on 29th Street and Ninth Avenue, which featured Middle Eastern cuisine, music and belly dancing, and reminded her of her many visits to Cairo during her younger years as a Paris-based flight attendant with Trans World Airlines.

She began there in 1965, traveling to Europe, the Middle East, and the Far East. During her fifth year at TWA, while on a Boeing 707 jetliner flying from Paris to Rome, her persuasive manner helped to convince an armed hijacker to change his mind about ordering the pilot to land in Damascus, Syria, where she believed they would be treated cruelly by the airport personnel, and fly instead to Beirut, Lebanon—where, it later turned out, they were civilly received without any loss of life or property to the passengers or crew.

But if she thought that charming a hijacker had better prepared her for persuading the Bartha family to change its mind about evicting tenants, she had greatly underestimated the single-mindedness and fortitude of Dr. Bartha's sixty-two-year-old mother, Ethel.

In Romania during the 1940s, before the Nazis and then the Communists had confiscated her family's domicile and gold-mining business, Ethel Bartha had served as the firm's accountant and resident bookkeeper; and now, in January of 1980, while assuming similar responsibilities regarding the newly acquired brownstone, she also took the initiative in clearing it of its tenants in order to allow the renovation and remodeling to begin.

It required more than a year for her to achieve her goal while being challenged all the way by the opposing lawyer and the singular efforts of Monika Barbier—who, in addition to her petitioning letters to Mrs. Bartha and her strategizing with the tenants' attorney—decided to confront her lady landlord face-to-face, appearing one day without an appointment at the beauty parlor where Mrs. Bartha was then temporarily employed. It was on the ground floor of a high-rise at 209 East 56th Street. She planned to work there until she had the opportunity to open her own place within the brownstone.

When Monika Barbier arrived at the salon, Mrs. Bartha was busy with a customer; but after the customer had gone, and Monika stepped forward to introduce herself—the couple had never met—Mrs. Bartha quickly turned away, and, with arms folded, she stood rigidly still while avoiding eye contact. For many moments this would be her posture and mindset, remaining listless and remote.

Since the little contretemps in the center of the room was soon getting the attention of the other beauticians and their seated customers, and since Monika more or less realized that the immutable Mrs. Bartha was unlikely ever to negotiate, she eventually made her demure departure while writing that night in her journal:

"Naive as I was, I hoped I might convince her to let me stay in my apartment if I talked to her personally . . . But what I encountered was a stone-faced, unapproachable, well-groomed woman with a meticulously done hairdo."

Six months later, Monika was living in a sublet apartment on the fifth floor of a twenty-one-story building near 34th Street and Park Avenue. She had been vacated along with all her erstwhile 62nd Street co-defendants in the aftermath of a civil court ruling that entitled the Bartha family to be the brownstone's sole occupants.

Although the ruling brought considerable relief and satisfaction to the entire family, there was one member who had reservations about leaving Queens. This was the doctor's wife, Cordula. Transferring to Manhattan engendered fears that the increased real-estate taxes and higher costs of insurance and living might gradually overwhelm them. She had quit her job at the Dutch consulate in 1977 to raise the children, and though she would be rehired in 1988, it would be part-time. She was also upset that her husband refused to include her name on the brownstone's deed. He and his parents' names were listed on the original ownership document, but not hers despite their marriage. She complained of this often and brought it up decades later during the divorce trial, telling the judge that she always felt financially at risk because "if something happens to him" she might have problems because she was not a U.S. citizen. She preferred retaining her Dutch nationality, she explained, but still believed her name belonged on the deed even though her husband always said "he doesn't trust me and he's not going to die."

Always and entirely it was "his house," she continued, adding: "He was obsessed with the house. It was his only hobby."

And after the Bartha family had emptied the brownstone of its tenants, Nicholas appointed himself the general contractor so that he could oversee everything that the workers did in renovating the house, and he also placed a tool box and lathe in the sub-basement and began making some wooden furniture. For example, he designed and constructed his daughter's beds, built a few tables, reinforced the chairs and other furniture that had been purchased in stores, stabilized the staircase in a way that rendered it soundless to footsteps, and he put up a floor-to-ceiling bookshelf in the family's living room complete with a ladder on rollers.

He chose the paint colors for the walls, decided on where all the fixtures and furniture would be placed, and made it clear that everything was to remain where he put it, and not be moved elsewhere by anyone.

He also served as the building's custodian: He cleaned the gutters, shoveled the snow, fixed whatever was wrong with the toilets, air-conditioning, and kitchen sink. His wife helped too—she watched over the workmen while her husband was on hospital duty, and she had also contributed $45,000 of her own money toward the acquisition of the brownstone in 1980. (The money had been a gift from her father.) But again, whatever contribution she made was taken for granted, she testified, repeating: It was "his house."

In order to pay for the monthly upkeep of the house, Nicholas had to earn about $9,000 a month from his medical services, which he did by hiring himself out sometimes to two or more hospitals simultaneously—a day shift at one hospital, a night shift at another, and extra hours on weekends at yet another hospital—receiving a regular weekly salary from the one while serving at other hospitals on a per diem basis, usually at the rate of between $60 and $80 an hour. His average annual income beginning in the mid-1990s was slightly more than $200,000, but it meant that he worked six or seven days a week and spent little time at home with his wife and daughters.

"He was a workaholic," said his computer teacher, Alejandro Justo. In addition, Dr. Bartha had to spend many hours each day and night on the road because the only hospitals where he could find steady employment were in emergency rooms located beyond Manhattan, at such places as the Lutheran Medical Center in Brooklyn, the Mount Vernon Hospital in Westchester County, St. Anthony's Community Hospital in Warwick, and the Mercy Community Hospital in Port Jervis. It took him one hour and ten minutes to drive from his brownstone to Warwick, and one and a half hours to reach Port Jervis.

For nearly twelve years, until he bought a new Toyota Echo in 2000, he covered hundreds of miles each week in an old red Honda hatchback with the driver's seat shoved all the way back to accommodate his girth (he weighed about 240 pounds) and with nothing to listen to on the radio because someone had stolen it shortly after he had bought the automobile. Deciding he could live without the radio, Dr. Bartha never replaced it, nor did he even cut off the dangling four-inch-long strand of sliced wiring that hung from the dashboard's empty section where the radio had been.

One afternoon, riding in the passenger seat, his friend Dr. Mantia tried to enhance the dashboard's appearance by tucking the wires back into the opening, but Nicholas interrupted him, saying, "Don't bother. Leave it like it is."

Mantia obeyed, without seeking an explanation. Maybe Nicholas wished to exhibit the fact that his car had already paid its dues to vandalism, Mantia thought, and therefore deserved a free pass from the next potential thief. Or maybe Nicholas, whom Mantia saw as an "eccentric" foreign father motivated by old-world influences, was mentally linked somehow to severed connections or stolen objects, not the least being the Bartha family home in Romania.

Still, Dr. Bartha remained the most influential figure in Paul Mantia's life. He imitated Bartha when it came to the kind of shoes he wore, the type of car he drove, and the places he patronized when buying what he needed.

Mantia remembered complaining to Bartha about his aching feet while wearing Italian loafers on the hard floors of the Bronx Lebanon emergency room. Dr. Bartha immediately recommended that he switch to soft leather rubber-soled Rockport shoes, which would indeed eliminate the pain; Bartha also told him where to purchase them at the best price at a store near Canal Street. Aware that Dr. Bartha always favored a small-sized economy car because, in addition to the mileage, he could maneuver it more easily into narrow parking spaces, Mantia bought a snub-nosed ten-foot-long Toyota Scion IQ that, if tilted all the way upward, would barely touch a standard basketball rim. Bartha told Mantia where to buy the best vegetables at the Harlem Market, where to acquire the most reliable metal roofing material at a plant in the Bronx, and where fine-quality cabinets were available at a store in Maspeth, Queens.

Bartha cultivated friendships with many hospital workers whose backgrounds were African American, Asian, and Hispanic, and he enjoyed a special kinship with a fellow physician named Rodolfo A. Nazario, who was born in Puerto Rico and earned his medical degree in the Dominican Republic.

Dr. Nazario was a short, dapper, gray-haired, sometimes cocky but never discourteous individual who was close to Bartha's age and who shared with him a skepticism of the expressed good intentions of powerful people. Dr. Nazario's father was a prominent lawyer in Puerto Rico, and he often quoted one of his father's favorite sayings: "Law and justice do not work hand in hand. Law is law. Justice is justice. Law is supposed to protect justice. But it does not."

Nazario first met Bartha in 1989 when they began working in the emergency room of Bronx Lebanon.

"Bartha was an excellent doctor who took very good care of his patients," Nazario said. "But he was also very strict. If people were doing things right, he was very nice. But if not, he was very critical. But he would tell them directly. He would never go higher and say, 'Fire this person!' No, he would say: 'This is wrong. You do not do it that way. You do it this way,' and people usually appreciated it."

When they were not limited to dining in the hospital cafeteria, Bartha, Nazario, and sometimes their younger Italian American colleague Paul Mantia would eat outside the hospital in such places as Dominick's Italian restaurant and Patsy's Pizzeria in the Bronx; or, on the rare occasions when they were off duty together, they might meet at a Romanian restaurant in Yorkville that Bartha knew, or his favorite, Uncle George's Greek Tavern in Astoria; or, at the suggestion of their computer-fixing, Buenos Aires–born pal Alejandro Justo, at an Argentinian steak house called La Fusta, in North Bergen, New Jersey, not far from where Justo lived and worked on computers.

"Dr. Bartha loved the tripe there," said Justo, a lean, brown-eyed, dark-haired man in his midthirties who left Argentina at seventeen to attend the University of Massachusetts Amherst, where he earned a degree in electrical engineering. "He was a good eater," Justo said. "He'd eat anything."

Dr. Nazario added that this included such Latin American specialties as pernil—a slow-roasted marinated pork shoulder or leg often seasoned with dried oregano, kosher salt, ground black pepper, and a couple of garlic cloves per pound of pork. Dr. Bartha was so fond of pernil that he had

Nazario provide him with a recipe; and on the following Christmas Eve, when Bartha was on duty, he treated the medical staff to a pernil dinner that he had cooked earlier at home, then transferred to the hospital in containers placed in the back of his Honda.

While Nicholas Bartha enjoyed cooking and socializing at meals, he and Cordula rarely went out to restaurants together, and during the last four or five years of their marriage they dwelled quite separately within the same building. He spent most of his time in hospitals, where he concentrated his attentions on his patients and his friends on the staff. When he returned home late at night his wife was usually asleep and often irritated if he awakened her with such requests that she get out of bed and type a letter for him or perform some other chore. "I'm tired," she might explain, to which he would likely reply, "You're always tired," and he might not speak to her at breakfast on the following day—if, indeed, she had not already left the residence at seven in the morning for her job at the Dutch consulate. She had resumed full-time employment there in 1994 and often worked until seven at night. Sometimes she attended cultural events later in the evening at the consulate or elsewhere in Manhattan.

Cordula drove around town in her own car, a Ford Festiva, and she was on her way to becoming the consulate's office manager, earning more than $80,000 a year. Still, she relied on her husband's income for paying most of the bills, including the monthly living and household maintenance costs, the taxes, the insurance, the children's upbringing and education, and the one or two visits she took each year to visit her family in Europe, often accompanied by one or both of the daughters.

Her husband claimed that he had no time for vacations. He also had no time for entertainment. He had accompanied Cordula to the movies only twice during their long marriage, and he could not remember the names or plots of either film. He never attended the theater, the opera, the ballet, a concert, or a sporting event. Once when his computer servicer, Alejandro Justo, was rebooting a medical operations system, and at the same time keeping an eye on a televised World Cup soccer match involving his beloved Argentina, Dr. Bartha sat next to him in a state of muted bewilderment whenever Alejandro would jump to his feet and roar with approval following every successful move by one of the players from Argentina.

"He just couldn't understand my enthusiasm," Justo said.

IV

Alejandro Justo was a frequent visitor to the 34 East 62nd Street brownstone, responding to Dr. Bartha's call for help whenever the home computer froze, or the printer stalled, or when there were malfunctions with any of the many mobile devices that Bartha had purchased in bargain stores, such as his BlackBerry, PalmPilot, or Startac phone.

When Dr. Paul Mantia and Bartha opened an office together on the sidewalk level of the brownstone—where they were later joined by two periodontists, who rented space in the rear—Justo arrived to install six new computers, and he was once summoned to eradicate the work of hackers who had introduced pornography into the software.

Whenever Justo could not find a parking space within the 62nd Street neighborhood, he would park illegally in front of Bartha's brownstone and wait for the doctor to send down one of his teenaged daughters, Serena or Johanna, to sit in Justo's car while he was working in the house. Justo found both daughters to be friendly and accommodating, and, on at least one occasion, he serviced their computers as well.

But he rarely felt welcome whenever Cordula was at home. If she greeted him at all, she was curt and perfunctory. Once she walked past him near the staircase without saying a word. This happened sometime in late 1996, when she and her husband were often quarreling, although Justo remembered Cordula as being quite gracious when he first met her a year or so earlier at Dr. Nazario's birthday party in Fort Lee, New Jersey. She had been introduced by none other than her husband. It might well have been the couple's final evening out together, because shortly after the party Justo and Nazario learned from Bartha that he and Cordula were no longer on speaking terms.

Both men were very understanding, since each had undergone similar difficulties in the past. Dr. Nazario's first marriage had ended in divorce. And Alejandro Justo was a historian on the subject of broken marriages. His wealthy father, an Argentine of Italian extraction who lived in Florida, had been married six times. Alejandro's mother was his father's first and fifth wife. A few years after graduating from college, Alejandro himself married a woman from Uruguay, with whom he had a daughter. This marriage ended bitterly. Even more than a decade after the breakup his daughter refused to speak to him. Justo initially sought escape from his marital misery by getting a pilot's license and flying at great distances above the clouds in his single-engine plane. Eventually he found happiness with a woman in Costa Rica who would become his second wife.

Dr. Bartha's other close friend, the onetime happily married Paul Mantia, was equally sympathetic to his colleague's marital woes but at the same time counseled him to be more patient with Cordula and not to succumb so willingly to his unproven suspicions that she had a lover in Europe and was siphoning money from their joint account and banking it in the Netherlands. One day Mantia softly chided him: "Nick, please try not to be paranoid." Nicholas Bartha replied: "If you live in a Communist country, you have to be paranoid to survive."

In the spring of 1997, believing that Romania had long risen beyond the authoritarianism of its postwar Soviet history, Bartha's mother, Ethel, at seventy-nine, decided that she must now or never try to reclaim the family's home and other property that had been stolen during the 1940s and 1950s. Her husband, Janos, had died at eighty-three in New York in 1993, and since then Ethel had been living alone in the second-floor apartment within the brownstone.

Dr. Mantia, who had met her, remembered how hopeful she had been prior to her trip abroad; but once she arrived, he said, she encountered only bureaucratic resistance and renunciation. "She had all the documents proving that the Bartha family owned the property, but they wouldn't listen and prevented everything that she tried to do. This caused her to have a stroke during the trip, and soon she died right there in Romania. I imagine that her blood pressure went through the roof because no one would listen to her."

Prior to her death, she and her son had been listed as co-owners of the brownstone. In her will, she bequeathed half of her share to him and the other half to be divided equally between his daughters, Serena and Johanna. Cordula received a cash gift of $25,000, which she deposited, although not eagerly, in the couple's joint bank account, acceding to her husband's expressed expectations.

During these years the daughters were residing uncomfortably within their parents' frosty relationship, and the issue of how well the girls were doing (or not doing) in school and in life was crossly debated within the brownstone and later became part of the public record during the divorce trial.

Dr. Bartha always believed that his wife was coddling the girls, allowing them to do as they wished instead of meeting his demanding standards. He was appalled that Serena, who had received a superior education at the Bronx High School of Science, would later flunk out of Fordham and then enlist in a culinary school (with tattoos on both shoulders) hoping to become a chef. His younger daughter, Johanna, had gone from the Brooklyn Technical School to the Fashion Institute of Technology, with expectations of becoming a custom designer.

"I do not think that a cook and a seamstress is a very good result," he told his wife. But his daughter Serena—who testified against him in court—accused him of being verbally abusive both to her and her sister and undermining their self-confidence. "My father expected us to be the kind of people who were leaders and go-getters," she told the judge. "A lawyer or doctor or something of that nature."

When Bartha took the stand, his attorney, Ira Garr, reminded him: "Your daughter testified that you were disappointed with your daughters' academic achievements."

"I think they should have done better than I did," he replied. "I came from a village, from a political background that didn't help me on the other side. So I thought that they will go a step further than I would have done. They didn't use the opportunity . . . that's all."

His wife disagreed.

"How can you do better?" she asked Ira Garr. "My younger daughter is a fashion designer. She prepares costumes for two avant-garde performances in Brooklyn . . . Serena is excellent in her job, trying to be a chef . . . They are very artistic, fantastic children."

Although she did not testify at the trial, the sixty-year-old Ileana Cora, an elegantly dressed receptionist who ran the Bartha-Mantia office in the brownstone, had firsthand knowledge of Dr. Bartha's disruptive family life because at times it was on display in front of her and the patients in the waiting room.

Ileana Cora recalled one afternoon when Johanna, who had apparently been using one of her father's credit cards without his knowledge, objected so much to his canceling the account that she barged into the office and loudly confronted him while he was attending to a patient. He was slow to react, perhaps caught by surprise or embarrassed, but Ms. Cora stepped forward to take charge and single-handedly ushered Johanna out of the office.

Ms. Cora was probably the only woman who felt protective and admiring of Dr. Bartha at this time. She had been one of a dozen women who had applied for the receptionist's job and, according to Dr. Mantia, was hired by Bartha because she reminded him of his late mother, Ethel. Ileana Cora always arrived for work well groomed in tailored attire with a scarf around her neck (Ms. Cora's mother in Puerto Rico made dresses for prominent women), and in addition she was an excellent bookkeeper and adept with the computer.

"Dr. Bartha had a fixation about his mother," said Dr. Alan Winter, one of the two periodontists who rented space in the back. "He would say, 'This is my mother's building,' or 'This was my mother's whatever'—'my mother my mother my mother.'" Dr. Winter mentioned that a photograph of the movie star Anthony Quinn, inscribed to Bartha's mother, hung above Ms. Cora's reception desk, and stored in the basement were the hair dryers that Bartha's mother had used when her beauty salon was there.

"I'm conjecturing," Dr. Winter went on, "and I have no right to do this, but had his mother never had her business here, and had she and he not lived in this building, he might have handled it differently. [That is: instead of taking the building to his grave, he might have put it on the market.] As I said, he had this thing: 'It's my mother's. I can't give it up.'"

One of the reasons he lost the building was undoubtedly due to the courtroom strategy of Cordula's attorney, Donna Bennick, a tiny but formidable blue-eyed blonde in her midforties who uncovered and exploited some very damaging evidence during the trial, which portrayed Dr. Bartha as such an unsavory character that the judge eventually ordered him to pay $4 million to Cordula.

The evidence arose out of an argument the couple had during November of 1998; but what was meaningful about this to the attorney, Donna Bennick, was that it provided her with two scraps of paper that Dr. Bartha had torn from a small notebook sometime after the argument; and later, when his wife was not around, he covered the papers with offensive words and drawings and then placed them on the kitchen cabinet where Cordula would sooner or later surely see them. On the paper he had printed: "You

Are A Bully!" And next to these words he had drawn the Soviet symbol of the hammer and sickle, as well as a swastika.

Cordula was alone when she discovered his message, and, although confused and quite upset—especially by the swastika and its relationship to her family during the occupation—she did not immediately confront her husband to demand an explanation when he returned home. In fact, she said nothing after removing the scraps, although she did save them and kept them hidden for more than three years. Then, before the divorce trial in 2002, she gave them to her attorney, Ms. Bennick, who later introduced them in court as "Plaintiff's Exhibit One"—which became part of the evidence intending to prove that although Dr. Bartha's mother was half-Jewish, and his maternal grandfather was a rabbi, he himself bore the soul of an anti-Semite.

Shortly after the 1998 argument and her receiving the "Bully" message, Cordula left for the Netherlands for her father's birthday, as she always did in early winter. On being greeted at the airport by her sister-in-law, Cordula mentioned the swastika and indicated that her marriage was over. But during her month-long visit abroad she discovered she had cancer. On returning to New York in January of 1999 and visiting Sloan Kettering, it was confirmed: She had second-stage cancer.

As she would later testify, her husband was "shocked" by the news, and he suddenly began showing signs of concern and affection. He took time off from work on one occasion to join her for a hospital visit, and one evening he surprised her by cooking a special dinner for her. She also recalled the excitement he had shown in telling her that he had just met a physician at Harlem Hospital who had a new cancer treatment that would benefit her.

But there was no follow-up, she went on, and she was "very disappointed." Her husband also refused to participate in the couples' therapy sessions for cancer survivors at Sloan Kettering, she added. He claimed that "he had nothing to say."

In the middle of August 1999—following eight months during which time Cordula acknowledged that her husband had "supported her somewhat"—the couple had another serious argument. Later in their courtroom testimony, neither could precisely recall how the quarrel began or what it was about, other than that it concerned their daughters, Serena and Johanna. "I took the side of Serena and my wife overrode me and took the side of Johanna." That was all he remembered.

As a result of the argument, he and his wife stopped talking for many months. Each day she went to her job and he to his, no longer sharing the marital bedroom at night on the fourth floor. He moved down into the third-floor living room, sleeping on a sofa. He saw their daughters from time to time and they briefly conversed. But it was a broken household that the girls were now part of—although they did not keep this fact entirely secret from some of their friends and acquaintances.

One person with whom Serena discussed this was the sous chef at the Links Club next door. His name was Brian Sugrue. A line cook at the Russian Tea Room before coming to the Links in 1997, Sugrue was a robust, hazel-eyed son of Irish immigrants who stood five-eleven, weighed about two hundred pounds, and kept his close-cropped brown hair spiky with daubs of gel. On his left arm was a small tattoo bearing his nickname, "Grue."

He and Serena, also tattooed and with professional aspirations in the culinary world, quickly struck up a congenial relationship, usually chatting along the sidewalk near the brownstone's staircase while he was taking a smoke break from the club's kitchen. Brian Sugrue was a pack-a-day appreciator of Marlboro Lights. Sometimes, for more privacy, he and Serena would meet under the staircase near the entrance to Dr. Bartha's office. Once or twice she gave him a tour of the interior when no one else was around.

Actually, he was already on speaking terms with her father. The two men first met unintentionally one afternoon when Sugrue, puffing on a cigarette while sitting alone on one of the brownstone's lower steps, suddenly heard the sound of the steel door opening, and, turning, he saw Dr. Bartha emerging. Before the doctor could say anything, Sugrue stood up and called to him: "Oh, sorry, I'm blocking your steps."

Not responding, Dr. Bartha kept his eyes focused on his shoes as he carefully made his way down, pausing and taking a breath after each step, holding on to the rail with one hand and a canvas satchel with the other. He wore a blue blazer, a button-up shirt with no tie, and a pair of extra-large-sized khaki pants. Hatless, with his gray hair blowing slightly in the wind and his steel-rimmed glasses balanced on the thick nose of his sturdy face with its solemn expression, he then stepped heavily down onto the sidewalk, almost colliding with the younger man who stood in front of him, holding a burning cigarette down at arm's length.

"Sorry to be invading your space," Sugrue repeated.

Saying nothing, Dr. Bartha regarded him with passive curiosity for a few moments. Sugrue was wearing a baseball cap, checkered trousers, and a chef's white jacket.

"No problem," Dr. Bartha said finally. "You can sit on the steps whenever you wish." The doctor's accompanying smile surprised Sugrue, who had been told by Serena of her father's brusque disposition.

"And so goodbye," the doctor said, with a little wave. "I must be on my way." He stepped around Sugrue and headed toward his car parked at the curb nearby. And from then on, Brian Sugrue took the doctor at his word and laid claim on a daily basis to the brownstone's steps—where, from time to time, he had other brief exchanges with the doctor. It might be references to the weather, or to some minor occurrence in the neighborhood, or to how Sugrue was doing at his job.

The doctor never mentioned that his late father, Janos, had once been a kitchen worker at the Plaza hotel. But when Sugrue later learned of it, he guessed that it might have factored into the doctor's cordiality toward him.

Although Sugrue had expressed regrets to Serena after she had described her parents' troubles, he—and some of his fellow workers at the Links—had already had a close-up view of her family's difficulties, along with times when there appeared to be harmony in the household. From the fourth-floor window of the club's Auchincloss Room, where the members' meals were served during summer months, the kitchen staff would sometimes see the doctor's younger and more slender daughter, Johanna, sunbathing in her bikini on the rear terrace of the brownstone's third floor. At other times, both daughters might be seen standing together at the top of the brownstone's staircase, apparently trying to distance themselves from their parents' noisy arguments within.

One afternoon in mid-October of 2001, Brian Sugrue himself caught a glimpse from a window of Cordula and her daughters leaving the brownstone, and he did not see them return that day, nor the next, nor during all the days and weeks that followed from then on. In fact, Sugrue would never see Serena again. Of course he made no inquiries about this situation during his chance meetings on the steps with her father, nor did the doctor volunteer any information—most often passing by with little more than a nod of recognition. But Sugrue soon concluded that Dr. and Mrs. Bartha were no longer living together.

V

Dr. Bartha did not want a divorce, but his wife did, and he therefore felt obliged to hire an attorney. He selected one of the leading matrimonial lawyers in New York City, Ira Garr. In his early fifties, Mr. Garr was a refined, slender, soft-spoken individual whose green eyes were framed with wire-rimmed glasses and whose courteous manner made him popular with most of the judges and lawyers he met.

When the Manhattan federal court judge Kimba Wood needed legal representation in ending her fourteen-year marriage to the political columnist Michael Kramer, she summoned Ira Garr. He also stood by Ivana Trump in her divorce from Donald Trump, and he handled the divorce case of publisher Rupert Murdoch following his fourteen-year marriage to his third wife, Wendi Deng.

Even when he himself was a personal participant in such situations—Ira Garr's two marriages ended in divorce—he managed to proceed without any manifestations of rancor between himself and his ex-wives-to-be. The terms were promptly and fairly settled, and, in his first divorce case, his wife trusted him to draft the agreement, which was quickly approved by opposing counsel.

He was introduced to Dr. Bartha by a fellow attorney and friend of Dr. Paul Mantia, the latter experiencing much concern about his mentor's morale and need of legal guidance in the aftermath of the sudden departure of Cordula and the daughters from the brownstone. On October 17, 2001, after she and her daughters had moved briefly to Brooklyn before renting an apartment in Washington Heights, she left a note on a chest of drawers that read:

Nicholas, it is clear we cannot live together.
    More than two years of no communication seems enough. All the best for your future. Cordula.

There actually had been some communication between them during those two years but it had been mostly mean-spirited and accusatory.

In 2000, he had complained bitterly when she refused to file a joint tax return, as they had customarily done in the past. He suspected, not for the first time, that she had been routinely diverting sums of money from their savings into her own banking account registered in the Netherlands, while at the same time she was living entirely on his earnings, which he dutifully deposited into their joint checking account.

During the summer of 2001, while Cordula was on a prolonged visit to Europe (her father had died there in July), her husband took it upon himself to temporarily rent out the second-floor brownstone space that had been vacant since his mother's death four years earlier. He also removed his wife's name from the joint Chase credit-card account that she had been using. He claimed to be desperate for money, unable to keep pace with the monthly costs of operating the house and paying the taxes—plus his daughters' student loans, the cable and telephone bills, the *Times* daily delivery, the maid, and his wife's trips overseas—with his earnings as a double-shift, and sometimes triple-shift, emergency room doctor, and the small sums that he and his partner, Paul Mantia, were receiving from their newly opened office in the brownstone.

While Cordula was in Europe, he once telephoned to accuse her of being with a lover; and just prior to her trip—in June of 2001—he resumed taunting her in a manner similar to what he had done back in November of 1998, when he pasted scraps of paper to the kitchen cabinet and printed out the words: "You Are A Bully!" and illustrated them with his drawings of the hammer and sickle and a swastika.

He did not repeat "Bully" on this occasion but instead scribbled some difficult-to-read remarks on four torn-out articles from the *Times* (all printed in June of 2001) that he apparently believed reflected negatively on her homeland, the Netherlands, and by extension on herself as a citizen. On each article he also printed a swastika.

One article mentioned that a privately financed 130-foot Dutch ship, *Women on Waves*, was equipped to carry out abortions in international waters near countries where the procedure was banned, adding that the vessel's first port of call would be Dublin.

Another article reported: "Since 1996, the number of young Eastern

Europeans, Africans and Asians seeking asylum in the Netherlands has more than doubled . . . China was the largest source of immigration by minors into the Netherlands."

A third article was a follow-up to the *Women on Waves* story, amending that the Dutch abortion shop lacked proper registration and "may sail back to the Netherlands for its missing license, then return to Ireland in July, or it may sail on to South America or Africa to continue its campaign in places where the regulations on abortion are greatly restricted."

The fourth article had nothing to do with the Netherlands; instead it was a profile on President George W. Bush's fifty-four-year-old policy adviser, Stephen J. Hadley, and his efforts "to convince the Atlantic allies and Russia that scrapping the 1972 Antiballistic Missile Treaty for a shared missile defense makes sense for superpowers, former superpowers and skeptical allies."

Since Cordula herself would testify that she was bewildered by whatever his intentions were in posting these news articles with the swastikas, her husband's attorney hoped to find a way for Dr. Bartha to plausibly explain himself, although Ira Garr conceded outside the courtroom that the display of a swastika "was the death knell in Jewish New York City. If you maybe did that some place in the Midwest, they might applaud you." But still, he added: "I do not believe he was an anti-Semite. I don't believe there was any implication of trying to instill fear. It was just a foolish thing that he wrote on those notes."

Ira Garr, himself Jewish, suggested that Dr. Bartha was responding "to something he felt oppressive about the Dutch government," and on the witness stand he guided Dr. Bartha in that direction.

"Did you have any conversations with your wife concerning people of the Dutch heritage being anti-Semitic?"

"Yes," said Bartha.

"What was the substance of that conversation? What did she say to you? What did you say to her?"

"Many of them were anti-Semitic. The husband of the queen used to be a Nazi sympathizer."

"Your wife told you that?"

"Yes."

But when Garr asked Cordula to confirm this, she would only say: "I don't recall."

When he asked her to explain why her husband had written "You Are A Bully," she replied: "I don't understand what this means."

"Dr. Bartha had meant that you were using Nazi tactics toward him," Garr said. "You were bullying him." Getting no response, he continued: "Do you think Dr. Bartha is overly concerned about having enough money to live?"

"I think there would be enough money, if it would be organized differently," she said.

"Did you ever tell him to work less?"

"I live in a situation with a man that you cannot discuss anything with," she said.

Overseeing the courtroom proceedings was Joan B. Lobis, the first openly gay female judge in New York. She was a founding member of the New York City Bar Association's Committee on Lesbian, Gay, Bisexual and Transgender Rights. She would not have been Garr's first choice to preside in this case, for reasons he explained in a pretrial letter to Dr. Bartha on August 12, 2002.

Dear Dr. Bartha: I appeared in court in connection with the pre-trial conference. It is clear that we do not want Justice Lobis to try the case as she has already formed a negative opinion of you.

But even though Judge Lobis would remain, Ira Garr believed he had a strong case in supporting Dr. Bartha's view that Cordula lacked the legal grounds for a divorce in New York and thus was not entitled to an equitable distribution of marital property. New York was not a no-fault state.

"In order to get a divorce here there are limited grounds," Garr explained. "One is adultery. Dr. Bartha wasn't seeing anyone. One is abandonment. He didn't move out. One is cruelty. Under the statute, cruel treatment is defined as conduct that makes it unsafe or unfit to co-habitate. That's a very high threshold. It almost means you have to have the crap beat out of you. There are two cases: *Hessen* and *Brady*. These are the seminal cases from the court of appeals in the 1970s, and they say you're required to have a high degree of proof of cruelty."

During their nearly twenty-four-year-marriage, there had never been complaints to the police, or restraining orders, or medical evidence of physical abuse. Prior to his "Bully!" posting in November of 1998, Dr. Bartha had done nothing like that in all the years he had known Cordula, beginning in 1973. Never during their long marriage had either spouse so suffered from depression that they were unable to efficiently do their jobs or pursue their daily routines.

"Cordula took care of herself," Garr went on. "She didn't miss vacations. She went several times a year to visit her family in Europe. She moved out after seeing a lawyer, and left Dr. Bartha a letter which says: 'Nicholas, it is clear we cannot live together. More than two years of no communication seems enough. All the best for your future.' There's not a word about abuse here. There's not a word about anything other than she was upset."

On the witness stand, he asked her: "Have you ever been treated for depression?"

"No."

"Never, from 1996 to 2001?"

"No, I'm usually a very cheerful person."

"Mrs. Bartha, why didn't you seek therapy?"

"Because that is not really in our background to do that. And as often as it is used in the United States, you don't go immediately to a psychiatrist. You mostly solve your situation how you deem it fit to do."

When Dr. Bartha was on the witness stand, Garr directed his attention to Plaintiff's Exhibit One—the drawings of the hammer and sickle and swastika, and the words, "You Are A Bully," and asked: "Is there any reason why you left that for Mrs. Bartha?"

"There must have been some kind of argument, and I said, 'You are a bully.'"

"Did she ever bully you?"

"Yes."

"Did you leave that document to impart any type of ethnic slur?"

"No."

"Did you ever discuss this document with Mrs. Bartha? Did she ever mention it to you?"

"Since I don't remember why I put it there, the only thing I can tell you is that there was an argument before, where I probably suffered."

"I show you Plaintiff's Exhibit Two—a newspaper article. It says: 'Dutch ship offers abortions to make Ireland its first call.' The back says Monday, June 11, 2001 . . . and [it] looks like a swastika on the top.

"Did you leave the article for Mrs. Bartha to read?"

"Yes."

"Was there a reason why you did that?"

"Objection," interrupted Cordula's attorney, Donna Bennick.

Garr resumed with Dr. Bartha: "I'll show you Plaintiff's Exhibit Three. Something seems to be cut off . . . Is this your handwriting? Did you ever have any discussion with Mrs. Bartha about any of these three documents?"

"No."

"Did you talk to her frequently?"

"If I didn't see her frequently, I couldn't talk to her frequently."

"She testified that you regularly abused her. True?"

"No."

"Ever hit her?"

"No."

"She alleges in her complaint that you treated her like a slave."

"I don't know what it means."

"On the occasions when you did have an argument, how did it make you feel?"

"I tried to avoid these discussions because it would interfere with my work."

"So you avoided her?"

"I tried to do that."

"Was there any reason you didn't accompany [your wife and daughters] more often on trips abroad?"

"If I wouldn't have worked, we wouldn't have had the money." He added: "My mother-in-law didn't like me."

"Mrs. Bartha complains that you did things on the house and you didn't ask her about what you were doing."

"She really didn't care about the house. She always thought it should be sold because we cannot afford it. And later on, we just didn't talk."

"She wanted to sell the house?"

"All the time."

"Did you ever take an afternoon off from your shift so you could accompany your wife to the [cancer] treatment?"

"I don't know how I could have helped," Dr. Bartha answered. "I just can't tell various hospitals that I'm not going to come in. I was per diem. I didn't have a contract. I don't have medical insurance. Nothing."

None of these excuses were acceptable to Donna Bennick, Cordula's attorney, because she was convinced that Dr. Bartha was guilty of neglecting his wife when she was suffering from cancer. In addition, she believed the swastikas he had exhibited to his part-Jewish wife were tantamount to "cruel and inhuman treatment"—thereby justifying her divorce and her claim to a fifty-percent share of his property and other assets.

"Brutality need not be physical," Ms. Bennick declared, disputing Mr. Garr's argument that Cordula did not bear the marks of a beating, had never contacted the police, had not sought therapy, and had never actually asked her husband to escort her back and forth to the hospital where she was receiving treatment. She had to rely on her daughters and friends, Ms. Bennick continued, "because she knew it was pointless" to seek help from her husband.

Donna Bennick was a fiery, fair-haired, five-foot-one native of North Carolina who had practiced law in New York for twenty years, first as a public defender with the Legal Aid Society and then as a matrimonial attorney with a special interest in battered women—among whom she definitely included Cordula Bartha.

It was "psychological torture" for Cordula to remain married to an "ill-tempered bully," Ms. Bennick declared, adding that the only reason Dr. Bartha opposed the divorce was "to save himself from its financial consequences." She went on: "Surely he does not expect this Court to believe, based on the evidence, that the marriage meant anything to him emotionally . . . [It] was merely a supplemental flow of cash necessary to permit him to fulfill his dream of living in an Upper East Side town house."

While Mr. Garr had earlier suggested that Cordula falsely sought sympathy in the courtroom by depicting herself as a Nazi victim—"She was only three at the close of World War II," he said, and yet the "transcript is replete with references to her experience as a Holocaust survivor [that permitted] her to testify to events she could not possibly remember"—Donna Bennick responded: "She truthfully describes herself as an individual of Jewish origin born in the Netherlands in 1942, three years before the end of the war . . . [She] never once referred to herself as a Holocaust survivor despite the fact she was."

The arguments, the counterarguments, the appeals and postponements, the negotiations with regard to spousal maintenance, the equitable distribution of property, and other debatable matters made their way for almost four years through the slow-moving and overworked court system. When the case was finally resolved, in 2005, Cordula gained everything she could have desired.

Judge Lobis granted her a divorce from Dr. Bartha on grounds of "cruel and inhuman treatment." The judge then referred the determination of the financial issues to a judicial official known as a "special referee"—in this instance, Marilyn Dershowitz, a sister-in-law of Harvard law professor Alan Dershowitz. Following a hearing, Ms. Dershowitz concluded that while the brownstone was Dr. Bartha's "separate property"—i.e., it belonged to him—she wanted to compensate Cordula for her contributions to this long marriage, and awarded her $1.2 million.

This was unacceptable to Dr. Bartha, and, as a result, his attorney Garr attempted to get the appellate court to negate the Dershowitz judgment as well as Judge Lobis's earlier granting of the divorce. The appellate court, however, affirmed Judge Lobis's ruling while it did concede that Ms. Dershowitz's analysis was wrong; and then, in a finding that absolutely stunned and devastated Dr. Bartha, it held that the brownstone (the doctor's only significant asset) was "marital property"—meaning that its worth would be divided between the doctor and his ex-wife at a later hearing.

Mr. Garr immediately contacted Dr. Bartha to urge an appeal to the court of appeals, New York's highest court, hoping to correct what Garr believed was an example of gross injustice. At this point, however, Dr. Bartha had lost all faith in the system and stopped communicating with his attorney.

Approximately six months later, at a new hearing before Judge Lobis to decide the couple's property division—a hearing that Dr. Bartha refused to attend—Cordula was awarded the sum of $4 million. This figure was arrived at after Cordula's attorney, Donna Bennick, had introduced a real estate appraiser in court who claimed that the brownstone was worth $7 million. Cordula was therefore due $3.5 million, her half of the total. But the court also added another $500,000 in ancillary relief, such as support payments and counsel fees.

Dr. Bartha had stopped paying his lawyer after the divorce was finalized, and therefore he had no legal representation in court to denounce the settlement as excessive and demand a review by the court of appeals. Mr. Garr himself only learned about Cordula's $4 million award because Donna Bennick had telephoned to inform him.

"I tried to reach him, but he didn't answer his phone or my letter," Garr recalled. "I was no longer his lawyer, but that wasn't my big concern. My concern was you have a certain number of days from the decision to file a motion for leave to appeal to the court of appeals. That time was expiring. Then it expired. He had exhausted his remedies. He was stuck. It was like shooting fish in a barrel. Donna puts on an expert: 'What's the house worth?' 'Seven million.' She puts the wife on: 'What do you want?' 'Half.' 'Fine.' He's completely screwed. Instead of having his house, he'll get less than nothing."

Garr went on: "Assuming the house was worth $7 million, its sale would have resulted in an enormous capital gains tax liability. The Bartha family purchased the house for approximately $400,000 in the 1980s and spent more than $1 million renovating it. Therefore, the tax basis would have been $1.4 million. Assuming a 5 percent brokerage commission, which would be $350,000, together with closing costs of approximately $150,000, the gross proceeds of the sale would have netted no more than $6.5 million. However the sale would be subject to a $5.1 million capital gains tax. Assuming a blended federal and state tax rate of 30 percent, the tax liability would have been $1.5 million, leaving the net proceeds at $5 million.

"But Dr. Bartha only owned three quarters of the house," Garr continued, noting that when his mother died in 1997—she and her son had been co-owners up to that point—she willed half of her share to him and the other half to be divided between her granddaughters, Serena and Johanna. And so Dr. Bartha would receive $3.75 million and the girls would split $1.25 million.

"The court, not having been presented with Dr. Bartha's fractional interest in the residence, or the tax ramifications resulting from the sale of the residence, awarded Cordula what she requested. The bottom line is that, due to Dr. Bartha's inability to come to grips with the situation, he was now required to pay his wife $4 million when in fact he would not have realized more than $3.75 million from the sale. Simply stated, she would have received more than 100 percent of the net proceeds of the sale of his separate property residence. Apparently, it was more than he could bear."

Mr. Garr referred to Dr. Bartha's situation as "the saddest case" so far in his nearly thirty years as a lawyer. "We have clients who are, you know, self-important. Wall Street guy comes in, he makes a lot of money, thinks he's smarter than everyone, sometimes he doesn't take your advice. Okay, I don't take your advice. Okay, I understand that. Sometimes you represent a wealthy Upper East Side woman married to someone who's made hundreds of millions and they have a certain entitlement.

"But Dr. Bartha was nothing like that. There were no frills. He was casually dressed all the times I met him—nothing like many of our clients in designer clothing. He wore khaki pants, a simple shirt, maybe a jacket. I always ask litigants to wear a suit and tie to court, and women to wear a modest skirt and not too much jewelry. But when Dr. Bartha appeared before Judge Lobis, he wore no tie. A jacket, but no tie. He was not about to dress up as a sign of respect for someone in whom he had lost all confidence.

"He was a large man with a gruff exterior," Mr. Garr went on. "But I don't recall, when we spoke, his ever raising his voice, or using foul language. He was a solitary man, distant, almost unapproachable. I guess that's partly why I always called him 'Dr. Bartha,' and he called me 'Mr. Garr.' My clients usually call me 'Ira.' I'm loose with my clients, on a first-name basis, and some of them become my good friends, and we have conversations about many things: books, films, theater, and how did you like Kevin Kline in *Present Laughter*? But Dr. Bartha never talked to me about anything but his case and how the court system was destroying him—and it was. It did fail him.

"But judges make mistakes. It was a wrong decision. I think I could show it to any competent lawyer today, and they'd say: 'But that was separate property. How'd they get there?' Oh, I would have liked to continue the case, and if Dr. Bartha had gotten back to me I'd have told him: 'We're going to appeal. This is incorrect as a matter of law.' But I also would have told him that there are no guarantees. You never know if a judge is going to like you or believe you. And there's no guarantee that the appellate court that has thirty cases a week is going to give adequate time to consider your case thoroughly enough.

"But, as I said, Dr. Bartha had given up. He basically said, 'The system is rigged, it's like Communism was in Romania, and the New York judge is a lesbian who favors Cordula and Donna Bennick, and they're all against me.'"

And these sentiments accompanied Dr. Bartha to his grave a year later and were among the final thoughts found in his computer.

- Judge Lobis decided to evict me from the house for which my mother, my father and myself worked and paid. My parents and I lost out for the second time . . .
- Cordula claimed that she was tormented by the swastika in the kitchen with the New York Times articles, intended for Dutch extremists . . . I do not know why Dutch extremists have to export their social ways to another country . . . As far as Judge Lobis is concerned, the swastika was there to torment Cordula, not to show the thinking of some groups in Holland—one group exporting abortion, the other group importing minors for sexual exploitation.
- I survived Adolf and the Iron Guard . . . but this is how [Judge Lobis] treats a senior citizen who is 12.5 to 25% Jewish . . . I think I deserve a $7 million dollar crematorium/coffin. I worked for it for 65-plus years.
- Fascism=Communism=Politically Correct

VI

During the final year of his life, Dr. Bartha would continue to chat briefly with his next-door neighbor, Brian Sugrue, whenever they met on the brownstone's steps while the latter was taking a smoke break.

The already stout Dr. Bartha had gotten even heavier of late, it seemed to Sugrue, perhaps exceeding three hundred pounds. The doctor was not only moving slowly and haltingly while gripping the rail for support, but he also was climbing down the steps backward.

One dark and chilly afternoon in February 2006, Dr. Bartha paused for a moment as he reached the sidewalk, and, turning to Sugrue, he said in an offhand manner, "You know, February is the most popular months for suicides." He paused again, then asked: "Do you know why?"

"No," Sugrue replied.

"Lack of vitamin D," Bartha said. "Lack of sunshine."

Without waiting for Sugrue's response, Dr. Bartha turned away and proceeded to trudge toward his parked car. Sugrue gave no further thought to this strange exchange until five months later.

It is quite possible that Bartha had contemplated doing this in February or at some other time in the past. Dr. Paul Mantia remembered entering his office in the Bartha brownstone one morning and noticing that all of his framed medical certificates that had been hanging on the wall were now removed. After walking into Bartha's office next door to report this, the latter at first said nothing. Then, reaching slowly into his jacket pocket for his car key, he handed it to Mantia.

"They're in the back seat of my car," Bartha said.

"What's my stuff doing in the back of your car?"

"Don't ask," said Bartha.

Mantia was perplexed. He stood facing Bartha for a second, waiting for an explanation. Bartha remained straight-faced and silent, so Mantia accepted the key and headed out to scout some of Bartha's favorite parking spaces in the neighborhood. Within a block or so, finding the Toyota Echo, he retrieved the certificates and returned to the office to rehang them on the nails that were still in place. He then donned his white lab coat and sat behind his desk, waiting for the receptionist, Ileana Cora, to bring in his first patient.

In the front office sat Bartha behind his computer. He was wearing a suit and tie, as he always did here and never anywhere else. Owning a private practice within his home was for him a prideful and celebratory experience. Unlike serving in emergency rooms, here it was by appointment only.

When he first purchased lab coats for himself and Dr. Mantia, he had their names in front stitched in red scroll lettering. Normally taciturn if not obstinate, he made every effort to greet his patients with a smile after they had been initially welcomed by the gracious Ms. Cora, whose special skill was in running the office in a manner pleasing to both Dr. Bartha and everyone else, a feat made easier by the recent departure of the not-always-happy tenants who had been renting space in the back.

For almost four years, beginning in 2002, a pair of periodontists—doctors Alan Winter and Alan Pollack, accompanied by their hygienist—had rented the rear area, where they also placed a CAT scan machine for dental implants. Because of the radiation, their patients had to sit waiting in the front along with the Bartha-Mantia patients, which was okay unless there was a shortage of chairs, in which case there might be murmurings of displeasure expressed by Dr. Bartha.

He and Dr. Winter were often at odds over the air conditioner's temperature setting—even on warm days Bartha insisted that the machine function at a low-energy level—and he also wished to keep the atmosphere around the office devoid of whiffs of perfume, having lately become highly allergic to the fragrance. His patients had been forewarned about this by Ms. Cora, but apparently Dr. Winter had not gotten the word, and in any case this was one of many reasons why he and his partner moved out in June of 2006.

"He was such a difficult person," Dr. Winter said. "He was also irrational at times. Sometimes he'd say, 'I don't want you here anymore,' and finally we said, 'No, we can't deal with him anymore.' If you got to know him, I think there was some humor there . . . When Mantia was there, he'd lighten up a bit. He liked Mantia a lot . . . [but] things had to be his way."

Bartha at this point had been living alone in the brownstone for nearly three years. He lived frugally, cooking with a microwave and hot plate. The tenant who in 2001 had taken a one-year lease in his parents' apartment had departed and not been replaced.

This was probably just as well with Dr. Bartha, whose lack of enthusiasm for renters was suggested years before in a list of conditions he initially submitted to a rental agent: tenants must not have pets, not play music, not smoke indoors, never move the furniture.

Even in his solitude, the irritations of the outside world reached him. With limited success, he closed his front windows in an effort to avoid the smoke filtering in from the grill operated by the food vendors of a super-sized pushcart on 62nd Street and Madison Avenue. He also stayed away from his terrace because it overlooked the coal-burning pizza ovens that functioned in the outdoor dining area in the back of the Serafina restaurant, on East 61st Street. In his computer he wrote:

Mayor Michael Bloomberg is a customer of Serafina. Whenever he eats a pizza there it makes the breathing more difficult for people with respiratory problems. Coal burning pizza ovens are banned for decades in Rome, Italy, but restaurants in New York City cannot build them fast enough.

Directly across the street Dr. Bartha observed with displeasure the headquarters of the multi-millionaire businessman and investor Ronald Perelman. On the same block where Dr. Bartha's mother had been forced to close her beauty salon due to presumed zoning violations, Mr. Perelman oversaw his commercial empire.

The Fleming School [35 East 62nd St] was bought by Mr. Ronald Perelman and is now office space for Revlon. At 37 E. 62 another office building . . . East 62d Street is a residential and public-use zoned street. It is not for connected people.

During the late afternoon of Friday, July 7, 2006, while Dr. Bartha was on duty at Mount Vernon Hospital, in Westchester County, a messenger visited the brownstone office and placed an envelope into the hands of the receptionist, Ileana Cora. It had come from the New York City Sheriff's Office. It contained a final warning instructing Dr. Bartha to vacate his residence. Ms. Cora placed it on his desk, and later in the afternoon she left the office for the weekend.

At this time Dr. Mantia was vacationing in Canada with his wife and nine-year-old son. He was due back to the office at nine o'clock on the following Monday morning, July 10. But less than an hour before he was scheduled to arrive, Dr. Bartha was preoccupied with polluting his place with infusions of gas diverted from a pipe in the basement.

Dr. Bartha was alone in the building when it eventually blew up. To prevent anyone from entering, he had positioned himself at the front window of the reception room of his street-level office. Having already read the sheriff's eviction notice set for Monday, he had contacted Ms. Cora and told her to cancel all of that day's appointments. There was no doubt that he planned to die early that morning in the brownstone that he valued more than his life.

Before dawn he had already emailed to a select circle of individuals, including his ex-wife and Dr. Mantia, a suicide note that he had typed earlier on his computer. It was doubtful that anyone had yet read it as he now stood waiting behind his office window facing the street, having no idea how long it would take for the gas to circulate throughout the interior and achieve its desired result.

Shortly before six thirty, the flow of gas was strong enough to have penetrated the basement and main floor of the building next door, the Links Club, a five-story classical brick structure at 36 East 62nd Street to the east of Bartha's property. The first person to smell gas there was a forty-year-old waiter and native of Ecuador named Jack Vergara, who was on duty to help with the breakfast that would be served to the members beginning at seven thirty

That morning at five thirty, Mr. Vergara had taken the train at the Grant Avenue station near his residence in Maspeth, Queens, and, after exiting about forty minutes later, at 59th Street and Fifth Avenue, he briskly walked three blocks uptown, turned right to cross Madison Avenue, and soon was passing under the green canvas marquee of the sixteen-story Cumberland House co-op, at 30 East 62nd Street.

A few steps ahead, extending across the sidewalk, was a nine-foot-wide driveway that led down to the Cumberland's underground garage; the driveway also bordered the western wall of Bartha's brownstone. As Jack Vergara passed the brownstone and advanced toward the Links Club's entrance, he might well have been among the last of those whom the doctor would see alive.

After entering the vestibule of the Links Club shortly before six thirty and exchanging greetings with the night watchman, Vergara said: "I smell gas." As the watchman shook his head, indicating that he smelled nothing, Vergara hastened past him toward the staircase, and he did not stop climbing until he had reached the kitchen on the fourth floor.

He suspected that someone on the staff had carelessly left the oven on all night; and even though this turned out not to be true, he immediately saw to it that Con Ed was notified and that an urgent request was made for inspectors to come as soon as possible.

Within twenty minutes two inspectors had arrived, along with members of the fire department; but although the Con Ed inspectors' handheld detectors registered the presence of gas they were unable to trace its source. Meanwhile, as the kitchen workers were downstairs setting the tables in the third-floor dining room, Vergara told the cook: "We're serving only a cold breakfast today"—meaning that while there would be juice, fruit, cereal, pastry, and hot coffee from the electric machine, there would be no ham, eggs, pancakes, or anything else that was usually prepared on a gas range.

The cook objected: "The chef will be angry when he shows up and sees we don't have the bacon ready," adding that the members would probably also be unhappy with the restricted menu.

"Cold breakfast today," Vergara repeated. He was only a waiter, but in the absence of his boss, the general manager, he was imposing his status as a senior employee. He had been working at the Links Club for nearly twenty years. And so on this morning a cold breakfast was served, and, with him having explained the circumstances to each arriving member, there were no complaints.

It was during the latter part of the breakfast service, somewhere close to eight thirty, that Vergara first heard what he later described as a "big tremor," a loud noise accompanied by a quivering sensation within his body that he initially attributed to the collision of a dump truck outside, or maybe a major malfunctioning of its engine.

However, as he peered down from the fourth-floor window, overlooking the street in front of the club, he saw nothing amiss. Then, after going down to the third floor and looking through one of the side windows, he saw huge clouds of dark dust rising into the atmosphere and then realized, much to his amazement, that the familiar sight of the old brownstone next door, a fixture since 1881, was no longer there.

Crumbled by the explosion, dismantled in size and shape, it was now vaporized within a mirage of cascading chaos, a fiery heap of fallen floors that steadily covered the sidewalk and curb with an ascending mound of charred and splintered remnants of Dr. Bartha's household fixtures and personal possessions—his burned books, his crushed computers, tiny pieces of his shoes, clothing, spectacles, his bed, microwave, eating utensils, bathroom tiles, carpeting, banisters, door knobs, chunks of the half-intact stone stoop, the battered newel posts, the contorted and loosely hinged French-style iron front door. Christopher Gray of the *Times* wrote that it "staggers like a drunk at the top of the stairway." There were also spread throughout the remains of a few of Dr. Bartha's late mother's hair dryers that he had stored in the back of his office as a memento from when she briefly ran a beauty parlor there; and mixed in with the piles of splintered wood there might have been chips from the wainscoting of The Room in which Vincent Astor had once presided over his elite group of espionage aficionados; and amid the several glass-less window frames flung here and there was the one behind which Dr. Bartha had been standing just prior to his body being buried in the avalanche of wreckage.

Completely unaware of the occurring calamity—which would in time injure ten firefighters as well and five passersby, and damage the interiors of thirteen apartments within the eighty-four-unit Cumberland House—was a sixty-six-year-old financier and Links member named Eric Gleacher, who, as Bartha's house was tumbling down, was fully concentrated on soaping himself under a shower in one of the club's guest rooms on the fourth floor. He was staying at the Links because he was getting a divorce and his new apartment was not yet ready for occupancy.

"The two rooms at the Links which are used for overnight stays have not been renovated for many years," Mr. Gleacher said. "They seem right out of the 1960s, reflecting old school WASP gentility. The good news is the water pressure is great. I'm slow when I shower in the morning because I shave in the shower. While I was shaving I heard a loud noise. It sounded like a backfire in a furnace system. I was not concerned, as the noise was not particularly loud and I had been trained in explosive ordnance while on active duty with the Second Marine Division at Camp Lejeune, North Carolina, in the 1960s. I know what a blast from C-4 plastic sounds like, as well as dynamite and hand grenades. This noise wasn't close to the percussion from those explosives.

"I looked out the bathroom window and saw a white unmarked panel truck parked in the middle of 62nd St. directly in front of Ronald Perelman's office. I could see debris in the street and a woman lying on the sidewalk almost at the northeast corner of Madison and 62nd.

"My first reaction was that someone tried to blow up Perelman's office," he said, referring to the frequently litigious and four-times-divorced mogul. "Ronald was a client and a friend with whom I had worked many times. I helped him acquire Revlon in the 1980s and I knew him well. He was thoroughly honest and very tough in his business dealings and, as a result, had made enemies who would like nothing more than to see him taken down a peg or two.

"I dressed quickly and opened the door to my room. Much to my surprise right outside stood a New York firefighter, ax in hand. He told me I'd better hustle down the stairs and vacate the premises. There was broken glass in the front door area and the attendant on duty was cut and bleeding. I picked my way around the debris and crossed to the north side of 62nd Street.

"I immediately saw the flames, which looked ferocious and climbed all the way up the west firewall of the Links, licking the roof after reaching the top. I immediately assumed that the Links building was surely going to be consumed by the flames. Within seconds of that, though, the NYFD demonstrated what it could do. They turned on the hoses and washed the side of the building with water, and the flames fell away with remarkable speed."

Ronald Perelman was not in his office at the time of the incident, but his secretary, seated at her desk, said that the impact knocked her off her chair and the explosive sounds she heard reminded her of when she had lived in Israel and worked for twelve years in the office of the mayor of Tel Aviv. Another employee in Perelman's office, a native of California named Ashley Stackowski, thought at first that she was in the middle of an earthquake. She did manage to take a photo of the destruction across the street, and it ended up on the front page of the next day's edition of the *New York Daily News* (with a photo credit).

Throughout the afternoon, television-news helicopters hovered over the neighborhood, and although the White House announced that the blast did not appear to be the work of terrorists, Dr. Bartha's notoriety quickly spread around the world via television and the print media. Some headline writers began referring to him as "Dr. Boom." At Camp Fallujah, west of Baghdad, a Marine Corps lieutenant named Renny McPherson saw images of the burning brownstone on the television set in his mess hall, and he immediately emailed his parents, who resided on 62nd and Park Avenue—his father was also a member of the Links—and asked: "Are you all right?"

When Dr. Paul Mantia arrived at the building surrounded by the police vehicles and fire trucks, he was relieved to learn that Ms. Cora had not been inside. Although his office was buried under piles of rubble, he had fortunately made duplicate copies of his medical certificates and kept them at home. Also at home, on his computer, was a message that Dr. Bartha had emailed him an hour or two before the explosion.

Paul, I am sorry, but I cannot put up with this situation any more. I am glad you passed your board recertification. It made my decision easier. I hope your vacation was good.

Dr. Bartha had also emailed two final messages to his ex-wife. In one he wrote:

Cordula, my further staying alive does not make any sense.
Work as described above is pure punishment. I will lose my office. Getting sick even in the most optimal conditions is not easy. Alone is certainly terrible.

The other message to Cordula read:

When you read these lines your life will change forever. You deserve it. You will be transformed from a gold digger to an ash and rubbish digger.

After the firemen had recovered Dr. Bartha's unconscious body from the rubble, it was rushed to the emergency room of the New York–Presbyterian Hospital. Almost half of his body was charred with second- or third-degree burns, and during his time in the hospital he was unable to speak or communicate in any way. He died there on July 15, five days after he arrived. On the following week, he was buried in Queens.

"It was a small ceremony for family-only," said the funeral director, meaning that none of Dr. Bartha's close friends (such as doctors Mantia and Nazario, and the computer-servicing Alex Justo) were invited. Cordula did appear at the grave site to lay some white baby roses on the tombstone, but the gravedigger at the Cypress Hills Cemetery told the *New York Daily News*: "There weren't any tears. Nobody was really busted-up . . . A preacher read a short prayer from the Bible, then we lowered the white coffin."

Following the funeral, Cordula (who later bought an apartment outside Manhattan) refused to grant interviews to the press, and this would be her policy from then on. Anyone trying to contact her or her daughters would be contacted by Cordula's law firm and warned about invading the family's privacy.

Although Dr. Bartha did not leave a will, his daughters (who already owned 25 percent of the property) inherited his remaining 75 percent share, along with his posthumous debts—which included his $5,000 hospital bill, a $5,730 tab for the Queens funeral, and the sum of $230,000 that New York City was charging for scooping up the mounds of debris and carting it away in dump trucks.

There were also several lawsuits levied against the estate to cover the costs of property damage to the neighboring Links Club and the Cumberland House co-op, as well as the personal injuries to such individuals as twenty-two-year-old Jennifer Panicali, who underwent surgery after being sprayed with shards of glass and bits of splintered wood while walking along 62nd Street toward her summer job with the Parks Department.

Even Dr. Bartha's office manager, Ileana Cora, filed suit against the estate, seeking unspecified damages for "persistent emotional and mental distress" as a result of approaching the building ("key in hand") as it came crashing down. She suffered no physical injury, her attorney explained, but she was offended by the fact that the doctor had earlier instructed her to cancel all appointments for Monday, July 10, "but never warned her not to come to work."

Among the other publicized complaints at this time was an Associated Press story in which one of Cordula Hahn's attorneys, Polly Passonneau, objected to her client being referred to in the doctor's suicide note as a "gold digger," a description that was widely repeated in the media, including in the *New York Times*. The late Dr. Bartha had objected to a fair settlement, Ms. Passonneau said, and thus he suffered "the consequences of his own behavior."

There was also an article in the *New York Post* referring to a wrongful-death suit brought by the son and daughter of a woman who had died due to an overdose of medication issued at the Lutheran Medical Center in 1999. Dr. Bartha was mentioned as one of the physicians involved in the case, which resulted in the hospital agreeing to a settlement fee of $50,000

each to the son and daughter, although the article added that "it was unclear who administered the overdose."

The largest debt owed by the estate was the one that Dr. Bartha chose
to not live long enough to deal with: the court-ordered sum of $4 million
awarded to Cordula in the divorce case.

No money would be available, of course, until someone bought the
lot—which was, in fact, worth more because Dr. Bartha had transformed
his brownstone into two thousand square feet of empty space. If he had
not made it disappear, his revered 124-year-old building might have sold
for around $7 million, which was the sum quoted by the real-estate ap-
praiser who evaluated it during the divorce trial.

But, as an empty lot, it represented a much more lucrative opportunity for real-estate developers—and indeed, within a year of the explosion,
a creative and ambitious developer bought the lot for $8.3 million from
Serena Bartha, the executor of the estate, and then announced plans to
erect on the spot a luxurious five-story town house that would go on the
market within a few years at an asking price of between $30 million and
$40 million.

The new buyer of 34 East 62nd Street was a glamorous forty-year-old
Russian-born blonde named Janna Bullock.

VII

Leaving behind an unhappy marriage and a young daughter in the temporary care of her mother in Saint Petersburg, Ms. Bullock—whose married name in Russia had been Boulakh—arrived in New York in the early
1990s and settled in the Brighton Beach section of Brooklyn, known for its
sizable Russian-speaking population. There she held various jobs, among
them working as a clerk in a delicatessen and serving as a nanny in the
household of an Orthodox Jewish gentleman who had seven children and
a wife in a mental institution.

Later Ms. Bullock was hired as a paralegal and translator by immigration lawyers in Brooklyn whose clients included a Russian economist who
in 2000 would become the finance director of the region surrounding

Moscow. He was a tall, suave, and bespectacled individual in his late thirties named Alexei Kuznetsov.

When Mr. Kuznetsov was scheduled to visit New York on business, Ms. Bullock's employers dispatched her to the JFK airport to greet him. This greeting eventually led to an affair, and then to a marriage, and within a few years she was running a real-estate enterprise in Moscow and New York whose value she estimated at one point to be as much as $2 billion.

In an article in the *New York Times* it was reported that her fortunes began to rise in 2003 after she began "acquiring vast tracts of land around Moscow to develop malls and homes, and eventually forming a partnership managed by her husband's department."

Beginning in 2005, the *Times* continued, she began buying, renovating, and reselling Upper East Side town houses at great profits—"flipping," it's called in the trade; a good example was the town house at 54 East 64th Street that had been the home of the *New York Observer* weekly newspaper. Ms. Bullock bought the building for $9.5 million in January of 2005 and, after spending about $1 million on renovations, resold it eleven months later for $18.75 million.

Shortly after buying the Bartha property Ms. Bullock said that the new town house would have a limestone and glass exterior, a geothermal heating and cooling system, a bamboo-fenced roof garden, a courtyard waterfall, and a 12 × 36–foot swimming pool in the basement. There would be an all-glass elevator, four bedrooms, a formal dining room, a butler's pantry, a wine cave, and a spa with a steam room.

Perhaps seeking favor with the Links Club next door, Ms. Bullock's architect designed the town house with a recessed entranceway that was likewise set back five feet from the property line, and the fifth-floor roof of the new building would be built back eight feet so as not to intrude upon the mansard roof of the Links.

Still, the Links president, John S. Pyne, was unimpressed after seeing the plans for Ms. Bullock's property. "The design plans bear no resemblance to any building on our block," he said, emphasizing that this area existed within the Upper East Side Historic District—and its membership promptly supported him with a 27–5 vote declaring that the design was "not in keeping" with the neighborhood. Mr. Pyne also pointed out that the town house's facade of limestone was "jarring and overbearing" when placed next to the redbrick construction of the ninety-one-year-old Links Club.

Nevertheless, Ms. Bullock continued to promote the desirability of her proposed town house by displaying illustrations of it in Sotheby's real-estate brochure and touting it in the many newspaper interviews that came her way. When a *Times* reporter asked her if buying the old Bartha property presented her with an "image problem," she replied, "I don't want any association with the tragedy. To me it is an empty lot." Her broker added: "Memories are short. Things happen every day in New York. How often can you get a brand new house built on the Upper East Side?"

One day, stepping out of her chauffeured limousine at the curb of 34 East 62nd Street, Ms. Bullock strolled past a chain-linked fence and entered the empty lot wearing a white Valentino suit, a pearl necklace, and black kitten-heeled shoes. Then she sat down, legs crossed and hands clasped, in an Arne Jacobsen Egg chair that her press agent had delivered there sometime earlier, balancing its four-star aluminum base in the dirt not far from the west wall of the Links Club. Surrounded by low-growing weeds, pebbled rocks, spreads of sand, and a few droppings and footprints of rodents, Ms. Bullock posed for a *New York Times* photographer and spoke to a reporter while reclining comfortably within the 20 × 100–foot lot that had not been bathed in natural light for more than one hundred years.

The *Times* article described her as looking like "a socialite or an heiress," adding that she was "ubiquitous on the social circuit." In a later article in the same paper: "There she is at the American Ballet Theatre spring gala wearing elegant black; at a Society of Memorial Sloan Kettering Cancer Center spring ball in white; at a Guggenheim gala in blue."

Reference was also made to her once having ridden a motorcycle from Saint Petersburg to Moscow accompanied by the actors Jeremy Irons and Dennis Hopper, as well as Thomas Kerns, formerly the director of the Solomon R. Guggenheim Foundation. She herself had joined the Guggenheim board in 2007, and it was reported that she possessed a distinguished selection of contemporary paintings and sculptures as well as some late-nineteenth-century Russian artwork. In addition to her homes and holdings in Russia, Manhattan, and the Hamptons, she was said to own an apartment in Paris, property in Switzerland, a yacht, and a hotel in the ski resort of Courchevel in the French Alps.

But her good life went into decline after Alexei Kuznetsov, with whom she had her second daughter, resigned from his government position in 2008 and soon sought refuge in France. Meanwhile an associate of his in Russia was targeted in what the press called a contract murder attempt.

In time, not only Kuznetsov but also his wife were accused in Russia of corruption—partnering in fraud, money laundering, and embezzling at least $26 million in Russian state funds. Ms. Bullock's real-estate development company in Russia was seized and taken over by a rival group that included Vladimir Putin's former judo coach. Her extradition was sought, but U.S. authorities ignored the request, since Janna Bullock was an American citizen.

Her husband claimed publicly that he was forced to resign from his post in Moscow because government investigators had discovered irregularities in his wife's real-estate activities, but she characterized all the charges levied against her as politically motivated and symptomatic of Russian envy. "Just because I did better than others," she told the *Times*, "somebody had the appetite to take it all away from me."

In February of 2012, in a vacant East 80s Beaux-Arts mansion that she was trying to sell, she held a photo exhibition featuring two dozen images of influential Russians—individuals in business, the law, the media, or politics, including Mr. Putin—and the captions accompanying these images were rarely flattering.

"Ms. Bullock has taken on nothing less than the Russian power elite," wrote a reviewer from the *Times*, while the critic from *Art in America* magazine added: "The content in the exhibition reads more like propaganda than fact, and it's likewise difficult to tell whether or not Bullock has been wronged, or if she was complicit in her own downfall."

She was now separated from Alexei Kuznetsov, and would soon become divorced, and she was also struggling to arrange financing for the new town house she planned to build on Dr. Bartha's old property. Her architect blamed the delay on the recession and real-estate slowdown, explaining: "The economic downturn coincided almost immediately with the plans to begin. I think every time there's a glimmer of hope in the economy, it turns the other way." Still, he went on, regarding Janna Bullock's desire to erect a luxury residence at 34 East 62nd Street, her "enthusiasm had not waned a bit."

He said this in 2012. But even a year later, and more than two years after that, the empty lot remained empty and unoccupied—except for the growing weeds, the scampering rats and mice, and occasionally some homeless men who slipped through an opening in the chain-link fence and huddled at night within the northwest corner of the slot. Many neighbors on the block were displeased by this unseemly sight, and few people were more so than the normally patient and mild-mannered sixty-two-year-old James Savage, a bespectacled and studious-looking wealth-management consultant and a Cumberland House board member whose fourth-floor apartment windows, located along the eastern wall of the sixteen-story co-op, overlooked the junkyard.

Before working in finance at such places as Merrill Lynch, James Savage had spent decades within the New York City Police Department, beginning as a cop in 1966 and six years later as a plainclothesman who went on to serve as a trustee of the Patrolmen's Benevolent Association's pension fund, until 1999.

He and his wife, Marie, a blue-eyed brunette whom he married in their native Brooklyn in 1969, had been vacationing in Montauk when Dr. Bartha blew up his brownstone on July 10, 2006. After being flabbergasted by the news, the couple quickly drove back to the Cumberland House, where they soon joined crowds of other residents on the sidewalk behind a police barricade while firefighters were packing up their gear and dump trucks were hauling away piles of crushed masonry and soot.

After receiving word from engineers that the building was safe for occupancy, the residents filed through the lobby and took elevators up to examine their living quarters.

"Our front door was bashed in by firefighters," James Savage recalled. "Our walls and ceilings were black from the smoke. Paint was peeling from the heat of the fire. Our windows were gone, frames and all. It was the weirdest feeling. It was as though we were stepping outdoors. There was broken glass all over. Our apartment was a mess. We found signs of blood in a bathroom. Apparently a fireman cut himself somehow. A box of Band-Aids was left in the sink. We managed to retrieve all the valuables we could carry. But our pet cat, Rosie, was nowhere to be found."

After learning that their cat had been taken by one of the first responders to a nearby animal shelter, James and Marie Savage collected their cat carrier and the $120 in cash that they had left for the cat sitter, and appeared at the front desk of the shelter—only to learn that their cat had just died while being tested for rabies.

"My wife was devastated at the news," he said. "So was I. We returned to our car with the empty carrier. We realized we were homeless. So we decided to drive back to Montauk where we had left our things. This was the first day of our vacation and worst day of our lives."

In the weeks and months that followed, the couple bunked with relatives, stayed at the New York Athletic Club, and then moved into an East Side condominium. In January of 2007, six months after the explosion, their apartment at the Cumberland House was finally ready for them to reoccupy, and as they did so they were greeted by an unexpected bonus. Since Dr. Bartha's building next door was no longer blocking their view, their fourth-floor residence was now bathed in extra light. This was true not only of their space but as well for many of their neighbors.

A half block south, overlooking the rear of Suzanne Newman's millinery, at 27 East 61st Street, streams of supplementary light now reflected upon the heads of people making hats, and next door at the Serafina restaurant the diners on the patio had an unobstructed view of Ronald Perelman's mansion located on the north side of 62nd Street. The horizon was also extended northward for the rear-window beauticians at the Minardi hair salon, at 29 East 61st Street, where Marie Savage was a regular customer.

Having sudden access to the two thousand square feet of added viewing space in New York undoubtedly represented a rare and valuable amenity, but no one could put a price tag on it in an ever-expanding and soaring city in which it so often seemed that the light was on loan.

Marie Savage first became aware of this sometime during 2015, when she began noticing that the clarity of the sky beyond her dining-room window was now being penetrated by a narrow climbing shaft of darkness. Her dining room was in the rear of the apartment, and it was where she sat in the afternoons doing portrait painting, a talent cultivated years earlier at the Art Students League.

The source of the rising shadow was actually five blocks south of the Cumberland House. It was a newly constructed ninety-six-floor condominium at 432 Park Avenue, between 56th and 57th Streets. At a height of

1,396 feet, it boasted of being the city's tallest residential property, but not far away, at 217 West 57th Street, there was under development the 1,550-foot residential-commercial property called the Central Park Tower. It would be second in height only to One World Trade Center, which, thanks to its spire, reaches 1,776 feet. (The Empire State Building, completed in 1931, is 1,250 feet.)

"This is a golden age of construction in American metropolitan areas," said Gian Luca Clementi, a New York University associate professor of economics at the Stern School of Business. He went on to say, being quoted in an article published in the *Times*: "The U.S. is still less urbanized than similar countries, so if anything, we will probably see more and more construction."

The New York City Department of Buildings issued an all-time-high 179,320 construction permits throughout the five boroughs in 2017. Earth-moving equipment, towering cranes, and workmen wearing hard hats and tool belts (and speaking different languages) seemed to be everywhere, spread throughout thousands of construction sites and actively engaged within the wall-anchored scaffolding and safety nets of new buildings as well as old ones in need of repair or restoration.

One old building whose outer walls were now lined with multi-decked scaffolding housed the central offices of the New York City Department of Buildings, at 280 Broadway. It's a seven-story mid-nineteenth-century structure that started as a department store, then served for decades as the headquarters of the *New York Sun*, and finally was acquired by the city in 1966. (The defunct newspaper's slogan: "*The Sun* . . . It Shines for All.")

But in 2016 the building's marble facade had deteriorated so badly that it was deemed unsafe for pedestrians, and so a multi-year restoration project was begun. In addition to the suspended scaffolds and safety netting, the site was further protected from falling debris by a sidewalk shed made of steel pipes, beams, planks, and a heavy-duty plywood parapet.

Scaffolding was reportedly a billion-dollar industry in New York. There were more than sixty firms specializing in the trade, and the buildings department had issued permits for the creation of approximately 7,700 sheds. If they were all lined up in tandem, about 280 miles of New York sidewalk would be shaded by sheds. The parapet of every shed was painted green because in 2013 Mayor Michael Bloomberg decided that the color coordinated well with the city's Million Trees initiative and its huge investment in parks.

In the early winter of 2017, Marie and James Savage were horrified by the sight of a green plywood shed going up on the sidewalk next door to their Cumberland House apartment, and also by the presence of several workmen wearing hard hats and toting tool boxes and planks of heavy timber and steel beams into the empty lot at 34 East 62nd Street.

Unbeknownst to the Savage couple, and nearly everyone else in the neighborhood, the lot had been privately sold a year or more before by the Russian-born contessa of flippers, Janna Bullock, to a real-estate development firm in Rye, New York, named the Woodbine Company.

One of the two owning partners at Woodbine, Theodore Muftic, was a stocky, fifty-year-old, blue-eyed blond native of Colorado who graduated from the Harvard Business School in 1992 and was the son of a doctor born in Montenegro. Theodore's politically active mother, born in Oklahoma, ran unsuccessfully for mayor of Denver in 1979.

The other partner at Woodbine was Francis Plummer Jenkins III, a preppy, dark-haired six-footer in his midforties who was born in Tarrytown, New York, and, after graduating from Suffolk University in downtown Boston, earned a master's degree in business at the University of London.

It was Jenkins who did most of the face-to-face negotiating with Janna Bullock, and, having been reminded by his attorney of her compatibility with Russian oligarchs, he attended each meeting wearing a fine suit and tie accessorized with an Hermés scarf and a borrowed Rolex watch.

He ultimately convinced Ms. Bullock in 2015 to sell her lot for $11.95 million. Even though she had acquired it for $8.3 million in 2007 from the Bartha estate, she was not happy with her profit margin on this occasion. But her resources and bargaining power had been greatly diminished in recent years following the financial scandal in Moscow involving her and her imprisoned ex-husband, so she assented to Woodbine's final offer—which marked at least the twelfth time since the late 1880s that this small but desirable residential space had been transferred from one owner to another.

VIII

The building was first advertised for sale during the spring of 1882, for the price of $10,000, by a pair of developers named Joseph B. Wray and Samuel P. Bussell. At the same time they built two adjoining, and similarly priced, neo-Grecian brownstones at 32 East 62nd and 30 East 62nd. These two would be demolished in the late 1950s to make room for the sixteen-story Cumberland House co-op, which took its address as 30 East 62nd.

The first buyer and occupant of the brownstone at 34 East 62nd, according to a *Times* article written by the architectural historian Christopher Gray, was a fruit dealer named Charles H. Parsons, who in 1884 moved and remained there for nearly ten years before selling it in 1893 for $45,000 to John S. Robinson. The latter might have then experienced bad times; in any case he unloaded the property a year later for $28,500 to one Peter Brady, who just as quickly passed it on for the same price to another buyer, Oliver J. Wells.

Wells was a Brooklyn attorney and later a municipal court judge who had served as an infantryman in the Union army during the Civil War. He and his heirs maintained ownership of 34 East 62nd Street for more than half a century, finally selling it in 1952 for $60,000 to a real-estate investor in Yonkers, New York, named Vatcho Kobouroff, a native of Bulgaria.

Between 1952 and 1975, Kobouroff retained control of the building, but, like Oliver J. Wells and his inheritors previously, he sometimes leased out the brownstone to prominent New Yorkers who were often mentioned in the press and it was sometimes noted that they resided at 34 East 62nd Street.

Among the early leaseholders during the Wells family ownership period was a gallant six-foot-three individual named Walter Gibbs Murphy, an importer of champagne and son of Thomas Murphy, a state senator who had been collector of the Port of New York during the presidency of Ulysses S. Grant. The younger Murphy was an avid golfer, sailor, and competitive marksman who won some amateur shooting matches, including one in Monte Carlo. He never married, which might explain why in later years access to the 34 East 62nd address fell into the hands of his relatives within the Aldcroft and O'Kane families.

In 1930, for example, there was an article in the *Times* society section that began:

> Mr. and Mrs. Richard Bradbury Aldcroft of 34 E. Sixty-second Street have announced the engagement of their daughter, Miss Elena de Rivas Aldcroft, to Robert Fisher Kohler, son of Mrs. Emil Kohler of 830 Park Avenue and New Canaan, and the late Mr. Kohler.
>
> Miss Aldcroft is a member of an old New York family and of the well-known de Rivas family of Cordoba and Madrid, Spain. She is the great-granddaughter of the late Thomas Murphy, a leading merchant in New York in the '60s, who was a close friend of Presidents Lincoln and Grant.

In 1939 there was another *Times* piece on its social page with this lede:

> Mr. and Mrs. Thomas Francis O'Kane of 34 East Sixty-second Street entertained with a buffet supper last night in their home for their daughter, Miss Helen Marcia O'Kane, who will leave soon to make her home in Hartford, Conn., while studying there for a year.

During this time Vincent Astor and members of The Room were meeting periodically in the unmarked suite on the parlor floor, while another distinguished tenant renting in the building was the industrialist Siegfried Bechhold, whose company during World War II developed the Sherman tank.

It is unclear when exactly the brownstone was converted from primarily a one-family dwelling into a tenant building, but it is known that sometime after Vatcho Kobouroff took over from Oliver Wells's inheritors in the early 1950s he created ten half-floor apartments, between the basement and top floor, and provided each with a bathroom, a refrigerator, and a gas range.

One of his tenants who fell behind in her $225 monthly rent during the late 1950s was named Virginia McManus, although elsewhere she identified herself as Karen Moore and other names as well; and Vatcho Kobouroff, believing she was a prostitute, one day padlocked her door and took her to court, complaining to the judge of the ongoing "influx of masculinity" leading up to her third-floor apartment.

The judge ruled that he had a right to the unpaid rent but admonished him for locking her out and denying her access to her clothing and other personal property. "One must not take the law into his own hands," said the judge. "Justice is indispensable in our society and its importance is so great that even those who are evil-minded are entitled to its consideration."

In 1976, Vatcho Kobouroff sold 34 East 62nd Street for $256,000 to Joerg Klebe, a Berlin-born, New York–based investment banker in his midthirties who, among other enterprises, headed the Agate Realty Corporation at 666 Fifth Avenue. Mr. Klebe kept the brownstone for four years and then sold it to the Bartha family in 1980 for $395,000.

A little more than a quarter of a century later, Nicholas Bartha would turn the building into the empty lot that Janna Bullock would sell in 2015 for $11.95 million to Woodbine's Theodore Muftic and Francis Jenkins, who in turn would hire an architect to transform the lot into a luxury town house that it was hoped would sell for at least $30 million.

The architect was named Henry Jessup. He was a lean and agile man in his midsixties who stood six-two, wore tortoise-shell glasses, cut his gray hair short, and kept his comments brief and to the point.

As a young teenager growing up in Greenwich, Connecticut, Jessup earned summer money by painting the houses of people who lived in the area, and sometimes they would ask him to fix the garage door, or replace the shutters, or even enlarge upon parts of their property.

Learning as he went along to master the skills of carpentry and also bring mature shape and form to his childhood preoccupations—"I was always drawing and painting as a kid"—Jessup started a construction company at nineteen that would pay for his four-year tuition at Brown University, in Providence, Rhode Island, which he entered in 1970 as an art-history major.

He had not yet decided to become an architect. In fact he then had "no clue" about his future goals, and so, after high school and before entering college, he spent eight months touring Europe on a bright yellow motorcycle he bought in London for about $600 and rode as far as Turkey and Greece. His parents had separated when he was thirteen, and while he divided his upbringing agreeably between the two of them, he mainly measured himself against his own expectations.

After leaving Europe he brought his motorcycle home and used it for a while before going off to Providence, where, in addition to his studies, he played for Brown University's highly touted soccer team well enough to be offered, after graduation in 1974, a contract in the American Soccer League with the Rhode Island Oceaneers.

Although he never made more than $500 per game, and far less in later years as a semi-pro player, Henry Jessup continued playing soccer until he was forty years old—by which time he was the father of two daughters and married to a woman from New Jersey who, when he met her, was an aspiring screenwriter and young actress with a few small parts in Hollywood films and a dancing role in the 1977 Broadway revival of *The King and I*. They were married in 1984.

Jessup's decision to attend the Columbia Graduate School of Architecture, from which he graduated in 1978, had been encouraged by a satisfied customer (an architect) for whom he had once built a house in Katonah, New York. In the nearly forty years since then, most recently working out of his office on lower Broadway, he completed approximately five hundred projects of varying sizes in different parts of the world. These countries include Australia, Costa Rica, Spain, Germany, and France—although a vast majority of his clients lived in New York City or the Tri-State area.

One exception was a financier from Vermont named Peter Novello, who, in 2008, paid $10.8 million to buy a century-old six-story brick town house at 21 Beekman Place and later hired Jessup to gut the place and redo the thirteen-room building from top to bottom. Jessup designed a new entrance with a covered portico of limestone and, on the roof, a pergola and garden. In between, he ordered new windows, new staircases, three fireplaces, and additional brickwork and cornices, and he excavated the cellar to add a gym.

But just as the construction work on the town house was completed and the furniture was about to be installed, the owner suddenly died in Vermont at the age of fifty-six. "I was shocked and saddened that he was never able to enjoy the place and convince his family in Vermont to spend more time with him in it," said Henry Jessup.

A year later, in July of 2013, Novello's heirs sold the property for $34.35

million to the state of Qatar—a record price at $4,754 per square foot for a twenty-foot-wide Manhattan town house. One result of this transaction was the increased awareness by New York developers of Jessup's work, and soon he was hired by Woodbine's Francis Jenkins and Theodore Muftic to redesign a town house for them on East 64th Street, and then another on East 66th Street, and finally to design an entirely new building on the lot at 34 East 62nd Street.

"He's the best architect I've ever run into," said Muftic. "Most architects are trying to strive for that picture that makes it into *Architectural Digest*. He just wants to do a building that all the tradesmen respect him for and that the client likes."

"There are a lot of architects that push the boundaries of the art world," Jessup said, "but I'm not one of them. I'm a professional. I do what I say I'm going to do. Because I have this construction background, I can be pretty realistic about everything that's going on. And so apparently that combination of factors has served me well, in terms of clientele."

Among the first things he did after accepting the 62nd Street commission from Woodbine Company was to produce a computer-generated image of the town house he had in mind and then estimate what it would cost to complete and what type of client might buy it.

Since current rules mandated that no building on the block could have apartments, Jessup and the two owners believed that their proposed five-story town house might serve as an ambassadorial residence or consulate, or it might appeal to some of the wealthy people from China, Russia, or such Middle Eastern countries as Qatar, the latter of which, in addition to Novello's property, had earlier spent many millions buying other town houses in Manhattan.

"The original design was geared toward this," Jessup said. He explained that in the preliminary sketches of the town house he had designated a "separate staff entrance, which is essential for many Middle Eastern cultures," and also "large entertainment rooms with possible staff services in the cellar to accommodate a possible sale to a diplomat." Finally, he and the owners contemplated changing the address from 34 East 62nd to 32 East 62nd because 4 is not considered to be a fortuitous number in Chinese culture.

But in subsequent months, as the shifting real-estate market in New York produced fewer international buyers—partly due to less favorable tax regulations and tighter capital controls in China, Russia, and elsewhere—Jessup reshaped his floor plans in anticipation of American ownership. For example, he eliminated a service-staff-oriented entertainment room that might be needed by a diplomat and replaced it with a large family kitchen.

Regarding the exterior, Jessup foresaw his imagined town house in the Beaux-Arts tradition, but he also wanted it to blend in somehow with the two very divergent architectural styles that stood on each side of his work-in-progress. On the west side was the sixteen-story, brick-built 1950s Cumberland House co-op, with its lower two floors fronted by Indiana limestone. On the east side was the century-old neo-Georgian Links Club, which in Jessup's opinion was a "really beautiful representation of a historic building."

To the degree possible, Jessup believed that he could bridge the gap with the Cumberland House by designing a brick wall on the western side of his town house that overlooked the co-op's nine-foot-wide parking ramp and matched the Cumberland's bordering brick wall. He also hoped that his future town house's facade of creamy white French limestone might co-mingle with the Cumberland's Indiana limestone base, although Jessup conceded that the co-op's type of limestone somewhat resembled concrete.

He had an easier time imagining compatibility with the Links Club, believing he "paid homage" to it in providing his town house with a mansard roof and copper dormers that were harmonious with the historic building next door. He also sketched into his design such visual enhancements as cornices, dentils, and quoins, which are decorative edges of masonry giving the impression of clamping the corners of a wall.

Still, he insisted, he was designing his town house for "today," as a building that at first glance might pass for historic but was actually "historically derivative," meaning that while the scale, proportions, and materials were based on classical precedent he remained ever mindful of being contemporary—demonstrating this, for example, by fronting his building with black casement windows made of steel instead of wood, as "a nod toward a more modern feel that we want the place to have."

There were a total of fourteen openings on the front of his proposed town house—two on the fifth floor, which would be a pair of arched copper dormers set into a mansard roof of black Vermont slate tiles; three windows on the fourth floor, all capped by a cornice with dentils below; three windows on the third, where the shape of the building was designed to have a bow front; and on the second floor would be three French doors opening onto a Juliet balcony with a metal railing.

On the first floor he had two windows overlooking the sidewalk, and to the east of the windows would be the town house's simple modern entrance, a plain door painted black, flanked by metal railings, and reached after climbing two very low-set, squatter-discouraging granite steps, the lower step being two inches high, and the upper step three inches high—a major example of downsizing when compared with the almost eight-inch-high, nine-step staircase that Dr. Bartha took with him in 2006 and thus deprived the Links's sous chef of a favorite hangout during smoke breaks.

When an architect such as Henry Jessup designs a building that he calls "historically derivative," he is conceding at the same time the existence of historical works worthy of derivation, and, in his opinion, many of these were created in New York between the late 1880s and early 1900s—a period he calls "the heyday of town house construction."

Among the architects from that era that he said inspired him were Charles A. Platt, who in 1907 designed Sara Delano Roosevelt's town house in the East 60s; Chester Holmes Aldrich and William Adams Delano, who in 1916 created the Colony Club for women on Park Avenue and 62nd Street; and Mott B. Schmidt, who in 1927 built Vincent Astor's town house on 80th Street between Park and Lexington Avenues.

Astor lived there when he was a frequent visitor to 34 East 62nd Street to meet with his fellow members of The Room, and Jessup decided to cover the front of his coming town house with the same type of limestone that Astor's architect had used nearly a century earlier, which Jessup himself associated with prestigious projects. It is called French roche.

Jessup would obtain his supply from a quarry in Euville, a village in northeastern France, and then have it delivered, tons of it, to a factory in Corgoloin, located in the eastern center of the country, where, during the next five or six weeks, it would be cut to size and be shaped to conform to what Jessup had specified earlier in his construction drawings. His illustrations would show not only what his finished town house would look like, but they would also single out and enumerate each and every chunk of limestone that would cover the front of the building. This would amount to a total of approximately three hundred pieces, ranging from a cornice that might weigh six hundred pounds to a smaller example of decorative molding, or a windowsill, or roof coping, which might weigh anywhere from fifty to a hundred and fifty pounds.

After all the chunks of limestone had been fabricated to Jessup's speci- fications at the factory in Corgoloin, they would be wrapped, packed, and dispatched to the port city of Le Havre, where, in twenty-foot shipping containers, they would be forwarded to a terminal in Staten Island. The cargo would spend about fourteen days at sea. Trucks in Staten Island would later take it into Manhattan.

Each of the three hundred pieces would be marked by a number (which would match the number appearing on Jessup's construction drawing) in order to help the workmen on 62nd Street, who would later receive the limestone and then carefully hoist it, hang it, bracket it, and finally inter- lock it into a predetermined numbered space within the building's steel- fronted frame. For the workers it would be like doing a jigsaw puzzle with variously shaped cuts of limestone.

The cost of all the limestone would be nearly $500,000. The amount of money needed to complete the entire building—material plus labor— would be $5 million. The target date to finish the town house was expected to be no later than January of 2018.

But before any of this would happen—indeed, even before Jessup would place his order for the limestone in France—he had to devote full attention to the tedious and time-consuming task of getting permits from the Department of Buildings for everything he hoped to accomplish. This also required, among other things, sharing his construction drawings with the Upper East Side Historical Society and the Landmarks Preservation Commission in the hope of obtaining their support. At the same time, he was hiring expeditors, engineers, and lawyers to help him deal with the DOB's many zoning and structural restrictions as well as concerns with the plumbing, electricity, sprinklers, and the new elevator that Jessup had designed for use between the basement and the fifth floor. (The old brown- stone did not have an elevator.)

Jessup would also have to assure the Department of Transportation that the sidewalk and street would be repaired if damaged during the construc- tion period, and have to consult with the Department of Environmental Protection regarding water connections to the street, and the Department of Energy prior to any drilling of the structural pilings, and the fire department to confirm that there would always be roof access in case of an emergency.

IX

A typical pedestrian strolling past a construction site has little idea that such architects as Jessup must spend nearly a year on paperwork before the first nail of a carpenter is hammered into timber or the first gallon of concrete is funneled out of a mixer truck. And it is probably also true that few individuals pause and ponder that perhaps under each newly poured concrete foundation there exists a potter's field of terminated and conventional people who long ago inhabited and enjoyed that space as part of a farm, or a park, or a friendly front porch, or a room with a view, or some other desired and desirable place now landmarked in obscurity.

The Greeks built on top of Phoenician temples, and the Romans built on top of Greek temples, and thus it has gone thereafter. And now in New York, Henry Jessup was planning to put a town house on top of Dr. Bartha's ashes.

Yes, it is true that everywhere there are street signs, plaques, statues, buildings, and transportation hubs reminding us of the departed noteworthy: Carnegie Hall, LaGuardia Airport, George Washington slept here, Herman Melville lived here, Dylan Thomas drank here, John Lennon died here.

But in order for the name of an ordinary person long deceased to remain in print within the voluminous and dusty files of the Department of Records and Information Services, at 31 Chambers Street, it would help if that person had once owned a piece of property.

This might partly explain why owning property mattered so much to Dr. Bartha. World wars arise from disputes about land and property rights, and indeed Bartha's family in Romania had lost its land to the Nazis and Communists during the 1940s. And perhaps it is why, much later in New York, Dr. Bartha went to war with his ex-wife, and her attorney, and the judge, and finally with the sheriff who nevertheless prevailed, and exiled him into homelessness, and left him an all but forgotten New Yorker whose name endures in the city files and press records today principally because he once owned property that he believed was worth dying for.

The plot of Bartha's story is about a 20 × 100–foot plot of land not much longer, and not as wide, as a tennis court. But while it is merely a dot on the map of the Upper East Side it is, no less than anywhere else, marked by the footprints and fingerprints of multitudes of diverse people who, since colonial times, have represented the will and ways of the larger city along with its propensity for differences and disagreements over politics and property.

It is likely, if not entirely verifiable, that the soil under Bartha's brownstone was acquired at some point during the late 1700s by a prominent Irish-born New York printer, publisher, and property owner who, during the Revolutionary War, became controversial because he had shifted his allegiance from the American rebels to the occupying British. His name was Hugh Gaine.

Born into a struggling family near Belfast around 1726, he was employed as a printer's apprentice in Ireland for about five years; and then, in 1745, at the age of eighteen or nineteen, he arrived alone in New York. He soon found work as a journeyman printer for James Parker, the official printer of New York province, who, years before in Philadelphia, had been mentored and befriended by Benjamin Franklin.

Hugh Gaine continued under Parker for seven years—from 1745 to 1752—and then went on his own, eventually becoming very successful in downtown Manhattan not only as a printer of official documents and decrees, and as the publisher of a weekly newspaper called the *New-York Mercury*, but also as the proprietor of a bookshop and general store named the Bible and Crown.

In his three-story building in Hanover Square, south of Wall Street, he filled his shelves and bins with an eclectic selection of merchandise: books of all kinds (Bibles of the Old and New Testament, Fielding's *Tom Jones*, Montesquieu's *Letters*, Pope's translation of Homer's *Iliad*, John Pomfret's poetry, school texts, and a variety of almanacs, printed in both English and Dutch); household and office supplies (stationery, quills, ink, wafers for sealing letters, lead pencils, corkscrews, playing cards); and, in addition, other sundries that might appeal to customers' needs and desires (doeskin gloves, cotton hose, boots, shoes, London razors and straps, scissors for trimming horses, body powder, patent medicines, musical instruments such as fiddles, flutes, and fifes, lottery tickets, and also tickets to concerts and the theater).

He was a great supporter of (and, indeed, paid the rent for) the John Street Theatre, which, until it closed in 1798, after thirty-one years, was the first and only theater in Manhattan. Among those performing on stage was Eliza Arnold, mother of Edgar Allan Poe.

Gaine was also involved with civic and philanthropic organizations, including the New York Society Library and New York Hospital, and he served as a vestryman at Trinity Church. There, in 1759, when he was about thirty-two, he celebrated his marriage, which eventually produced three children.

While he joined other New York newspaper publishers and printers in expressing displeasure at some of Britain's policies, such as the Stamp Act in 1765, he nevertheless advocated restraint and continuing respect for the Mother Country, and this no doubt encouraged his British hosts in 1768 to appoint him the public printer of the province of New York, a profitable position from which James Parker had retired years earlier.

Gaine now began enlarging his property holdings, purchasing a six-thousand-acre farm in upstate New York in 1770, and a few years later he bought into a partnership at a paper mill in Long Island. But when the war began in 1775, and with British troops about to attack New York, Gaine sought to save himself and his family from danger by moving to the rebel-controlled city of Newark.

He had remarried in 1769 following the death of his first wife, and, having fathered two more children in addition to the earlier three, he had a large household for which to care, and he was eager to be on the winning side of the war. It was his belief that the Continental Army would inevitably drive out the British.

Meanwhile his property in Hanover Square—his Bible and Crown shop, his living quarters, and his printing operation—had been taken over by the invading British, and their pressmen assumed control over his newspaper (which he had recently renamed the *New-York Gazette and Weekly Mercury*) and turned it into a decidedly pro-Tory publication.

A year later, with the British occupation ongoing and the Continental Army in retreat, the Tory authorities promised amnesty to anyone pledging loyalty, and one individual who agreed to these conditions was

Hugh Gaine. His decision was of course widely ridiculed within the rebel community of Newark and elsewhere; Anthony R. Fellow, in his book *American Media History*, describes Gaine as a "Turncoat Editor" and "Opportunistic Irishman."

While he was welcomed back to New York by the British, he no longer held the title of public printer; and although he regained control of his property and his newspaper, his editorial authority was scrutinized from above. This did not appear to offend him. He remained a loyalist throughout the eight-year period of British occupation, although not an outspoken one, ever wary of being singled out by zealots formerly associated with the Sons of Liberty, a secret society of patriots who during the revolutionary era had chapters spread throughout the thirteen colonies.

When the British were finally driven out in 1783 and New York City came under rebel control, Gaine removed the word "Crown" from his store sign, ceased publishing his newspaper, and counted his blessings. He still had his book business and considerable wealth to his name, however tarnished, and during the remaining two decades of his life he took full advantage of the opportunities available to people with money in a new city consisting of vast amounts of uncultivated land that required investors and developers.

When he arrived as a teenager in 1745, Manhattan's population was about eleven thousand, with nearly everyone clustered downtown close to the water and traveling along some of the same cobblestone roads that the Dutch first laid down a century earlier. In 1783, though the population had risen to about thirty thousand, the downtown area remained an overcrowded center of civilization, while for miles to the north—from about 23rd Street and Madison Square all the way up to Harlem—it was largely an abandoned wasteland sharing its unaffiliated space with swamps and underdeveloped forests and outspread farms with grazing animals and horse-cart lanes over what had been Indian trails.

This was not yet taxable territory, but if it were made more habitable and marketable, it would potentially be a major source of income for a city needing funds for public improvements. Somewhere between the 1780s and 1800, Hugh Gaine bought some land for investment purposes in what today would be part of the Upper East Side, including 62nd Street between Park and Madison Avenues.

But in those days buying land uptown was an ambiguous undertaking.

Despite the best efforts of surveyors and their chain bearers, boundaries were often imprecise. Draftsmen made errors. The details shown on maps might be misrepresentative or merely approximate.

Also, being a surveyor then was a difficult and dangerous occupation. Casimir Goerck—who in 1785 personally charted great stretches of territory at the behest of municipal authorities and was producing an amended city layout a decade or so later—died in 1798, while in his midforties, due to yellow fever prompted by the numerous mosquito bites he received while working long hours in the filthy and swampy places he was exploring.

At the same time the city was selling lots ranging in size from about five to nine acres that were four-sided but not rectangular. Consequently, the uneven edges sometimes led to disputes over property lines between adjacent owners.

According to public records, something like this occurred in the East 60s in the early 1800s between Hugh Gaine and one of his nearest neighbors—the scion of a prominent merchant family, Peter P. Van Zandt. During the Revolutionary War, Van Zandt had served as a major in the Continental Army. He was active in the Dutch Church and a member of the state assembly. He had inherited his land from his father, Johannes Van Zandt, who in earlier times had become engaged in quarrels with other property owners elsewhere and been cited by authorities for frequently encroaching upon and laying claim to property that he did not own.

But before Hugh Gaine's dispute with the younger Van Zandt had been resolved, Gaine died in 1807, at the age of eighty-one. In 1812 Peter Van Zandt himself was dead, at eighty-two—but not before his land, and that of every property owner in the city, had been dealt with in ways that finally brought added clarity and preciseness to the often misunderstood map of Manhattan.

What produced this change was the so-called Commissioners' Plan of 1811, which was based upon some of Casimir Goerck's earlier recommendations and, in the words of the architectural historian Christopher Gray, writing in the *Times*, "made Manhattan's streets an iron fist of right angles."

Except for allowing Broadway to continue pursuing a wavering course through the center of town, most of the rest of the city's sprawling space was sculpted into a rectilinear grid system consisting of twelve parallel north-south avenues that were crisscrossed by 155 east-west side streets. The grid of 1811 covered two thousand blocks and extended for about eleven thousand acres, and the commissioners believed that it would encourage the creation of smaller and smaller lots, which in turn would make them easier to buy, to sell, and to build upon.

In time this would happen, but decades would pass before real-estate developers would emerge to lure homeowners to this area. Just because the streets were clearly marked on a drawing board did not mean that people would live on them, especially since there was still no reliable means of public transportation between uptown and downtown. It was a rare case when someone who bought property actually intended to put a house on it. More often than not they were speculators, people like Hugh Gaine, who bought the inexpensive acreage and held on to it in the hope that someday a rising economy and population would increase its value.

One notable exception was William Stephens Smith, who—married to one of President John Adams's three daughters—was planning to construct a mansion on the land he had purchased in 1795 near the East River and 61st Street. But then he and a few of his acquaintances were indicted by a federal grand jury for violating the recently introduced Neutrality Act. They had supported a movement attempting to free Venezuela from Spain. Although Smith was found not guilty, he never built his mansion, and after selling his property in 1796, he moved upstate to Lebanon, New York. However, a carriage house that he did build on 61st Street still exists and is currently in use as a museum.

In 1816, more than nine years after the death of Hugh Gaine, his heirs sold his still undeveloped property to an individual named Henry Dickers, who held on to it for a while before releasing it to the city, which in 1823 sold it along with other land to an elite merchant downtown on Pearl Street named John Mason.

After making his fortune in dry goods and leading a bond drive in support of the U.S. government during the War of 1812, John Mason began buying land with a voracious appetite almost rivaling that of his older contemporary John Jacob Astor. While the latter was consuming much of the Lower East Side and Times Square area, while spending little to improve it, Mason was directing his interests farther uptown and would eventually own much of the space that extended from 53rd Street to 64th Street, between Fifth and Park Avenues. Some of what he bought had formerly belonged not only to Hugh Gaine but to Peter P. Van Zandt and other landholders as well.

At this time John Mason was also a shareholder of the Chemical Bank, on the way to becoming its president, and in 1832 he began operating the New York and Harlem Railroad along a route that would later be paved over by parts of Park Avenue. Whenever the boilers of his trains malfunctioned, he would summon his horses.

Mason did not live long enough to see the Upper East Side transformed into a luxurious district favored by the socially prominent and wealthy. He died in 1839, at sixty-six. But one of his daughters would eventually build a white marble chateau on the northeast corner of Fifth Avenue and 57th Street and become one of the area's trendsetters.

She was Mary Mason Jones. Her husband, Isaac Jones, whom she married in 1818, succeeded her father as president of the Chemical Bank. At the time of the marriage the couple resided in a house she owned downtown on Chambers Street. Before that she and her two sisters owned three adjoining houses on lower Broadway at Waverly Place, in which the entertainment rooms could be opened to one another whenever it was necessary to accommodate a ball or other large social event.

A grand-niece of Mary Mason Jones was the novelist Edith Wharton, who, as a young girl in the mid-1870s and early 1880s, would sometimes visit her rich aunt, who moved into the chateau at 1 East 57th Street in 1870. Mary was then a widow in her sixties. Her husband had died in 1854, leaving her with three children. According to 1880 census data, Mary was living in the chateau with one of her daughters, a granddaughter, and five servants. The residence was alluded to in Edith Wharton's 1920 novel, *The Age of Innocence*, in which a character based on Mary appears as Mrs. Manson Mingott:

> It was her habit to sit in the window of her sitting room on the ground floor, as if watching calmly for life and fashion to flow northward to her solitary door . . . She was sure that presently the quarries, the wooden greenhouses in ragged gardens, the rocks from which goats surveyed the scene, would vanish before the advance of residences as stately as her own.

In actual fact, Mary was never an isolated socialite in downtrodden territory waiting for life and fashion to flow northward to her solitary door; indeed, even before she decided to build her chateau in 1867, several among her set had already moved uptown, and her younger sister Rebecca was on the way.

Rebecca's inheritance of two city blocks consisted of 55th and 56th Streets between Fifth and Park Avenues, and, assisted by an architect, she designed a row of eight Fifth Avenue houses made of olive-colored Ohio limestone that she hoped would suggest the spirit of a Parisian boulevard. After claiming a corner house for herself, she would sell or rent the other houses to friends and acquaintances, following a plan that Mary had already initiated a year earlier on Fifth Avenue between 57th and 58th Streets.

Mary's development, called Marble Row, was more architecturally elaborate than her sister's, conforming in style to Mary's own corner house, at 1 East 57th, which was inspired by the palace of Fontainebleau. But both sisters were financially successful with their real-estate investments, and among Mary's distinguished tenants (at 745 Fifth) was Dr. Charles Leale, who as a surgeon in earlier years had worked at a hospital in Washington and was the first to arrive at Ford's Theatre to treat the fatally shot President Lincoln.

With the completion of Central Park in 1873, property values north of 59th Street rose by 200 percent. Between the 1860s and 1880s, largely due to the influx of immigrants, the population of Manhattan increased from about 800,000 to more than 1 million. Many immigrants were among the 20,000 Central Park workers who provided the muscle that moved the rocks and shoveled the soil and planted more 270,000 shrubs and trees.

In earlier years, the city evicted several hundred squatters and shanty dwellers who had long lived along the rocky outcroppings, with their pigs and goats, within areas extending from 59th up to 106th Street, bounded by Fifth and Eighth Avenues. In its final stages of completion, Central Park's northern edge touched upon 110th Street and its scope encompassed 843 acres. During winter afternoons visitors skated on lakes that had once been the site of swamps.

In 1881, Mary Mason Jones died in her chateau at the age of ninety. Her sister Rebecca had died two years earlier. Within twenty years, as their heirs and other wealthy people moved further uptown, 57th Street and its surroundings were taken over by commercial enterprises. Replacing the demolished residential properties of the Mason sisters and other patrician families were office buildings, banks, department stores, fashionable shops, and boutiques.

During Mary's heyday as a social doyenne, her corner neighbors on 57th Street and Fifth were named Whitney, Huntington, and Vanderbilt. More than a century later, her former home address of 1 East 57th Street would be inherited by Louis Vuitton's luxury goods store. The other three Fifth Avenue corners would be occupied by jewelers—Van Cleef & Arpels on the northwest corner, Bulgari on the southwest corner, and Tiffany on the southeast corner—and south of Tiffany would stand Trump Tower.

X

The year of Mary's death marked the start of the construction of what a century later would become Dr. Bartha's brownstone. The 20 × 100–foot plot at 34 East 62nd Street, together with other land, had been bought in 1881 by the partnership of Samuel D. Bussell and Joseph B. Wray. The construction crew they hired to erect the five-story residence did not fortify it with a concrete foundation, possibly because the land then was rocky enough to support the structure. Or maybe in that time and place the regulators were not very particular, especially since the city was so supportive and needy of uptown development.

In any case, in the spring of 2016, after the architect Henry Jessup requested and reviewed a soil report, he decided that the lot at 34 East 62nd Street was too sandy and incapable of holding a house in place, and therefore it was essential to provide a concrete foundation.

The first step was to remove all the sandy soil, litter, and other refuse from the lot, requiring several men with shovels and another man sitting in the cab of a hydraulic digging machine, which has a claw that can hoist about a hundred and fifty pounds of material in a single scoop. The material the men and machine collected was deposited into a dumpster twenty-two feet long and parked at the curb; when full, this was replaced by an empty dumpster delivered on a flatbed truck.

Two weeks were spent loading the dumpsters with waste. What was deposited weighed in total about nine hundred thousand pounds. With this gone, there was a hole in the ground eighteen feet deep. Eventually this low-level and flattened terrain would become the locale of a basement and cellar, but first it was invaded by a pile driver that, one at a time, pierced and buried twenty-four concrete piles into the surface. Each pile was thirty feet long and nearly a foot thick.

The twenty-four piles were spaced four to a row across the width of one end of the lot, and it took six rows of four to cover the entire lot. Then the lot was overmounted with pile caps, which are hollow troughs placed horizontally over the rows of pilings and filled with steel rods for reinforcement before being inundated by tons of flowing concrete delivered by two trucks.

One was a mixer truck, the other a pump truck. The latter had a boom supporting a rubber hose that could reach across the sidewalk and extend over the entire lot and, in a day's time, pour seventy-two thousand pounds of concrete down upon it—but not before the workmen had snaked through some drainpipes and conduits for electrical wiring.

After the poured concrete was spread out and smoothed over by men using long-handled tools, and after it was dry enough to be walked upon, which might take more than a week, the foundation floor was finished.

Next came cement-block walls enclosing the four sides of the basement and cellar floors, and, after steel beams were installed horizontally to support the basement's roof, that roof helped to prop up the tier above—and, in turn, lend support to the four higher levels to follow within this five-story steel and wooden structure on the rise. The upward thrust was covered on the outside by scaffolding, and erected on the sidewalk was a green plywood shed to protect pedestrians from falling tools and debris.

Since the town house was being built within a historic district, regulations demanded that its owners—in this case, the Woodbine Company partnership of Theodore Muftic and Francis Jenkins III—provide and pay for the distribution of vibration monitors to be affixed to the exterior of all buildings within ninety feet of the construction site.

These monitors, not much larger than smoke detectors, carried wireless sensors that were intended to warn neighboring owners if their buildings were being adversely affected by what was going at 34 East 62nd Street. Ten buildings were requested to have at least one monitor, and those approached were the Links Club, Cumberland House, Ronald Perelman's mansion across the street, and seven other properties within the ninety-foot radius. The monitors were to function throughout the duration of the town house's construction. The cost to Muftic and Jenkins for this precautionary measure would be about $75,000.

The sums paid in salaries to all the workers participating in the project—those responsible for the carpentry, painting, wiring, plumbing, brick and steel work, et cetera—came out of the pocket of a veteran contractor named Steve Mark, a vigorous and meticulous individual in his early seventies who enjoys a longtime reputation in New York for producing the best work at the best price and, as a result, is often hired to oversee as many as half a dozen or more construction sites at the same time, which is why he is a longtime millionaire.

Steve Mark is a blue-eyed, gray-haired, trim and bespectacled man of five-foot-nine who bears the craggy windblown look of a road cyclist, which, in a way, he is. He travels from job to job each weekday on his bicycle, peddling from the town house he owns in the East 70s to various parts of the city, sometimes as far south as Greenwich Village, but more likely within the Upper East Side, where, since 1978, he has built or renovated hundreds of single-family homes and mostly duplex and triplex apartments located within multi-story cooperatives.

The architect Henry Jessup joined him on some of these projects, and it was Jessup who recommended to the owners that Mark take on 62nd Street. Whereas Jessup's salary as the town house's architect was about $400,000, the cost of hiring Mark was $800,000, which is his standard fee for such a single assignment. In addition, the owners advanced Mark $5 million to cover the costs of the building's materials as well as the payroll of approximately 150 workers and the bonuses that he frequently adds.

That he can both be generous to others and profitable to himself testifies to his budgeting abilities (he is the son of an accountant) and to the fact that he knows from personal experience the value of manual and skilled labor—and, indeed, he can use every implement in a tool box at least as well as anyone in the construction gangs he oversees around the city.

When he was thirteen, and growing up in East Meadow, Long Island, his parents hired a contractor to build an extension on their house, but the man disappeared midway through the project. And so young Steve borrowed some tools from his uncle Max, who was a plumber, and more from a neighbor who was an electrician, and, with some guidance from both, managed to complete the extension.

From then on he kept a small workshop in his parents' garage and from there he once used his burgeoning skills as a carpenter to repair a leaky wooden sailboat and made it sufficiently seaworthy for gliding through Long Island Sound.

At school he was found to have a high IQ but was also labeled an underachiever and lazy, disappointing his mother, who was a teacher; yet he was otherwise very motivated and reliable when it came to holding jobs after school and during summer vacations. One summer he worked at a corner luncheonette on Broadway and Nassau Street delivering orders and helping in the kitchen, where he particularly enjoyed the camaraderie of the diverse group of fellow employees, which he would later re-experience as a construction boss.

During another summer he worked in an accounting office under the supervision of his father. His father, born in New York as Morris Margolies, had graduated from law school but, according to his son, "couldn't find work at a law firm until he changed his name from Morris Margolies to Murray Mark." But he so disliked his work as a lawyer that he eventually shifted to accounting.

Both of Steve Mark's parents were the children of Jewish immigrants. His mother's kin were Austro-Hungarian and her father, Harry Strauchler, ran a fruit and vegetable stand in the Bronx. His paternal grandparents were from Poland, and his father's father, Joe Margolies, owned a coffee shop in the Bowery. Steve's mother, Roslyn, was an elementary school teacher and served for thirty years within the city's public school system.

Steve received a degree in accounting in 1968 from Adelphi University in Garden City, Long Island, attending school at night while holding jobs during the day, including one at a ski shop in Great Neck. He devoted some of his earnings toward flying lessons, and after graduation from Adelphi he enlisted in the air force, planning to attend an officers training school for pilots.

But while based in San Antonio he became injured while playing recreational football, and after his recovery at a military hospital he dropped out of the program. His interest in flying continued, however, and he currently owns a single-engine propeller plane that he flies for pleasure whenever he can get his mind and body away from his construction business. In his plane he ventures as far north as Canada and southward into Florida.

After his discharge from the air force he married a young woman he had known from school, and he single-handedly remodeled the couple's first home in Flushing and their second in Larchmont, sharing it with their two daughters.

For two years he ran a bath and kitchen remodeling business at the A&D Building in Manhattan, on East 58th Street, and then with much encouragement and a few loans from some of his wealthiest customers, he started his construction business. Within four or five years, he had a working crew numbering between eighty and ninety men, and as many as nine project managers, all of them women.

"Women are so much better managing projects than men," he said. "They have no egos. Or, if they do, they don't bring them to work every day." The managers' mission was to provide him with logistic and liaison support, splitting their time between his office and the job site while making sure that everything was operating on schedule, on budget, and that harmony prevailed among the suppliers, workers, architects, consultants, and clients.

One of his project managers is his daughter Rebecca, a married woman in her thirties with two children. His other daughter, Alissa, also married with two children, is a gastroenterologist. Both daughters are from his first marriage, which lasted twenty years. In 1992 he remarried and has two daughters and a son, all of them currently in college. His son also has a pilot's license and sometimes flies with him on weekends.

Steve Mark and his crew finished working on the 62nd Street town house in late December of 2017, spending a little more than a year on the job. Fortunately, none of his workers experienced fatal falls or serious injuries, and, except for the tardy delivery of the windows, all of the subcontractors fulfilled their obligations on time.

After it was completed and the scaffolding was removed, there was a sense of relief and contentment expressed by those living in the area. Now there was an end to prolonged traffic jams and honking horns caused by delivery trunks and machinery blocking the street, and finally pedestrians were no longer walking between vertical steel pipes and through the dim light imposed by a sidewalk shed.

The officers of the Links Club, who a decade before had been so condemning of the modernistic mansion that the Russian woman, Janna Bullock, had proposed for 34 East 62nd Street, now welcomed Henry Jessup's historically derivative design as compatible with their own neo-Georgian building.

Most of the co-op owners within the Cumberland House are also satisfied with the new town house. These include James and Marie Savage, whose fourth-floor apartment overlooked the job site and had endured a year of noise and flying dirt while the couple observed nearby, through their windows, the sparks of welding torches, the mist of steel particles rising from circular saws, and the hoisting of insulation panels, air-conditioning units, and chunks of limestone.

The daily clamor reminded James Savage of when he lived in Bay Ridge, Brooklyn, during the early 1960s and his neighborhood was invaded by workers building entranceways to the soon-to-be-completed Verrazzano-Narrows Bridge. But he also remembered living next to the filthy rat-infested empty lot at 34 East 62nd Street for a decade, and so this new town house was a desirable replacement.

The next step was for the owners to sell it, so Theodore Muftic and Francis Jenkins contacted the Sotheby's real-estate office on East 61st Street and listed their town house for $32.5 million. A full-page ad showing the building appeared in the *New Yorker* magazine, and there were articles in newspapers with such headlines as: "Former Upper East Side Blast Site Will Give Way to $32.5 M Beaux Arts-inspired Mansion," and "Manhattan Townhouse Built on Site of Gas Explosion Asks $32.5 Million."

But during this period, from late 2017 through 2018, there was a slump in the housing market, prompting Muftic and Jenkins to reduce the asking price to $27.9 million. Even so, it remained unsold. As a *Wall Street Journal* article explained in November of 2018: "New York is facing the convergence of several large economic forces: an oversupply of new condos, a drop in international buyers as some countries impose capital controls, changes to the tax law that cap state and local deductions, and rising interest rates. There is also a shift in taste from uptown to downtown."

Early in 2019, with the town house still empty—a headline in the *Wall Street Journal* read: "Slump in Housing Market Deepens"—the owners were obliged to take on an annual expense of $80,000 on taxes and maintenance fees, which includes security, washing the windows, and excluding bugs and rodents from the premises.

While disappointed by their inability to sell, Muftic and Jenkins remained confident that sooner or later they would make a deal. "We could sell this building within a day or two if we'd accept something in the high teens," Jenkins said, meaning around $18 million or $19 million. But he and his partner found this unacceptable. And so the blue sign that the Sotheby's real-estate agents hung in front of the town house—"Newly Built Mansion For Sale"—was still hanging nearly three years after the completion of its construction.

Hoping for a better financial outcome, the partners in late 2019 switched real-estate agents from Sotheby's to Douglas Elliman. But as another two years passed without producing a sale, the displeased owners became increasingly negotiable. Finally, in October of 2021, the *New York Post* reported exclusively that the "Dr. Boom mansion" had finally found a buyer, a man who resided in the Chicago area named Marcus Lemonis. The negotiating agent at Douglas Elliman, T. Roger Erickson, confirmed that the town house had sold for $18.2 million.

Mr. Lemonis, who refused to grant interviews, was described as a Lebanese-born, twice-married, forty-seven-year-old entrepreneur who, among other endeavors, produced a reality series for CNBC called *The Profit*. Since he was unwilling to comment, it is unclear whether Mr. Lemonis and his wife intend to sell their residence in the Midwest and relocate full-time to New York, or whether they would commute back and forth. But it is a fact that, while they spent huge sums throughout 2022 into 2023 renovating the interior of their new acquisition, they had yet to inhabit it as their domicile.

During this period when it continued to be unoccupied, Dr. Bartha's onetime divorce lawyer, Ira Garr, happened to walk by one Saturday afternoon after shopping with his girlfriend at the Hermés store on the corner of Madison Avenue and 62nd Street. Mr. Garr does not live in the neighborhood and so had rarely frequented it since the days when he used to visit the brownstone and urge Dr. Bartha to make concessions to his divorced wife, to avoid endless hours of aggravation and the soaring costs of litigation.

In a way, Mr. Garr could sympathize with his stubborn and inflexible client, understanding how the doctor had been so emotionally attached to his home site that he could not, under any circumstance, abandon it—or allow his former wife, who never enjoyed living there, to share in any of the revenue from its enforced sale. Like the lawyer in Melville's story who cared about Bartleby while being confounded by him and ultimately unable to help him, Mr. Garr now stood for many moments lost in his own thoughts. Finally, his girlfriend nudged him from behind and asked: "Is something wrong?"

"No," he said, after a pause, "but I was just thinking that this is the place where a client of mine once had a brownstone."

He then reached out, took her arm, and resumed walking.

"Yes, this is where it was," he said, "and the sad thing is that all he had to do was settle the case, and he might be living in that old brownstone today. It would be worth $12 million today. He'd be made in the shade."

His confused girlfriend turned toward him and asked: "What are you talking about?"

"Oh, it's a long story," he said. "I'll tell you some other time."

1-- **3d floor front**--a rent-controlled apartment, 1½ rooms, that Gay Talese subleased in 1958 for $70 a month from gossip columnist, Joseph Dever, who moved into a larger apartment further downtown.

2-- **2nd floor front**--In 1959, having married Nan Ahearn, an editorial assistant at Random House, Talese took over a 1½ room rent-controlled front apartment in the same building at the same rent after the tenants, attorney Herbert Blacker and his wife, Gloria, left the city for the suburbs.

3-- **The first floor's walk-through apartment**, at $200 a month, became available a few years later when its tenant, the fashion model, Hope Bryce, left the building to be with the Hollywood director Otto Preminger, whom she eventually married. The Talese couple took over her lease, but could not afford three apartments at the same time and so sublet the 2nd floor front in 1962 to the novelist, William Styron, whose main residence was in Roxbury, Connecticut but wanted a pied-a-terre in the city. He was then writing "Confessions of Nat Turner."

4--In 1964, with Nan Talese expecting her first daughter, and Gay Talese receiving a generous contract for his new book, "The Bridge," the couple reclaimed 2-F from Styron and turned his pied-a-terre into a place for the baby and her nanny.

5--In 1967, with the birth of Nan's second daughter, the Talese couple were already in possession of the 4th floor rear apartment since the tenant, a flight attendant named Deborah Cartright, was evicted after leaving her dwelling one day with her toaster burning and setting off a small fire.

6--In 1973, with the money from his two best selling books, "The Kingdom and the Power" and "Honor Thy Father," Gay Talese purchased the entire four-story brownstone from its owners, a Park Avenue cooperative, for $173,000 and continued to live there for the next half century and they're still there.

AUTHOR'S NOTATIONS ON A PHOTOGRAPH OF HIS
NEW YORK CITY BROWNSTONE

My New York City Apartment

FROM *New York Magazine*, 2011

VERY MORNING AT THE age of 79, I wake up in the same bed, in the same third-floor apartment, in the same four-story brownstone on the East Side of Manhattan that I first moved into in 1958, when I was 26 and feeling older than I do now. At 26, I was constantly worried about things that worry me no longer. Where was I going? What was my next move? Now I never question myself about my next move, I know the answer. *Don't move.* Change nothing. Let the world come to you.

On a sunny afternoon 53 years ago, a man invited me to see, and perhaps sublet, his one-and-a-half-room apartment in this once-elegant, 1871-built brownstone with its cracked molding, its rusty water pipes, its DC current, and its termites. His name was Joseph Dever, a refined and smartly dressed man who had a job a block away, near Madison Avenue, working as a ghostwriter for a syndicated gossip columnist. Dever was about to quit and allow his young co-worker, Liz Smith, to assume all the responsibility. He had just been offered a column of his own at the New York *World-Telegram*, which would feature *his* name and *his* picture at the top, and allow him to rent a larger and more modern place. So he said I could take over this smaller, rent-controlled $70-a-month apartment with the understanding that he would keep the lease under his name (and I would be ghostwriting his checks). He would also be giving me a few things at no charge, including, hidden under a towel in a bureau drawer, an unloaded Luger P08 pistol. Dever said he had gotten it when he was in the Marines and did not want to be taking it outside. I said I didn't want it. He said he would soon return to collect it.

The first thing I did after Dever had given me the key was to invite my girlfriend, Nan Ahearn, a Random House editorial assistant (she was then living at the Barbizon Hotel for Women, on Lexington and 63rd Street), to come and see my apartment. She was unimpressed with the building's downtrodden exterior and foyer, and offered suggestions on how the apartment might be rearranged. We had been dating for more than a year, and I was worried about the prospect of being married. On my lowly reporter's salary, how could I afford it?

But Nan wanted to get married, and in 1959, we got married. After three months of living together in Dever's apartment, the couple who occupied the second-floor front—a young lawyer named Herbert Blecker and his wife, Gloria—decided to move out, and I quickly persuaded them to allow me to take it over. Nan and I would make the Bleckers' space our bedroom and utilize Dever's as our living room and study. Nan convinced me that we could afford the two apartments because I had been making extra money writing magazine pieces. Herbert Blecker was aware of this because sometimes late at night, bothered by the sound of my typewriter, he would register his disapproval by banging against his ceiling with a broomstick. When Nan and I moved into his apartment, I noticed three small indentations in the ceiling.

Within a year or so, there was another vacancy: the tenant on the first floor, a fashion model named Hope Bryce—who was dating and would eventually marry the Hollywood director Otto Preminger—moved out and allowed me to take over her lease even though I could not really afford all three apartments. So I sublet the Bleckers' old 2-F place to the Connecticut-based novelist Willliam Styron, who wanted a pied-à-terre in the city. I charged Styron the same $100 a month that I had been paying after the Bleckers' departure, and I moved our marital bedroom back to 3-F, while moving our dining room and studio down to Hope Bryce's former dwelling. But in 1964, with Nan expecting our first daughter, we had to reclaim 2-F for reconversion into a place for the baby and her nanny; and when a second daughter was born in 1967, we had already acquired 4-R, where an airline stewardess named Deborah Cartright used to live. One morning while rushing to catch a flight, she left her toaster blazing, which caused a small fire resulting in her eviction and my good fortune.

By 1973, with dozens of violations lodged against our building for faulty maintenance, and with the Park Avenue cooperative willing to sell the brownstone, Nan and I bought it for the low price of $175,000—50 grand of which was absorbed by the seller to be used to repair and restore the floundering property. Now, when I arise each morning in my marital bed in 3-F, my surroundings do not seem all that different in appearance from what I remember being shown a half-century ago by Joseph Dever. Who never returned, incidentally, to pick up his pistol.

ABOUT
MARINER BOOKS

MARINER BOOKS traces its beginnings to 1832 when William Ticknor cofounded the Old Corner Bookstore in Boston, from which he would run the legendary firm Ticknor and Fields, publisher of Ralph Waldo Emerson, Harriet Beecher Stowe, Nathaniel Hawthorne, and Henry David Thoreau. Following Ticknor's death, Henry Oscar Houghton acquired Ticknor and Fields and, in 1880, formed Houghton Mifflin, which later merged with venerable Harcourt Publishing to form Houghton Mifflin Harcourt. HarperCollins purchased HMH's trade publishing business in 2021 and reestablished their storied lists and editorial team under the name Mariner Books.

Uniting the legacies of Houghton Mifflin, Harcourt Brace, and Ticknor and Fields, Mariner Books continues one of the great traditions in American bookselling. Our imprints have introduced an incomparable roster of enduring classics, including Hawthorne's *The Scarlet Letter,* Thoreau's *Walden,* Willa Cather's *O Pioneers!,* Virginia Woolf's *To the Lighthouse,* W.E.B. Du Bois's *Black Reconstruction*, J.R.R. Tolkien's *The Lord of the Rings,* Carson McCullers's *The Heart Is a Lonely Hunter,* Ann Petry's *The Narrows,* George Orwell's *Animal Farm* and *Nineteen Eighty-Four,* Rachel Carson's *Silent Spring,* Margaret Walker's *Jubilee,* Italo Calvino's *Invisible Cities,* Alice Walker's *The Color Purple,* Margaret Atwood's *The Handmaid's Tale,* Tim O'Brien's *The Things They Carried,* Philip Roth's *The Plot Against America,* Jhumpa Lahiri's *Interpreter of Maladies,* and many others. Today Mariner Books remains proudly committed to the craft of fine publishing established nearly two centuries ago at the Old Corner Bookstore.